EMOTIONAL COMMUNICATION

In *Emotional Communication*, Paul Geltner places the pre-linguistic type of communication that is shared with infants and animals at the core of the psychoanalytic relationship. He shows how emotional communication intertwines with language, permeating every moment of human interaction, and becoming a primary way that people involuntarily recreate painful childhood relationships in current life.

Emotional Communication integrates observations from a number of psychoanalytic schools in a cohesive but non-eclectic model. Geltner expands psychoanalytic technique beyond the traditional focus on interpretation and the contemporary focus on authenticity to include the use of feelings that precisely address the client's repetitive patterns of misery. The author breaks down analytic interventions into their cognitive and emotional components, describing how each engages a different part of the client's mind and serves a different function. He explains the role of emotional communication in psychoanalytic technique both in classical interpretations and in non-interpretive interventions that use the analyst's feelings to amplify the therapeutic power of the psychoanalytic relationship.

Offering a clear alternative to both classical and contemporary Relational and Intersubjective approaches to understanding and treating clients in psychoanalysis, Paul Geltner presents a theory of communication and maturation that will interest psychoanalysts, psychotherapists, and those concerned with the subtleties of human relatedness.

Paul Geltner is a psychoanalyst in private practice in New York City, USA. He specializes in individual and group supervision of psychoanalysts and psychoanalytic psychotherapists.

EMOTIONAL COMMUNICATION

Countertransference analysis and the use of feeling in psychoanalytic technique

Paul Geltner

LONDON AND NEW YORK

First published 2013
by Routledge
27 Church Road, Hove, East Sussex BN3 2FA

Simultaneously published in the USA and Canada
by Routledge
711 Third Avenue, New York NY 10017

Routledge is an imprint of the Taylor & Francis Group, an informa business

© 2013 Paul Geltner

The right of Paul Geltner to be identified as author of this work has been asserted by him in accordance with sections 77 and 78 of the Copyright, Designs and Patents Act 1988.

All rights reserved. No part of this book may be reprinted or reproduced or utilised in any form or by any electronic, mechanical, or other means, now known or hereafter invented, including photocopying and recording, or in any information storage or retrieval system, without permission in writing from the publishers.

Trademark notice: Product or corporate names may be trademarks or registered trademarks, and are used only for identification and explanation without intent to infringe.

British Library Cataloguing in Publication Data
A catalogue record for this book is available from the British Library

Library of Congress Cataloging in Publication Data
Geltner, Paul.
 Emotional communication: countertransference analysis and the use of feeling in psychoanalytic technique/Paul Geltner.
 p. cm.
 1. Countertransference (Psychology) 2. Psychoanalysis.
 3. Psychotherapist and patient. I. Title.
 RC489.C68G45 2013
 616.89'17—dc23   2012019659

ISBN: 978-0-415-52516-9 (hbk)
ISBN: 978-0-415-52517-6 (pbk)
ISBN: 978-0-203-08128-0 (ebk)

Typeset in Garamond
by Florence Production Ltd, Stoodleigh, Devon

Printed and bound by CPI Group (UK) Ltd, Croydon, CR0 4YY

DEDICATED TO THE MEMORY
OF SARAH LEUZE

WITH PROFOUND APPRECIATION
FOR THE 31 YEARS OF
ANALYSIS, WHERE I TRULY LEARNED
THE REALITY AND THE POWER
OF THE PSYCHOANALYTIC
RELATIONSHIP

CONTENTS

Preface ix
Acknowledgments xiii

1 Introduction 1

2 The evolutionary and developmental origins of objective countertransference 10

3 The concept of objective countertransference and its role in a two-person psychology 22

4 Emotional communication and its relationship to the basic concepts of psychoanalysis 36

5 Differentiating objective and subjective countertransference 53

6 Narcissistic countertransference 79

7 Object countertransference 101

8 Countertransference in projective identification states 129

9 Anaclitic countertransference 137

10 Emotional communication in psychoanalytic technique 159

11 Narcissistic emotional communications 204

12 Techniques of object emotional communications 239

CONTENTS

13 Techniques of emotional communication with
    projective identification 261

14 Anaclitic emotional communications 272

15 Conclusion 300

Notes 305
Bibliography 318
Index 327

PREFACE

This book is about the concept of emotional communication in psychoanalysis – what it brings to the analyst's understanding of the patient, and how it can be used to enhance the effectiveness of psychoanalytic technique.

In the context of this book, the term *psychoanalysis* is defined as the conceptual framework for understanding the patient that is based on transference and resistance (Freud, 1914a). (Of these two concepts, the far greater focus is placed on transference.[1]) The terms *psychoanalyst* and *analyst* refer to a psychotherapist whose technique is based on this conceptual framework. Thus, the terms *psychoanalysis*, *psychoanalyst*, and *analyst*, are not tied to any particular technique (e.g., use of the couch, high frequency of sessions, or exclusive reliance on interpretation or any similar restriction), to any particular certification, or to any particular style of training.

The book is a synthesis of the work of many analysts from a wide range of schools that make up (as described in Chapter 1) a minority tradition within psychoanalysis. The seeds of this tradition can be found in aspects of Freud's work but the tradition may be said to begin with Ferenczi's late modifications of Freud's rules of technique.

While the historical evolution of these ideas has been fascinating, the focus of this book is theoretical and clinical – to construct a coherent and consistent synthesis of a minority tradition in psychoanalysis that I will describe in Chapter 1. As such, my focus has not been historical, and my particular way of thinking and working has not allowed me either to follow their development of these ideas closely or to comprehensively reference all of the contributors. I hope it will suffice to say that I don't claim to have discovered any of the particular ideas presented here, and I don't know how much of it is wholly original, except, of course, the overall conceptual framework of the work.

The greatest theoretical influence on this book has been the work of Spotnitz[2] and the other Modern Psychoanalytic theorists, especially A. Bernstein (1992), J. Bernstein (1981, 1993), Ernsberger (1979, 1990), Hayden (1983), J. Kirman (1983,1998), W. Kirman (1980), Laquercia (1992, 1998), Liegner (1980,1991,1995), Margolis (1978, 1979, 1981), Marshall (1982), Meadow (1987, 1988, 1989, 1991), Sherman (1983), Weinstein (1986), and many others. Spotnitz was the first analyst to combine a systematic use of the epistemological value of countertransference analysis with a range of techniques, and more importantly, a theory of technique that explicitly incorporated emotional communication and differentiated its function in the treatment from that of interpretation. Spotnitz's work is notable for his use of specific and ever-changing emotional communication in working with individual, moment-to-moment transference situations and displays his readiness to use the full range of human feeling in his work with patients. Furthermore, Spotnitz fully integrated his use of emotional communication with the supervisory process, which subsequently became an integral part of the training process.

Although Spotnitz's work and that of other Modern Psychoanalytic theorists is the foundation of much of the present work, I have departed from traditional Modern Psychoanalytic theory and practice in a number of areas and expanded the range and the function of emotional communication in the technique. For this reason, the book should not be viewed as an exposition of Spotnitz's work nor of Modern Psychoanalytic theory as it has traditionally formulated.

Although Modern Psychoanalysis has a significantly different clinical temperament and aesthetic than Object Relations, the two schools developed in parallel in many significant areas. Spotnitz delivered his first paper on countertransference in 1949 (although it was not published until 1976 [Spotnitz, 1976]), the same years as Winnicott's (1949) more famous "Hate in the Countertransference," and he subsequently adopted Winnicott's term – *objective countertransference* – to describe induced feelings. Winnicott's (1949, 1978) use of negative feelings in the treatment (although less thoroughly elaborated) is also similar to Spotnitz's work. It is unclear whether these were parallel developments or examples of direct influence one way or the other.[3]

The phenomenological framework for conceptualizing objective countertransference that I have developed in this book has been directly inspired by and derived from Racker's (1957) pioneering delineation of two types of countertransference: the complementary and the concordant identifications. Although I have changed his terminology,[4] the idea of differentiating countertransference based on the type of object relationship – or, as I call it, the *relational mode* – that underlies it was a seminal insight and serves as the basis of all of my descriptions of both countertransference and types of emotional communications. In this respect, my work is an extended footnote to Racker.

Many of the ideas in this work also parallel those of Ogden, one of the few theorists outside of Modern Psychoanalysis to make reference to Modern Psychoanalytic theory in his work. Ogden's (1979) early paper on projective identification, which combined Object Relations theory with a Modern Psychoanalytic bent with exquisite clarity, was an important influence on this work. I have also come to see that aspects of Spotnitz's work on some types of countertransference, and consequently my own, is similar to Bion's work on projective identification and his concept of beta elements – with some clear differences as well. However, I have no evidence that Bion had any direct influence on Spotnitz, and his influence on my work has been secondary through other writers.

There have been significant parallels between aspects of Self Psychology (Basch 1983; Kohut 1971, 1977), intersubjectivity (Atwood and Stolorow 1984; Stolorow, Brandchaft, and Atwood 1987), and Modern Psychoanalysis (Marshall 1991). Although the use of emotional communication is far more restricted in these schools than in the present framework, Kohut's (1971) emphasis on the curative value of the idealizing and mirroring transferences has been an important influence on my thinking about the importance of certain types of narcissistic emotional communications.

At present (2012) the use of emotional communication in technique and emotional induction in epistemology is far more widespread than it was when I first began my psychoanalytic training in 1980. At that time, only a minority of the Object Relations analysts, Searles, and the Modern Analysts used these concepts consistently. Since then, many ideas that were (in most cases) first posited by these groups in the 1950s through the 1970s were later formulated, no doubt independently, in different terminology and in the context of somewhat different overarching theoretical frameworks, by theorists in other schools, including the Intersubjectivists, the Relationalists, and the contemporary Freudians. Writers such as Aron (1996), Bollas (1987), Chused (1991), Davis (1994), Ellman and Moskowitz (1998), Gabbard and Wilkinsin (2000), Giovacchini (1979), and Mitchell (1988) are only a very few of those whose ideas overlap with what I am presenting. In particular, Maroda (1991, 2009), Kumin (1996), and Slochower (1996) elaborated ideas that overlap closely with aspects of Modern Psychoanalytic theory and with the present work. Unfortunately, I have been unable to keep track of these parallel developments, and even less able to keep track of the often conceptual and terminological distinctions between others' and my own evolving theories. For this reason, I have only minimally referenced contributions of these other writers. Again, I regret the lack, and apologize to anyone whom I have not acknowledged, and hope that a more historically minded scholar than I will carefully document the evolution of these issues.

The structure of this book

This book contains two parts. The first – Chapters 1 to 9 – discusses the epistemological use of emotional communication from the patient to the analyst as manifested in the objective countertransference; the concept of objective countertransference; an approach to differentiating objective countertransference from subjective countertransference; and an in-depth phenomenology of objective countertransference.

PREFACE

The second part — Chapters 10 to 14 — begins with a theoretical discussion of the role of emotional communication in psychoanalytic technique, followed by chapters describing a range of techniques of emotional communication and their relationship to the more traditional techniques of interpretation.

There is, of course, another major manifestation of emotional communication in the psychoanalytic relationship — the impact of the analyst's unconscious, involuntary emotional communications on the patient. Although I discuss this issue intermittently — and somewhat extensively in Chapter 5 — it is not the primary focus of this book. This isn't to say that I don't think it's important, but other writers, classic and contemporary, have extensively explored this territory, and the little that I have to add on the topic is discussed as it relates to the two other issues.

A final comment before we begin: my method throughout this book has been to make distinctions, initially global, but increasingly fine-grained, between various forms of feeling and relating. Some readers will no doubt welcome this level of examination, while others may find that it ventures well past the border of obsessive hair-splitting. Whatever one's opinion of the level of detail that I have brought to the work, I wish to emphasize that I have never sought to make differentiations for purely academic reasons. Rather, my level of analysis has been guided solely on the clinical utility it has brought to my practice and that of my supervisees. It has been my experience that the more precisely the analyst understands his feelings in relationship to the patient, the more precisely he will be able to formulate a curative intervention, and it is to this end that I have worked.

ACKNOWLEDGMENTS

To my patients for entrusting me with the stories of their lives, and to my supervisees for entrusting me with their feelings about their patients.

To my wife, Mendie Cohn, for the years we have spent discussing cases, human relationships, our therapy and analysis, and everything else under the sun that has shaped so much of this work. She also cleaned up some very swampy verbiage and helped me to clarify a number of theoretical issues. Her love and support, as well as that of my sons, Henry Cohn-Geltner and Michael Cohn-Geltner, have sustained me through the 12 years I wrote this.

To Dr. Stanley Hayden, whose supervision over the decades continues to enlighten and support me. His graceful touch, his comfort with every feeling in the human spectrum, and his ability to see the dynamics expressed in the countertransference fog are a constant source of inspiration.

To James Peterson, the brilliant food writer, whose love, encouragement, and understanding are unstinting and always renewing.

To Valerie Frankfeldt and Bob Unger, with whom I've been discussing cases – and so much else – weekly for over 20 years, and with whom many of these ideas have been worked out and clarified. And it was Valerie, in a comment in a class so many years ago, who really helped me to understand the curative value of living through horrible feelings with a patient.

To Joseph Cancelmo, who has encouraged me from the beginning, who has read numerous chapters and re-writes, and who helps me to understand the richness of the contemporary Freudian school.

To Joseph Scalia, who has also encouraged me from the beginning, read and helped me to revise a number of chapters, and allowed me to present a huge chunk of the work to the Northern Rockies Psychoanalytic Institute. One day, perhaps, he will help me to finally understand Lacan.

To Judy Levitz, for love, encouragement, and for reading and making helpful comments on so many of the chapters.

To Laurie Sloan, for reading some of the chapters, for helping me to understand (I hope) the Relational school, and for spurring me to write Chapter 3.

To Harriet Pappenheim for reading a number of chapters and reminding me of the importance of defining all terms so that the book would be accessible to analysts of all persuasions.

ACKNOWLEDGMENTS

To Marilyn Lamonica, Joan Brady, Beverly Amsel, and Catherine Lindenmen for reading chapters, completely out of context, and working hard to make sense of them.

To Michael Dow, who did some of the final proofreading, and who might understand this book better than I do.

To Coletta Perry for the final proofreading and manuscript preparation and for helping me to clarify some ideas that nobody in the analytic field saw needed clarification.

To Tara Marion, for doing the heavy lifting on the proofreading.

We gratefully acknowledge permission to reprint the following articles:
Chapter 2: Geltner, P. (2000) "The Evolutionary and Developmental Origins of Patient-induced Countertransference," *Psychiatry*, 63:3, 253–63.
Chapter 3: Geltner, P. (2006) "The Concept of Objective Countertransference and Its Place in a Two-person Psychology," *American Journal of Psychoanalysis*, 66:1, 25–42, March.
Chapter 6: Geltner, P. (2003) "The Dynamics of Narcissistic Countertransference," *Annals of Modern Psychoanalysis*, 2:1, 87–113.
Chapter 7: Geltner, P. (2002) "Varieties of Object Countertransference," *Annals of Modern Psychoanalysis*, 1:2, 215–50.
Chapter 8: Geltner, P. (2005) "Countertransference in Projective Identification and Sadomasochistic States," *Modern Psychoanalysis*, 30:1, 25–41.
Chapter 9: Geltner, P. (2003) "Anaclytic Countertransference," *Annals of Modern Psychoanalysis*, 2, 2.
Chapter 10 (in part): Geltner, P. (2007) "Finding the Right Feeling: Objective Countertransference and the Curative Emotional Communication," *Modern Psychoanalysis*, 32:1, 66–78.

1

INTRODUCTION

Language and feelings: the two channels of human communication

Analysis is the talking cure, but the words only tell only half of the story. They communicate the particulars of the patient's existence. They recount the events, detail the circumstances, and name the feelings that make up the patient's life story. As the patient talks, she also stimulates feelings in the analyst that are beyond the scope of the patient's words. Sometimes the words and the feelings tell the same story; sometimes they tell different stories, and other times they contradict each other altogether. Neither can be understood without the other. The analyst must listen to the patient's words and experience the feelings to fully comprehend the full story of the patient's life.

What happens when two people talk? They use spoken language, which often looks and feels as if it were a unitary process, but is, in fact, a densely interwoven amalgam of two distinct components: language and feelings. The language expresses information about the speaker's thoughts symbolically and transmits these thoughts to the listener. The feelings express information about the speaker's emotional state through non-symbolic dimensions of speech such as tone and the rhythm of the words. The language is a form of *cognitive communication*. The feelings are a form of *emotional communication*.

Until the 1980s, most psychoanalytic theory focused on the role of cognitive communication in the psychoanalytic relationship. However, there was a minority tradition within psychoanalysis that recognized the importance of emotional communication and held that both channels of communication play a role in psychoanalysis.

It has only been within the last two decades that most contemporary schools of analysis have shown an increasing interest in emotional communication – both as a channel of understanding and as a vehicle of cure.

This book is about emotional communication in psychoanalysis as it is manifested in two important areas of the psychoanalytic relationship: countertransference and psychoanalytic technique.

INTRODUCTION

Before we can delve into the role of emotional communication in psychoanalysis, we must look more closely at the role emotional communication plays in everyday life.

Cognitive and emotional communication

Cognitive communication is the channel of communication that makes use of the purely symbolic elements of language: a set of symbols (words) and rules for using them (grammar) that generate consensually agreed upon meanings. Many types of information – including facts, observations, commands, opinions, requests, and questions – can be expressed through cognitive communication. The speaker (or sender) expresses this information in bits, encoded in the symbols, and the listener (receiver) understands these symbols and experiences this understanding as thought. Cognitive communication is effective to the extent that both people share the same understanding of the meaning of the words and the grammar.

Emotional communication, on the other hand, is the channel of human communication in which one type of information – information about the sender's feeling (or emotional state) – is conveyed to the receiver through the non-symbolic dimensions of spoken language such as tone, prosody, rhythm, and silence, as well as through facial expressions, posture, and non-symbolic gestures. When a person feels happy and conveys this state through emotional communication, the happiness is expressed through the brightness or lightness of tone and/or through her smile and the expression in her eyes. Conversely, when a person is angry, the anger is expressed through the harshness of her tone and/or through the narrowing of her eyebrows and tightness of her mouth and face. Emotional communication not only conveys information about the sender's emotional state but also about her intentions, desires, or impulses. The sender's expression of feeling stimulates feelings in the receiver. Whereas cognitive communication is experienced as thought, emotional communication is experienced as feeling.

Unlike cognitive communication, which is the distinctly human channel of communication, emotional communication is used by other mammals. It is also the first form of communication in human development, pre-dating the acquisition of language. After language has been acquired, emotional communication remains entwined with cognitive communication in spoken language. (This topic will be discussed at greater length in Chapter 2.)

Emotional communication is primarily goal-oriented or manipulative (Mithen 2006). Its function is to have a specific impact on the receiver. This can be seen clearly in the first emotional communication that all healthy human beings express at birth: the anaclitic cry – the cry that signals distress in the context of physical and emotional dependency (MacLean 1990). The newborn's cry not only signals the need for nurturance and attention, but its goal is also to elicit a specific cluster of feelings in the mother: sympathetic empathy with the newborn, which enables her to understand what she needs, and nurturing love that leads her to want to soothe her distress and satisfy her needs. Her feelings are a logical and predictable response to the infant's cry, and they lead her to give the infant the specific cluster of the feelings she needs to experience in an interpersonal context in that moment – the feeling that her needs are known and will be satisfied and the feeling that she is loved – all of which are as crucial to her as the physical care the mother provides.

This interaction, in which the baby's emotional communication stimulates the cluster of nurturing feelings in the mother that, in turn, motivate her to meet the infant's dependency needs, is an example of the process of emotional induction. Emotional induction is the outcome of a successful emotional communication. It occurs when the sender's emotional communication induces a feeling in the receiver that is logically and predictably related to the sender's goals and intentions. It is analogous to a successful cognitive communication, which occurs when the receiver understands the sender's language.

As we shall see in later chapters, emotional communication does not always result in emotional induction. For a range of reasons, the feeling that the receiver experiences may be a distortion of the sender's emotional communication, or it may be completely incorrect. These are examples of emotional interactions in which no emotional induction has taken place, despite the fact that the sender has expressed an emotional communication.

This sometimes happens even with newborns and their mothers. Some babies are less able to successfully induce the necessary feelings in the mother, and some mothers never experience the necessary feelings after having heard the baby's cry. But in this earliest, yet still fully operational example, emotional communication usually results in induction. The core of the infant's message gets through and has the right effect on the mother's feelings. Sometimes it takes a few weeks to get the communication working properly, but the vast majority of new mothers – even those who didn't feel maternal during pregnancy and feared that they wouldn't want their babies – hear their newborn's cries and are moved to nurture and soothe, a set of feelings that usually evolves into maternal love.

As we shall see throughout this book, what transpires between the baby and the mother is only one type of emotional communication and induction – the anaclitic type. Three other types will be described: narcissistic, object, and projective identification. However, the significance of emotional communication at the start of life illustrates that emotional communication is the one of the most basic of human experiences.

Emotional communication and psychoanalysis

Cognitive communication is largely responsible for the precision of human communication and the development of human culture. However emotional communication is the very stuff of human relatedness. Psychological maturation is largely dependent on the child getting the necessary emotional communications – the maturational feelings – from the parents at the critical points in development.

The idea that early relationships form the templates for later relationships is fundamental to the psychoanalytic perspective, and emotional communication is one of the most important means by which a person's emotional past is both repeated and recreated in the present. Emotional communication enables the successes from the earliest days to be carried over into the future. It also recreates the failures. And it is usually these failures that lead a patient to seek analysis.

Emotional communication is integral to the psychoanalytic process, as it is to all human relationships. Emotional communication functions in analysis in the same way that it does in everyday life: The patterns of emotional communication that were established in the patient's childhood shape the patient's patterns of emotional communication with the analyst, affecting the way the analyst experiences the patient and the way the patient experiences the analyst. The difference is that these patterns occur spontaneously and (usually) unobserved in everyday life, whereas the psychoanalytic relationship is structured in a way that allows the patient's repetitive patterns of emotional communication to be activated, observed, and most importantly changed through the impact of the analyst's interventions.

The concept of emotional communication is closely related to a number of more limited concepts in psychoanalysis: *thought transference* (Freud 1925), *empathy* (Greenson 1960; Kohut 1971), *trial identification* (Fliess 1942), *projective identification* (in Bion's [1959] sense, not Klein's [1946]), *the beta-screen* (Bion 1962, 1963), *reverie* (Bion 1962, 1963; Ogden 1997b) *coenestheic functioning* (Spitz 1945), *the infantile nonverbal affect system* (Krystal 1988), *role-responsiveness* (Sandler 1976), *nonverbal transmission of affects* (Schore 1994), *affective attunement* (Stern 1985), *intermodal matching of affect states* (Kumin 1996), *self-disclosure* (Aron 1996), and *emotional engagement* (Maroda 1991), *implicit relational knowing* (Boston Change Process Study Group 2008). However, each of these concepts is discussed in the context of a particular stage of development, form of pathology, type of defense, relational mode, type of feeling, or technique.

In contrast, *emotional communication* is a more general concept that encompasses all these phenomena. The concept of emotional communication describes the expression and the reception of all forms of emotion, in humans and animals, throughout the lifespan, in everyday life and within the analytic relationship.

Understanding the role of emotional communication in psychoanalysis is critical to understanding the patient and curing her. Through an understanding of emotional induction from the patient, the analyst has access to dimensions of the patient's experience and problems that the patient is unable to communicate directly in language. Through the use of emotional communication to the patient, the analyst gives the patient the feelings that she needs in order to resolve the problems that brought her into the analysis. In life, these needed emotional communications are called maturational feelings; in analysis, they can be called the curative feelings.

Brief history of the role of emotional communication in psychoanalytic technique

The role of emotional communication has been a point of difference between two traditions within the history of psychoanalytic technique: the classical tradition made use of a limited range of emotional communication but stressed the overriding importance of cognitive communication in the form of interpretation. The minority tradition, on the other hand, made use of a wider range of emotional communication in technique, viewing it as equally important – and sometimes more important – than the cognitive communication.

The classical tradition was established by Freud, who delineated two components in psychoanalytic technique. The primary component was interpretation. Through interpretation, the analyst communicated the latent meaning of the patient's symptoms, dreams, fantasies, memories, and feelings to the patient (Laplanche & Pontalis 1973). Interpretation was designed to make the unconscious conscious, enlarge and strengthen the ego in relationship to the id and the superego, and thus allow the patient to regain "its mastery over lost provinces of his mental life" (Freud 1940: 173).

Interpretation, for Freud (1919: 168), was the distinctive element in psychoanalytic technique – the "pure gold of analysis." But as powerful as interpretation was, what "turns the scale" in the patient's struggle against the neurosis "is not his intellectual insight – which is neither strong enough nor free enough for such achievement – but simply and solely his relation to the doctor" (Freud 1917: 445). Thus, the second component of psychoanalytic technique was the psychoanalytic relationship. Freud (1913: 139) suggested that if "one exhibits a serious interest in him [the patient], carefully clears away the resistances that crop up at the beginning, and [listens with] ... sympathetic understanding," positive, non-erotic transference will develop. He argued that this type of transference enabled the patient to make use of the interpretations and eventually adopt the analyst's "conviction of the inexpediency of the repressive processes established in childhood" (1919: 159). With this transference in place, the analyst could encourage and soothe the patient[1] in his efforts to overcome his resistances helping him persevere with the analytic process (Freud 1940: 178). The analyst could also, to a limited extent, make use of this transference to provide a degree of "after education" to the patient, correcting some of the parents' mistakes with the patient (Freud 1940: 175).

The first component – the work of interpretation – in which the analyst conveys precise information in language to the rational part of the patient's mind – the patient's ego – is conveyed through cognitive communication. The second component – the serious interest, sympathetic understanding, encouragement, and soothing – is conveyed through emotional communication. The work of emotional communication is secondary to and supportive of the work of interpretation, but it is essential to the analytic process. When the non-eroticized positive transference cannot develop, as in Freud's (1940) narcissistic neurosis, analysis is impossible.

Privately, Freud discussed a wider use of emotional communication. He wrote to his friend Ludwig Binswanger.

> What is given to the patient should indeed never be a spontaneous affect, but always consciously allotted, and then more or less of it as the need may arise. Occasionally a great deal, but never from one's own unconscious. This I should regard as the formula. In other words, one must always recognize one's countertransference and rise above it, only then is one free oneself. To give someone too little because one loves him too much is being unjust to the patient and a technical error.
>
> (Binswanger 1957: 50)

However, there is no hint of this idea in his published writings, which established the parameters of the classical psychoanalytic theory of technique. This can be seen in the work of Strachey (1934), who elaborated a more refined account of the role of emotional communication in the psychoanalytic process. He argued that the patient introjects the analyst as an auxiliary superego; this introjection modifies the patient's superego, which allows the patient to make use of the analyst's interpretations. What the patient introjects is not any particular interpretation but rather the manner in which the analyst relates to her. Strachey does not describe what the analyst actually does to facilitate this process, but Glover (1955: 370), referring to Strachey, says that the analyst maintains a "humane" attitude to the patient's instincts. He even suggests that, "in the deeper pathological states, a prerequisite of the efficiency of interpretation is the attitude, the true unconscious attitude of the analyst to his patients" (Glover 1955: 372).

This attitude is again conveyed through emotional communication. Nevertheless, the type and the range of deliberate, conscious emotional communication advocated by Strachey (1934) is extremely limited, even more limited than Freud's prescription. The mutative interpretation involves the transference, and its effectiveness is catalyzed when the patient's sense of reality differentiates between her transference fantasies and the analyst's actual behavior. In order for this to work, the analyst's behavior must not resemble the patient's fantasies – whether positive or negative – in any way. Despite differences in emphasis,[2] Strachey's (1934) description of the therapeutic process was consistent with Sterba's (1934: 324) idea that interpretation offered the patient's ego a "new point of view of intellectual contemplation": cure was affected through cognitive communication.

Later theorists within the Freudian mainstream (such as Greenson 1967) further explored the importance of the "real" emotional relationship between the analyst and the patient. However, these discussions continued to emphasize only one type of emotional communication; feelings that facilitate a "working alliance" between the analyst's analyzing ego and the patient's reasonable, observing and analyzing ego (Greenson 1967: 193). The most mature aspects of the analyst's personality are in contact with the most mature aspects of the patient's personality. No attempt was made to make direct emotional contact with the forces within the patient's mind that drove the repetitions. There was no consideration of the possible value of communicating feelings outside this "rational, desexualized, and de-aggressified" (Greenson 1967: 46) emotional spectrum. In this model of the psychoanalytic process, transference was activated within the analysis so that the patient and the analyst could observe it, but the analyst did not participate in it in any way. Emotional communication remained secondary to interpretation, which was viewed as the "ultimate and decisive instrument" (Greenson 1967: 39) of change.

This remained the mainstream Freudian position on emotional communication until the early years of the twenty-first century. There was, however, a minority tradition within psychoanalysis that began with Freud's friend and colleague, Sándor Ferenczi. Ferenczi (1931) dramatically enlarged the range of emotional communication in psychoanalytic technique when he responded to the patient within the context of the transference regression as though the patient was a child, rather than simply interpreting her childlike behavior to her adult ego. While never rejecting the importance of interpretation and insight, Ferenczi (1931) experimented with using a wide range of feelings to cure the patient. This spawned a theory of technique that emphasized the importance of the analytic relationship itself as a primary curative factor. Alexander (1925) described psychoanalysis as a corrective emotional experience. Balint (1968) argued that with more disturbed patients, the analyst needed to provide an object relationship, not a description of an object relationship (i.e., an interpretation). Sechehaye (1951) demonstrated that symbolic realization of the patient's fantasies could be curative with a schizophrenic patient. Kohut (1977) stressed the importance of the analyst's empathy in restarting the stalled developmental process.

While these analysts focused on the role of positive and/or loving emotional communications in analytic treatment, Winnicott (1949, 1978) took the radical and counterintuitive step of using hateful emotional communications in the analytic relationship, based on his understanding of the role of hate and aggression in early emotional development. Searles (1979) also described vivid and intense emotional interchanges that involved both loving and aggressive feelings. Spotnitz (1967, 1969, 1976) formulated a well-developed theory of technique in which both positive and negative emotional communications were used to systematically resolve pre-oedipal resistances without the use of interpretation. Furthermore, Spotnitz reversed the usual understanding of psychoanalytic cure by suggesting that insight was the product – and not the cause – of emotional growth and argued that emotional communication from the analyst was necessary to stimulate this growth.

Brief history of the role of emotional communication in countertransference analysis

A related disagreement involving emotional communication also arose in relationship to understanding the countertransference – the analyst's feelings about the patient. The classical position was again defined by Freud (1910), who viewed countertransference as a manifestation of the analyst's unresolved neurosis. As such, it was an obstacle to be recognized and overcome. There is no suggestion in anything Freud published that the countertransference contained anything that might be valuable to the treatment.

> Freud (1912: 115–116) did suggest that the analyst should use his own unconscious to understand the patient's unconscious. The analyst should "turn his own unconscious like a receptive organ towards the transmitting unconscious of the patient. He must adjust himself to the patient as a telephone receiver is adjusted to the transmitting microphone."

He also suggested the possibility of telepathic thought transference, but these ideas were about the analyst using the thoughts, not the feelings, that arose in course of listening to his free associations (1925).

These ideas formed the basis of the majority position in psychoanalysis up until the 1990s, when some classical analysts began to consider other ideas on the subject.

However, a few early theorists did consider using the countertransference as a source of information about the patient, in a way that can be conceptualized as emotional communication. Deutsch (1926: 127) argued for the utilization and goal-directed mastery of the countertransference. Hann-Kende (1933: 167) stated that the countertransference "not only does not inhibit, but actually facilitates the analytic work."

A pivotal point in countertransference theory was Winnicott's (1949) theory that a part of the analyst's feelings should be understood as a realistic emotional reaction to the patient and used to understand her. Winnicott called this type of reaction the *objective countertransference*. This will be the term that is used in this book to describe the feelings that are induced in the analyst by the patient's emotional communications.

Two years after Winnicott introduced the concept of objective countertransference,[3] Spotnitz (1976) argued that the analyst should feel and be able

INTRODUCTION

to utilize the feelings induced in her by the patient. Heimann (1950) further elaborated the view that aspects of the countertransference could be understood as specific communications from the patient. These communications, which in the present framework can be described as emotional induction from the patient to the analyst, served an important epistemological function in the analysis; they conveyed things about the patient that the patient was unable to put into words. From the 1950s through the 1980s, numerous writers, including Gittleson (1952), Tower (1956), Racker (1957), Bion (1959), Kernberg (1965), Giovacchini (1979), and Rosenfeld (1987), discussed countertransference as a form of communication from the patient. Countertransference became a crucial piece of clinical data.

Despite these developments, the classical position on emotional communication, both in technique and epistemology, dominated American psychoanalysis until the early 1980s. At that point, a slow but steady shift took place; by the first decade of the twenty-first century, the pure version of the classical position was on the verge of becoming a historical relic. All schools of psychoanalytic thought have accepted some role for countertransference as a legitimate source of information about the patient (Cancelmo 2009), and all schools have integrated some use of the analyst's feelings, however limited, in psychoanalytic technique as well.

2
THE EVOLUTIONARY AND DEVELOPMENTAL ORIGINS OF OBJECTIVE COUNTERTRANSFERENCE

> Articulate language is, however, peculiar to man; but he uses in common with the lower animals inarticulate cries to express his meaning, aided by gestures and the movements of the muscles of the face. This especially holds true with the more simple and vivid feelings, which are but little connected with our higher intelligence. Our cries of pain, fear, surprise, anger, together with their appropriate actions, and the murmur of a mother to her beloved child, are more expressive than any words.
> (Darwin 1872: 54)

Spoken human language combines two channels of communication: cognitive communication, which is composed of a system of symbols – words – and rules for using them, and emotional communication, which is expressed through the non-symbolic dimensions of speech, such as tone and rhythm of the words.

Emotional communication is by far the older form of communication, both evolutionarily and developmentally. Reptiles, birds, and mammals communicate through emotional communication, and babies communicate with their mothers through emotional communication before they acquire language. It later becomes interwoven with cognitive communication in language, and its importance is retained throughout the life cycle.

Objective countertransference, conceptualized as that part of the analyst's feelings about the patient that are viewed as being induced by the patient's emotional communications,[1] is nothing more than the manifestation of the emotional communication in the analytic relationship. The only difference about it in analysis is the same thing that is always different about everyday phenomena in analysis – experience that is ordinarily unconscious is made conscious and harnessed in the service of emotional growth.

A study of the evolutionary and developmental aspects of emotional communication positions the phenomenon of objective countertransference within the broader context of human communication and illustrates the consistency of the findings of clinical psychoanalysis with recent work in the field of evolutionary psychology. This chapter will explore the relationship of cognitive and emotional communication in greater detail and discuss the role that each plays in language. It will further describe the relationship between emotional communication, the repetition compulsion, and objective countertransference.

Emotions and emotional communication in non-human mammals

Evolutionary psychology provides a useful perspective for conceptualizing the process of emotional communication. While psychoanalysis provides a picture of how emotions develop and change over the course of an individual life, evolutionary psychology provides a biological framework for understanding how and why emotions arise and the function they serve in human and non-human animals. Although reptiles and birds have emotions, emotions are most highly developed in mammals (Darwin 1872). The area of the brain involved in emotional processing – the limbic system – expanded greatly with the advent of mammals, making complex emotional functioning a distinguishing feature of mammalian behavior (MacLean 1990). It is in communication among non-human mammals that the roots of human emotional communication are found.

Working from the perspective of evolutionary psychology, Damasio (1994), Pinker (1997), LeDoux (1998), and Panksepp (1998) have all argued that emotions evolved as survival mechanisms. While both Freud and the evolutionary psychologists have viewed emotions as motivating human behavior, the evolutionary psychologists posit that emotions evolved to serve specific survival needs, and all are reality oriented. Emotions are complex neurological and behavioral patterns that direct an animal's activities towards self-preservation and reproduction. Emotions set "the brain's highest-level goals," prioritize these goals, motivate behavior towards them, evaluate experience, and guide reactions to external events in light of these goals (Pinker 1997: 373).

When emotions function as motivations, they translate internal stimuli derived from basic biological needs – such as physical security, nutrition, elimination, and reproduction – into behavior designed to satisfy those needs. Emotions make the animal do what it needs to do. They give meaning and direction to life, providing the underlying hedonic framework for establishing goals and preferring one course of action to another (Damasio 1994).

Emotions also serve to evaluate external stimuli according to their potential benefits or threats and then generate behavior designed to manage the situation. Emotions are shaped by survival needs, as determined by genetic endowment and life experience. Emotional reactions are as essential to an animal's functioning as sense perceptions. As with sense perceptions, they must be accurate, appropriate, and predictable in order to serve their function of protecting and guiding the animal's behavior.

Much of the external stimulus that emotions serve to evaluate is inanimate, such as the sight of fire or the taste of an orange. The fear aroused by the fire indicates that fire is a danger, and the pleasure aroused by eating an orange (in species for which oranges are nutritious) indicates that oranges are good to eat. Both emotional responses then serve as motivations for future behavior.

The other types of external stimuli interpreted through emotions include interactions with other animals. Emotional reactions to other animals — especially with other animals of the same species, with which social interactions are possible — will vary more than reactions to inanimate stimuli because the correct response will depend on the other animal's emotional state, as indicated by its emotional expressions.

Darwin (1872) described how facial expressions, grunts, posture, vocal pitch, erection of hair, and gestures serve as pre-linguistic vehicles for the expression of emotions. Darwin argued that "emotional expressions were designed to convey information about the sender's emotional or motivational state" (Hauser 1996: 19). Thus, emotional expressions are a form of communication.

Communication is a two-way process; in order for an expression to serve a communicative function, it must be perceived and understood accurately. However, ethological studies of animal communication have focused far more attention on the expression of emotion than on the perception of emotion. Darwin (1872) suggested simply that the ability to understand the expression of emotions is instinctive. If the ability to express emotion is selected because it is adaptive, then the ability to understand emotional expressions must be selected as well. The communication of emotion has an effect on the behavior and emotions of the animal(s) that perceive the emotion (McConnell 1990; Hauser 1996). An animal's ability to accurately understand another animal's emotional state is crucial to its survival. Griffin (1984) suggests that empathy may be an animal's most efficient way of gauging another animal's emotional state. An animal's own emotional reactions are the means through which it perceives, evaluates, and responds to the other animal's emotions.

This process may be described as emotional communication. In non-human animals, emotional induction is a non-symbolic, non-linguistic means of communicating emotional states. The process of emotional communication has two parts: an emotional expression by a sender and an induced emotion in the receiver. The sender expresses an emotion to the receiver through any of the means that Darwin and others have described; this induces an emotion in the receiver, which corresponds in a specific way to the emotional state of the sender. Through this interaction, the sender has communicated an emotion, and the receiver has perceived it. Thus, emotional communication is a channel of communication that conveys information about one animal's emotional state through the expression to and the induction of emotion in another animal.

The communication is not necessarily intentional. Communication can take place as long as the receiver is within communicative distance of the sender (MacLean 1990).

Animals are selected to be accurate perceivers of other animals' emotional states – "good mind readers" (Krebs & Dawkins 1984: 380). Idiosyncratic reactions, whether caused by abnormal neurophysiological functioning or atypical past experiences, such as trauma, are indicative of flaws in the animal's ability to perceive other animals' emotions. Non-human animals with a propensity to misread other animals' emotional states will be quickly eliminated from the gene pool. In the wild, there is little margin for error in emotional reactions.

Understood in this way, not all emotions that animals experience in relationship to other animals are inductions. Some emotions are internally motivated by the animals' survival needs. Others, less frequently, will be idiosyncratic emotional reactions to other animals. Only those reactions that are accurate and appropriate reactions to the sender's emotions should be considered inductions.

Induction and maternal behavior in non-human mammals

Although emotional processing can be seen in reptiles and birds, it has especially flourished in the evolution of mammals. This appears to have been tied to three particular behavioral developments that evolved in mammals: nursing, which led to the establishment of the family; the use of audiovocal communication in maintaining maternal/offspring contact; and play (MacLean 1990).

Emotional communication would seem to be an essential component of these behaviors, especially those related to the maternal/offspring relationship, and probably evolved in synchrony with them. The most obvious form of emotional communication is infant crying, which induces nurturing emotions in the mother. Emotional communication between baby mammals and their mothers appears to be extremely effective. Even casual observations of mother/offspring relationships in a mammal as primitive as the gerbil suggest what appear to be exquisite levels of attunement between the mother and her offspring. The attunement and complexity of communication increases in non-human primate mother/baby interactions, which are extraordinarily expressive in easily recognizable ways. Few people who have seen mother chimpanzees nurturing their offspring have failed to be touched by their strong kinship with human mothers and babies.

Darwin demonstrated that the strongest continuity between non-human animal and human modes of communication lies in the expression of emotions (Hauser 1996). The first mammalian vocalization may have been the separation cry, which alerted the mother to her infant's location "on the dark confusion of the forest's floor" (MacLean 1990: 394). The complexity of human emotional communication had its origins in the primeval mammalian mother's need to care for her young.

Emotional communication, language, and cognitive communication

Emotions evolved far earlier than consciousness, and in most, if not all non-human animals, they are experienced without consciousness or reflective awareness. Although humans have the capacity to experience emotions consciously in the form of feelings, emotions themselves are a part of the mammalian heritage. Even in humans, evolutionary biologists argue that much emotional processing occurs unconsciously – a position that is consistent with Freud's model of the mind.

Emotions also evolved long before language. And there is no consensus on the question of why language evolved in humans. However, while animal communication is primarily oriented towards communicating information about emotions, language may have evolved in order to communicate information about the world.

The need for information about the world is a distinctive component of human intelligence (Pinker 1997) and the neo-cortex, the part of the brain that contains the neural substrate of language, appears to be oriented largely towards the external world (MacLean 1990). Tooby and Devore (1987) suggest that the distinctive human adaptation is the ability to engage in cause-and-effect reasoning, a survival strategy in which thought can model reality and consider that different actions can have different outcomes. This enables humans to occupy the "cognitive niche." According to Pinker (2003: 27), "such reasoning enables humans to invent and use new technologies (such as weapons, traps, coordinated driving of game, and ways of detoxifying plants) that exploit other living things before they can develop defensive countermeasures in evolutionary time."

Pinker (2003) argues that language is an adaptation to the cognitive niche. He observes that the value of the information that humans acquire through reason is dramatically increased when it can be shared. Language allows information to be passed on to others – to be exchanged, and to accumulate – instead of having to be independently acquired and learned by each individual. It also facilitates broader, more flexible, and more precise levels of cooperation between humans, and thus a greater degree of social complexity, than are seen in nonlinguistic species. Language, therefore, is one of the essential traits that have made the creation of human culture and the steady advance of human knowledge possible.

Although Pinker does not exclude (nor does he mention) the use of language to convey information about internal emotional states, his conception of language emphasizes its utility as a channel of communication about facts about the world. Pinker (2003: 160) states that "[t]he most remarkable aspect of language is its expressive power: its ability to convey an unlimited number of *ideas* [emphasis added] from one person to another via a structured stream of sound."

These ideas are a different type of information than the feelings that are transmitted through emotional communication: ideas are experienced by both the sender and the receiver as thought. In keeping with the notion of the "cognitive niche," this type of information may be described as *cognitive* information. And language, the conduit of this type of information, can be described as a channel of cognitive communication.

Cognitive communication conveys ideas through a system of symbols that generate consensually agreed upon meanings. In cognitive communication, the sender expresses bits of information in symbolic form, usually through words and a set of rules for using them, but sometimes through signs or gestures with specific meanings. The receiver understands these symbols and experiences this understanding as thought.

Cognitive communication, therefore, functions differently than emotional communication, which operates through the expression and induction of feeling.

The symbolic system that characterizes cognitive communication is the essential core of human language – the aspect of language that distinguishes it from mere vocalization. Natural spoken language (as opposed to computer language or mathematical notation) is not, however, a purely cognitive channel of communication. In addition to its symbolic content, it also contains non-symbolic elements that serve as a conduit for emotional communication. These non-symbolic elements include tone of voice, prosody, and both cognitive and emotional associations to words that are not symbolized by the words themselves.

Conceived in this way, language is composed of two distinct channels of communication: cognitive communication and emotional communication. This may have occurred because cognitive communication, as manifested in language, evolved in such a way that it was melded into the pre-linguistic forms of vocal communication. Mithen (2006) speculates that these pre-linguistic forms were primarily channels of emotional communication. Nevertheless, cognitive communication is what distinguishes language from the grunts, howls, and songs of other animals.

Emotional communication and language in the infant–mother relationship

Cognitive communication serves many crucial functions in human life, but infants cannot use it to communicate with their mothers. Human infants, like all young mammals, are born without language. Pre-human forms of mammalian emotional communication are recapitulated in the period of human development before the acquisition of language. Infants communicate through mechanisms similar to those used by animals (Spitz 1963, 1965). Their earliest communications are driven by the limbic system (Hauser 1996) which is the same part of the brain that drives emotional expressions in non-human mammals. Infants communicate information about their affective state before they are able to communicate about the external world (Hauser 1996). Research is confirming what analysts have long theorized and mothers have always known: different cries communicate different feelings (Lester & Boukydis 1992). The infant's first vocalizations "provide a window in the infant's heart," expressing states of pain, hunger, and joy (Hauser 1996: 325).

During the preverbal period, emotional communication is the primary mode of communication from the infant to the mother. Emotional communication is expressed through the infant's crying and vocalizations, facial expressions, gaze interactions, and body movements, which gives meaning to these nonverbal signals and conveys needs and emotions with palpable specificity. The mother does not simply observe and hear the baby, she feels what the baby feels and needs, and her feelings guide her interactions. Her induced feelings – maternal empathy – are the means through which she perceives and understands the infant's nonverbal communications.

Although the most visible aspects of this pre-cognitive, purely emotional communication (particularly in earliest infancy) are focused on concrete needs for food, sleep, and gastrointestinal relief, the emotions that infants induce are a good deal more varied than just that. Even early infant facial expressions exhibit a wide range of complexity (Messer 1994). Adults also have complex reactions to infants. Although empathy is one way in which adults experience the infant's induced feelings, some of the inductions are so intense that they stimulate more primitive forms of experience, such as merged narcissistic states (see Chapter 6). Some of the most powerful feelings experienced by parents of young infants – suicidal and homicidal impulses when the baby is agitated; feelings of profound contentment and peace when the baby is calm – are often identical to Klein's (1946) account of the infant's primitive mental states and may be inductions of the infant's extreme emotions, as Bion (1962, 1963) proposed in his concept of reverie. Once the baby begins to smile, the baby's emotional life becomes richer and more sophisticated, and a whole set of more moderate emotions related to playfulness, delight, and humor are induced in the parents.

Similarly, the mother (and other adults) induce emotions that communicate feelings for which the infant does not yet have the words. Ellman and Monk

(1997) emphasize the importance of taste, touch, smell, and sound in the earliest months of mother/infant communication. Mothers and other adults who speak to babies use a distinctive vocal pattern that varies very little across cultures (suggesting an innate, evolutionarily determined biological process) that directly induces emotions in the infant (Fernald 1992). These inductions alter the infant's emotional state, as when the mother's voice and touch are soothing, or in less fortunate moments, when they are irritating or depressing.

Schore (1994) emphasizes the importance of eye contact and gaze interactions in developing and regulating affect in the 10-to-12-month-old infant. These may be viewed as special instances of induction.

Numerous psychoanalytic infant researchers have detailed the ways in which the infant and mother communicate emotions without language in the prelinguistic period of life (Stern 1985; Trevarthen 1993; Messer 1994; Beebe *et al.* 2005).

In addition to regulating the infant's own emotional state, the mother's voice provides the infant with information about her emotional state (Fernald 1992). During a period in earliest infancy, the baby is able to imitate adult facial expressions, which may help the baby to feel and understand the adult's emotion (Messer 1994). Mothers and babies vocalize together in nonconversations without language, imitating, modifying, and playing off each other's sounds. Later, the mother shares the infant's emotional states and communicates this through affective attunements (Stern 1985).

Optimal mothering – and optimal loving – would consist, in part, of the ability to experience the emotions the infant induces, to interpret them accurately, and to respond to the infant through communications that induce the "right" feelings in the infant – the feelings that the infant needs in order to grow and mature (Bion 1962).

Many of the infant's emotional communications, like those of non-human mammals, are vocal but non-linguistic. Similarly, many of the mother's emotional communications to the infant are also vocal but non-linguistic. This is a consequence of the mother's ability to adaptively regress to the infant's level of communication, and is a manifestation of her merged attunement with the infant. The mother, however, also uses language to train the child in the use of cognitive communication. She talks to the child before her words are understood, with her emotional expressions accompanying the cognitive elements of speech. The emotional communication coupled with the cognitive communication in spoken language serves as a bridge between the infant's purely nonlinguistic modes of emotional communication and developing use of cognitive communication through language.

Over the first several years of life, the infant's communication becomes increasingly conscious, deliberate, and purposeful. The use of cognitive communication through language gradually supplants the nonlinguistic, nonsymbolic forms of emotional communication and becomes the dominant channel for communicating information about the external world. To some extent, maturation is characterized by a transition from emotional communication to cognitive communication, thus forming a part of the gradual transition from an id-dominant mode of functioning to a more ego-dominant mode of functioning.

However, cognitive communication never completely replaces emotional communication. And emotional communication pervades human interaction whenever emotions and feelings are involved. The two channels become increasingly intertwined as language develops. Many of the same routes of emotional expression used by non-human animals and preverbal infants, such as facial expressions, variations in breathing, posture (and possibly pheromones through olfaction) remain in use after the acquisition of language, but the tone and rhythm of speech gradually become the primary channels of emotional communication in speech. Furthermore, emotional communication interpenetrates language through affective associations to words and ideas. Certain types of written language – primarily expressive prose and poetry – can induce feelings independent of the literal meaning of the words, as can referential symbols.

In spoken language cognitive communication and emotional communication are closely intertwined in a "multi-channel communication" (Stern 1985: 181). The two channels function differently within spoken language: cognitive communication conveys the facts; emotional communication conveys something about the speaker's feelings. Cognitive communication stimulates thought; emotional communication induces feeling.

The relationship between them is particularly intricate when the content of cognitive communication expresses the speaker's conscious feelings. When a feeling is expressed in words, the emotions that are induced along with the words determine in large part how the communication is experienced and understood. Induction multiplies the shades of meaning that can be expressed through language. The meaning of the words "I love you" will be experienced differently depending on whether they are said with warmth, coldness, or indifference. In these situations, each channel conveys different information about the sender's emotional state. In accordance with consensually agreed upon meanings, the cognitive communication transmits "categorical information" about emotions (Stern 1985: 179), and conveys, with precision, the abstract type of emotion that is expressed. The emotional communication, on the other hand, conveys the personal, phenomenological particularities of the emotion as it is privately experienced.

Cognitive communication describes life. Emotional communication conveys how it feels in its immediacy. Language combines both dimensions.

Indeed, it is not clear whether emotions – as opposed to information about emotions, references to emotion, or description of emotion – can be conveyed directly without emotional communication. Emotions, like sense data, can be described or reported in words but must be experienced in order to be known.

The ability to understand through emotional communication is closer to the capacity to perceive sensory data than it is to the capacity to understand language.

At the same time, it is probably impossible to experience emotional communication in isolation from language after language has been acquired. Even a purely nonlinguistic emotional expression, such as a shriek or a moan, will usually stimulate thoughts and associations formulated in language after an initial non-linguistic emotional reaction. The relationship between the two is more on the order of a chemical solution than a compound. They sufficiently interpenetrate each other to create the effect of a single element, but they remain distinct components of verbal communication and can be separated from each other.

Within a single linguistic communication, the cognitive communication and the emotional communication can be congruent or incongruent. When the cognitive and the emotional communications are congruent − when the affective tone matches meaning of the words − communication is simple, straightforward, and effective. But when the words and the feeling are incongruent − when the affective tone contradicts the words or is irrelevant to them − a host of complexities ensue, ranging from confusion and ambiguity to covert communications and double messages. The cognitive and emotional communications simultaneously express different messages, and the total communication can be properly understood only if both components are taken into account.

Induction and repetitions

Emotional communication is often a conscious, deliberate process. The actor working at developing a character, the politician refining the delivery of a speech, and a mother considering the correct tone to take with her child are examples of emotional communication under conscious and voluntary control. Even in more ordinary interactions, however, emotional communication may be deliberately modulated. Congruence between the words and the feelings can be carefully emphasized in order to increase the clarity and the effectiveness of a communication, while incongruities can be exploited in order to express ambiguity, sarcasm, and humor.

But most often, emotional communication is expressed and induced spontaneously, on a pre-conscious or unconscious level. In everyday life, cognitive communication is the more visible component of most linguistic communication. Emotional communication usually operates unobtrusively, almost silently, sometimes reinforcing the meaning of the words, sometimes subverting it.

In addition to being an integral part of moment-to-moment, present-day communication, emotional communication is important as a vehicle of the repetition compulsion − the almost irresistible tendency to repeat patterns of feeling and behavior derived from early life experience – especially its pathological components. As Stern (1985) suggests, the split between language and pre-linguistic experience creates a space for neurosis to grow. The pre-existing, evolutionary-based tension between cognitive and emotional communication becomes a fertile culture for the expression of arrested or distorted psychic development and psychodynamic conflict.

Emotional communication linked to past experience is the interpersonal dimension of the repetition compulsion, a powerful force that causes the current people in a person's life to experience a wide range of feelings that originated in early life. Repetitions expressed through emotional communication actively recreate the emotional past in the emotional present by inducing old feelings in new objects. Current people respond to the inducer just like the old ones did, seemingly automatically, without either party quite understanding what is happening.

In everyday life, these kinds of inductive interactions are almost always involuntary and either pre-conscious or unconscious, both for the sender and the receiver. And they are often painful for the sender, who initiates the repetition. The induction is a signal – with instructions – to the current object to repeat an interaction the sender is often loathe to repeat but powerless to prevent. Induced feelings are often manifestations of unwanted behavior patterns of which the sender is desperate to be free.

Emotional communication and objective countertransference

If much about the role emotional communication and the repetition compulsion play in everyday life sounds familiar to the analyst, it is because it is nothing more than an account of objective countertransference as described by Winnicott (1949), Heimann (1950), Searles (1979), and Spotnitz (1985) and applied to everyday life. In life, the feelings that patients induce constitute a significant part of how other people feel about them; in analysis, the induced feelings become the raw material of the objective countertransference. Like transference, objective countertransference is a commonplace phenomenon that occurs regularly in everyday life but receives special attention in analysis. When it comes to the play of emotional forces, analysis is just like life, only more so.

Of course, not all of the analyst's feelings about the patient are induced by the patient. Some of the analyst's feelings are subjective countertransference (Spotnitz 1985) – those feelings that are the result of idiosyncrasies in the analyst's character, emotional life history, or neurophysiology. The subjective countertransference is not a product of the patient's emotional communications and thus contains no information about the patient. But many of the analyst's feelings are induced by the patient, and these will be accurate and informative emotional reactions to the patient.

These inductions are the analyst's perceptions of the aspects of the patient's life experience that the patient is unable to put into words. All inductions are important, including those that the patient uses consciously and deliberately. However, the inductions related to the repetition compulsion are of special interest because these lead to the patient's most painful and intractable problems in life. By focusing attention on the induced dimensions of the repetition compulsion, the analyst has firsthand experience of how the patient's misery is constantly recreated in a way that the words alone can never fully communicate.

Emotional communication is often a particularly prominent part of the analytic process in the early years of an analysis, especially at times when the transference intensifies and new material is brought into the analysis. Conversely, the role of emotional communication often diminishes as the process of working through issues progresses and the patient learns to express feelings in words.

Nevertheless, this process is never complete. Although an increasing ability to use cognitive communication to express the whole range of human feelings – to put the story of one's life into words – is a hallmark of analytic progress, the cognitive dimensions of language cannot completely supplant emotional communication in analysis any more than they can in life. Not all emotional communication is tied to the repetition compulsion, and many aspects of human emotion cannot be communicated except through induction. Throughout the analysis, the analyst must make use of the objective countertransference in conjunction with the patient's words in order to understand the full story of the patient's life.

3

THE CONCEPT OF OBJECTIVE COUNTERTRANSFERENCE AND ITS ROLE IN A TWO-PERSON PSYCHOLOGY

Before plunging into the technical language, let's start with an analogy. The concept of objective countertransference is based on a one-person-and-a-piano psychology. The analyst is the piano. As the analyst listens to the patient, she opens her keyboard and invites the patient to play. Each key that is struck, each string that sounds, is the analyst's own, but it is the patient who strikes it. The objective countertransference is a melody played on the analyst's feelings by the patient.

In order for the analysis to work, the analyst must have experienced many different feelings in the course of her life: psychotic feelings and autistic feelings; borderline rage and narcissistic insult; sadism, masochism, altruism, and cowardice; grandiosity and despair; exhilaration and apathy; nurturing love and blistering contempt; aggression and sexuality of every possible description; the feelings of the youngest baby and the most mature adult. The more strings the piano has to offer, the more accurate the patient's melody will be.

Each piano has a distinctive tone and a distinctive range – not to mention a few out of tune strings and broken keys – so the patient's melody won't sound the same with every analyst. But when the analyst is basically attuned to the patient, the setup is always the same: the patient hits the notes, the analyst makes the sounds, and together they make the music of the objective countertransference.

The objective countertransference isn't the only tune in the room. While the patient plays on the analyst, the analyst also plays her own tune, both on her own keyboard and on the patient's. It takes a lot of practice to hear the patient's melody amidst the din, but it's worth the effort. It makes the analyst feel things that the patient cannot remember, cannot control, and cannot understand. Above all, it communicates feelings the patient cannot describe in words. It's the siren song the patient has lived life by – the song that charms its listeners into recreating the patient's emotional past in the emotional present. When the analyst can hear it without being seduced by it, the analyst feels the feelings the patient carries from the past – the feelings that hurt the patient, as well as the feelings that are craved and the feelings needed in order to be healed.

Objective countertransference

The objective countertransference is that part of the analyst's feelings that is pragmatically understood to be caused by the patient's inductions. Through the objective countertransference, the analyst emotionally participates in the problems that brought the patient into treatment. It allows the analyst to know what the patient feels, what other people who have been involved with the patient feel (and have felt in the past), and what feelings were missing from the patient's early life experience. By understanding the objective countertransference, the analyst understands aspects of the patient's experience that the patient may never be able to put into words.

The concept of objective countertransference was formulated by Winnicott (1949), and further developed (with differences in theory and terminology) by Heimann (1950), Kernberg (1965), Spotnitz (1969) and other Modern Analysts, Giovaccinni (1979), Searles (1979), and Ogden (1982) and more recently by a number of contemporary classical theorists (Ellman & Moskowitz 1998). However, it has not been defined as a product of emotional communication. For this reason we will begin with a precise definition of objective countertransference and then place the concept in the context of contemporary theories of one- and two-person psychologies.

Objective countertransference – definition and scope of the concept

Objective countertransference may be defined as follows:

> Objective countertransference is a feeling that is induced in the analyst by the patient's emotional communications and is a repetition of a feeling that originated in the patient's emotional life history.

The objective countertransference feeling may have originally been the patient's own feeling, or it may have been a feeling that somebody had about the patient. In either case, it is a feeling that somebody – either the patient or somebody involved with the patient – experienced in the past. Because the feeling is a repetition of a pattern that predates the analytic relationship, it is most fruitfully understood in the context of the patient's life – not the analyst's – and it is viewed as a crucial piece of information about the patient.

Subjective countertransference – a definition

The objective countertransference must be differentiated from the subjective countertransference (Spotnitz 1969, 1985), which comprises the feelings that the analyst experiences either towards the patient or in relationship to the patient that are shaped by and rooted in the analyst's emotional life story and not the patient's. In contrast to the objective countertransference, the subjective is not viewed as a source of information about the patient and is of no value in understanding the patient, although the analyst must be aware of it to be able to work with the patient effectively.[1]

The place of objective countertransference in the analytic relationship

In a sense, each analytic relationship, like all interpersonal relationships, is unique and distinctive. Both the patient and the analyst bring their personalities – as shaped by their life stories – to the analysis, and through their interaction create a new relationship that is different in its details from any relationship that either one of them has encountered. But everyone's relationships, when viewed across time, can be seen to contain interpersonal patterns that continually repeat with a wide range of people. Some patterns lead to ongoing satisfaction and fulfillment. Others are bottomless wells of frustration and misery. The frustrating patterns are usually at the root of a patient's decision to seek treatment, whether the patient is aware of the repetitive origin.

Because these negative repetitions are the target of psychoanalytic treatment, it is critical to distinguish three primary interpersonal currents within the analytic relationship. These three interpersonal currents make up all interpersonal relationships, not just the analytic relationship. The terms transference and countertransference are used to highlight functional roles of the patient and the analyst within the therapeutic process.

The first current comprises the feelings, repetitions, and emotional communications that the patient contributes to the relationship. In this current, the patient's contribution to the dynamic between them is maximal and the analyst's is minimal. This current is the transference, in all of its expressions and manifestations.

The second current comprises the analyst's emotional contributions to the analytic relationship. These are of two sorts: the first is the subjective countertransference. The second is analytic style, conceptualized as the ensemble of the analyst's communications as shaped by clinical and theoretical thinking. This current includes feelings that the analyst induces in the patient, either inadvertently through the subjective countertransference, or deliberately through technique. In this current, the analyst's contributions to the dynamic between them are maximal and the patient's are minimal.

THE CONCEPT OF OBJECTIVE COUNTERTRANSFERENCE

The third current includes the feelings, dynamics, and inductions that grow out of the unique interaction between the patient and the analyst; it differentiates the analytic relationship from any of their other relationships. In this current, the contributions of the patient and the analyst are approximately equal, if not on a moment-to-moment basis, then over time.

Objective countertransference is a product of the first current, which is shaped primarily by the patient's repetitions – the transference. In objective countertransference, the patient's contribution to the interpersonal dynamic is largely active, and the analyst's contribution is largely receptive. The analyst's feelings are the interpersonal dimension of the patient's repetitions.

Objective countertransference is not the only form of emotional communication in the analytic relationship. As noted above, the analyst induces feelings in the patient as well. These are rooted to the subjective countertransference, as well as the analyst's analytic style, and are best understood in the context of the analyst's life story. Similarly, both the patient and analyst induce feelings in each other that are more purely related to their unique, here-and-now interaction than to either of their repetitions.

Objective countertransference, therefore, is only one component of the analytic relationship. It is distinctive because it connects the analyst's feelings in the analysis to the patient's interpersonal patterns outside the analysis, providing information beyond what the patient can communicate through language. While the other forms of emotional communication may be either constructive or destructive to the outcome of the analytic process, they do not reveal anything about the patient outside the context of the analytic relationship and thus do not enrich the analyst's understanding of the problems that brought the patient into treatment.

Objective countertransference, like transference, is the technical label for a ubiquitous component of human emotional interaction that is a focus of special attention in psychoanalysis. Although the analytic setting can be arranged to make the experience more visible than under ordinary circumstances, the ability to feel objective countertransference has nothing to do with whether the analyst is either well analyzed or well educated. Nor does the analyst have privileged access to this experience. Everyone regularly experiences emotional induction related to repetitions in everyday life in nearly all emotional interactions with other people. What the analytic method contributes is a framework for recognizing the induced feelings amidst the larger stream of the analyst's emotional experience and for understanding it in the context of what the patient communicates to the analyst.

The theory of objective countertransference is used to generate hypotheses about the relationship between the analyst's feelings and the repetitive interpersonal patterns in the patient's life that can be of value in clinical practice. However, it is impossible to know for certain which feelings are primarily induced and which are rooted primarily in the analyst's own subjectivity. Thus, objective countertransference must be treated as a model – an epistemological construct – and ideas about objective countertransference must be treated as working hypotheses, not statements of scientific fact.

The role of the analyst's subjectivity in objective countertransference

If the objective countertransference is caused by the patient, what is the role of the analyst's own subjectivity – his own life history and emotional experience – in this phenomenon? What about the cases in which the analyst's feelings appear to be as consistent with her own repetitions as with the patient's?

First, it must be acknowledged that such situations are the rule, not the exception. Almost invariably, the analyst's repetitions appear to overlap with the patient's, at least at some point in the analysis. This is either an astonishing rate of coincidence, or a different process is at work.

The induced feelings are not like the images projected onto the fabled blank screen. Rather, the analyst's subjectivity is the medium through which she experiences the patient's inductions. The patient's emotional communications activate dimensions of the analyst's subjective experience – thoughts, feelings, memories, impulses, and fantasies – that resonate with or resemble in some way the patient's emotional communications. Sometimes, bits and pieces of the analyst's experience will be activated in a way that has never before been experienced, and the feeling will feel novel or foreign. More often, familiar aspects of the analyst's experience – including the analyst's own repetitions – will be activated.

In either case, the analyst's subjectivity is the raw material, the substrate of the objective countertransference. Without it, no induction can occur. If the analyst doesn't have within her biological endowment and life experience the emotional components necessary to experience a feeling that can be activated by the patient's transferential communications, the patient's message will not get through. No feeling can be induced in the analyst that is completely foreign, any more than the analyst can hear a tone that is outside of her auditory range.

There is rarely anything in the raw experience of the objective countertransference that distinguishes it from the rest of the analyst's feelings. The analyst cannot determine, on the basis of her emotional experience alone, whether a particular countertransference feeling is objective. Countertransference serves as objective information about the patient only to the extent that it is consistent with patterns in the patient's life outside the sessions.[2]

Furthermore, an objective countertransference is never a perfectly attuned or consistent response to the patient. It is always marbled with aspects of the subjective countertransference (the analyst's subjectivity) that are irrelevant to the patient's repetitions and distort the patient's communications. But what defines an objective countertransference is the signal, not the noise, and the signal is identified by its similarity to a pattern from the patient's life.

Up to this point, we have considered the analyst's experience only to the extent that it receives and is activated by the patient's communications in a way that repeats a feeling from the patient's life. This moment in the analytic process is the limit of the scope of objective countertransference. But this moment is, of course, an abstraction. Once the analyst feels the induction – whether consciously or unconsciously – it becomes a part of her subjective experience. It is probably inevitable that the analyst expresses the feeling to the patient, if only in a very subtle way. Indeed, by the time the analyst becomes consciously aware of the induction, it is probable that she has already expressed the feeling in her interaction with the patient, which, in turn, would have an impact upon the patient's experience of him. Most of the time, this mutual process tends to reinforce the dynamic that the patient initiated through the induction.

Strictly speaking, this behavior (which is usually unconscious) is no longer objective countertransference; it is now an action – countertransference acting-out or enactment, depending on the choice of terminology. But because this behavior is inevitable, the distinction between the countertransference and the action is not clinically useful. As long as the analyst's feelings (including both the unconscious expression and the resulting interaction with the patient) are primarily consistent with the patient's past, they are still most usefully understood within the framework of objective countertransference, that is to say, as a source of information about the patient.[3]

The concept of objective countertransference in relationship to opposing theories of countertransference

Classical analysts rejected the type of emotional involvement with the patient that objective countertransference requires. Although they acknowledge that the analyst will have feelings about the patient, countertransference is viewed exclusively as an expression of the analyst's neurosis (Kernberg 1965) – a source of distortion in the analyst's thinking that should be "overcome" (Freud 1912). Although some classical analysts (e.g., Reich 1951) who followed Freud argue that the analyst's spontaneity and natural warmth may be important technical elements in the analytic process, the countertransference feelings themselves contain no information about the patient. The epistemology of classical psychoanalysis relies on cognitive and intellectual appraisals of the patient, ideally uncontaminated by the analyst's feelings or emotional biases.

Underlying this position is the attempt to conceptualize psychoanalysis as a discipline modeled on the methodology of the natural sciences, combined with a theory of the emotions that views feelings as expressions of drives that inevitably strive for discharge, not understanding. From this perspective, feelings can no more be objective reactions to the patient than they can be

THE CONCEPT OF OBJECTIVE COUNTERTRANSFERENCE

objective reactions to the laws of physics. Only thought, as opposed to feelings, can accurately reflect upon and interpret facts and thus provide a framework for an objective understanding of the patient. The classical position is based on a view of the analytic relationship, and human interaction, in which it was possible for the analyst to minimize the influence of her subjectivity, both on her thinking about the patient and on how she relates to the patient.

Contemporary critics, drawing on theories of a two-person psychology,[4] argue that the analyst's subjectivity not only shapes feelings about the patient, but also her thoughts, theories, and interactions with the patient as well. They reject the idea that the analyst – a subjective human being – somehow put on a white analytic coat and turned into an emotional Geiger counter, evaluating the effect of the patient's subjectivity on herself without having an impact upon it. The analyst cannot be objective about the patient because she can neither step out of her subjectivity nor step out of her relationship to the patient. The analytic relationship, like all relationships, is a tangled web of mutual influence. The analyst shapes the patient's experience as much as the patient shapes the analyst's. The emotional reality in the analytic relationship is co-constructed by both. The analyst's feelings about the patient grow out of the interplay of her subjectivity with the patient's feelings, not out of any supposedly realistic response to the patient.

Where does the concept of objective countertransference stand in the face of these critiques? The primary problem with the classical position lies in the view of human emotion that focuses exclusively on issues of motivation and discharge, to the neglect of its role in receptive and expressive communication, as conceptualized in evolutionary psychology. As I have argued in Chapter 2, induced emotional reactions to others are the products of evolutionary and developmental processes and serve vital survival purposes as a channel for understanding other people's non-verbalized emotional states. Evolutionary considerations suggest that this understanding should be comprehensible, consistent, and accurate. To ignore the analyst's feelings about the patient as a source of information about the patient is to deliberately exclude crucial dimensions of human communication from the analytic process.[5]

The relationship of objective countertransference to the objections of the two-person theorists is more complex. They seem to be aimed at a concept of objective countertransference in which the analyst can simply know, on the basis of her superior self-knowledge (supplemented, perhaps, by psychoanalytic theory) which feelings are objective and which ones are not.

In contrast, the concept of objective countertransference presented here is an intersubjective concept. The experience of objective countertransference is co-created by patient and analyst. It cannot manifest without the analyst's subjectivity. It cannot be understood without a biographical understanding of the patient's subjectivity, either in itself or in relationship to other people in the patient's life. What determines whether a countertransference is objective has nothing to do with the quality of the analyst's training or

THE CONCEPT OF OBJECTIVE COUNTERTRANSFERENCE

maturity but rather its consistency with the repetitive patterns in the context of the patient's life.

The two-person theorists emphasize that the analyst's impact on the patient is equal to the patient's impact on the analyst. This is not disputed when the relationship is viewed in its totality. However, the concept of objective countertransference requires that the patient's influence on the analyst be viewed greater than the analyst's influence on the patient at the particular moments in the analytic relationship when objective countertransference occurs, and that at those moments, the analyst's subjectivity be seen as the raw material through which the objective components of countertransference are experienced. This is incompatible with the idea, central to many two-person theories, that the emotional components[6] of the analytic relationship are co-created equally by both patient and analyst.

I do not believe that this interpretation of the concept of co-construction is either a valid or necessary feature of a two-person psychology.[7] On the contrary, I believe that the three-part description of the analytic relationship (or intersubjective field) offered earlier provides a more precise, more clinically useful model of the analytic relationship: (1) some dynamics are influenced primarily by the patient, (2) some are influenced primarily by the analyst, (3) some are more purely a product of mutual influence.

Within these three major currents, objective countertransference analysis describes only those dynamics in which the patient's influence on the analyst's subjectivity is the greater. Conceptually, it is an essential component of a two-person psychology. Without it, the repetition of the patient's interpersonal patterns within the analytic relationship cannot be explained except as coincidence. But it does not describe the entire analytic relationship, nor is it intended to. It is a part of the whole – a phenomenological and conceptual subsystem. On a clinical level, it can often be usefully applied in a semi-autonomous way that does not make overt reference to the two-person perspective or to the other currents in the analytic relationship. On a theoretical level, however, it is consistent with, and indeed must be understood within the broader context of, a two-person psychology.

Differences in the practical application of the standard two-person model and objective countertransference

Although I believe that the concept of objective countertransference is fully compatible with a two-person psychology, the idea that some dynamics in the analytic relationship are primarily shaped by the patient leads to a very different understanding of the analyst's feelings than the current two-person models. A two-person analysis is designed to give an account of the contributions of both subjectivities in the analytic relationship. In contrast, an analysis of objective countertransference is designed to answer a specific cluster of questions: What is the patient communicating, remembering, longing for, or fearing, but unable to put into words? What does the patient induce in others that leads to the perpetual re-creation of the experiences the patient dreads? What maturational feelings were missing from the patient's early environment? What is the relationship between the analyst's feelings and the patient's inability to get what she wants from her life? Moreover, what feelings does the patient need to feel with (or from) the analyst in order to succeed? All of these questions may be subsumed under a more general question: What is the relationship of the analyst's feelings to the repetitive interpersonal patterns in the patient's life?

Consider the case of a man whose analyst is disappointed in him for not making more progress in the analysis. Part way through a session, the analyst realizes that he is impatient because the patient is so concrete. Nothing goes anywhere. The analyst asks a question like, "How did you feel when your wife wouldn't have sex with you?" – she's been rejecting him for months – and the patient responds, "It wasn't great, but it was okay." He goes on to say blandly that what really bothered him was that it snowed that night, and he had to get out of bed 15 minutes early to shovel the walk. (This, the analyst thought with exasperation, after three years of analysis!) There doesn't seem to be anything that the analyst can do to get this patient to have a real feeling. The patient just lays there, a loyal lump, coming to his sessions regularly week in and week out, never getting anywhere.

The analyst feels that he would like to help him, but also realizes that he has ignored the patient. The analyst has never mentioned him in supervision. He has to admit that the patient has no more presence in his mind than the not-so-good coffee he gets twice a week from the café next to his office.

He has heard the patient's life story, and he knows that the patient has seldom been treated warmly. His mother transparently preferred his older sister and repeatedly told him that she had always hoped for two girls. The father wanted a boy, but the patient wasn't the little macho the father expected. He was always anxious, always shy. His parents were both high-fliers – successful professionals who assumed their children would follow suit. His sister did, but not him. He wasn't the best in school. He wasn't great in sports. He wasn't very popular. Most people found him boring. He was passed over for promotions at work; he didn't get the girl of his dreams, and his wife has withdrawn from him.

On the other hand, the patient's life had not been totally bleak. He was his grandfather's favorite and often went to him for comfort. Some teachers liked him better than his sister, appreciating his sweetness and generosity more than her hard-edged competitiveness. He always had one close friend. His wife had been more loving before their baby was born.

The analyst also knows that he can be impatient. He is a bit of a perfectionist himself, just like the patient's father. He knows where it comes from. His mother was passive, and left him prey to his father's insatiable demands.

His father insisted that he produce, and he complied in spades: all As throughout school, Ivy League college, the best graduate school. It was a nightmare from which he finally awoke only after a long, intense analysis (that the analyst thought was very successful analysis). He expects less from himself than he used to, and he is able to be patient with his other patients. He's gentle with his kids. He once sat with a schizophrenic for six months without asking anything of him. He knows how to contain in silence. He understands the patient's pain. He is uncomfortable with how he feels about the patient, but he can't change the way he feels, not at that moment anyway.

An analysis of this situation from a two-person perspective would start by assuming, as a heuristic principle, that the patient must be viewed within the context of the relationship with the analyst, and that this relationship was co-constructed. In this case, both the patient and the analyst went into the relationship primed for their interaction, and the relationship is rich with mutuality. The patient has a long history of disappointing others, but each person was disappointed for their own reasons. The patient's mother wanted a girl, and the father wanted more of a boy. Each teacher who viewed the patient as mediocre, each employer who overlooked his presence, and even his wife who has withdrawn from him, have been involved in a unique relationship with the patient that was constructed by each of them. Many people were disappointed in the patient, but each for their own reasons.

Although the continuity between the feelings that other people in the patient's life have felt towards him and the analyst's feelings would be recognized, the contribution of the analyst's subjectivity would be emphasized. The analyst's history reveals a strong tendency to be disappointed, and this patient would appear to be a likely target. The fact that the analyst is patient with other patients is irrelevant, for each relationship is unique. Something about his interaction with this patient has led to this state of affairs. It may be something about the patient that triggers these feelings in the analyst. Or the analyst may have done something that initiated the patient's feelings. Perhaps the analyst's tone was intimidating, causing him to be less expressive than he might be in a different relationship. Perhaps the analyst expected more from him than from his other patients and communicated this to the patient, either subtly or overtly. In any case, what is transpiring is an enactment – a product of both subjectivities. It doesn't make sense to ask who caused what. How can we know the dancers from the dance?

From the perspective of objective countertransference, the situation is conceptualized differently. As a heuristic principle, it would begin by analyzing the analyst's feelings in the context of what is known about the patient's life, focusing primarily on what was common throughout the patient's relationships. It would emphasize that many important people in the patient's life were disappointed in him. It would recognize that some people did have good feelings about the patient in the past but would not view this as immediately relevant to the analytic relationship because those feelings were absent from the countertransference. For the purpose of understanding objective countertransference, the most salient feature would be the continuity between the analyst's feelings and those of the other people in the patient's life. An objective countertransference analysis would agree that an enactment was taking place and that the analyst's behavior – at least until he became aware of it and did something about it – no doubt reinforced and maintained (and possibly triggered) the repetition of the dynamic in the analysis. But it would hypothesize that the enactment originated primarily as an expression of the patient's repetition compulsion – an unconscious, involuntary tendency to induce his parents' early disappointment in him in other people who were important to him, including the analyst.

But what is the role of the analyst's subjectivity in the interaction? How should his clear propensity to be demanding and disappointed be understood? Why consider this merely raw material for an induction, rather than the initiating factor in the enactment? Why not hypothesize that the analyst induced the feelings of being a disappointment in the patient and view both countertransference and the transference as products of the analyst's repetition compulsion?

This would be considered to be a serious possibility if the patient didn't have a history of being a disappointment to others or if the analyst was regularly disappointed with most of his patients. Because neither scenario was true, the working hypothesis that the patient induced the feelings in the analyst – rather than the other way around – would be considered more likely.

Having said that, why not take a thoroughgoing two-person perspective and view the situation as being co-created equally by both of them? Why focus on the patient's contribution to the dynamic when there is ample evidence from the analyst's life history that this is a repetition for him as well? Why not view the analyst as a full participant in the interaction and assign him an equal measure of responsibility in creating the emotional climate?

The answer depends on the interpretation that is given to the patient's history of having been involved in relationships in which he is considered a disappointment. Is it a series of unique relationships that coincidentally had the same painful outcome – a lifelong string of bad luck? Or is it a pattern? And if it is a pattern, what is the most useful way of understanding that pattern?

It is true that within the broader two-person perspective, each of these relationships was a unique interaction between distinct subjectivities. Furthermore, the patient has not remained exactly the same over time. At times he has evolved and matured, and at other times, he has regressed. The repetition compulsion is not a software program. Each repetition is a little different from the previous one; each is marked by the stamp of the relationship in which it takes place. In this example, there is no doubt that everyone who was disappointed in this patient brought their own individual reasons into the

THE CONCEPT OF OBJECTIVE COUNTERTRANSFERENCE

relationship. The patient's experience of being rejected was a product of each relationship; he was never solely the cause.

The patient's problem does not lie in the unique features of each relationship but rather in the common thread of rejection that runs through all of them. His problem is that no matter where he goes, no matter whom he meets, most of the important people in his life – even his analyst – have the same reaction to him. Each new relationship is an experience of being hurt in the same old way. This is the problem that brought him into treatment.

The key to this problem cannot be found in the other peoples' subjectivities – they are all different – or in the distinctive aspects of the intersubjective matrix each co-creates with the patient. It can only be found in the patient – in the pattern of emotional communication that he brings to these relationships – because the patient is the only constant. Consequently, an objective countertransference analysis tends to discount the idiosyncratic features the analyst brings to the relationship, including coincidental overlaps between her emotional life history and the patient's. If the goal is to understand the patient, then the focus must stay on the patient. From this perspective, the most salient point is that the patient induces the same type of feeling in the analyst that he had previously induced in others. That is the core of the patient's recurrent misery. And for that reason, it is the core of an objective countertransference analysis.

Multiple objective countertransferences

In this example, the patient induced a particular cluster of feelings related to disappointment and neglect. However, a study of the patient's life story suggests that at least one more repetition was possible – a repetition linked to the more positive, loving feelings that a minority of people in his life had experienced towards him. Had the analyst experienced those feelings instead of the disappointed feelings, that countertransference would also be viewed as objective.

There is never a single objective countertransference because no person's life is limited to a single repetition. Most people engage in a number of repetitions throughout their lives, and to the extent that each of these various repetitions is related to an interpersonal theme in the patient's life, each will be linked to a distinct objective countertransference.

What causes a particular transference/countertransference configuration to emerge? It's difficult to say. Some patients experience such a powerful compulsion to repeat a specific aspect of their life history that they will develop essentially the same transference with almost any analyst and consequently induce essentially the same countertransference in all of them. For other patients, subjective elements in the analyst – her subjective countertransference, the usual effect of her interventions, and her receptivity to the different types of transference and induction – play a significant role in triggering a particular transference/countertransference configuration. As long as its content is primarily a repetition from the patient's past, however, the countertransference would still be considered objective and most usefully understood in the context of the patient's life.

The place of objective countertransference in the analytic process

Understanding is one thing, curing is another. Once countertransference is recognized and understood, the analyst must use this understanding to help the patient work through, overcome, or be cured of the repetitive patterns that perpetuate unhappiness. An objective countertransference analysis girds this process but provides no instructions. In the example given, the results of the analysis do not tell us whether to:

- interpret the situation to the patient without disclosing the feeling;
- disclose the feeling without interpreting it;
- disclose the feeling dispassionately while interpreting it;
- disclose the feeling while taking personal responsibility for it;
- disclose the feeling while making the patient responsible for it;
- express the feeling with affect;
- tolerate the feeling while consciously relating to the patient in an accepting and appreciative manner;
- contain the feeling while behaving neutrally towards the patient;
- acknowledge the feeling silently while developing and communicating an empathic understanding of the patient's subjective experience;
- make an intervention that expresses a different feeling than the one that was induced, based on an analysis of what the induced feeling indicates about the patient's emotional needs;
- make any other sort of intervention that might work.

In contrast to understanding the objective countertransference, questions of technique always require an equal focus on the analyst's contribution to the relationship. Objective countertransference describes one aspect of the patient's problem, but clinical decisions must still be made based both on the analyst's subjective proclivities – theoretical orientation, character style, and personal level of comfort – and (equally importantly, one hopes) the individual patient's specific needs. How the analyst expresses feelings determines whether the analysis is another in a long string of repetitions or becomes the road out.

Objective countertransference analysis is, therefore, an epistemological tool, not a theory of technique. Its clinical utility, while profound, is limited to understanding certain dimensions of the patient's problems. Its importance in the analytic process varies from case to case. With some patients it is the central feature of the work; with others, it remains in the background through most of the treatment, coming to the fore only occasionally. These differences usually have nothing to do with the nature of the patient's problem or the prognosis. Independent of all these variables, there are differences in peoples' propensity to induce feelings, just as there are variations in the range of notes that people can sing. Some patients are strong inducers; others communicate more purely through language. Some patients' problems are linked primarily to emotional communication; other patients' problems are linked primarily to language. In a single patient, some problems may be expressed through induction and other problems through language. Similarly, some analysts are more receptive to emotional communication, and others are more receptive to words.[8]

Summary

Both the patient and the analyst bring the weight of their life stories to the analysis and create a complex relationship that combines repetitions from each of their life stories with novel elements that are unique to their relationship. The objective countertransference is an interpersonal effect of the patient's repetitions on the analyst. It is not the only important interpersonal current in the relationship, but it is significant because it is closely linked to the problems that brought the patient into the treatment.

Objective countertransference analysis is a theory of understanding, not a theory of technique, and it is not linked to any particular way of intervening with the patient. An understanding of the objective countertransference allows the analyst to experience aspects of the patient's experience and repetitions that language alone can never convey.

4

EMOTIONAL COMMUNICATION AND ITS RELATIONSHIP TO THE BASIC CONCEPTS OF PSYCHOANALYSIS

1 THE QUALITIES OF EMOTIONAL MOMENTS AND RELATIONAL MODES

Although the concept of emotional communication has been used (in different terminology) throughout the history of psychoanalysis, it has not been conceptually integrated with the psychoanalytic concepts of repetition, transference, and countertransference.

This chapter will introduce the idea that emotional states – feeling (or affective) states that involve other people – can be described by two qualities: the specific feeling and the relational mode, which defines the general way the other person is experienced in relationship to the self, within which a wide range of specific feelings are possible. Used in conjunction, these two qualities allow a fine-grained analysis of human emotional communication and increased precision in formulating interventions.

These qualities can also be applied to concepts of repetition, transference, and countertransference. This chapter will define these basic psychoanalytic concepts in a way that links them to the concepts of emotional communication, specific feelings, and relational modes. While the definitions themselves will be familiar to readers who are familiar with basic psychoanalytic theory, the importance here is the integration of these concepts with the theory of emotional communication.

The defining qualities of emotional relatedness

Human emotional experience that involves other people in any way – in thought, fantasy, dreams, or actual interaction, whether conscious or unconscious – is an unending succession of emotional states. These states comprise both subjective, intrapsychic experience, and expressed, observable behavior.

Each emotional state is characterized by two closely entwined qualities: a specific feeling (or feelings) and a specific relational mode.

BASIC CONCEPTS

The specific feeling is the content of the emotional state, the affective tone that gives it its particular flavor. Specific feelings include the whole range of human emotion – love, hate, anger, fear, longing, desire, irritation, sadness, hilarity, disappointment, humiliation, exaltation, potency, helplessness, and every other feeling or combination of feelings that anyone has ever experienced. Although specific feelings are not always conscious, they are usually the aspects of the emotional state that are most accessible to conscious, subjective experience.

Specific feelings, however, are experienced in the context of a relational mode,[1] which determines how a person experiences and relates to another person in a global way. The relational mode is defined primarily by whether the other person is experienced as being similar to, or different from, the self.

The specific feeling that characterizes an emotional state determines the moment's affective tone, while the relational mode determines the target and the meaning of the affective tone in relationship to the other person. Let's consider an example in which the specific feeling is hate: a woman – let's call her Penia[2] – hates both of her parents, but the feeling of hate is different with each of them because she experiences them within two different relational modes.

This woman hates her mother because her mother neglected and abused her as a child. She experiences her mother as cruel, withholding, and intolerant, while she experiences herself as kind, generous, and accepting. She believes that her feelings are completely different from her mother's in any given situation. She's glad when her mother is in pain because it means that there is a measure of justice in the universe. Her mother is a target of her hatred, and when she hates her mother, she does not hate herself. In fact, she feels good about herself. She does not feel that her mother's identity is in any way related to her own. The specific feeling she experiences is hate, which she feels within the context of experiencing her mother as being separate and different from herself.

She hates her father because he has all of the same qualities she hates in herself. He's just as intimidated by her mother as she is. He's passive and frightened, just like she is. Her self-image and her identity overlap with her image of her father and with her sense of his identity. Both she and her father are targets of her hatred. When she hates her father, she hates herself, and when she hates herself, she hates her father (although the whole constellation of feeling is not always conscious). She and her father are the target of her hate. The specific feeling she experiences is hatred, which she feels within the context of experiencing her father as the same as herself.

The relational mode, therefore, describes how a person relates to another person based on whether the other person is experienced as being the same as or differentiated from the self. In the example above, the woman experiences her mother as being separate from, and therefore differentiated from herself, while she experiences her father as being the same as, and therefore undifferentiated from herself.

37

This woman's experiences of hate towards her parents are two distinct emotional states. In both moments, she feels the same specific feeling – hate – but the meaning, the target, and the subjective feel of the hate are different because the hate is experienced in the context of two different relational modes.

These two entwined qualities – specific feeling and relational mode – are ever-present in human emotional life. Together, they define and describe the emotional state. They can be discerned in subjective experience and in observable behavior.

Emotional communication takes place within the context of the emotional state, and it is characterized by the same qualities. Every feeling that is communicated expresses a specific feeling within a specific relational mode, and every feeling that is received is also experienced as a specific feeling within a relational mode.

As we shall see, repetitions, transference, and countertransference can all be conceptualized as patterned clusters of emotional states. As such, they are also characterized by specific feelings and specific relational modes. For this reason, these concepts will be used throughout this book to describe, classify, and understand the many ways people experience themselves and others.

The basic relational modes

There are five basic relational modes. These represent a synthesis of the clinical and theoretical observations made by the Freudian, Kleinian/Object Relational, Modern, Interpersonal, Self Psychological/Intersubjective, and Relational schools. Not all schools would acknowledge the existence of all five modes; some have privileged particular modes and defined others as variants. However, I believe that each of these schools has made valuable contributions and taken together, they provide a more complete picture of human relatedness than is provided by any one school.

Although some people experience others primarily through a single relational mode, all people typically experience others through all relational modes at different moments throughout their lifetimes (with the exception of the present-anchored mode that develops relatively late in development and is not experienced in infancy or early childhood). And while certain diagnoses may be characterized by a preponderance of particular relational modes, the concept of the relational mode is not a diagnostic classification. Rather, the relational mode is fundamentally a description of how the other person is experienced in particular emotional states. In the example given, Penia experiences her mother as different from her and her father as the same as her. Whether these experiences are pathological is another question altogether, and it is determined by the overall quality of her relationships with them and the impact of these relationships on her current relationships and functioning, her life goals, and her overall level of satisfaction with her life.

The five relational modes can be grouped in two main categories: the undifferentiated modes, in which the other is experienced and related to, as being the same as or similar to the self and the differentiated modes in which the other is experienced and related to, as being different, separate, or distinct from the self.[3] Within most modes, there is a spectrum of manifestations, ranging from states that are infantile and primitive to states that are mature and adult. (The present-anchored mode is the exception, in that it is experienced only in maturity, and thus has no primitive manifestations.)

The undifferentiated relational modes

There are two undifferentiated relational modes: the narcissistic and the projective identification modes.

The narcissistic mode: In the narcissistic mode, the person experiences a feeling of sameness between his self and the other person. The feeling of sameness may or may not be based on realistic similarities; what defines the narcissistic mode is that the person feels the sense of sameness. The other is experienced as being merged with, a part of, an extension of, a twin of, identical to, or similar to the self – either wholly or in part. There is an overlap between some aspect of the self – in feeling, identity, or ego boundaries – and the other.[4]

In all but the most intense states of fusion, a person in the narcissistic mode experiences some sense of self as being distinct from the other person, but this is experienced through the prism of sameness. The degree of the sense of sameness with the other defines the spectrum of narcissistic relatedness: largely undifferentiated states of fusion or merger with the other are at the primitive end of the spectrum, while states of conscious empathy are at the mature end of the spectrum. Experiences in the narcissistic mode can be affectively positive or negative. Thus, the feeling of sameness can be pleasurable and serene or painful and anguished. Or it can be almost unnoticeable – an invisible and seemingly neutral backdrop to the specific feelings. Examples of relatedness within the narcissistic mode include emotional states:

- the fantasy of merging with a celebrity, imagining one's own identity is mingled with the celebrity's, and living vicariously through the celebrity's life;
- the feeling of intimate symbiosis with another person, such as in moments of romantic intimacy in which one has the sense of having the same feelings in synchrony. Or as in moments of shared self-hatred: "we are a pair of pathetic losers";
- the feelings of twinship or shared identity with another person, such as adolescents who dress and talk in identical ways and experience strong feelings of affiliation;

- the feeling of being understood empathically, in the sense that one feels that the other person has shared or experienced the same feeling;
- the feeling of empathy with another other person, in which a similarity between one's own feelings and those of the other is experienced but without overlap in identity or ego boundaries.

The projective identification mode: The projective identification mode[5] arises when a person is unable to tolerate a particular feeling and defends against it by projecting it onto the other person. He then experiences the other person as being characterized primarily (if not exclusively) by the projected feeling. For example, a person cannot tolerate feeling weak and projects the feelings of weakness onto another person. Consequently, the person consciously feels no weakness; rather, he feels strong and experiences the other person as weak. Although the projection is an attempt to eliminate the feeling, the feeling remains an essential component of his identity. The projective identification allows the person to remain connected to the feeling by remaining connected with the person who receives the projected feeling. There is a strong overlap in ego boundaries – a lack of differentiation – in relation to the projected feelings: aspects of the person's own identity, the projected feelings, have become a part of his experience of the other person's identity. However, this overlap is only experienced unconsciously; consciously, the other person's identity is experienced as the polar opposite of his own, in one or more critical ways. There is no conscious feeling of sameness, despite the lack of unconscious differentiation. Projective identification (as it is defined here),[6] differs from the other modes in that it arises exclusively as a defense.

Some examples of experiences in the projective identification mode are listed below:

- A man projects all feelings of strength onto his girlfriend. He then experiences himself as being weak and helpless and relates to her as if she were powerful and strong.
- A mother can't tolerate her shyness and fear of other people and projects these feelings onto her daughter, who she then experiences as being fearful and socially incompetent. She further feels contemptuous of her daughter for feeling so fearful.
- A teenage boy, who feels awkward and unattractive, projects all of his feelings of power and potency onto a sexy, seductive movie star. Then he feels envious of the idealized star but feels that he can never be like him.

Moments of emotional relatedness in the projective identification mode can be stable and ongoing, but they also tend to be intense and volatile. Although they can be affectively positive or negative, they usually have a desperate, anguished quality or an unusually rigid and stereotypic quality.

BASIC CONCEPTS

The differentiated relational modes

There are three differentiated relational modes: the object mode, the anaclitic mode, and the present-anchored mode. In all the differentiated modes, the other person is experienced, consciously or unconsciously, as separate and different from the self and not a part of or connected to the person's own self. In more primitive differentiated states, the other person may be experienced as either a part of the environment, like the air that one breathes (Balint 1968), or simply as "not me." In less primitive states, the other is experienced as a different person, a different center of initiative, a different subjectivity.

The object mode: As in all the differentiated modes, the other person is experienced as separate and different from the self. The distinguishing feature of the object mode is that the differentiated relatedness occurs within the context of an interaction that is experienced as pathogenic or traumatic. During development, the object mode is often experienced in the context of maturational needs being unsatisfied, either subtly or grossly, by the other. The reasons that the needs are unmet range from a well-intentioned misattunement to sadism or aggression. No matter the reason, the effect is injurious. Emotional states in the object mode are affectively negative – wholly or in part. Relatedness in the object mode is illustrated in the following examples:

- a baby's feeling when he is cold and needs to be warmed up, but gets fed, walked, or changed instead because the parent doesn't intuit that he needs warmth;
- a girl's feeling when she is frightened and wants to feel protected by her parent but is instead ridiculed because the parent is afraid of spoiling her;
- a boy's feeling when he needs admiring attention from a parent but receives none because the parent is depressed and pays no attention to the boy;
- a woman's feeling when she wants her girlfriend to understand why she is hurt but instead is criticized by her because her girlfriend hates it when she cries;
- a man feeling hurt and disappointed because he wants his father to be proud of him for surpassing him but receives his father's anger and resentment instead.

The concept of the object mode is implicit in all classical theories of transference in which a person's experience of the other person is (a) distorted due to displacement of past experiences with other people; (b) the other person is experienced as being separate and different from the self; and (c) the other person is experienced in a way that was originally pathogenic, or currently maladaptive.

The anaclitic mode: As in the object mode, the anaclitic mode is a differentiated relational mode in which the other is experienced as separate and different from the self. The defining feature of the anaclitic mode is that it occurs in the context of an interaction that is nurturing and supportive.

In development, the anaclitic mode is associated with the experiences in which maturational needs are being met. The anaclitic mode is characterized by healthy dependency, maturation, and growth.[7] Relationships in the anaclitic mode are usually experienced as affectively positive, either wholly or in part. Examples of anaclitic relatedness are listed below:

- a baby's experience of feeling cold and then having a parent wrap him up comfortably in a blanket;
- the experience of a girl who is frightened about performing in a play who receives the right combination of support and encouragement from a parent that enables her to go on stage and play her part;
- the feelings of a boy who is panicked about learning his multiplication tables and has his mother patiently help him memorize them;
- a teenager who feels anxious and regressed when she has the flu is comforted and pampered by her parent, even though she is old enough to care for herself;
- a man who is proud of having surpassed his father receives his father's loving admission that he did even better than his father.

The present-anchored mode: Relatedness in the present-anchored mode is characterized by the minimal influence of repetitions and unmet developmental needs on interpersonal perceptions, reactions, and interactions. Thus, a person relating in the present-anchored mode engages in an emotional exchange that is grounded in the present, not the past. Others can be experienced primarily as separate people in their own right, and can be viewed realistically, three dimensionally, and fully differentiated from the self (Jacobson 1964; Mahler *et al.* 1975). Interactions with others are not predetermined by previous patterns.

This is not to say that interactions with others are uninfluenced by past experience – that is impossible – but rather that this mode is characterized by a degree of flexibility, spontaneity, and freedom that is not possible in the other modes. The present-anchored mode affords the highest degree of free and conscious choice that humans can attain.

The present-anchored mode can provide the basis of full intersubjectivity (Benjamin 1998; Mitchell 2000), a sub-mode marked by the potential for truly equal partnership, cooperation, authenticity, and mutual recognition of the other's subjectivity. On the other hand, relatedness in this mode can also take the form of neutral emotional interactions as well as non-cooperative conflict and intolerance (albeit conflict that is not based on repetitions).

This mode is the result of optimal negotiation of early developmental stages and probably emerges in middle-to-late childhood, and can be viewed as one of the hallmarks of maturation. For most people, however, this mode alternates, to a greater or lesser extent, with the repetitive modes in everyday life. It is the rare (probably mythical) person whose life is unaffected by repetitions.

Patients in analysis go in and out of this mode. Moments of relatedness in the present-oriented mode are rarely the primary target of analytic treatment because analytic treatment is focused on repetitions and repetitions are not manifested in this mode. Thus, a patient must be able to relinquish this mode in order to engage in the analysis. Nevertheless, he will usually have to return to this mode at various points in order to be able to observe himself and to experience moments of self-awareness and insight.

The analyst, however, must be able to maintain this mode for a significant part of the time in the analysis. It is within this mode that the analyst can experience the patient's emotional communications as objective countertransference and also be able to pull back from them and understand them.

Examples of emotional states in the present-anchored mode are listed below:

- A woman listens to her partner's sexual desires, understands that they are different from and in some ways antithetical to her own needs. She strives to accommodate her lover's needs without sacrificing her own.
- A person listens to a friend discuss his cultural background and how it influences his perspective on abortion. He appreciates how his friend might have come to a different point of view than he has and is accepting of his friend, despite the intensity of their differences on this issue.
- A woman discusses the possibility of sharing an apartment with a friend and realizes that they would be extremely frustrated living with each other in light of the difference in their lifestyles. Although she feels disappointed and frustrated, she does not feel rejected when her friend agrees with her and they decide not to live together.
- A socialist discusses the issue of taxation for health care with a libertarian that he has met at a party. He understands that the libertarian is sincere, intellectually honest, and embraces his position with integrity. Nevertheless, he thinks it is a selfish point of view, he hates the man and his politics, and remains resolved to struggle against this ideology which he finds abhorrent. (The libertarian felt the same way about the socialist, and he was also in the present-anchored mode.)

2 REPETITIONS, TRANSFERENCE, AND COUNTERTRANSFERENCE

Relational modes, relationships, and repetitions

Emotional states, characterized by specific feelings experienced in the context of a relational mode, are here-and-now experiences that include every moment of human relatedness. However, many here-and-now emotional states are shaped primarily by prior patterns of emotional relatedness that evolved, primarily but not exclusively, in childhood, which determine how current relationships are experienced. These moments can be described as repetitions. The concept of a repetition was introduced by Freud (1914c), and has been used, with modifications, extensions, and differences in vocabulary, by nearly every psychoanalytic theorist since then.

Let's go back to Penia and consider how the patterns of relatedness with her parents affect her other relationships.

When she relates to her mother – whether in reality or in her mind – she experiences her as being separate and differentiated from herself. She is in the object mode, and she hates her mother because of the way her mother treated her, both in the past and in the present. These two facts color every communication moment of relatedness that she has with her mother – both how she understands what her mother tells her and how she talks to her. If her mother asks her how her search for a new job is going, she understands this as a criticism. As far as she is concerned, her mother is a predator, and she's prey. She thinks about screaming at her mother – a pleasurable fantasy – and she doesn't feel guilty about it. She hasn't completely given up on the idea that someday her mother will be nice to her. Sometimes she has fantasies that her mother will be proud of her or will give her something wonderful. But most of the time she despairs about the possibility of getting through to her. She feels that it would be easier to teach geometry to an orangutan than to get her mother to understand her. When she has any distance from the relationship, it seems like they are both locked into a script from which neither of them can escape. But most of the time it just feels like life – life with her mother.

Life with her father is different. With him, she is in the narcissistic mode. She hates herself, and she hates him because they are both the same. It's a muted hatred, an enmeshed hatred. When he complains about her mother, she remembers the helplessness that she felt every time her mother screamed. Sometimes she'd watch her mother rail at him for being a worthless loser while she cowered in the corner. After her mother's rage was spent, and she had retreated to the kitchen to finish off her pitcher of martinis, she and her father would sit on the couch and watch TV in silence. A friend suggested that she must hate him for not protecting her, but she bears him no grudge because they are cut from the same cloth – two pathetic cowards. It's his weakness that she hates, his horrible passivity so like her own. She hates him but never says a word for fear of wounding him. She would feel too guilty. He's so kind – too kind to criticize.

Both of her relationships with her parents are the templates for other relationships. Her relationship with her mother forms the basis for some of her relationships with women, such as teachers and bosses, and also with some of her boyfriends. She initially feels that they appreciate and adore her but soon she feels rejected and attacked by them in the same way that she feels rejected by her mother. Not every detail of her relationship with her mother is repeated in these relationships; there are always some new details that are different – sometimes better than the original, sometimes worse. But the broad outlines of the relationships are the same. They all share the object relational mode: she experiences the other people as different from herself, and she experiences these relationships as if they are pathological or traumatic for her. These relationships all comprise a range of feelings that resembles those she feels in relationship to her mother.

Her relationship with her father forms the basis for some of her non-romantic relationships with men and with some of her female friends as well. She often thinks that she and her friends are a pack of losers, just like her father. She feels comfortable with them but wishes that they had some backbone. But she would never say a critical word to any of them. These relationships all share the narcissistic mode, in that she sees the other people as all being same as or similar to herself.

The relationships that are based on her original relationships with her parents are repetitions. A *repetition* is an unconscious cluster of emotional states, a pattern of feeling, thought, behavior, and relatedness that is characterized in the following ways:

- originated in a particular period of a person's life, usually in relationship to another person;
- arose as an adaptation of the person's emotional state at the time – conscious and unconscious, experiential, behavioral, and interpersonal – and the external conditions of his environment during that period;
- is retained involuntarily through later periods in the person's life during which external circumstances have changed.[8]

Repetitions persist in the face of changes in the environment. They lack the fluid reactivity to the actual external world that characterizes present-oriented emotional interaction. A person experiencing a repetition feels as if he is living in the present, but he acts, reacts, and relates as if he were he were living in the past. Repetitions recreate the emotional past in the emotional present.

This all happens unconsciously. The power and tenacity of repetitions derive from their unconscious origin. A person engaged in a repetition may be consciously aware of the similarity between the past and his current emotional state, but he has little or no conscious awareness that he is engaged in a repetition unless he has been in psychoanalysis or has developed a degree of self-understanding through other means.

For example, Penia knows that she feels the same way with a woman in her present life as she did with her mother. Penia thinks this is just a coincidence, another piece of bad luck or fate. Despite her awareness of the similarity, she doesn't know that her perceptions – her subjective reactions and her interactions with the woman – create the similarity. She doesn't know that she is in the grip of a repetition, an unconscious emotional state that shapes her present experience to fit patterns that developed in the past.

Causes of repetitions

Repetitions are rooted in the following experiences.

Unmet maturational needs: Repetitions can be caused by the failure of the parent (or the environment) to provide an emotional or a behavioral experience that was needed in order to allow normal maturation to unfold. However, the need continues. Examples of unmet needs include, but are not limited to, a lack of emotional consistency, emotional attunement, inadequate mirroring, improper soothing or lack of structure, discipline, affection, admiration, or love.

Trauma: Repetitions can be caused by a trauma that impaired or injured the person's ability to cope with or integrate the injury and retarded, regressed, or stalled development. Traumas include physical or emotional abuse, environmental catastrophe, over- or under-stimulation, or any experience that overwhelms a person's defenses.

Intrapsychic conflict: In accordance with the various versions of the classical theory of neurosis, repetitions can be caused by conflicting feelings, unresolved ambivalence, or an inability to tolerate wishes, impulses, thoughts, or feelings.

In practice, these three categories of experience overlap and usually contribute jointly to the development of any particular repetition. Conceptualized in this way, all types of psychopathology that have been described by the various schools of psychoanalysis can be described as repetitions.

How repetitions become enacted in present-day relationships

A repetition is a sort of unconscious memory that is lived out continuously in the present. It is always experienced subjectively and is usually expressed in behavior and patterns of interpersonal relatedness as well. Repetitions become enacted in the present through three unconscious processes that can operate alone or in combination with each other.

The first process, the most fundamental of the three, involves displacement and distortion: feelings from past relationships are displaced onto current relationships, which are then distorted in accordance with the patterns from the past. For example, Penia often feels that other women are hostile and rejecting, just as she experienced her mother; this propensity overrides evidence to the contrary. Her feelings about her mother are displaced onto the current relationships. These current relationships are then understood and experienced in a distorted way that fits the template established in the past. Information that does not confirm her distortions might be ignored or interpreted in ways that are inaccurate in terms of current reality but are consistent with how she experienced her mother.

The process of displacement and distortion affects subjective experience, both conscious and unconscious. But it does not, in the absence of the following two processes, recreate the patterns of the past in her actual interactions. For example, this process leads Penia to feel that women in her current life are hostile, but it does not lead her to be involved with women who are actually hostile, or to stimulate hostile behavior in other women towards her.

In the second process, repetitions are enacted in the present when a person unconsciously seeks out relationships with people who actually do resemble the people (usually the parents) who were involved in the original relationships. For example, as much as Penia feels repelled by her mother, her repetition sometimes impels her towards women who are as hostile and rejecting as her mother. These real similarities reinforce the process of displacement and distortion.

Third, repetitions can be enacted through the process of emotional induction, as described in Chapters 2 and 3. Through emotional induction, a person can induce the feelings that characterized past relationships in the patient's current life. For example, Penia sometimes induces feelings of hostility and rejection in women who might not, in other circumstances, be spontaneously inclined to feel that way towards her. Emotional induction actively recreates the patterns from the past in the present. This process will be described more fully below. But first we must discuss the characteristics of repetitions that affect the process of emotional induction.

Characteristics of repetitions

Repetitions are a type of emotional state; as such, they are characterized by a specific feeling and a relational mode. In Penia's case, the repetitions based on her relationship with her mother may be described as object repetitions. In these repetitions, she is in the object mode; she experiences other people as being separate and distinct from her. Furthermore, she experiences the specific feelings that she has with these people as being traumatic or pathogenic. Not every one of her object repetitions is characterized by the same specific feeling, but in all cases the specific feelings she experiences are in some way traumatic, pathogenic, or frustrating.

Similarly, the repetitions that are based on her relationship with her father can be described as narcissistic repetitions. In these repetitions, she experiences the other as being like herself, and the specific feelings that characterize these repetitions are also rooted in the feelings that she has about herself in relationship to her father. Thus, in narcissistic repetitions, she usually experiences the other person as being weak, inadequate, or incompetent – in the same way that she experiences herself and her father.

She has other types of repetitions as well. Occasionally, she finds the level of weakness that she experiences to be absolutely intolerable. If, at these times, she meets somebody whom she feels is even weaker than she is, she tends to project her feelings of weakness onto that person and then feels strong in comparison to that person. In those moments, the other person has become the receptacle of all of her weak feelings, and she experiences him only as weak, and she experiences herself only as strong. In these moments, she is engaging in a projective identification repetition in which she feels the polar opposite of the feeling that she has projected onto the other person.

And while most of Penia's life has been painful, she still feels a strong craving to be loved and cared for in a way that she only occasionally experienced with her mother. She has a powerful memory of baking cookies with her mother when she was very little. Her mother was gentle and sweet with her and patiently showed how to use cookie cutters and decorate the baked cookies. She remembers how her mother helped her make light pink flowers with icing and then handed her the brightly colored jellybeans that they placed in the center of the flowers. Sometimes this emotional state – a memory of joyful play and dependency – forms the basis of a repetition with a teacher, in which she feels guided, nurtured, and instructed. In these moments, she experiences an anaclitic repetition, an interaction in which she experiences the other person as being different from her but nurturing in a way that meets her unmet dependency needs.

No one's life is limited to a single repetition. In the absence of unusual forms of severe pathology,[9] everyone has the potential to engage in a minimum of three distinct repetitions:

- a narcissistic repetition
- an object repetition
- an anaclitic repetition.

In addition, a person may engage in repetitions related to projective identification but not all patients do so to a significant degree.[10]

Repetitions do not occur in the present-anchored mode because this mode is, by definition, shaped primarily by present oriented, here-and-now interactions in which the influence of past patterns is fleeting and non-constricting.

The different types of repetitions are usually not of equal importance in a particular person's life. Some people have a dominant relational mode and a dominant type of repetition. For example, a person might relate primarily in the narcissistic mode, experiencing most people as being the same as he is and engage in object or anaclitic relatedness only minimally. Many combinations are possible.

Relational modes, repetitions, and emotional communication

When two people relate to each other, each experience, understand, and communicate with the other through the prism of the emotional state active in them at that time, as characterized by the specific feelings and the relational mode. But as they interact, each person's emotional communications can have an impact on the other. Sometimes the sender (the person who initiates an emotional interaction) makes an emotional communication that is ineffective and has no impact on the emotional state of the receiver (the person who is the target of the sender's emotional communication). At other times the receiver's reaction is idiosyncratic: the receiver's emotional state is impacted by the sender's emotional communication in a way that is unrelated to what the sender has expressed. But often the sender's emotional communication successfully induces a change in the receiver's emotional state, changing the receiver's specific feeling, his relational mode, or both.

Let's consider examples of each of these reactions. Penia is the sender in this emotional interaction – the person who initiates the emotional communication under discussion. In this moment, she feels the kind of self-hatred that she usually feels in relationship to her father: she feels weak, incompetent, and depressed. She is experiencing a narcissistic repetition. She is relating to a male colleague with whom she works. He is the receiver. At this point in time, she relates to him in the narcissistic mode; she experiences him as being similar to her own self. Thus, she feels that he is as weak and incompetent as she is. Moreover, the specific feeling she experiences is self-hate in the context of a narcissistic repetition.

Now let's consider the receiver. He too often feels weak and incompetent. But in the past, Penia has been helpful and encouraging when he feels like that, reassuring him and making him feel better. He expected her to be the same this time. His self-confidence was fragile – that was his specific feeling – and he expected her to shore up his self-esteem. He approached her experiencing her as being different than him and with the expectation that she would nurture him. Thus, he was initially in the anaclitic mode with her.

At the start of their interaction, therefore, they are experiencing different specific feelings and different relational modes. He hopes Penia will help him. But instead of her usual encouraging smile, he sees despair in her eyes. He tells her what he is feeling and she says, "You know, I've been thinking that this stupid, low-paying field we are in is really for losers. It's amazing how we can work and work and never accomplish anything."

The colleague is surprised. This isn't the Penia that he's been hoping for. He's disappointed, but he immediately disengages from her and goes back to his work. He's still feeling insecure and maybe a little more in need of nurturance than before, but basically his response to her is unchanged. Her emotional communication has been ineffective; it has had no impact on him.

Now let's consider an idiosyncratic response. In this case, the colleague sees that Penia is filled with self-hate, and he's reminded of his father who was also filled with self-hate. His response to his father was to try to do something to help him – to give him something. He responds to Penia in a similar way, and asks if he can get her a cup of coffee. This response has no analogue in Penia's experience. Her emotional communication changed his emotional state in a way that activated one of his own repetitions but had nothing to do with what she was feeling. His response is idiosyncratic.

Finally, let's consider what happens when Penia's emotional communication induces a complete change in her colleague's emotional state, both the specific feeling and the relational mode. In this case, when the man looks into Penia's eyes and hears her self-hating response, his already fragile self-confidence is transformed into outright self-hatred. He too feels depressed, and he has lost all faith in her to help him. She is as messed up as he is; they are like two rotten peas in the pod, and he feels kinship with her on that basis.

What has happened? Penia's comment, her bitter depressed tone, and the expression on her face, generated a strong emotional communication. It conveyed her feeling – self-hatred – in the context of the narcissistic mode within which she experienced him as being similar to her, in a negative way. In doing so, she induced both the specific feeling and the narcissistic mode in her colleague, who then experienced the same emotional state that she did. This is an example of a complete emotional induction: the sender induced both dimensions of her emotional state in the receiver.

Let's consider another example of a complete emotional induction that occurs in the context of a different repetition, which takes place in a different relational mode. Again, Penia is the sender, and in this example, she is relating to her supervisor. She feels paranoid. She goes to her supervisor trembling with apprehension and anger in anticipation of a reprimand. She is in the grip of an object repetition that is rooted in her relationship with her mother. Consequently, she experiences her supervisor in the object mode: she experiences her supervisor as different from herself, with the expectation that their interaction will be hurtful.

Her supervisor, on the other hand, genuinely likes Penia. She thinks Penia is bright, creative, and hardworking. She would like to see her rise in the organization and sees her as a bit of a protégé. She is usually in the anaclitic mode with Penia: she experiences Penia as separate and different from her own self, but she wants to nurture her. But she has noticed that she sometimes criticizes Penia unfairly.

In this interaction, Penia approaches her supervisor with a strange look of abject fear mixed with a hint of defiance and tells her that a project that was due that morning isn't completed. The supervisor snaps at Penia, without realizing what she is feeling: "Can't you ever get anything done on time? I can't ever trust you to do anything right, can I?" Penia responds defensively, with real hostility, but gives her a perfectly acceptable explanation for why the project isn't done. Her supervisor is astonished. She asks herself why she has yelled at one of her favorite employees. She doesn't yell like that at other people whom she likes a lot less than Penia. In fact, she yells very little. Why does it always seem to happen with Penia?

What has happened? A successful emotional communication has taken place: Penia has induced the specific feeling and mode of relatedness in her supervisor that characterize the repetitions that are patterned by her relationship with her mother.

Finally, let's look at a third example. Again, Penia feels paranoid and approaches her supervisor with apprehension and dread, in the object mode. This time, however, the supervisor has had a chance to reflect on their interactions. Although she doesn't understand why she snaps at Penia, she is determined to avoid it. In other words, she is planning on remaining in the anaclitic mode in relationship to Penia. Penia begins to talk in the same provocative tone. This time the supervisor recognizes it; she can feel the contemptuous anger rising in her. Nevertheless, she deliberately talks to Penia in a calm, loving tone and asks her what caused the problem. Penia responds to her nurturing tone and words and explains the situation. Her supervisor smiles and tells her not to worry about it. Penia leaves feeling relieved and nurtured, and her supervisor feels satisfied that she has tamed the dragon within her.

In this instance, Penia began to induce the feelings related to the object repetition in her supervisor, but her supervisor resisted the induction and responded with a stronger emotional communication in the anaclitic mode. Instead of Penia inducing the specific feeling and mode of relatedness in the supervisor based on her repetition related to her mother, the supervisor induced a specific feeling and mode of relatedness in Penia. Penia has become the receiver. Her supervisor's successful emotional communication disrupted and interrupted Penia's repetition.

Repetitions as the basis of transference and countertransference

Repetitions are a significant component of all people's lives, at all stages of development. They are an aspect of general human psychology. When a repetition is activated within the analytic relationship, it is described as *transference.*

As with all repetitions, *transference* is characterized by a specific feeling and a relational mode. When a patient experiences a transference, he experiences and relates to the analyst within the context of the specific feeling and the relational mode that characterizes the repetition. This means that the patient relates and reacts to the analyst in the context of the repetition. Furthermore, his emotional communications to the analyst are also characterized by the same specific feeling and relational mode. The repetition shapes every aspect of his experience of the analyst.

An *objective countertransference* is an emotional state that is induced in the analyst by the patient's emotional communications that express the transference: it is conceptualized as the interpersonal dimension of the patient's transference/repetition. The objective countertransference is characterized by the same specific feeling and relational mode that characterize the patient's transference. In the objective countertransference, the patient's transference comes to life within the analyst's subjectivity and provides information about the patient that the patient is unable to put into words.

A *subjective countertransference* is a repetition from the analyst's life that is experienced in relationship to the patient. It is either an idiosyncratic response to the patient's transference, or it is a displacement from the analyst's life that arises irrespective of the transference. In either case, it is exactly analogous to the patient's transference and provides no information about the patient.

The emotional forces that drive the transference and countertransference in psychoanalysis are exactly the same as those that drive the enactment of repetitions and emotional communication in everyday life. Everyone engages in repetitions, and everyone responds to other people's repetitions with a combination of feelings that include inductions, idiosyncratic reactions, and emotional states rooted purely in one's own repetitions. All of this occurs spontaneously and (usually) unobserved.

Psychoanalysis differs from everyday life in that the psychoanalytic relationship is structured to allow the patient's repetitions to become activated within the relationship as transference[11] so that the patient can experience and verbalize them, and the analyst can observe and understand them. The analyst studies his own feelings to differentiate the inductions that are interpersonal dimensions of the patient's repetitions – the objective countertransference – from his idiosyncratic reactions and the feelings rooted in his own repetitions (the subjective countertransference). He then makes cognitive and emotional communications to the patient designed to loosen the compulsive grip (Spotnitz 1976) the repetitions have on the patient's life.[12]

5

DIFFERENTIATING OBJECTIVE AND SUBJECTIVE COUNTERTRANSFERENCE

Broadly speaking, the analyst experiences three sets of feelings in the course of the analysis: the objective countertransference, the subjective countertransference, and the feelings that are unique to the relationship with the patient.

The objective countertransference comprises the feelings that repeat a dynamic from the patient's past. It is most usefully understood within the context of the patient's life. It is primarily caused by the patient or, more precisely, by aspects of the patient's transference.

The subjective countertransference comprises the feelings that repeat dynamics from the analyst's life but not from the patient's life. It is most usefully understood in the context of the analyst's life. It is primarily caused by the analyst's idiosyncratic reactions to the patient.

The feelings that are unique to the relationship are those feelings that are different from those experienced in the analyst's other relationships (both personal and professional). They are most usefully understood in the context of current mutuality between the analyst and the patient. They are viewed as being caused equally by the patient and the analyst.

Although all three sets of feelings are co-constructed by both the analyst and the patient, the analyst's contribution is minimal in objective countertransference, maximal in subjective countertransference, and equal to the patient's in the feelings that are unique to the relationship. In other words, objective countertransference is a part of the story of the patient's life, subjective countertransference is a part of the story of the analyst's life, and the unique feelings are a part of the story of the life they create together.

Although these definitions are clear, identifying objective countertransference is not as easy as finding sapphires in the mud. In reality, the analyst (like everyone else) experiences a seamless stream of consciousness. These concepts are abstractions designed to highlight patterns in the flow, and their use entails the limitations inherent in all abstractions – oversimplification and reductionism. Thus, it is important to remember that this conceptual framework is a tool that generates clinical hypotheses, not an oracle that reveals absolute truths.

With this proviso in mind, the goal of countertransference analysis is to separate the objective elements in the analyst's feelings from the rest of her emotional experience for the purpose of understanding which dynamics from the patient's past are being repeated in the analysis. At first glance, this might seem like trying to isolate violas in the orchestra while listening to a Beethoven symphony – a learnable skill, no doubt – but one that would require a tremendous amount of practice. In fact, the process is fairly simple; the challenge is applying it consistently.

Several questions arise from this process: What does objective countertransference feel like? Does it have inherent, experiential qualities that differentiate it from other feelings? Does it pop out on its own from the background of the analyst's consciousness? Occasionally it does, and these cases will be discussed, but the most important characteristic about induced countertransference is how ordinary it is. It feels just like any other feeling. The gray despair that the analyst feels in the presence of the anaclitic depressive is just like the helpless apathy she has herself felt in moments of prolonged deprivation. The intimidation induced by the haughty narcissist is the same feeling of inadequacy she has struggled with all of her life. The tedium of listening to the obsessive–compulsive is what she always feels when forced to attend to masses of detail. There is usually nothing about objective countertransference, viewed in isolation, to distinguish it from the overall tapestry of the analyst's consciousness.

Emotional induction is possible because the spectrum of human feelings is limited. Everyone – patients and analysts alike – shares the same basic emotional palate. There are only a few primary emotions and a somewhat larger number of basic defenses. An individual's personality is defined not by her feelings in and of themselves but by the particular combination of feelings, experiences, defenses, and fantasies that make up her life story. Truly unique feelings can be induced in the objective countertransference, but these are exceptions – especially for the relatively well-analyzed[1] analyst to whom (hopefully) nothing human is alien.

Countertransference feels like any other feeling because it is the analyst's own feeling. Although the patient induces the countertransference, the experience of the countertransference is constructed out of the analyst's subjective experiences. At times, it is a mosaic composed of such disparate bits and pieces of the analyst's feelings, memories, and fantasies that it does not resemble anything the analyst remembers experiencing. At other times, it is completely familiar to the analyst, and she marvels at how similar her feelings are to the patient's. And at other times still, it is made up of unmodified swaths of the analyst's experiences that seem unrelated to anything the patient has done or said. However familiar or unfamiliar the countertransference feels, the patient cannot induce a feeling that the analyst doesn't have somewhere within her subjectivity any more than a pianist can play a note for which there is no string.

So how then does an analyst determine whether a countertransference feeling is objective if it is not experientially different from anything else the analyst feels?

Keeping in mind that an objective countertransference is a feeling that is consistent with the patient's life history, it stands to reason that objectivity can only be established in the context of the analyst's knowledge of the patient. The analyst has two sources of information about the patient: the content of the sessions, which includes everything the patient does and says in the sessions, and her feelings about the patient, which include, but are not limited to, objective inductions. The content of the sessions serves as the standard against which the countertransference is compared. The objective elements in the countertransference are consistent with the content of the sessions; the subjective and the mutual elements are not.

The task of differentiating them is straightforward: first, study the countertransference; then study the content of the sessions; finally, compare the countertransference to the content, looking for areas of congruence – similarities, analogies, and patterns – in common. The objective countertransference seldom fails to become visible, provided the analyst looks at the material carefully and allows the analytic process enough time to unfold.

We will begin with a simple example to illustrate the process. In one case early in my career, the patient had suddenly decided to leave town, and thus would be leaving treatment three months later. She had made the decision without discussing it with me, and she was indignant that I might question it in any way. She was unwilling to even explore the idea that there might be something more to this decision than a desire for a change of scenery. I was left feeling intensely frustrated that I could do nothing to influence her decision in any way.

In the following session, she talked about some problems she had once had with a boyfriend. Although these problems had nothing to do with her plans to leave town, she described them in the same tone of stubborn defiance that I heard the previous week. She became angrier and angrier as she described their fight, finally exclaiming, "He said that he couldn't do anything at all to influence me! Can you imagine that?!" I certainly could.

Her association revealed that my feeling was the same as her ex-boyfriend's. The countertransference, therefore, was consistent with material in the content of the sessions. This suggests that the patient had induced the same feeling in both of us and that this induction was the product of a repetition. It later emerged (she did not leave town, after all) that she had induced this feeling in other people in numerous important relationships in her past as well, so, the countertransference was a manifestation of problematic patterns throughout her life[2] story.

DIFFERENTIATING COUNTERTRANSFERENCE

This case had several features that made the induction particularly easy to identify and understand. The countertransference itself was vivid and easily definable within my experience. It was clearly and obviously related to how she actually related to me in the session. Finally, the consistency between the countertransference and her life emerged quickly in the process.

A surprising number of countertransferences can be clarified this easily; a quick comparison of the analyst's feelings and the content often reveals the repetitive pattern. In more complex cases, however, the process must be approached more deliberately. For this reason, it is worth examining the steps of the process in more detail.

Countertransference feelings – specific feelings and modes of relatedness

A countertransference feeling, like all emotional moments, is characterized by three qualities: the specific feeling, the relational mode, and the intensity. Of these three, the specific feeling and the intensity are usually the easiest qualities of the countertransference to identify. The analyst feels bored, happy, hungry, or irritable. And she feels very bored, a little happy, ravenously hungry, or mildly irritable. Of course, sometimes the analyst is confused about what she feels, but the confusion itself is often part of the specific feeling. In any case, the specific feeling is usually the part of the experience that is most present in the analyst's mind – the part that makes her aware that she is feeling something.

Sometimes the relational mode is easy to identify as well. For example, the patient angrily tells the analyst she should be sued, and the analyst feels frightened of the patient. It's fairly obvious that the specific feeling is intense fear. It's also fairly obvious that the analyst is afraid of the patient and that the fear is experienced in the object relational mode, which is to say that the analyst and the patient experience each other as separate and different, and they are experiencing different feelings. However, even when the relational mode is easy to identify, it is usually something that the analyst concludes about her feeling, as opposed to its immediate quality. Thus, the relational mode is always more theoretical than the specific feeling. The specific feeling is the quality of the countertransference that most immediately colors the analyst's experience, and for this reason, we begin the work of countertransference analysis by identifying the specific feeling.

Identifying the countertransference

Although it is often obvious what the countertransference feelings are, at times it can be surprisingly difficult to identify the feelings within the continuous flow of the analyst's experience. The countertransference feeling may be subtle, not intense enough, or not different enough from her emotional baseline for her to be consciously aware of it. For example, the analyst may find that her mind wanders ever so slightly but dismiss the feeling because her mind has a tendency to wander, especially right before lunch when she sees the patient. It is only after the patient has rescheduled for a time of day when she is normally more alert that the distinctness of her wandering mind with this particular patient becomes apparent.

Similarly, I recall one case in which my conscious feeling was that I enjoyed the patient and looked forward to seeing her every week but often had a vague fear that I would be found inadequate. However, this feeling has always floated in and out of my consciousness, and there didn't appear to be anything unusual about feeling it with this patient. During one session, however, she laughed when she noticed that I'd had a haircut, and I felt distinctly uncomfortable and anxious. It was only then that I realized the extent to which I fell prey to her sexuality, a feeling that she had felt often as a young girl with her mother.

Many inductions are primitive, involving preverbal or nonverbal feeling states and require considerable self-reflection to capture. States of vague and diffuse longing, mild anxiety layered with irritability and depression, and feelings of dissociation and depersonalization may flash in and out of the analyst's consciousness before she has even realized she has felt them. One supervisee matter-of-factly discussed what she thought was a trivial question in a case: should she return a patient's call regarding an insurance-related question the patient wanted to discuss in the next session when the patient had not explicitly requested a response? Although the question was initially framed as a general question about case management, she realized that she was far more anxious about this question than she had realized. The patient was a former substance abuser who had reported, in an offhanded manner, a minor slip in the previous session. The supervisee had barely reacted to this and had not been aware of the extent to which she was frightened by this information. When questioned, the supervisee couldn't describe the anxiety. It was a sort of an encompassing, nagging fear that things were not right. She felt that she couldn't really name this feeling but realized that it was motivating her question whether she should return the phone call. Furthermore, it was similar to a pattern that the patient had of asking questions instead of expressing feelings.

This kind of situation is typical of many countertransference feelings. It is often impossible for the analyst to know what she is feeling until she has discussed the case with either colleagues or a supervisor. In this respect, being an analyst is no different than being a patient; it is hard to identify what an analyst feels without putting the experience into words.

Sometimes the analyst can search the associations she had while with (or thinking about) the patient in order to uncover what she was feeling. Ogden (1997a) describes how the analyst's reverie contains the clues needed to capture the distinctive feeling the analyst has about a particular patient.

On the other hand, the countertransference can also be difficult to identify because it is so intense. The intensity of the countertransference can essentially blind the analyst from connecting what she is feeling to what the patient is saying. One patient spent a session describing a number of self-destructive actions he was taking in all parts of his life, such as quitting his job and taking out a new loan to spend money on stocks. I was well aware of what he was doing and was even waiting to see how this would come into the transference. When he announced at the end of the session that he wanted to take the month off from the analysis due to lack of funds, I really shouldn't have been surprised. But I was flabbergasted. The fact that I had been anticipating a maneuver just like this, only minutes before, meant absolutely nothing. I asked myself, "How is he ever going to stop acting self-destructively if he stops coming to treatment?" – as if that wasn't the reason he was leaving treatment. The intensity of my feelings completely overwhelmed me, making it impossible (at least in the moment) to identify my feeling as being about the patient, to see it as objective countertransference.

Perhaps the greatest obstacle to identifying the countertransference, however, is the premature assumption that the feeling has nothing to do with the patient. The analyst feels irritable with the patient; instead of connecting the feeling to the patient, she assumes that she is just edgy that day. She feels anxiety about money when the patient is discussing his new salary and refers it back to the fact that his personal expenses have been high that month. She feels sexually aroused by a patient because the patient is just her type.

All of these things may be true; any countertransference may turn out to be subjective rather than objective. But it is unwise to assume this out of hand because there is nothing in the raw experience of an induction to distinguish it as objective. Any association, no matter how personal and idiosyncratic it may appear, can be a manifestation of an induction. With one patient I had a persistent image/fantasy of standing naked and holding a sword. This image was similar to one that had arisen in my analysis at a point when I was struggling with issues related to integrating aggressive feelings, and I had come back to it many times since. However, I was not naked in the original image from my analysis, and the feeling was different as well. During one session, the patient told me that his mother used to read him stories out of *Hamilton's Mythology*, a book that had been important to me as well. He had been particularly intrigued and horrified by the story of Perseus killing Medusa. I realized that my image, while substantially constructed of thoughts of my own, was also very similar to the Cellini Perseus who had been on the cover of Hamilton's book when I was a child.

While this is a distinctive example, most are mundane. Even feeling unusually hungry around lunchtime may be more related to a patient's feelings of deprivation than to having eaten too little at breakfast. As Ogden (1997a) suggested, any personal issue that arises in the countertransference should be contextualized to the particular patient with whom the analyst experiences it. Even when the analyst is preoccupied with some personal matter, more often than not it will be experienced differently with each patient, and this will be reflective of how the feeling is shaped by the specific inductions from each patient. While it is impossible for the analyst to analyze every thought and feeling she experiences in relationship to the patient, it is worthwhile examining anything that is experienced regularly.

Comparing the countertransference to the content of the sessions

Once the countertransference has been identified within the analyst's emotional experience, the next step is to compare it to the content of the sessions,[3] looking for areas of congruence and incongruence. Congruence is the key to identifying and understanding the relationship between the countertransference, the content of the sessions, and the patient's repetitions.

Congruence

Congruence is the quality of agreement of feeling or meaning between the countertransference and the content of the session. When a countertransference is congruent with the content, it has an easily comprehensible relationship to the content. Sometimes, the congruence is obvious. For example, the patient reports that his mother has cancer, and both the patient and the analyst feel very sad. The analyst's feeling is clearly and obviously related to both what the patient has said and to what the patient is feeling.

However, the congruence is not always so clear, and it is often necessary to consider the possible relational mode of the countertransference in order to see the congruence. In the narcissistic relational mode, the patient and the analyst will have the same feeling (or will have analogous feelings), as in the aforementioned example in which the patient and the analyst are both sad. But in the object relational mode, the analyst will have a different feeling than the patient – a feeling that forms the counterpart of the patient's feeling in an interpersonal relationship, and the feeling will usually be painful or uncomfortable in some way. For example, if the patient feels hurt by the analyst, the analyst might feel guilty. In the projective identification mode, the analyst will experience a feeling that is the polar opposite of the patient's feeling, which is understood to be a feeling that the patient is heavily defended against. Here the patient might feel very powerful, and the analyst feels powerless. Finally, in the anaclitic mode, the analyst will feel a different feeling from that of the patient. But it is one that the patient needs to experience from the analyst to meet a developmental need. For example, the patient is feeling agitated and the analyst has the impulse to soothe him.

A feeling may seem to be incongruent with the content of the session when viewed from the perspective of one relational mode but may appear to be quite congruent when viewed from the perspective of a different relational mode. Let's consider the example in which the analyst feels powerless and the patient feels powerful. If the analyst is assuming that the relational mode is narcissistic, the analyst's feeling appears to be incongruent with the content. But viewed from the perspective that the relational mode is projective identification, the analyst's feeling is completely congruent.

In all of these examples, the relationship between the countertransference and the content is obvious, and objective countertransference theory assumes that the patient's feeling has induced the analyst's feeling. The nature of the congruence explains the meaning of the countertransference in the analytic relationship. Suppose the analyst and the patient both feel sad. The congruence – the information that gives meaning to the analyst's feeling – is that she has the same feeling as the patient. From this, the analyst concludes that she is in a state of narcissistic countertransference. She understands the sadness she feels to be the patient's sadness as experienced in a state of narcissistic transference.

In this example, the content of the sessions – in this case, the patient's sadness – expresses a single feeling. However, the content has two components – the words (and the facts that they convey) and the affective tone. And each of these components may express different feelings. The affective tone usually carries the emotional communication. When the words and the affective tone communicate the same feeling, the affective tone matches the words – strengthening, amplifying, or highlighting the emotional meaning communicated through the language. When the words and affective tone communicate different feelings, the affective tone contradicts, undermines, or communicates a different emotional meaning than the words. For example, the words and the affective tone communicate the same feeling if the patient shouts that the analyst ought to be taken out and shot. But they communicate different feelings if the patient uses the same words in a lilting, sonorous voice.

If the words and overt affective tone communicate different feelings, then the induction can be congruent with either one component or none. If the patient expresses his threat sweetly, fear would be congruent with the words, while affection would be congruent with the tone.

In these examples, the patient is expressing feelings directly to and/or about the analyst. When the patient is talking about something else, it is possible for the induction to be incongruent with the words themselves but congruent with the facts communicated by the words.

One patient dreamily described walking down a country road where she had found a beautiful almond tree under which she wanted to bury her girlfriend. Her affective tone was sensual, but I was horrified. No funerals were planned. The girlfriend wasn't sick. Her fantasy revealed how intensely she wanted her girlfriend dead.

Conversely, the countertransference may be congruent with the affective tone but not the facts. For example, a supervisee described the manic optimism

DIFFERENTIATING COUNTERTRANSFERENCE

she felt when a penniless philosophy student breathlessly announced his plan to get rich by writing a television mini-series about the life of Immanuel Kant.

Congruence with either the affective tone or with the words that describe the patient's here-and-now feelings – whether about herself or about the analyst – indicates that the feeling is a product of the patient's effect on the analyst. For example, fear in response to a violent threat from the patient, expressed through either the tone or the words, is a congruent feeling that is obviously a response to the patient.

This type of congruence does not, however, indicate whether the induction is a repetition. If the patient's threat had been a reaction to a feeling the analyst induced in her or a product of their mutuality, it would be an induction but not a repetition from the patient's past.

But if the patient describes facts about her outside life – past or present – that are congruent with the countertransference, then the countertransference is a repetition. For example, if the threatening patient says that his wife is terrified by his anger or that his father's screams frightened him as a child, then it can be hypothesized that the countertransference is a repetition of his interactions with his father.

Searching for congruence between content and countertransference – a preliminary example

As previously mentioned, there are a number of different ways in which the countertransference can be congruent with the content, and these are intrinsically related to the various types of countertransference that will be delineated in the following chapters. For present purposes, however, we will not attempt to classify the specific type of congruence, but rather will use the different forms of congruence as a set of guidelines for identifying areas of congruence anywhere in the material.

The task is to compare this feeling to the patient's words, to the facts she describes, to her affective tone, and to the countertransference. I have outlined the process as a sequence, but in real life no such sequence is necessary. It doesn't matter where the analyst begins or what order she follows.

We will begin with a simple, single, countertransference feeling: the analyst feels like a failure as an analyst. She doesn't feel like she is very good at what she does. The feeling is of a moderate intensity. She isn't completely preoccupied with the feeling, but it comes up regularly when she is with the patient. Thus, we know the specific feeling – failure – and we know the intensity. We do not know the relational mode, which is to say that when we consider the feeling of failure, we do not know how the analyst is experiencing herself in relationship to the patient. Thus, we will examine the feeling in the context of different modes of relatedness.

DIFFERENTIATING COUNTERTRANSFERENCE

We should first ask whether the feeling might be experienced within the narcissistic relational mode, which would mean that the analyst has the same feeling as the patient. Let's look for obvious similarities between the analyst's feeling of failure and the patient's feeling about herself. Does the patient say – either overtly or covertly – that she feels like a failure in her life? If not, does she say that she feels like a failure in some area of her life – whether it is as big as her marriage or as small as a frustrating phone call to customer service at a credit card company? Does the feeling of failure come up in her dreams? Does she describe other people in her life – friends, relatives, and politicians – as failures in a way that suggests that she feels a kinship with them? Do other people treat her like a failure, or does she feel that they do? Does she express analogous feelings, such as powerlessness, impotence, or weakness or ascribe them to others?

If no clear similarities emerge, consider whether the feeling of failure is being experienced in the object relational mode, in which the analyst and the patient would have different feelings but would be logically related to each other. Is the patient constantly reassuring the analyst – or does she describe reassuring others in her life? Does the patient make a lot of demands on the analyst or on others in her life? Does she feel disappointed in what others do for her? Does she make suggestions to the analyst in ways that undermine the analyst's confidence? Does she insinuate that her friends in therapy are making tremendous progress – more than she is? This particular form of congruence – object congruence – is often difficult to locate because almost any feeling can be the counterpart of any other feeling within the context of an interpersonal relationship. The analyst must always listen for any evidence that anyone else in the patient's life feels like a failure in the context of their relationship with the patient.

Another possibility is that the feeling of failure is the product of a projective identification, in which case the feeling would be the polar opposite of the patient's feeling. Is the patient confident – or overly confident? Does she brag about her successes? Is she grandiose? (At times this can be very subtle, only emerging after a very long time.) One patient with whom I felt like a failure was not overly grandiose about herself, but she constantly talked about her relationships with celebrities. Does she present her life story as a heroic struggle in which she always wins – or as an epic failure in which she wins by suffering the most? Does she describe situations in which she should feel like a failure but somehow manages to give a positive spin? Does she refer to others as failures, losers, or wimps? Does she seem like she always gets what she wants?

Finally, we need to consider whether the feeling could be experienced in an anaclitic relational mode, which is to say, as a feeling the patient needs in order to mature. For example, the patient might need the analyst to feel like a failure in order to help her distinguish the analyst from a parental figure, not in the sense of denigrating or devaluing her but rather in the sense of accepting that she is not an idealized figure that she cannot hope to live up to.

Now let us consider the affective tone, looking for similarities, again starting with the narcissistic mode. Does she sound like a failure – depleted, hesitant, or resigned? Is her tone self-lacerating even if her words express confidence or realism? Is there anything at all in the tone, perceptible if not describable, that harmonizes with the feeling of failure? Any of these would suggest a degree of congruence based in the narcissistic relational mode.

And if not, look for a feeling tone that is the counterpart, or the opposite of the feeling – either the object mode or the projective identification mode. Is there anything in her tone that is demeaning, haughty, or contemptuous? Does she sound impatient or condescendingly patient? Does she compliment the analyst from a position of superiority? Is there anything in the patient's interaction with that analyst that could be discouraging? Does she denigrate therapy in general – or doctors or other professionals as quacks or charlatans? Does the patient say "yes, but" to everything the analyst says, stating or implying that there is something wrong with all of her comments – that they always miss the mark. Does she feel consistently misunderstood by the analyst? Does the patient agree with the analyst while always taking the point a step further in a subtle manifestation of competitive one-upmanship? Does she refer to a friend who is making astonishing progress in her life, or in her therapy, without overtly complaining about her progress or her life? Does she praise the analyst's comments, while remaining curiously unaffected by them? Any of these ways of relating to the analyst could induce feelings of failure in the countertransference in the object relational mode.

It is remarkable how often these types of questions reveal the parallels between the analyst's feelings and the patterns in the patient's life. When I listen to cases in supervision – or when I myself am describing my cases in supervision – I am often astonished at how frequently the congruence is right on the surface of the material. When the analyst can describe the feelings she has about or with the patient – even a little bit – and discuss the case in an open-ended way, the congruencies are often luminous.

Of course, the congruence is easiest to see when its similarity with the content is detailed and explicit. If not, the material needs to be examined more carefully in order to perceive the similarity. At times, the problem is separating the global feeling from the specific context in which the analyst experiences it. For example, a supervisee described a case in which she felt critical of a patient for being somewhat sneaky and dishonest with her. The analyst thought the countertransference was subjective because the patient never reported that anyone had said anything similar to her, nor was this a complaint that she had about others. While this was true, a closer study of the patient's communications revealed that almost everyone in the patient's life was critical of her for some circumscribed aspect of how she related. Some felt that she was irresponsible, some that she was pushy, and others felt that she was disingenuous. But everyone was critical of something. The relevant component of the countertransference – the part that correlated to the patient's repetition – was not the idea that the patient was sneaky but rather that the analyst felt critical of her for any reason.

In all of this, it is most important not to dismiss any similarity as mere coincidence, no matter how seemingly irrelevant it seems to the thrust of the content. Many times an association that appeared to be no more than a distracting tangent will bloom into a full-blown pattern provided the analyst keeps listening for it. The point is to listen for anything anywhere in the material that resonates on *any level* with the feeling in the countertransference. The analyst builds up an increasingly complete understanding of the countertransference repetition by sifting through the mass of associations, memories, fantasies, and behaviors. The intelligibility of the countertransference emerges by passing the totality of the patient's communications through the sieve of the analyst's feelings. What is left over usually pops out vividly.

Unfortunately, the congruence is not always obvious. Sometimes it must be extracted more laboriously from the ore of the patient's material. This can be seen in cases in which the congruence lies not in the specific feeling the analyst experiences but in relational interactions derived from feelings the analyst acts-in (or enacts) with the patient. For example, let's go back to the feeling of failure in the countertransference. Suppose there is nothing in particular that seems to cause the analyst to feel like a failure. A careful study of the material reveals no specific congruence with the content of the sessions. But let's also suppose that the analyst's feeling of failure leads her to relate to the patient in a way that causes the patient to behave impulsively.

At first glance, it appears that the analyst's feeling of failure induces an impulsive reaction in the patient (and this of course might be the case). However, as the analyst listens further, she finds that the patient becomes impulsive after numerous interactions in which the other person has any emotional reaction to the patient's behavior. When he discusses his career with his father, his father gets annoyed, and the patient becomes impulsive. When he talks to his boyfriend about plans for the summer, the boyfriend gets obsessive, and the patient becomes impulsive. When he talks to his boss about his performance, the boss makes some recommendations, and the patient becomes impulsive.

What do we have here? We see the beginnings of a pattern. After having received a range of communications from others, superficially motivated by a number of different feelings, the patient becomes impulsive. Although the patient does not consciously experience these communications as problematic, they seem to have a problematic effect on him; his impulsivity creates serious problems for him in many areas of his life. Vague as the pattern is at this point, it is too serious to be dismissed as coincidence.

Here, the specific conscious countertransference is not the salient issue in the repetition. It is simply one of the feelings that other people experience in relationship to the patient that leads to an interaction that causes him to become impulsive. The congruence lies in this pattern of interaction, not the specific feeling that any one particular person has about the patient's behavior.

But what sets the process in motion? How is it that each person experiences different feelings that all have the same effect on the patient? The patient has clearly induced something in all of them, a propensity to relate to him in an unsatisfying way, which leads to the same result. But it is not possible to see this pattern more clearly because it is incongruent with what the patient is overtly saying, doing, or feeling in the session.

Incongruence

Countertransference is incongruent with the content to the extent that there are no evident similarities, parallels, or analogies between the countertransference and the content. Whereas congruence is a source of information about the relationship between the content and the countertransference, incongruence is a source of puzzles and questions. In general, the analyst's confusion – both emotional and intellectual – is directly proportionate to the degree of incongruence in the countertransference.

Things are fairly simple when the countertransference is incongruent with only one component of the content. Consider the situation in which the analyst dislikes the patient intensely, and suppose that the patient's words are friendly but his tone of voice is belligerent. The induction is incongruent with the patient's words but congruent with his affective tone. The countertransference is an obvious induction from one part of the patient's communication but not all of it.

The situation is more complex when the countertransference is incongruent with both the words and the language but congruent with other facts the patient reports. Consider again a scenario in which the analyst dislikes the patient. But, this time, suppose that there is nothing offensive in the patient's presentation: he is friendly, gentle, and cooperative. However, the patient also reports that other people dislike, mistreat, or reject him. The countertransference is congruent with these facts, which suggests that it is definitely a repetitive induction. The confusion is caused by the incongruence of the feelings with the patient's overt mode of relating to the analyst. It is impossible to see what the patient is doing that induces the countertransference. The process is too subtle to identify.

The most confusing configuration occurs when the countertransference is completely incongruent with the content. Nothing in the countertransference seems remotely related to what the patient is doing or saying. In this case, the analyst dislikes the patient, but there is nothing in the content that suggests a resonance. The patient is not only friendly, gentle, and cooperative, but he reports that everyone likes him and appreciates him. The patient describes other problems, of course. (Why else would he be in analysis?) But there is no evident link to the analyst's feeling of disliking him.

To some extent, this is a matter of how closely the material has been studied. It is always possible that the analyst has misidentified the countertransference feeling, overlooked details in the content, or ignored the patient's overt tone. The analyst may be blind to congruencies that are obvious to a supervisor or colleagues – or even to the analyst herself after careful reflection. Nevertheless, at some point it must be acknowledged that there isn't any comprehensible relationship between what the analyst is feeling and what the patient is doing or saying in the sessions, at least within the limitations of ordinary human intelligence.

There are two possible explanations for incongruence. One, of course, is that the countertransference is not an induction but rather a purely subjective response that contains no information about the patient. The other explanation is that there is a cleavage between the feelings communicated through induction and those communicated through talking and the more overt forms of relating.

There is probably a certain amount of biological variation in this area (as in all areas), with some people exhibiting more incongruence between their inductions and language – independent of dynamic issues – than others. For the most part, however, incongruence is due to the operation of defenses.

Incongruent inductions of this sort are often at the core of the patient's problems. Their origins are rooted in the earliest phases of preverbal development and underlie the most tenacious repetitions. Although they are incongruent with material the patient has consciously verbalized, they are actually congruent with unconscious feelings, impulses, or memories. This usually becomes apparent over time, as the analytic process modifies the defenses, and the patient comes to tolerate and verbalize the unconscious feelings and memories. However, the analyst must wait – often for a long time – for the material that reveals the hidden congruence.

Understanding incongruent inductions

The analyst's understanding of incongruent countertransference will be less certain than of congruent countertransference, and it is always possible that it is subjective. But the subjective explanation should be the last one to be seriously considered. As a working hypothesis, all countertransference – both congruent and incongruent – should be treated as potentially objective until proven otherwise.

The first step in analyzing an incongruent countertransference is to place it in the context of the analyst's emotional life history: is the feeling characteristic of the analyst's patterns of relating or is it distinctive? Although most feelings the analyst experiences will be familiar, some are unique, and these are usually objective.

For example, one analyst experienced an uncharacteristic difficulty talking whenever she was with a particular patient. She made slips of the tongue, had trouble finding words, and sometimes stuttered. She felt extremely unnerved by this incompetency. She had never had this type of confusion before. Her verbal communication was normally flawless. The problem arose as soon as the patient came into the office and abated when he left. It also occurred when she discussed the patient in supervision.

This difficulty must have had a subjective root somewhere. If the analyst weren't capable of feeling it, the patient would not have been able to induce it. The fact that it was so distinct from anything the analyst had ever felt, and was so regularly linked to a particular patient, suggested that it was induced. This was confirmed later in the analysis when the patient revealed that she had stuttered as a child, which had been extremely painful. She had learned to overcome the stuttering almost completely. The only shadow of it that remained was a subtle deliberateness in her speech. But the memories had left her with a profound feeling of vulnerability and incompetence, which the analyst experienced through the induction.

Even if the countertransference feeling is familiar, and even if it might be expected to occur in the context of what is happening in the moment between the patient and the analyst, its intensity can signal that it is an induction. Once I became annoyed with a patient who was tentatively boasting about a recent accomplishment. This woman was a timid and reluctant braggart if there ever was one. Indeed, we had recently worked on helping her to appreciate her abilities more fully, and this was the first time she had tried it out. Yet I was irritated at that moment by what I felt was her grandiosity. Now, it is not unlike me to be irritated by overt grandiosity. But my reaction was not only inconsistent with the main thrust of my feelings about her and the goals of our work, but it was completely out of proportion to how she actually expressed herself. This appeared to be an induction, and was confirmed as such in the months that followed when she described her parents' hostility towards anything that resembled (no matter how lightly) pride or exhibitionism.

Finally, what about situations in which the analyst's feelings are familiar and might be expected to arise at the intensity at which she experiences them? Here, it is beginning to look as if the feeling is an idiosyncratic subjective reaction – particularly if it is experienced only one time – rather than an induction. However, if it is a regular and repetitive feature of the analyst's feelings about the patient, I would still be reluctant to dismiss the possibility that it is induced. I would continue listening – for years if need be – for congruent material in the content.

Sexual arousal, for example, has not been a unique or unusual feeling in my life. But with one schizophrenic patient it seemed to be a more idiosyncratic response. She had been hospitalized for at least thirty years; she was disheveled and smelled bad, and spent most of her time sitting in a chair and muttering. Although she could talk, our range of topics was limited. When I asked what she liked to eat, she told me that she liked what was in refrigerators. (I wasn't able to determine whether this meant that she liked cold food, or if this just best described the foods that she did like.) There was nothing seductive or flirtatious in her behavior. Nevertheless, following a period in which very little seemed to being going on in the treatment, we had a session in which I had a number of very exciting sexual fantasies about her, which had a strong sense of taboo.

While I would not rule out the possibility of having fantasies about her unrelated to her life story, the conditions in which we met – the hospital dayroom, her overall appearance and odor, the level of our verbal communications – were not consistent with my own erotic patterns. This suggests that the feelings were induced. However, there was no material in the content of the sessions that supported this hypothesis. So my countertransference remained incongruent with the content. There was a note in her chart that indicated a possible history of sexual abuse, which – particularly in light of the taboo feelings in my fantasies – also suggests that these feelings may have been induced. However, this information was not certain. In any case, if I had continued to work with her, I would have continued to search the content of the sessions for material that might be congruent with the countertransference.

Time and again I have analyzed countertransference (my own and my supervisees) that initially appeared rooted in the analyst's life history that eventually was revealed to be an undistorted repetition from the patient's history. And I have rarely seen the converse. Idiosyncratic subjective responses to patients do occur frequently, and they can certainly be potent sources of distortion, but they are usually much less prominent in the countertransference than has traditionally been assumed. The analyst is seldom alone with her feelings when she is working with the patient.

Enactments

In enactments, an interpersonal dynamic from the patient's past is repeated in the current interaction between the patient and the analyst – not just on the level of feeling but in overt behavior. For example, if a patient's experience of being emotionally abused by his father is enacted in the treatment, the analyst does not just feel the father's abusive feelings; she actually behaves abusively towards the patient. This is not to say that the analyst's behavior is exactly the same as the original object's behavior; it is usually a symbolic analogue. Nor does it mean that the intensity is the same; it is usually significantly attenuated. But the behavior is real – it's not just a feeling – and it expresses the same feelings and meanings in the current relationship as the original object's behavior did in the original relationship.

This can be seen in the following example of a low-key enactment. A patient came in over a period of several weeks and complained about a number of calamities in his life. He was having trouble at work, his boyfriend was cheating on him, and he had lost control of his spending. My countertransference feeling was that I was numb with all of this. Although I sympathized with his problems, in a sort of abstract way, they really didn't move me. I realized that I also became preoccupied with my own thoughts and problems when he was talking.

In a subtle yet very real sense, I was neglecting him. He needed me (as I subsequently understood) to take an active concern for what was going on, and I was lying back and free associating as the spectacle of his life unfolded. Once I realized what I was doing, the meaning of it all was obvious: his mother had been frequently depressed when he was young and usually unresponsive to his needs and problems. She often forgot to make him meals, do his laundry, take him to the dentist, or get him a haircut. On a symbolic level, my neglect was a repetition of her neglect. But I had gone beyond just feeling neglectful. Through my passivity, I had actually neglected him – not in the way that a mother can neglect a young child – but in the way that an analyst can neglect a patient.

But here's the rub: it is probably impossible for the analyst to experience any feeling without expressing it to some degree in behavior. In this case, my actions went over the line to the point that they were visible. But they had been there, on a more shadowy level, at other points in the treatment as well. We talk about feeling a feeling without acting on it, but this process is never leak proof. Furthermore, the analyst may not know what she is feeling until after she has acted on it and can read her feelings in his actions. Induction is a powerful, unconscious process that always leaves the analyst a few steps behind. She will always be acting on the countertransference, sometimes visibly, sometimes imperceptibly.

For this reason, I do not find it helpful to distinguish between objective countertransference and enactments, and I use the term countertransference because it is more consistent with my overall theoretical framework. However, when the analyst expresses her feelings too floridly in behavior, she crosses the qualitative line separating countertransference/enactment from acting-out. How much action is too much? Analysts of different orientations are sure to disagree. From my perspective, the line has been crossed under three conditions: (a) the analyst is conscious of the meaning of her behavior in the context of the patient's life, and she has made no effort to modify her behavior to meet the patient's analytic needs (b) she has decided not to make the effort, or (c) she grossly violates an important ethical standard of practice, such as having sex with the patient.[4]

Subjective countertransference

Subjective countertransference are those elements of the countertransference that are primarily a product of the analyst's life story and do not contain any information about the patient. It can be manifested in three ways:

- subjective countertransference feelings, in which the analyst has feelings with or about the patient that are unrelated to the patient's life story;
- subjective misinterpretations of feelings that are objectively induced;
- the inability to tolerate feelings – whether they are objective or subjective – that interfere with the analyst's ability to relate to the patient therapeutically.

Subjective countertransference feelings

Thus far I have argued that every effort should be made to determine whether any countertransference that the analyst experiences is objective (or contains objective elements) and that this should be the analyst's initial working assumption in analyzing the countertransference. Eventually, after the countertransference has passed through this epistemological sieve, some elements will remain that have no meaningful relationship to the patient's life story. These are the subjective dimensions of the countertransference. They have been stimulated by emotional contact with the patient but are not otherwise related to her. These are the truly subjective countertransference feelings.

These feelings are always incongruent with the content, but there is rarely anything in the raw experience of a feeling that distinguishes it as subjective. Just as the objectivity of a countertransference becomes visible when it is placed in the context of the patient's life story, subjective countertransference feelings often become visible when they are placed in the context of the analyst's life history or more narrowly within the context of the analyst's feelings about her caseload as a whole.

Objective countertransference is an individualized response to a particular patient, and objective inductions should vary considerably from patient to patient. To some extent, this variability will be constrained by the fact that many patients have the same kinds of problems. If most of the analyst's patients are anaclitic depressives, she is more likely to experience monochrome hopelessness more frequently than if her practice were liberally sprinkled with borderlines, narcissists, bipolars, and melancholic depressives. But even with similar patients (and keeping in mind that on some days every patient really does say the same things), objective inductions will not be identical across her caseload.

In contrast, subjective countertransference is uniform and repetitive. The analyst tends to have the same feelings towards a wide range of different patients. There will be some variability, of course; some patients are more likely to arouse certain subjective issues rather than others, and there may be whole groups of patients that arouse a particular set of subjective issues in the analyst. But for the most part, subjective countertransference has a stereotypical quality that extends throughout the analyst's caseload. Most of the time, subjective countertransference feelings will be part of some discernible pattern from the analyst's life or character.

Subjective feelings arise when the analyst feels something that is related primarily to her own life and not to the patient's life story, transference, or repetitions. The least analytically interesting forms of subjective countertransference are the thoughts and feelings that form the bulk of the analyst's stream of consciousness. Hunger, for example, is a common induction from patients who feel deprived, but sometimes it is nothing more than a reflection of the analyst's psycho-physiological state at the moment. Similarly, many thoughts, feelings, and memories will have nothing to do with the patient. Although the analyst's reverie is usually an important source of information about the patient (Ogden 1997a), some of it is just noise.

More significant subjective countertransference arises when the patient is, does, or says something that triggers an emotional reaction in the therapist rooted in her history but not in the patient's history. In one simple example, an analyst feared her rageful, violent father who had a bushy red beard; the analyst consequently feared an inhibited, shy patient who had a bushy red beard. The feeling was stimulated by the patient but was not an induction.

This type of subjective countertransference can arise from more deeply embedded issues as well. Conflicts the analyst experiences regularly with all or most patients – and usually in her personal life as well – are a common source. For example, the anticipation of raising fees used to be extremely difficult for me. There were times in my own analysis when I hated having my fee raised and anticipated that my own patients would respond the same way. In reality, some patients responded the way I expected, others had little or no trouble with fee increases, and some even welcomed it. Until I had resolved some of my subjective issues about fee increases, however, I anticipated the same reactions from every patient whenever the issue came up, regardless of how any particular patient might realistically be expected to react.

More complex are the analyst's ongoing characterological traits. A need to compete with the successful, a desire to protect the abused, or a feeling of inferiority with the socially sophisticated – any issue of this sort creates feelings about the patient that have nothing to do with the patient. Strongly held opinions of all sorts – especially those that have a pseudo-psychoanalytic foundation, such as prejudices around raising children, sexuality, or impulse control – can all be potent sources of subjective countertransference feelings.

Another source of subjective countertransference feelings is the idiosyncratic aspects of the analyst's personality that place limitations on her ability to understand or accept the patient. Prejudices of any sort – ethnic, racial, religious, and diagnostic (e.g., a therapist who simply does not like and cannot tolerate drug addicts or child abusers) – are common examples. One supervisee was unable to describe why she was so revolted by a new patient in the first session. We couldn't find any congruence in the material, nor did I have the same reaction to the patient. We considered the possibility that there was a difference in the type of countertransference that we were each experiencing, yet it did not ring true. After an extended discussion, she rather shamefully admitted that she had a profound disgust for Southerners – and this patient was from rural Alabama: white trash, in her eyes. This appeared to be an example of a purely subjective countertransference in that no parallels to the material ever did turn up, and the feeling did not recur once the analyst's understanding of the patient as an individual predominated over her stereotypical response. Most of the time, these kinds of subjective feelings lose their intensity after they have been identified as such.

At the other end of the tolerance spectrum, infatuations and idealizations can be a source of subjective distortion. An over-affection for artists, for example, can lead the analyst to miss the uniqueness of a particular patient who is an artist. These idiosyncratic aspects of the therapist's personality do not necessarily represent pathology. Indeed, Jacobson (1964) argued that these types of quirks are vital to the functioning of a normal personality. But they do cloud the analyst's vision if she is not vigilant.

Occasionally, the analyst experiences subjective countertransference feelings uniquely with one patient that are not part of a visible pattern in her life. While these feelings grow out of the analyst's history, they are derived from conflicts that the analyst is either unaware of or has dealt with very little. These are hard to sort out. Looking at the analyst's reactions to other patients will not clarify the situation. I know of no good way – or even a fairly reliable way – of determining whether a particular unique reaction is objective or purely subjective. The best way to begin is consultation with a supervisor, colleagues, or a supervisory group in order to see whether anyone shares the analyst's countertransference feelings. If so, the feeling is probably objective. If not, the consultant's reactions may still illuminate the situation, as it may further clarify the analyst's feeling and reveal areas of congruence that were not immediately obvious. If it is not possible to reach an understanding about the feelings, the only solution is to monitor them carefully. They do not usually cause problems in the treatment as long as the analyst remains conscious of them.

Subjective distortions and misinterpretations of objective inductions

Even if the analyst experiences an objective countertransference feeling, subjective factors can cause her to misunderstand the meaning of the feeling. Induced boredom is a frequent example. Some analysts automatically assume that feeling bored means the patient is passive–aggressively killing them off. Others assume the patient is feeling depleted and helpless. Still others view it as a lack of engagement in the treatment process. Any of these interpretations of induced boredom might be correct. In the absence of more information that is based on a study of the content of the sessions, however, there is no way of knowing which one is correct. Each interpretation is valid as a hypothesis. As assumptions, however, they are subjective interpretations of objective countertransference.

Objective countertransference can be misunderstood for characterological reasons. Every analyst has a subjective propensity to experience the patient within one object relational mode more readily than others, which colors her perception of the inductions. Analysts with looser ego boundaries tend to identify (or merge) with the patient; consequently, they are more likely to assume the countertransference is narcissistic. Analysts with tighter ego boundaries, on the other hand, tend to experience the patient more readily as a separate object and to interpret the countertransference as being object or anaclitic. While no analyst I have ever met routinely experiences patients within the mode of projective identification, some are far more sensitive to it than others and interpret the countertransference more frequently in that direction.

Objective inductions can also be misunderstood for theoretical reasons. Object Relations theorists tend to interpret all countertransference as projective identification, Interpersonalists (and Relationalists, to the extent that they use the concept of countertransference) as object countertransference. Self Psychologists call the dimensions of it that they consider useful to be empathy and Modern Analysts are pretty evenly split between those who experience every feeling as a narcissistic merger, and those who see it all as the product of inhibited aggression against a frustrating person. Each orientation contains a measure of truth, but an exclusive adherence to any single one creates a disposition to misinterpret the raw emotional inductions in a doctrinaire way,[5] causing the patient's communications to be co-opted by the analyst's worldview.

The problem is more complex when the analyst not only misinterprets the induction but also defensively transforms it into a different feeling because she is unable to tolerate it. This situation can quickly stalemate a case, even if the intolerance is not expressed overtly in the analyst's behavior. One supervisee said that his mind always wandered with a particular patient. It sounded as if he was dissociating. I asked what he could remember about what they discussed. It was always about extremely violent arguments between her and her mother. This was a point of subjective vulnerability for the analyst. The thought of the mother behaving viciously towards the patient made him extremely anxious. (There was no indication that the patient was dissociating; she seemed to be fully immersed in her feelings.) Once he became aware of this, he was able to be more present in the sessions, and he opened himself to the fear and the anxiety that the patient felt. Although there was no actual change in his overt interventions, after his emotional shift, she started to describe the fights, and other aspects of the relationship, in more nuanced detail.

Intolerance of subjective or objective countertransference leading to errors in technique

So far we have considered subjective countertransference as it is manifested only in the analyst's feelings, independent of the analyst's behavior. The situation is different when subjective countertransference feelings affect the analyst in ways that lead her to intervene in ways that are potentially disruptive or destructive to the process.[6] The relevant subjective factor here is not the countertransference feeling itself – which may be subjective or objective – but rather the inability to tolerate it while relating to the patient therapeutically. One supervisee had tremendous anxiety about feeling hate towards his patients, but was able to handle it if the patient was overtly aggressive. One patient, however, induced intense hatred at times when she was feeling helpless and passive. The supervisee responded by becoming excessively nice to her. This aggravated the situation immensely. The nicer he got, the more helpless and pathetic she became, and the case was stalemated. In supervision, he realized that he was afraid that he would lose control of his hatred if he did not act nice, and he was concerned that this would damage her. His concerns about hurting the patient were well founded, but she didn't need him to be nice, either. The subjective element in the countertransference was not the anxiety, per se (which had both subjective and objective components), but the fact that it interfered with his ability to provide her with the right emotional climate in the session. After having discussed the problem, he became comfortable just feeling his hate, without being compelled to act on it or against it. They had a few sessions in which they both felt their feelings at full force – her helplessness and his hatred. Accurate emotional communication was restored in the analysis, and the case began to move again.

In some cases, the analyst is conscious of both the intolerable feeling and its impact on her behavior. More often, the analyst is unconscious of both, only noticing when the treatment is obviously disturbed or when she does something so out of character that it jolts her into awareness. Impulsive interventions – particularly if the analyst is not usually impulsive – are a strong indication that the analyst is having trouble tolerating the countertransference. Other clues include spectacularly bad interventions that create a lot of disruption in the patient; less spectacularly bad interventions that are made persistently (in spite of their ineffectiveness); inflexibility or rigidity of any kind that is not typical of the analyst; needing to be right or needing to be understood; needing (as opposed to deciding) to be honest, sincere, or authentic; making grand-sounding decisions to make significant changes in the treatment parameters, such as fees, attendance, or insurance; and giving ultimatums when they have not been carefully thought out.

Mistakes of omission are also suggestive of an intolerance of the countertransference. Examples include not enforcing a rule or a policy; not asking a necessary question or avoiding a particular topic; not responding to a verbal or emotional contact; not changing the treatment when the patient gets worse; relying on routine interventions – even if they obviously aggravate the patient; starting late, ending early; inattention; falling asleep; or confusion.

The list could go on and on, but the general rule is that any deviation from the way that the analyst usually functions, or any failure to deviate when it is clear that a deviation is necessary, should be examined to see whether the analyst is having trouble tolerating the countertransference feeling.

No single act or lapse is conclusive. The analyst might have good reasons for doing most of the above (yes, even falling asleep!). The issue is not what the analyst has done, but what motivates the analyst, and most importantly, to what degree the activity is under the analyst's conscious (or at least partially conscious) control. The more out of control it is, and the more repetitive it is, the more it is likely that subjective factors are at play.

Subjective intolerance of the countertransference

There is one last type of situation that might be classified as a form of subjective countertransference that is better described as an inability to experience the countertransference. This occurs because the analyst does not have the emotional raw material within her experience to resonate with the patient's feelings. At times, this is because the analyst has not shared the patient's experience. For example, childless analysts sometimes have trouble empathizing with parents, probably because their own primary identification in life is still as a child and there is not enough parental identification in their characters for them to be optimally responsive to a patient who is a parent. Cultural factors can come into play here as well, particularly in the area of culturally based religious or gender-related feelings. Finally, character styles are sometimes too different for the analyst to experience the feeling the patient is communicating. An analyst who is extremely easy-going and accepting, for example, may not be receptive to a patient who was raised in a rejecting environment and tries to induce rejecting feelings in the analyst.

According to the dictum that was current in Modern Analytic circles when I first began my training, the analytic environment has to be similar enough to the original environment in order for it to be emotionally compelling but different enough to be curative.[7] Subjective unresponsiveness to the induction is problematic when the environment is not similar enough to be compelling.

The effects of subjective countertransference on the treatment process

The effects of subjective countertransference on the treatment process vary considerably, depending on how strongly they are expressed in the analyst's behavior, how closely related they are to the analyst's core conflicts, and whether they are toxic to the patient.

In general, subjective countertransference feelings, which are only minimally expressed through the analyst's behavior, have a negligible effect on the analytic process. Analysts can usually experience all sorts of subjective feelings that have no apparent impact on the treatment, provided the analyst can contain them well.[8]

Subjective misinterpretation of objective inductions is more problematic. The misunderstanding can lead to serious technical errors. If the analyst understands induced boredom as an effect of inhibited aggression when it is actually an expression of anaclitic depression, she is likely to intervene, not just in the wrong way, but in exactly the wrong way. Even if the analyst does not make an intervention based on the misunderstanding, over certainty about the meaning of an accurately experienced induction can create an atmosphere in the analysis in which the patient feels understood enough by the analyst to become not only extremely attached but also hopeless about ever really getting through to her. I have found that cases in which the analyst accurately understands or sincerely tries to understand the patient's inductions flow much more quickly than those in which the analyst feels the inductions but weaves them into her own subjective agenda, even if this is not overtly expressed to the patient.

The most technically complex situations occur when the analyst cannot tolerate the countertransference and consequently relates to the patient in ways that are actually (or potentially) disruptive to the treatment. Two main factors determine the successful resolution of this situation. The first is the degree to which the patient has been hurt by the analyst's out of control behavior. Most of the time she is not hurt, or if she is, the damage is mild, and the patient and the analytic relationship are stronger from the challenge. But occasionally – and this is not always predictable – the patient has been so hurt by the analyst's behavior that the analysis cannot be saved. Of course, this is true of any incorrect intervention,[9] but the stakes are higher when the analyst's behavior is even momentarily out of control.

The second factor is the analyst's ability to control her behavior. This will depend to some degree on how deeply the loss of control is related to her core conflicts. But even when it is related to one of her entrenched conflicts, the analysis can still turn out well if the analyst is willing and able (it is hard to say which of these factors is more important!) to work on tolerating the countertransference and changing the emotional climate in the analysis. The analyst may feel under less pressure in this regard if she remembers that she is not obliged to resolve the characterological issues involved in all areas of her life, just during the time that she is in session with the patient.

The therapeutic results in these kinds of cases can be tremendous – often better than when the analyst tolerates the feeling as a matter of course – because the patient often knows and appreciates the work that the analyst has put into changing herself. The knowledge that the struggle was shared seems to increase the intensity of the benefits and gives the patient the unparalleled experience of having somebody important to them change in order to meet her needs.

On the other hand, the problems that arise when the analyst is unwilling or unable to learn to tolerate the countertransference can be profound. At the very least, the patient is limited in what she can accomplish with that particular analyst. If the feelings that the analyst cannot tolerate are unrelated to the patient's core problems, then the analysis can often proceed despite the analyst's limitations. While this is not ideal, it is not necessarily terrible. All patients need to learn how to live with situations in which their emotional needs are unmet because the person they are involved with cannot accommodate them. If the analyst can help the patient to do this in the analysis, this too can be an aspect of analytic growth.

However, if the analyst's problems are central to what the patient needs to work through in order to mature and get on with her life, then the problem is serious. At times, the patient can work around the analyst's limitation and resolve the issue on her own. This is a little bit like what occurs when a child is able to mature beyond her parent's need to hold her back in a particular area. More often, the patient needs to get another analyst – either instead of or in addition to the current one. Group therapy – sometimes with the same analyst, sometimes with another – is another possible solution.

This again is an unfortunate situation, but it need not be tragic, provided the analyst can face it without "a wardrobe of excuses" (Auden 1979: 92) and help the patient get what she needs elsewhere. While most analysts would probably like to help all of their patients through all phases of their development, this is an outlandish expectation. All analysts – even the most experienced and well-analyzed – have areas of subjective vulnerability. There are always limits to what one patient can accomplish with a particular analyst.

The real trouble starts when the analyst cannot tolerate the feelings but proceeds as if everything were fine – or worse, blames the patient when there are problems. The emotional atmosphere in the analysis becomes increasingly contaminated by the analyst's own repetitions. The other types of subjective countertransference – experiencing feelings unrelated to the patient's life story and misinterpretation of the induced feelings – proliferate wildly as the analyst hardens in her resistance to tolerating the countertransference and changing her behavior.

These are the kinds of situations that give analysis a bad name. They can be extremely damaging to the patient and can eventually corrode the analyst's integrity in her work with other patients as well.

The best prevention for this sort of thing is ongoing supervision, preferably with ongoing personal analysis as well. But alas, even that does not provide complete protection. Every analyst must engage in ongoing self-monitoring and self-reflection, especially at times when the going is rough in the treatment and the analyst finds that she is becoming increasingly vehement and inflexible in her responses.

Conclusion

Differentiating objective from subjective countertransference involves comparing the analyst's countertransference to the content of the session, for as long as necessary, in order to find consistencies between the analyst's feelings and the patterns within the story of the patient's life.

In order to do this, the analyst must be willing and able to allow herself to experience the full range of her feelings in relationship to the patient without regard to whether they first appear to be important or trivial, professional or unprofessional, empathic or malevolent. Only when she can experience all of her feelings in relationship to the patient, can she abstract the patterns that will elucidate the repetitions that constrict the patient's life.

The goal here has been beautifully described by Spotnitz (1985: 247) as "the freedom to function." This is the state in which the analyst has acquired the freedom and the strength to feel the full range of her feelings towards the patient while maintaining the ability to do the right thing – to see the transference and the countertransference clearly, to intervene with whatever techniques or emotional communications are required, and to not intervene when no intervention is necessary. While no analyst can possibly meet this goal all the time, it remains a practical point of reference and an admirable goal to attempt to achieve.

6

NARCISSISTIC COUNTERTRANSFERENCE

In objective narcissistic countertransference, the analyst identifies with the patient's feelings and experiences them as if they were his own. It is usually induced by narcissistic transference, in which the patient experiences the analyst as being like himself or as an extension of himself (Spotnitz 1985). Together, narcissistic transference and narcissistic countertransference form a relationship in the narcissistic relational mode, in which the patient and the analyst experience a profound sense of unity – an essential sameness of feeling. The analyst's feelings are a reflection of the patient's feelings. When the analyst understands the countertransference, he has a clear picture of the transference and of the patient's "fluctuating intrapsychic states" (Margolis 1979: 135).[1]

Narcissistic countertransference encompasses a broad spectrum of feelings, ranging from empathic attunement to preverbal regression and quasi-psychotic disintegration. It can be a difficult phenomenon to understand, as it often creates a sense of self-absorption that impedes the analyst's ability to understand its relationship to the manifest content of the session. And because the feelings experienced in the narcissistic mode originate in the preverbal period, they are often diffuse and difficult to comprehend in the moment.

However, a close study of the phenomenology of the narcissistic mode demonstrates that a highly structured mode of interpersonal relatedness underlies the murky experience of narcissistic countertransference. The mode of relatedness takes a number of clearly delineated forms, which give rise to distinct types of narcissistic countertransference. An understanding of these types of narcissistic countertransference allows the analyst access to highly specific information about the most primitive dimensions of the patient's emotional life, feelings that often cannot be accurately conveyed through language (Freud, A. 1969; Geltner 2000).

Basic types of narcissistic transference

Because the character of the narcissistic transference determines the character of the narcissistic countertransference, we will begin with a brief overview of the basic types of narcissistic transference. The distinguishing feature of all narcissistic transference is the patient's experience of an identity or similarity with the analyst, as a result of overlapping or blurred ego boundaries (Spotnitz 1985). It can take three primary forms: introverted narcissistic transference, extroverted narcissistic transference, and symmetrical narcissistic transference.

In introverted narcissistic transference, the patient feels a unity with the analyst – as if the analyst was a part of his own mind or body – and relates to him as if he were relating to himself. He often seems unaware that the analyst has an existence separate from himself.

In extroverted narcissistic transference, the patient is aware that the analyst has a separate existence but experiences him as being just like himself: a twin. He projects the features of his own personality onto the analyst without denying them in himself.

In symmetrical narcissistic transference, as in extroverted narcissistic transference, the patient projects his own thoughts, feelings, and fantasies onto the analyst. However, unlike in the extroverted state, he does not experience these qualities in himself. Consequently, he experiences the analyst as being different from himself – often the opposite of what he himself is like – because all the qualities that the patient cannot tolerate in himself have been projected onto the analyst.

Superficially, the introverted, extroverted, and symmetrical narcissistic transferences are quite different. What they have in common, however, is that in all three forms the patient needs to be involved primarily with an object just like himself.

These different forms of narcissistic transference give rise to different forms of narcissistic countertransference. We will describe each form in turn.

Countertransference induced by introverted narcissistic transference

In introverted narcissistic transference states, the patient experiences the analyst as being connected to him and relates to him as if he were a part of himself. Consequently, the analyst as a separate object is seldom the focus of his attention; the patient appears to be self-involved.

However, the intensity of this self-involvement varies considerably. When the intensity of self-involvement is low, the patient experiences a degree of overlap between his ego boundaries and those of the analyst while maintaining a clear awareness that the analyst is a separate object. He takes the analyst's presence for granted in a comfortable sort of way. The patient is clearly absorbed in his own thoughts and feelings; nevertheless, he is obviously connected to the analyst, even if he does not show any overt concern or interest. He talks freely, as if in a sort of dialogue with himself.

When the intensity of self-involvement is high, the patient's ego boundaries become blurred and confused. The patient often appears to lose all awareness of the analyst as a separate object. He shows little interest in the analyst and rarely makes contact through questions or requests. He is obviously self-absorbed. He may appear to be oblivious to the analyst, and to anything else in the room, such as intrusive noises or changes in the office. However, the appearance of indifference can be misleading. In most cases, the patient is – or becomes – deeply attached to the analyst, although not in a separated or conscious way. For the patient, talking to the analyst is like a monologue to himself, and at times of great intensity, talking itself may seem superfluous. The analyst is like a part of his body – implicit in everything he says and feels – but often unnoticed, except when its presence is disturbed.

The intensity of self-involvement in the introverted narcissistic transference usually determines the form of the induction. In low-intensity states, the analyst focuses on the patient, but in high-intensity states, the analyst focuses on himself. The low-intensity states, in which the analyst's attention is patient-focused, will be considered first.

Patient-focused narcissistic countertransference

When the narcissistic countertransference is patient-focused, the analyst's feelings are clearly about the patient; the patient is the target of the analyst's feelings. The analyst may feel that he understands the patient, may feel sympathy or antipathy for the patient, or may feel confused by the patient, but in all cases, the patient is clearly present as a distinct object in the analyst's mind.

The simplest type of patient-focused narcissistic countertransference is empathy with the patient's conscious or preconscious feelings. In such empathy, the analyst understands the patient's feelings by experiencing the feelings as though they were his own but in an attenuated way (Greenson 1960). The analyst may be consciously aware that he is using his own experience when he does this. For example, if the patient describes anxiety about whether to have a child, the analyst might recall his own anxiety about the decision to have a child. The patient's anxiety is not just a theoretically normal and understandable reaction, it is personally familiar to the analyst. The patient's feelings are the same feelings that he had, and as he remembers those feelings, he sees and feels a parallel between himself and the patient – a unity of experience that they both share.

Of course, it is not necessary for the analyst to have experienced exactly the same feelings or events as the patient (which, after all, is impossible). The analyst may have consciously experienced an event and/or set of feelings that may provide a close analogy to the patient's feelings, or the power of the induction may allow the analyst to experience the patient's feelings even without any biographical grounding in the analyst's own life. For instance, one patient described the realization that her boyfriend had concealed being HIV positive. Nothing in my own experience was closely analogous to the mixture of fear, rage, and betrayal that she was feeling, but I am quite certain that I shared her feelings as she talked. As soon as she told me what had happened, I could feel her terror at the thought of being infected, and I had images of wasting away in hospitals and of beating her boyfriend to death. Both of these images were almost identical to fantasies that she later described over the course of the session. I felt at one with this woman and could easily imagine myself experiencing everything that she was experiencing.

When the induction is congruent with the content of what the patient is discussing, as in this case, the relationship between the two is obvious. Although the patient may not verbalize every feeling that the analyst experiences in the countertransference, these feelings are nevertheless close to the surface of the patient's awareness. The patient is not strongly defended against the feelings that are foremost in her mind at the moment. If the analyst asks about a feeling with which he feels empathic, the patient is willing and able to acknowledge it.

Empathy is usually a well-controlled, self-limiting phenomenon. Although the analyst may feel that he shares the patient's feelings, his awareness of his own ego boundaries remains intact. He knows that his feelings, although similar to the patient's, are his own feelings; they are not confused with the patient's actual experience. His feelings do not cause him to lose sight of the patient altogether. In the case of the woman with the HIV-positive boyfriend, my empathic feelings were strong but not overwhelming. It was always clear in my mind that we were discussing her experience and that I was only observing it, albeit in an understanding and intimate way.

Empathy of this sort is common in many analyses. When it is a genuine emotional response to the patient (and not a posture artificially adopted for theoretical reasons), it is usually an objective induction from a low-intensity introverted narcissistic transference. The broad outlines of the patient's ego boundaries remain intact, as do the analyst's boundaries in the countertransference. The patient is strongly self-involved but not self-absorbed in a way that leaves her unaware of the analyst. There is enough overlap between self and object boundaries to create the feeling of similarity and understanding in both the patient and the analyst but not so much that there is a blurring of ego boundaries between them.

This feeling of empathy is usually positive. The patient experiences the analyst not as a clear or distinct object but as a diffuse, comforting presence, and there is minimal tension between the patient and the analyst. Although the patient may be in pain, the analyst is usually not experienced as the source of the pain. Nor is the patient rejecting of the analyst. The analyst's empathy, whether expressed through silence, interpretations, or purely emotional communications, is easily assimilated.

The transference–countertransference configuration that gives rise to uncomplicated empathy is a productive state for most patients and a pleasurable state for most analysts. Although empathy is not sympathy, sympathy often accompanies empathy, and the analyst tends to feel warmly towards the patient. This state can be so productive that many theorists (e.g., Kohut 1984) have argued that empathy is the ideal or even the only therapeutic emotional environment for all patients at all times. While this is certainly untrue – all types of objective countertransference can be used therapeutically depending on the patient's needs and the ability of the analyst to manage them appropriately – there is no denying the value of the empathic countertransference when it is a genuine reaction to the type of transference that has been described. The patient repeats a significant developmental need in the narcissistic transference, and the analyst's empathy can be deeply curative.

Empathy is the easiest form of narcissistic countertransference to recognize. A slightly more complex situation arises when there is less congruence between the content and the induction. For example, another analyst's patient flatly described to her a medical procedure that he was due to undergo. He showed no overt anxiety, and when the analyst inquired about it, he matter-of-factly reported that it was a common procedure and that he didn't see the point in worrying. The analyst, on the other hand, had a lot of intense feelings. She thought that she would be scared to death to have the procedure. How much work would she miss? What if it were painful? What if she had cancer? However, her focus did not remain on herself; she quickly and automatically returned to the patient and felt anxious for him.

In this case, the analyst's feeling of anxiety was congruent with the topic but not with how the patient discussed it nor with the patient's conscious experience of not feeling anxious.

The relationship between the patient's experience and the analyst's countertransference is clear. A certain amount of anxiety about a medical procedure is to be expected, and its absence was noteworthy. A reasonable hypothesis might have been that the patient was defending against his anxiety through isolation and intellectualization and thus induced the anxiety in the analyst. This was confirmed when the patient came to the next session consciously feeling very anxious about the upcoming procedure and described most of the same fears that the analyst had experienced the session before.

This is an example of empathy with the patient's unconscious feelings. It is similar to uncomplicated empathy, except that the analyst's feeling is incongruent with some aspect of the patient's presentation. Furthermore, the feelings the analyst experiences are usually more intense than in uncomplicated empathy. In uncomplicated empathy, the feelings are shared, but the patient experiences them more intensely; while in empathy with the unconscious, the analyst often carries the greater weight of feeling. As the patient becomes able to consciously tolerate the feelings, the intensity of the analyst's reaction usually decreases.

As in empathy with the patient's conscious experience, the relationship of the countertransference to the patient is still fairly obvious. Although the intensity of the analyst's feelings may be high, they are clearly related to what the patient is saying, and the analyst does not get lost in them himself.

He may incorrectly assume, however, that the intensity suggests that he is experiencing some subjective countertransference as well.

This type of countertransference is induced by the same type of low-intensity transference that gives rise to empathy, in which ego boundaries overlap but remain intact. In the case of empathy with the unconscious, however, the patient is more strongly defended and is unable to consciously tolerate the feelings that he induces in the analyst.

When the intensity of self-involvement in the transference is a little higher, the boundaries between the patient and the analyst become blurred both in the patient's experience of the analyst and the analyst's experience of the patient. The analyst's overall attention is still patient focused, but he identifies with aspects of the patient's mind in ways that are not immediately obvious. For example, the patient might not induce feelings that he experiences directly but rather his defenses against those feelings. One patient told me that his wife had unexpectedly decided to leave him. He said that he was a little bit sad but that basically it was OK; although he hadn't been prepared for it, he was feeling stronger than ever. He knew he'd be able to survive and to thrive. He would find a better wife. He would find a better life. There was a touch of elation in his voice when he told me this – a note of the triumphant joy that comes from overcoming adversity.

This was a bit strange in light of the fact that this man loved his wife dearly and depended on her for almost everything. But as he talked, I too felt elated, as though he really was going to get through this trauma and come out better than ever. I felt proud of the work we had done together, happy for all of his progress, and impressed with his ability to endure adversity.

This all came crashing down a few sessions later when he began to feel horribly abandoned and angry. He was completely bereft, and it was apparent that his previous feelings were, at least in part, a manic defense against loss.

This manic defense had been induced in me as well. My elation and my thought that the work we had done together would enable him to go through this separation painlessly were both aspects of this induction. My defense was induced by his defense – an effect of his narcissistic transference to me. In contrast with empathy, however, our ego boundaries had, in this area, become confused. I no longer shared his feeling; I experienced it as if it were my own.

This type of narcissistic countertransference can function on a more cognitive level as well. I once did a consultation in French with a man from Martinique who spoke in an extraordinarily precise manner. Every statement was part of a well thought out, carefully reasoned argument. Every sentence was beautifully articulated. Although my own French tends more towards a rather vulgar Parisian argot, with him, I became utterly pedantic. After about 15 minutes, we were both paragons of Cartesian rationalism, equally enthralled with the beauty and logic of our discourse. It was only after he left that I realized the strangeness of this encounter and the extent to which he had induced his style of thought and self-expression in me. (And, in this case, I acted it out.) I have had similar experiences with histrionic patients, attention-deficient patients, and others with distinct cognitive or communicative styles.

A particularly interesting type of narcissistic countertransference can arise when the analyst identifies with a part of the patient's mind that judges or evaluates the sense of himself as a whole or some aspect of his behavior (whether conceptualized as the superego, the ego ideal, an introject, or similar intrapsychic formation, or simply as a feeling the patient has about himself). Consequently, the analyst experiences – as if they were his own feelings – the same feelings (attitudes, opinions, judgments) towards the patient as the patient feels about himself. Thus, the patient and the analyst are in agreement about their feelings about the patient.

This type of narcissistic countertransference can resemble an object countertransference in which the analyst appears to be experiencing feelings towards the patient – whether idealizing or devaluing – as if he were a differentiated object. What suggests that the analyst is responding rather as if he were a part of the patient's mind (a hallmark of narcissistic countertransference) is that the analyst's feeling about the patient and the patient's feeling about himself are exactly the same. When the analyst is experiencing feelings about the patient as a differentiated object, there is usually some difference between the analyst's feeling and the patient's feeling.

This type of countertransference can manifest as either positive or negative feelings towards the patient. One supervisee described working with a man who was grandiose and thrilled with his own abilities as a painter. The supervisee also became thrilled with the patient's artistic abilities and felt the same pride in each new painting the patient produced. It often sounded like they were the same person, indissolubly united in their estimation of the patient's talents. The analyst had identified with the patient's positive self-evaluation and experienced this as positive feelings about the patient and his work.[2]

This type of countertransference is more striking when the analyst identifies with the patient's negative feelings about himself. Another patient of mine constantly berated himself for his spending patterns. This man felt that he was basically incapable of behaving appropriately in this regard. To hear him tell it, he was living far beyond his means – spending frivolously – completely out of control. After a few months, I completely agreed with him. I was angry with him every time he told me about a new purchase. He was aware of the problem, I thought, so why couldn't he just control himself? How did he expect me to help him if he wasn't going to even try to help himself? I began to believe that he truly was as weak and hopeless as he said he was.

At one point, I realized that although I was in agreement about how he was behaving, I really had no idea how much he was actually spending, so I asked him to go over his spending, and his income, in detail, describing exactly how much he spent and what he spent it on. As he did, I realized that he wasn't out of control at all. His debt was considerable, but it was almost exclusively for unavoidable medical expenses. He was also working far more and behaving far more responsibly than his constant self-attacks revealed. His evaluation of himself was wildly distorted, and he had induced the same distorted feelings towards him in me.

In both of these cases, the relationship between the patient's self-evaluation and his ego was replicated in the analytic relationship where the analyst identified with the patient's assessment of his own ego. In the first case, the patient had the sort of inflated self-regard characteristic of those types of narcissistic characters in which there is a fusion between the patient's real self-image and ideal self-image (Kernberg 1985). The patient thought the world of himself, and his analyst felt the same way about him. In the second case, the patient was experiencing the kind of antagonistic internal conflict characteristic of melancholic depression (Freud 1917). The patient was harshly critical of himself, and the analyst, induced with the feelings of the patient's primitive superego precursors, was also harshly critical of him.

In both of these cases, the intensity of self-involvement in the transference is higher than it is in the various types of empathy. Although the counter-transference is still patient focused in the sense that the analyst's attention remains directed towards the patient, the analyst has taken on an aspect of the patient's feelings about himself as though they were his own feelings. This process, a blurring of ego boundaries between the patient and the analyst, is more significant when the intensity of self-involvement in the transference grows higher still and the analyst experiences self-directed narcissistic inductions.

Self-directed narcissistic countertransference

As the intensity of the self-involvement in the transference increases, the analyst's subjective[3] experience becomes increasingly self-involved as well. The analyst's conscious awareness of the patient diminishes, and his attention shifts inward, onto himself. The analyst may lose sight of the patient altogether and become preoccupied with any number of self-focused topics – his own personal problems, his bodily sensations, his finances, his chores, or what he is going to have for lunch. His own feelings become the conscious focus of his experience of the patient. The patient feels secondary in his attention, and may seem to disappear altogether, as the analyst seems to be self-absorbed. It can be difficult to deliberately shift out of what feels like complete self-absorption. The experience is compelling, almost impossible to resist.

This sort of countertransference often arises at times when the patient is talking without any apparent awareness that the analyst is in the room, rattling on, completely self-absorbed and oblivious to the analyst's presence. Consider a typical example. The patient is preoccupied with feelings of helplessness and despair. Nothing is going right. He can't find a partner. Every woman he approaches rejects him. What's wrong with him? He can't make enough money. He feels like he will be poor forever. He feels too weak to ask for anything, and when he does, he feels ineffective. He can't sleep, can't find anything good to eat, yet he is fat and unable to exercise. When he looks around, everyone seems to be able to get what they want – everyone except him. The dominant feeling is failure. The patient is talking out loud to the analyst, but apart from that, he shows no awareness that he is in a room with a separate person.

The analyst hears this, and her initial feeling is empathy. She knows how he feels. She has been there. Quickly, however, she begins to think about herself. The patient's talk reminds her of how unpleasant her husband is. She just married him, she thinks, because she was desperate and too afraid to hold out for a better man. She too feels broke and unable to get ahead financially. She thinks about her colleagues, and they all seem to be making more money than she does. How do they do it? Her weight may be under control, but she could still afford to lose a few pounds. She never seems to be able to exercise either. Is her health deteriorating? If it is, she can't do anything about it. She's never been able to really take control of her life. She too feels like a failure. Every few minutes she is able to shift her attention back to the patient, who is still sunk in his depression. She notices that they are in similar physical positions: the patient is frail and flaccid on the couch, while she is collapsed and sprawled out in the chair. They seem to move in harmony, even to the extent of crossing and uncrossing their legs at the same time. But it is a terrible burden to remain focused on the patient. Occasionally, the thought occurs to the analyst that her life really isn't so bad; she is basically quite content. But then she sinks back into her own depression, only partially aware of what the patient has been saying.

At first glance, it would seem that patient and analyst are each encased in their own narcissistic cocoons, detached and emotionally isolated from each other. But the appearance is misleading. The induction is completely congruent with what the patient has been talking about. The analyst's feelings about herself are a mirror image of the patient's feelings about himself.

The patient has induced his whole state of being in the analyst. The analyst does not simply emotionally understand the patient's feelings in the differentiated way that occurs in empathy – she actually has the same feelings as the patient. This sameness is not limited to the details of the feelings. It encompasses the form of object relatedness in which the patient experiences those feelings. The patient is seemingly oblivious to the analyst's presence, and the analyst is seemingly oblivious to the patient's presence, yet they are in perfect harmony. The analyst's self-involvement is a consequence and a reflection of the patient's self-involvement. But this self-involvement is illusory. The analyst is not out of touch with the patient. No matter how unaware of the analyst he might appear to be, the patient is communicating effectively with the analyst, and the analyst, by means of her apparent self-involvement, is listening in a purely experiential way. Together, they are in a profound, if primitive, state of attunement.

However, the analyst rarely recognizes this in the moment when it occurs because the induction has rendered her self-focused and narcissistic. The indistinctness of the patient's ego boundaries has temporarily blurred the analyst's ego boundaries, and their identities are overlapping. The induced self-involvement makes it extremely difficult for the analyst to be aware enough of the patient to recognize the similarity between the patient's experience and her own.

This type of self-directed countertransference, in which the analyst seems to turn into the patient, occurs more dramatically with paranoid patients. One analyst described a patient who experienced typical paranoid fantasies. His boss was out to get him, his wife spied on him, and he was terrified of the IRS. The analyst was usually able to manage this, and indeed found it rather distant from her feelings, because it seemed stereotypical (although not overtly psychotic). At the end of one session, however, she felt distinctly uneasy and was concerned that something she had written on an insurance form earlier in the day might be misinterpreted as fraudulent. She continued to feel paranoid. Later in the day, this analyst went into a clothing store and tried something on but became fearful that there were cameras observing her in the changing room. It was only later that she connected this outbreak of paranoia with the patient, and realized that it was an identification with him. (The transference is different in those cases where it is the patient who becomes the object of the analyst's paranoia. These will be discussed in the section on symmetrical identifications.) I have found that this experience is most often a signal that the patient's transference has intensified, and the patient and the analyst have reached a deeper level of intimacy.

This type of countertransference can take a different form with the type of narcissistic patient described by Kernberg (1985). The patient may be overtly grandiose, and this may induce grandiose feelings in the analyst. With one narcissistic patient, whose reveries focused on the grandeur of his spiritual development, I often found myself marveling at what a wonderful analyst I was. I would tell myself that I had really mastered this craft in a way that was unusual and distinct, and none of my colleagues were anywhere near me in their skill. This was almost a word-for-word transcript of my patient's feelings, merely transposed from the world of spirituality to the world of psychoanalysis. This patient demonstrated little overt awareness of me, and I often went into a state in which I had little overt awareness of him, except to think that he was making remarkable progress and that I was doing remarkably good work with him.

In these cases, the analyst's narcissistic countertransference with the patient is complete. Through the induction, these analysts experienced their whole lives in the same way that the patients experienced theirs. However, the identification may also be limited to more specific areas of the analyst's experience. Another analyst described a patient who always felt like she was lost. She didn't know what to do or where to go next; her depression was like an endless black labyrinth. The analyst herself felt like she didn't know where to go in the case. She was too inexperienced to treat a patient like this. She didn't know what to say or what to do. In fact, she always felt like she was just winging it as an analyst. She never really felt like she knew what she was doing; she was always in the dark.

Here again, the patient and the analyst were feeling the same thing, except that the analyst's narcissistic countertransference was limited to the area of her sense of direction as an analyst. Similarly, it is not uncommon for a patient to feel that he is extremely successful in a particular area and for this feeling, in turn, to induce feelings in the analyst that he is extremely successful in a particular area of his analytic practice.

The induced narcissism in all of these types of cases makes the nature of the induction difficult to recognize, even though the induction is obviously congruent with the content. The induction is even more difficult to identify when the relationship between the induction and the content is congruent but not self-evident. This occurred in a striking way with one patient of mine, a psychology student who had recently come to this country. He was very well educated and especially well versed in Object Relations theory – far better versed than me. I felt that he was also much smarter than I was. He was perfectly nice, and I had a strong sense that he genuinely liked me and admired me, yet I was seized with terror that I would be intellectually lacking, uncultured, or in some sense a fraud. It was not his reaction that I feared. It was simply that I would be inadequate to accomplish the task at hand.

I had expected this man's analysis, given his background, to be intensely introspective and intellectual, and I was surprised when all he talked about were the most mundane details of everyday life: no dreams, no memories, no fantasies. Nothing but everyday minutiae. Still, my anxiety persisted.

Soon after the analysis began, he started to take cooking classes. Nothing fancy – just a basic French cooking class. I thought that this might make me feel more comfortable, as I am a trained French chef, and somehow I felt that we were on territory that would make me less anxious.

But it didn't. Each week, he would go over what he had learned in very careful detail – what recipes and techniques he had learned, how he had practiced them, what the results were. His affect was restrained. He was not overtly anxious or fearful, but the obsessive quality of his focus suggested that this was a difficult and important problem for him. I, in contrast, would be so consumed with anxiety that I could barely function. I could follow him, but I was swept with fear throughout these sessions. I felt stupid, fraudulent, unable to say anything worthwhile, and terribly, terribly vulnerable. At times I felt as if I had to hang on to my chair in order to avoid falling out (and keep in mind that I was sitting in a recliner).

Although I was almost always anxious in sessions with him, my fear was the greatest during his talk about cooking. Gradually, as he began to acquire a bit of competence and confidence in the area, I noticed that I was feeling less anxious. Eventually, it diminished significantly, as he began to cook with more and more confidence. After a certain point, he stopped talking about cooking altogether, and this particular countertransference reaction ended as well. The problem, for both of us, was resolved.

It became apparent that my anxiety was linked in some way to my patient's unconscious feelings about what he was talking about. After I realized this, the relationship between the induction and the content became clearer. The whole issue of learning to cook represented a life and death struggle for him, but the intensity of these feelings was not available to him consciously. His defense of being painstakingly thorough and somewhat obsessive kept his anxiety out of consciousness. However, he induced these feelings in me, through a narcissistic transference, and I felt his anxiety through a narcissistic countertransference with him. As his feelings changed, so did mine.

As in the case of the spiritually grandiose patient who induced fantasies of analytic grandeur in me, and in contrast to cases of empathy with the unconscious, my feelings were self-directed, which is to say that I was narcissistically oriented. What was different from the case of the spiritually grandiose patient was that the content – the subject and the affect – of his communication was not obviously related to what I was feeling in the countertransference.

Although I never determined what his anxiety symbolized, whether it was in some way connected to feeling competent about cooking and whatever else this symbolized – oral ambivalence, aggression and cannibalism, managing in the world – my own anxiety was experienced primarily in terms of my intellectual competence. It is probable, in this case, that the fact that I experienced his anxiety through anxiety about intellectual competence was shaped by my own, idiosyncratic anxieties; cooking, in and of itself, was not problematic for me, and I never had any information to suggest that his intellectual functioning was problematic for him, although it is possible that this would have revealed itself if I had worked with him longer. The anxiety itself however – its life and death intensity – was the objective induction. My area of personal vulnerability provided a resonant medium through which I experienced the induction of his emotional state. My anxiety was a close emotional analogue to his, and that was enough for his communication to be conveyed to me.

The situation is most complex when there is no congruence between the induction and the content. With another patient, I became extraordinarily sad as soon as she opened her mouth. But overtly, little of what she discussed was depressing. She talked about all aspects of her current life, which was filled with ordinary misery but was by no means unbearable, and I was close to tears. The sadness was completely out of proportion to the subject matter, and I felt it just as acutely when she talked about a fight with her girlfriend as I did when she mentioned buying some particularly good arugula from the green market. I felt sadness if she was angry. I felt it if she was bored. All of her feelings were somewhat flattened, but even this was not striking.

The sadness aroused almost no associations in terms of my own life. I didn't recall past disappointments, nor did I despair of my current life. It was self-directed, in that it was I who was sad, and I wasn't sad for her. But the sadness was without context and dissociated from everything in my life, except for her presence and the ever-so-slight monotone sound of her voice.

Eventually – and this took a long time – she recounted memories that provided a context. She had grown up in a working-class family in a gray industrial town, and her home life had been bleak in the extreme. Nobody talked; nobody communicated. Her father was an alcoholic, the kind who sat anesthetized in front of the television, every night, forever. Her mother was passive and depressed, and the patient was an only child. There had been no rage, no joy – just gray, dreary nothingness. She was taken care of, efficiently, with a minimum of fuss. And that was it for the first 17 years of her life. Somehow, she learned to get by. She functioned at a good level professionally and was not overtly depressed. Once she began to discuss her memories, however, she felt the sadness more and I began to feel it less.

I have seen this kind of situation often in cases of severe anaclitic depression, as well as in patients who dissociate. Here, the countertransference often takes the form of unbearable levels of sleepiness. The patient may talk about anything at all, but the analyst is at great pains to keep his eyes open.

In one case, I tried everything to stay awake. I consciously tried to catch every word the patient was saying. I pinched myself, stopped eating sweets the day of the session (as they make me sleepy), took naps before the session, and I even changed the time of the session to a part of the day when I had more energy. Nothing worked – not even a little. The fact that the tiredness was an induction became clear when, after a number of years, I realized that I was no longer getting sleepy with this patient, at least not all the time.

Her life had improved dramatically during this period. Now during most of the sessions with her I was alert the majority of the time. However, there would still be periods during which she would go back into the old state and I would immediately become exhausted. These periods lasted for a few minutes at a time, and then I would become alert again. This could occur a number of times during the session.

My exhaustion rarely had anything to do with the specific subject matter she was discussing. Yet there was increasing congruence between the induction and her overall affect at the times that I became sleepy. I was eventually able to see that I would get exhausted during periods in which her depression or exhaustion became slightly more overt. I was even able to identify a specific tone of voice – a very muted kind of moan – that she used during these states.

However, all of this was subtle, and my patient never fully verbalized any feelings, memories, or associations that corresponded to what I was feeling (except to say, perhaps, that her girlfriend found her boring). Nevertheless, my sense was that the tiredness was an identification with a very early depressive state – a kind of marasmus in which the will to stay awake, to live, has dried up, and the effort of maintaining awareness becomes too big a burden to carry. Although this depression remained dissociated from her consciousness, she communicated it through induction, and I experienced it consciously whenever I was with her.

This kind of experience is also common in cases where trauma is dissociated. One supervisee described becoming periodically overwhelmed with fear in the early stages of treatment of a male patient who eventually revealed that he had been severely physically abused as a child. The patient might be talking about a neutral exchange with a friend or something else that had nothing to do with violence. Yet the analyst would feel panic, paranoia, or outright confusion. The analyst consistently identified with these dissociated feelings that the patient verbalized over time.

A similar, though far less subtle, countertransference is frequently induced by schizophrenic patients. When working with hospitalized patients, I have often had the experience of sitting in total silence while thinking and feeling the craziest possible things. Feelings of depersonalization and disintegration, fantasies of eating bodies and excrement, and perverse sexual fantasies (in which the patient was not the partner) with intense sadomasochistic overtones were common.[4]

With a schizotypal patient, who required almost complete silence from me, I would often experience dissociated moments of bizarre, wild emotion. This patient could contain his persecutory madness only through obsessive measures to keep his Social Security number private. As I sat with him, entire strings of intense feelings would pass over me in waves. The most prominent, during a critical period, was a feeling of flyaway hilarity. I fantasized being on the moon, all by myself under the black sky, inhaling laughing gas or some such thing. I'd think, "What am I doing here?!," and would have to repress gales of insane laughter. I'd look around my office, incredulous at the weirdness of what I was doing – the patient carrying on in his crazy way and me carrying on (to myself) in mine. I am unclear as to whether the specific content of my fantasies had anything to do with what he was thinking, although occasionally there were eerie similarities. More often, however, it was his general state of fragmentation and unhingedness that was induced in me, which I then experienced through the lens of my own history and unconscious.

Extroverted narcissistic countertransference

Extroverted narcissistic transference

Extroverted narcissistic transference comprises the forms of transference in which the patient experiences the analyst as a separate – but not differentiated

– object outside of himself. In the extroverted narcissistic state, the patient experiences a developmental need for a mirror image of himself: a twin. This need may be conscious or unconscious, although it tends to be conscious more often than in the introverted narcissistic transference, but it is always present. The patient is aware that the analyst is out there, a clear and distinct presence in the patient's emotional life, but he is experienced as being identical to the patient (Aichhorn 1936; Kohut 1971; Spotnitz 1985). Alternatively, the patient can idealize or devalue the analyst purely on the basis of qualities the patient likes or hates in himself. (This is somewhat different from the types of idealization and devaluation based on projective identification, which will be considered later in the book.)

A patient in a state of extroverted narcissistic transference is focused on both himself and the analyst, almost interchangeably. The patient makes frequent contact with the analyst through asking questions, making comments, or making allusions to the analyst's presence; however, he focuses on areas of similarity between himself and the analyst, not on differences. The patient relates to the analyst as though the analyst was a mirror image or twin of himself and assumes they share the same opinions, qualities, and faults. The patient may think that he is the world's most talented actor and that the analyst, in turn, is the world's most talented analyst. Or he may think that he is uniquely inadequate and that the analyst is uniquely incompetent. The patient may feel that he and the analyst are both sensitive, that they are both cowards, or that they both have a special appreciation for the absurd.

This assumed similarity with the analyst may be based on projection, or it may be based on the real areas of similarity between himself and the analyst that the patient has been able to identify, sometimes with astonishing accuracy. However, even in cases where the patient's perception of the analyst is reality based, this perceptiveness is limited to areas of similarity. Details that contradict this experience of identity are ignored.

Countertransference induced by extroverted narcissistic transference

As in all narcissistic countertransference, the analyst's emotional state is essentially the same as the patient's. The extroverted state tends to induce the analyst to feel that he is just like the patient or that the patient is just like him. The patient may be a younger twin or an older twin; the analyst may also idealize or devalue the patient in the same way that the patient idealizes or devalues the analyst.

Just as the analyst is always a perceptible, albeit incomplete, presence for the patient, the patient is always a presence for the analyst. Consequently, countertransference induced by extroverted narcissistic transference is altogether different from countertransference induced by introverted narcissistic transference. While the patient may, at times, appear to lose awareness of the analyst, it is never to the same extent as in the most intense forms of introverted narcissistic transference. Similarly, the analyst rarely loses awareness of the patient, and usually does not sink into apparent self-absorption. The atmosphere in the room is less isolated, livelier.

Basic forms of extroverted narcissistic countertransference

As in introverted states, ego boundaries remain intact in the less intense forms of the extroverted narcissistic transference/countertransference configuration and become blurred in the more intense forms. In the less intense forms of extroverted transference, the feeling of twinship – its meaning and emotional resonance – is induced by the patient, but it is experienced by both patient and analyst through the actual similarities between them, either in feelings or personal facts. The ego boundaries between them remain intact.

One patient, for example, found a new job where he had to wear a suit for the first time in his life. Although he had not anticipated enjoying this, it soon began to symbolize the great strides he had made in his life. He wore his suits to our sessions with real pride and soon began to comment on my suits. Suits had symbolized an important developmental transition for me as well, and as he talked, I too felt enormously proud of my suits. I took great pleasure in the idea of the two of us both being in the room together, both wearing beautiful suits, both having brilliant careers, and both being the same.

In this case, the feeling of twinship grew out of an actual commonality. There was no confusion in my mind about either the extent or the reality of the commonality. It was clear to me that his feelings were his and that mine were mine, and it was on this basis that we felt alike. We had the same set of feelings under similar circumstances, and this mediated a feeling of twinship in which our egos were very much alike but still distinct.

Indeed, the configuration in these kinds of cases can appear to be based exclusively on real similarities between patient and analyst. The patient and the analyst may truly share very similar interests, experiences, and goals and may tend to look at the world in essentially the same way. But it is important to remember that while the actual similarities facilitate the feeling of twinship, they do not create it. I have had a number of patients who were extremely similar to me in some way or another but who did not induce this feeling of twinship. The countertransference experience of twinship is induced only when the patient is successfully expressing the developmental need for an identical separate object in the transference. When this induction is not present, any real similarities between the patient and the analyst may be interesting or perhaps even striking, but they are not emotionally compelling.

When the narcissistic transference becomes more intense, it can go beyond inducing the feeling of sameness. Such transferences can also distort the analyst's experience of his own identity in such a way that it conforms to the patient's transferential expectations. One patient was delighted to see a diploma in my office from a school in the state he had grown up. I felt a flush of that same narcissistic pleasure as he said it. The diploma, however, was not mine. His desire to share a similarity with me had led him to read only the part of the diploma that interested him. I reacted (to myself) as if what he had read were true, as if we really did share that experience.

Another patient, an analytic candidate, would frequently talk about how he and I shared the same kind of life. Although he focused on the fact that we were both analysts, in actuality this extended to all areas of our identities. When he said "we," it was saturated with such a feeling of unity that I would agree to myself that "we" did indeed feel the same way about something, even if I realized after the session that I actually didn't feel that way at all.

In both of these cases, there was a degree of distortion of my own identity; I had – momentarily, and in isolated areas – experienced aspects of my patients' egos as my own. Our ego boundaries had become blurred.

This distortion of the analyst's identity can become so intense that the analyst becomes deeply confused about how similar he and the patient actually are. This most often takes the form of an attitude that I have experienced myself and heard time and again from supervisees: "I can't treat this patient because he is so much like me that I can't be objective about him."

One supervisee reported uncanny similarities with a particular patient. They had the same feelings, the same thoughts, the same experiences, and the same histories, she said. They even looked and acted the same. She felt everything the patient felt, and she saw herself in everything the patient did. They were like the same soul in two bodies.

My curiosity aroused, I pressed for more details. Well, this analyst told me, they were both artists – although the analyst had been a printmaker, and the patient sang on Broadway. And they had both come from medium-sized towns on the coast – the analyst from the East Coast, and the patient from the West. They both first had sex at fifteen. The analyst had been involved with women, and the patient occasionally fantasized about this.

As might be expected, I was not entirely convinced that these two women were identical souls; and as we went through more of the details, it turned out that they weren't similar to each other emotionally. They had some of the same feelings – and what two people don't – but they handled them differently, and they led completely different lifestyles. Besides having brown hair, they did not look alike. In fact, there were few real-life similarities between them.

As is often the case with this form of induction, there was no obvious congruence between the content of the patient's communications and the countertransference. Only rarely did the patient make explicit references to feeling that the analyst was identical to her, and it is likely that this feeling was largely unconscious. Instead, the patient implied her feeling of sameness in the way that she communicated; her way of talking implied that the analyst already knew everything because she had been through the same experiences. The patient's need for an identical object was also apparent from her complaints about others, particularly boyfriends, who always did and felt things differently than she did in ways that upset her. She wished they were more like her and couldn't understand why they weren't.

Although the patient and the analyst retained awareness of each other, they were no longer distinct – at least not in the analyst's conscious experience. Here, the patient's transference induced not only the feeling of twinship but also an almost delusional belief that they were twins. The analyst experienced a profound confusion about the extent to which her identity actually overlapped with the patient's. The fact that the analyst really believed they were the same, despite the paucity of actual commonalities, indicates that a more pervasive blurring of ego boundaries took place here than in the previous cases.

Differential effects of positive and negative transference on the countertransference

To a much greater extent than in the introverted state, the analyst's experience of countertransference induced by extroverted narcissistic transference is significantly influenced by whether the transference is positive or negative.

When the transference is positive, the patient is feeling primarily positive about himself (whether defensively or profoundly), and thus feels primarily positive about the analyst. The countertransference in these cases is pleasant and comfortable, sometimes even ecstatic. The patient feels good, in a way reminiscent of Mahler *et al.*'s (1975) description of the exuberant 12-month-old, and views the analyst as his counterpart. A warm feeling of deep familiarity envelops both members of the analytic pair. When the patient idealizes the analyst in this state, the two feel they are a perfect team. Everything the analyst says or does works perfectly, and the patient's response is splendid. Should the analyst make a mistake, the patient understands because, after all, he would do exactly the same thing. Similarly, the analyst has infinite patience with the patient because he knows how hard things can be.

When there is significant congruence between the content and the induction in a positive transference state, the result can be a state in which the patient and analyst are filled with admiration and/or love for each other. This is common in the early stages of work with certain narcissistic patients,[5] and in later stages of the successful treatment with many other types of patients, especially anaclitic depressives. In these cases, the patient feels that they have the most wonderful, most loving, most insightful, most brilliant, or most sensitive analyst in the world, and the analyst thinks he has the most lovable, most talented, most delightful, most intelligent, or most easily analyzed patient in the world. Both feel lucky to have the other (although narcissistic patients tend to feel it is only their due, while depressives can't believe their good fortune).

This kind of situation can look a lot like an object mode in which each of them is the other's idealized object. What distinguishes the two states is how the patient and analyst feel about themselves in relation to the other. In the narcissistic states, both analyst and patient feel the same way about themselves as they feel about the other; each is a rose-colored reflection for the other. (This feeling, however, may not be fully conscious or articulated for either the patient or the analyst.) In the positive object state, on the other hand, there is a significant difference between how they view themselves and how they view the other, even if the overall feeling between them is still very positive.

When the content and the induction are not clearly congruent, positive extroverted countertransference can crest into bursts of exciting, narcissistic fantasies that involve the patient. I had one patient, an extremely attractive, campy, gay man, with whom the transference and the countertransference had been marked by mistrust and hesitation for the first several years of treatment. After about two and a half years, the transference shifted. The patient began to feel that I understood him, and I began to feel a strong affinity with him, despite our apparent differences. At one point, he started wearing a dark green leather outfit, something far out of the range of things that I usually wear. I was entranced and spent a number of sessions imagining the two of us swathed in beautiful green leather, romancing the nights away while camping it up outrageously in the clubs and the bars. We were the hottest couple in town. The fantasy was only superficially erotic, as it never shaded into sex. What was exciting for me was our identity, not our attraction.

In this case, there was little overt congruence between the content and the countertransference. While I was absorbed in my reveries, the patient talked about the details of his everyday life, just as he always did. The transference could be seen in his response to my interventions. Previously, he had either ignored my comments or disagreed with them, no matter what they were, but now, his response was always "That's so true! How do you know me so well?" I also knew that we had a mutual interest in classical music, which I had never revealed to him. However, he began to discuss it with me as if he had always known it was something that we shared, and I simply responded in kind. Furthermore, he had interests that I had never shared, but I suddenly acted as though I had always had them.

If positive narcissistic countertransference can be heaven, negative narcissistic countertransference can be hell. This is a transference–countertransference configuration that can be induced when the patient hates himself, in the way described first by Freud (1917) in relation to melancholia, and later by Spotnitz (1976) in relation to schizophrenia. The patient's aggression is directed towards himself, whether in the form of depression, schizophrenia, psychosomatic illness, or self-destructive behavior. He forms a narcissistic transference in which he experiences the analyst as sharing his own flaws and hates him for it, just as he hates himself. The patient picks up everything that is wrong about the analyst and attacks him viciously. The patient is miserable. He feels like a failure and proceeds to make the analyst feel like that same failure.

A supervisee described a patient who initially was admiring of her and contrasted her own ineptitude with the analyst's sparkling competence. The analyst, however, did not feel competent in sessions with her, and soon she began to feel extremely incompetent. The patient's conscious attitude changed rather quickly, and soon she began to suggest that the treatment was a failure, or rather that since she was a failure, it stood to reason that the treatment would be a failure as well. Although the patient left the analyst out of the equation when she first expressed these feelings, the analyst began to feel increasingly bad about everything she did. She felt weak, stupid, and incapable of communicating with the patient. These were the same feelings that the patient had about herself.

Soon, the patient began to express this directly, becoming sharply critical of every little detail about the analyst – her weak tone of voice, her tacky office, and her clichéd interventions. She wasn't surprised that a loser like herself had picked an analyst who was a loser, she said, and by this point, the analyst emotionally agreed with all of it. Every time the patient reported another failure in her life, the analyst agreed (silently) that she had indeed messed up yet another situation. At the same time, she felt powerless to help her and thought that most of what the patient said about her was true: her voice was weak, she did have tacky taste, and she probably wasn't much of an analyst. True, she had other patients with whom she worked well, but she felt like this one had somehow unmasked her and revealed her true uselessness. Before every session with this woman, the analyst would promise herself to try to get some perspective on the situation, and during every session she would fall back into this pattern.

This is extroverted narcissistic countertransference in full negative bloom. The patient hates the analyst for having all of the negative qualities that she hates in herself; the analyst, under the influence of the narcissistic induction, also believes this and hates the patient for tormenting her with it. They are identical, and they hate each other for it. The qualities the patient criticizes in the analyst are sometimes projections and sometimes accurate perceptions of the analyst's character. In either case, what drives the dynamic is the negative narcissistic transference. In the countertransference, the analyst feels the patient's self-hatred at its full intensity.

Countertransference induced by symmetrical narcissistic countertransference

Symmetrical narcissistic countertransference is induced when the transference state is strongly narcissistic and dominated by projection. The patient projects his own impulses onto the analyst and consequently views the analyst as differentiated from himself. Thus, the patient may appear to be relating to the analyst in a state of greater differentiation than he actually is. In response, the analyst experiences the patient as having the qualities that the patient has projected onto him and views the patient as being differentiated from himself. The patient and the analyst both feel the same in themselves, and they both feel the same way about each other. Their experiences are identical – mirror images in which they do not recognize themselves.

This can be obvious when the induction is congruent with the content. One woman whom I agreed to see for an exceptionally low fee would regularly accuse me of being cheap. This always made me feel like saying "Me? Cheap? Why, you are the cheapest person I have ever met!"

This countertransference frequently appears in paranoid transference states. One analyst described a patient who felt extremely persecuted by everyone, including the analyst. She refused to give the analyst her work number out of fear that he would call her at work and endanger her job security. She wouldn't tell him about an idea that she had for a novel because she was afraid he might steal it. She made frequent reference to patients who had been sexually abused by their analysts.

All of this made the analyst extremely uneasy. He became preoccupied with the idea that the patient would sue him. Maybe she would lie and say he had made sexual advances. Maybe she would just try to sue him for damages because she was getting worse, not better. Maybe the fact that she paid in cash would make it look like something illicit was going on. Maybe she would denounce him to the IRS. He became increasingly fearful about seeing the patient and wished that he could get her out of his life.

The similarity between the analyst's feelings and the patient's feelings is clear; both are in a state of fear of each other. Each feels paranoid, and each is the object of the other's paranoia.

Symmetrical countertransference is not limited to paranoia, and positive qualities can play a part as well. For example, one patient idealized his analyst while devaluing himself, and the analyst similarly idealized the patient while devaluing herself.

This kind of countertransference can be difficult to manage. One analyst described working with a patient with necrophilic tendencies. He described frequent fantasies that the patient had about dismembering people and about people having strokes while she was having sex with them. The patient was very controlling and insisted on having the chairs in the office in a particular alignment before she would talk and on having the shades drawn in a particular manner. Initially, the analyst agreed to this arrangement. However, he began to feel controlled, especially after the patient announced that she was falling in love with him. He refused to allow the patient to arrange the room in a way that was comfortable for her and explored her requests to do so in a way that, in retrospect, was similar to how the patient treated him. The treatment became a duel in which the analyst involuntarily mirrored the patient's every move.

In all of these cases, the induction was congruent with the content, although the induced paranoia and its accompanying self-certainty obscured the congruity. It certainly seems possible that symmetrical identifications can occur when the induction is incongruent with the content, but I have never seen it in myself or my supervisees. This may be due to chance, or it may be that exposure to this type of content is necessary to induce the countertransference.

7
OBJECT COUNTERTRANSFERENCE

In object countertransference, the analyst experiences herself and the patient in the context of the object relational mode. This means that (a) the analyst experiences herself and the patient as two separate and more or less differentiated people, and (b) the interaction between them repeats an interaction that was painful, traumatic, or in some ways pathogenic for the patient.

Object countertransference is usually induced by object transference, in which the patient experiences the analyst as a separate and more or less differentiated other person. (As we shall see, the patient may experience the analyst as a separate, but not as a fully, human presence in the object mode.) Furthermore, the patient also experiences the analyst in the context of a relationship that was painful, traumatic, or in some way pathogenic for her.

Object countertransference allows the analyst to experience two different types of feelings: either (a) feelings that emotionally important people in the patient's past felt towards the patient or (b) what the patient felt in her relationships with these emotionally important people. This contrasts with narcissistic countertransference that allows the analyst access to the patient's own feelings.

The object mode has considerably less attention than the narcissistic mode in schools that emphasize the importance of primitive transferences in treatment, such as developmental ego psychology (Jacobson 1964; Mahler et al. 1975; Kernberg 1985), Modern Psychoanalysis (Spotnitz 1976; Margolis 1978), and Self Psychology (Kohut 1971),[1] all of which emphasize the importance of the narcissistic mode both in infancy and in treatment.

As important as relationships in the narcissistic mode are, however, they are not the only important element in emotional development, pathology, or analysis. The observations of infant researchers, such as Stern (1985), as well as the experiences of parents who routinely observe and experience their children relating to them as being different from themselves, all suggest that the infant's earliest interactions with the world are not experienced exclusively through the narcissistic mode. Relationships with others that are experienced as, at least to some extent, separate and differentiated play a role throughout the life span – from infancy through old age. During analysis, the object mode recreates the world of the patient's separate pathogenic interpersonal relationships, from the most primitive to the most complex. By experiencing and understanding the inductions of the object mode, the analyst has access to the emotional information needed to free the patient from the involuntary repetition of her most painful experiences.

Characteristics of the object relational mode

The object relational mode is usually characterized by three features:

- the patient and the analyst experience different feelings;
- the patient and the analyst experience each other as different people;
- the analytic relationship is a repetition of pathogenic dynamics from an earlier relationship from the patient's past.

Difference between feelings experienced by patient and analyst

The first typical feature of the object mode is that the patient and analyst experience different feelings. The patient expresses a thought, feeling, or fantasy, and the analyst thinks, feels, or fantasizes something different. These feelings may conflict with each other. For example, the patient hated a movie, but the analyst loved it; the patient self-righteously describes a fight with his wife, and the analyst sides with the wife; the patient feels like she is making a lot of progress, but the analyst thinks she is stagnating. Alternatively, their feelings may be different but not conflicting, as when the patient feels happy during the session, but the analyst is depressed, or the patient becomes enthralled with homeopathy, while the analyst can't share his enthusiasm.

When patient and analyst focus on each other, their feelings are usually related. For example, the patient fantasizes that the analyst seduces him, and the analyst is aroused; the patient is frightened of the analyst because she is late, and the analyst feels punitive; the patient feels pressured, and the analyst feels that the patient should be working harder. Although their feelings may be related, they still remain different.

Patient and analyst experience each other as separate

In addition to experiencing different feelings, the patient and the analyst experience each other as different and separate from each other. Ego boundaries remain intact for both: there are two objects – two different people – relating to each other in the same room. This is not to say that the patient is necessarily aware of the analyst as a separate object, much less a fully differentiated three-dimensional, whole object, or subject. Indeed, most primitive states of object transference are neither elaborate nor clearly defined. The patient may simply

OBJECT COUNTERTRANSFERENCE

experience the analyst as a presence that is "not-me" – not a part of the experience that is connected to her consciousness or sense of self. This contrasts with the narcissistic mode, in which ego boundaries can blur, and the patient and analyst experience each other the same as, connected to, or a part of each other.

Although the patient in the object transference can re-experience the most primitive experiences of relating to a separate object, object countertransference is generally less regressive for the analyst. Because there is no blurring of ego boundaries, the analyst usually maintains a clear sense of the patient's presence.[2] Thus, the analyst tends to stay at higher levels of differentiation than the patient and does not lose track of her as a human object.[3] The patient (or another person who is a representation of or displacement from the patient) is always present in the analyst's mind, or as part of the context of the analyst's experience. Consequently, object countertransference is usually a less murky experience than narcissistic countertransference. The analyst, though rarely self-absorbed, is aware of her own feelings even if she does not understand why she feels them. Even when strongly self-focused – as in states of intense anxiety, fear, or sexual desire – his feelings are rooted in the relationship to the patient.

Patient–analyst relationship as a repetition of a pathogenic dynamic from the patient's past

The third characteristic of the object mode is that the feelings between the patient and the analyst are a repetition of an interpersonal dynamic from the patient's past.[4] This dynamic is pathogenic in the sense that it plays a causative role in the development or maintenance of the patient's current problems. The repetition of these feelings may be the overt focus of the interaction between patient and analyst. For example, the patient may say that she feels as guilty about canceling her last session as she did when she disappointed her mother, and the analyst may feel hurt, just as the mother would have been. Or the repetition may be reenacted between them covertly, as when the patient is subtly helpless and the analyst is unwittingly directive. In either case, the patient repeats the past not by distorting the present but by recreating her old relationships.[5]

It is not always easy to determine which dynamic is being repeated, however, or to know what the patient is feeling or how she is relating in the interaction. The analyst finds herself in an interpersonal drama in which her lines come easily, but their context remains unknown. She must hypothesize that the induction indicates her role in a differentiated interpersonal relationship, and she must then determine what the patient's corresponding role would be.

The repetitions in the object mode are derived from the patient's interpersonal relationships, primarily her early relationship with her parents, but also relationships with siblings and other intense relationships from her early life. Later intense relationships, especially traumatic ones, can form templates for new object repetitions. In some cases, the object countertransference that occurs is an accurate recreation of the patient's past relationship as it actually happened (or as the patient experienced the relationship). As we shall see in examples throughout this chapter, the analyst often has specific thoughts and feelings about a patient and subsequently learns that the patient's parent(s) felt exactly the same way towards her, and expressed it in exactly the same words.

The object mode can also be substantially different from the original relationship. Defenses may mask or distort repetitions of the original relationship. For example, a patient who had an exceptionally violent childhood with an impulsive and unpredictable mother may induce boredom in the analyst. In this case, the boredom is not a repetition of the original relationship. Rather, the boredom might have grown out of a defense that served two purposes: the first to block out memories of the original relationship and second to prevent repetition of the original relationship in subsequent relationships. As a result of this defense, however, the boredom would become a regular and repetitive feature of the patient's later relationships. Similarly, fantasies can create a new relationship that is a defensive solution to an earlier relationship. The patient with the violent childhood, for example, might have developed a fantasy of getting back at her mother by threatening to abandon her. This fantasy could be activated in the analysis (rather than the memory of her real relationship with her mother), with the result that the analyst ends up feeling in constant danger of abandonment.

Although it is hypothesized that the feelings experienced by patient and analyst in the object mode are repetitions, it is often impossible to know the origins of feelings experienced in the countertransference. Some patients can relate detailed memories of their past relationships that explain the feelings experienced in the mode. Many patients, however, do not provide such memories. For example, one of my patients constantly spoke in a loud, insistent tone that made me feel as if he was vomiting on me. Although he never told me about any interactions with his parents or anyone else in his past in which someone reported experiencing this feeling, one of his friends told him the same thing I felt, in the same words. Our interaction was clearly a repetition, even though its origin was never discovered.

Not all the separate object repetitions that occur in the analysis are necessarily pathological. There are positive repetitions as well, in which the patient induces feelings in the analyst that were maturational for him. These may include feelings of love, caring, delight, and protectiveness. These positive repetitions represent aspects of the original relationships that the patient did not get enough of at the time or for which she has experienced a renewed need due to later trauma or stress. In analysis, these positive repetitions are expressed in the anaclitic relational mode (see Chapters 4 and 8), in which the analyst provides the emotional communications that enable the patient to grow and mature (Spotnitz 1985). The concept of the object relational mode,

OBJECT COUNTERTRANSFERENCE

therefore, is limited to repetitive emotional interactions that were originally pathogenic for the patient and that continue to limit her ability to reach her full potential in life.

Congruence and incongruence

Object inductions can be congruent or incongruent with the content of the session. When the inductions are congruent with the content, the analyst's feelings are obviously and realistically related to what the patient is saying. For example, the patient screams that the analyst ought to be taken out and shot, and the analyst feels fear. The relationship of the analyst's fear to the patient's behavior is clear and understandable. A range of different object inductions may be congruent with the content in the object mode. In this example, other congruent reactions could include anger, indignation, desire to counterattack, or masochistic pleasure.

Incongruent inductions, on the other hand, are not obviously related to the content. Varying degrees of incongruence are possible. The analyst may have feelings about the patient that appear unrelated to what the patient is saying. This can be illustrated in an example where the induction was congruent with the content, but without the patient overtly enacting his role behaviorally in the session. A supervisee presented a patient who had been sexually molested for a number of years by an uncle. The patient mentioned this in the first session as one of his reasons for seeking treatment but never brought the topic up again. Instead, the patient discussed problems at work and with his family. He was generally restrained and inhibited. After about six months, the supervisee said that he had become sexually preoccupied during the patient's sessions. He had very explicit fantasies about having sex with the patient in a dominant, forceful way. There had been no change in the patient's demeanor, which was not provocative, seductive, or submissive, and there didn't appear to be any realistic reasons for the analyst's feelings. Not surprisingly, however, when the patient eventually did describe his molestation by his uncle, his account was very similar to the analyst's fantasies.

In more intense states of incongruence, the analyst's feelings appear to be completely unrelated to either the content or the patient. With one patient, for example, I persistently had memories of a friend from college. We had been close for several years, but I hadn't thought about him in a long time. As I sat with the patient, I thought that we had started to drift because I was disappointed in his lack of development after college. He never found a career, and he hadn't moved successfully into the adult world. I reproached him in my fantasies. Initially, this appeared to have nothing to do with the patient, who talked exclusively about day-to-day life, with no overt references to being a disappointment to anyone. Over time, however, I learned that his wife felt the same way towards him as I did towards my friend. The patient had not been fully aware of this, as his wife had not been open about these feelings.

Unconsciously, I had been thinking about the patient and had used an analogous relationship from my own past as a prism for experiencing the induced feelings.[6] This example illustrates how fantasies an analyst may have about other people during the session often prove to be incongruent object inductions.

Types of object countertransference

Simple object countertransference

Simple object countertransference occurs when the analyst experiences feelings that someone in the patient's past actually had about the patient or feelings that someone would have in accordance with the patient's defense or fantasy. The countertransference can repeat either the general form of a relationship or a discrete episode from a relationship. In either case, the patient maintains the same role in her relationship to the analyst that she did with the person from the past while the analyst experiences that person's feelings.

We will consider a simple example first. One patient described her father as a rigid perfectionist who was never satisfied with anything she did. (Parental attitudes often have nothing to do with the reality of who the child actually is, but this struck me as particularly odd.) The patient was talented, hardworking, and charming, and it sounded as though she always had been. She'd done well in school, never been in any kind of trouble, and if anything, it seemed like she was overly cooperative at home. What could the father possibly find to complain about in such a lovely child? True, the patient was not doing as well in her career or her relationships as might be expected – her self-esteem was devastatingly low – but this seemed to be an entirely predictable effect of the impossibly high demands her father had placed upon her.

Initially, I liked this patient a lot, and I expected the case to go smoothly – just a few drops of ordinary human kindness would be enough to get her on the right track. After a certain point, however, I became impatient with her progress. She continually got into bad relationships at work, and her judgment was consistently poor. What she did wrong depended on the circumstances, but she did exactly the wrong thing under most any circumstances. In one session, we discussed a way of dealing with a difficult situation with her boss and developed a plan; she did the opposite of what we'd discussed – with predictably disastrous results – yet seemed to think she had exactly followed our plan. I felt hypercritical of her: she was stupid, utterly lacking in common sense, and she was passive–aggressive, a die-hard masochist. Even when she managed to get a new job (which was a considerable achievement), I was annoyed that she hadn't negotiated a higher salary. In sum, I despised her for her failures and found her successes wanting. I had turned into her father.

This example illustrates simple object transference. First, my feelings were clearly about her as a person distinct from myself. I experienced her as a failure, but I did not experience myself as a failure, nor did I blame myself for her lack of progress. In my feelings, the problem was simple: she was socially inept. There was no blurring of ego boundaries. She was who she was, and I was who I was.

Second, her feelings were different from mine. She was depressed about not getting what she wanted. She cursed her fate and complained that she was being treated unfairly. Nobody would give her a chance. And when she sensed that I was critical of her, she told me I was just like all the rest. It was just her luck to find an analyst who felt the same way everyone else did about her. This difference in our feelings indicated that I identified with an object from her life and not with her superego.

Finally, we replayed an interpersonal relationship from her past. We each had our roles and followed her script closely: she was incompetent, and I was critical – my feelings echoing her father's criticisms word for word.

In this case, the induction was congruent with the content. My feelings were an understandable and logical reaction to hers. Furthermore, her feelings and memories of her father were conscious, and she had described their relationship in the analysis extensively. When I experienced them myself, the relation to her life history was clear.

One might expect that the clarity and congruence of this countertransference would make it easy to identify, but this was only partially true. Although I quickly recognized the resemblance between my emerging feelings and her father's feelings, my subjective experience was that my feelings about her were realistic reactions to her here-and-now functioning: she acted incompetently in the world, and she presented herself as incompetent in the sessions.

Clinging to reality-oriented interpretations of the feelings (or ascribing them to subjective issues in the analyst)[7] is a common obstacle to understanding the repetitive elements in the countertransference. Note that countertransference is only rarely determined by the patient's overt behavior and not all inductions are congruent with the content. There are numerous examples where patients act incompetent, obnoxious, or immoral, and the analyst reacts with nothing but love, patience, and acceptance. (These are usually anaclitic inductions.) Similarly, there are examples of patients whose behavior is impeccable, yet the analyst experiences aggression towards them.

Common simple object countertransference scenarios

While the object countertransference induced by each patient will be unique – a reflection of her own individual history of interpersonal relationships – some patterns arise fairly often. These transference/countertransference configurations are derived from typical developmental situations. I will describe several of them that I have found to be most common, both in my own work and in that of my colleagues. However, manifestations of simple object countertransference are by no means limited to these particular configurations.

Analyst as rejecting parent

The most primitive form of simple object transference induces the "boring baby" countertransference. In this configuration, the patient often talks with no apparent awareness of the analyst. The patient makes little or no contact, whether in the form of questions or other attempts to engage the analyst in interaction. The patient may be relatively silent and affectless, or verbal and animated. What is important is that she seems oblivious to the analyst's existence as a different person. The analyst's reaction is to be enveloped in a state of severe, almost paralyzing, boredom. The analyst finds herself doing his shopping list, planning vacations, adding up bills, or remembering forgotten errands. She returns from her reverie to find the patient still there, talking away, unaware that her attention ever drifted. The analyst may feel useless or interchangeable. She may feel resentful that her individuality isn't recognized – she might as well be a piece of the furniture, erroneously concluding that her presence is unnecessary.

Superficially, the patient in this state relates to the analyst as if in a deeply narcissistic transference state. The induction, however, is completely different. During narcissistic countertransference, the analyst experiences the same, deep self-absorption that the patient does. In contrast, during object countertransference, the analyst may think about herself a lot but is not self-absorbed. She may be acutely aware of the patient despite not being terribly interested in him. The analyst's feelings are a reaction to the sense that the patient is using her – engaged with her, perhaps, but not relating to her as a person in her own right. In fact, the patient in this state relates to the analyst as just another component of the same environment that sustains and maintains her identity. As such, the analyst is not quite human and lacks individuality and subjectivity, but her presence is as crucial to the patient's functioning as the air that she breathes. Like the air, her presence is taken for granted by the patient unless it is irritating or toxic. The patient in this state is deeply narcissistic, in the sense of being unaware of the analyst as a separate person. But she is not in a state of narcissistic transference because she does not experience the analyst as an extension of herself. Consequently, she does not induce her own feelings in the analyst.

This very primitive object transference state recapitulates the earliest relationship the infant has to the mother as a separate object – the object is "not me" but no more differentiated than that. The mother in these moments has no identity but is no less indispensable for the lack of it. As long as the object unobtrusively and consistently meets the infant's needs, it remains indistinct and impersonal until the infant matures into a higher level of interpersonal awareness.

Most parents have at least occasional moments of boredom when the infant needs them in this seemingly impersonal way, and some parents find these periods in which their individuality is not acknowledged to be completely unbearable. This range of bored, sometimes resentful, feelings is similarly induced in the analyst during these primitive object transference states.

Another common pattern of early object countertransference is the "disgusting baby" induction. The following is a typical example. A supervisee described a patient he had seen approximately six times. Something about this patient annoyed him. He couldn't say what. At first glance, the patient seemed relatively appealing: she was well dressed, attractive, and articulate. Yet he felt repelled by her. Her voice was choppy and peppered with slang that sounded artificial and affected. Nevertheless, his overall feeling was that he could work with her.

Over the next several sessions, my supervisee's objections to this patient increased exponentially: she didn't look quite clean, her hair was a mess (it would look much better if she combed it a little more), and her goals were nothing more than a patchwork of New Age clichés and talk-show psycho-babble. (Had she ever had an original thought in her head?) But her voice was the worst of all – grating, whining, and pleading. Almost every session, she cried about something in ugly, wrenching sobs. He knew she was in great distress, that her pain was genuine, and that she seemed to be benefiting from the therapy. Despite all of this, he shyly told me he felt little empathy or sympathy for her and that he found her to be completely repulsive.

As the supervisee described his feelings, I could picture an exasperated father unhappily holding a squirming, screaming baby. The baby is crying and vomiting, shitty and smelly. All the parent can think about is how horrible this small, noisy creature is. Why couldn't she be cute and adorable like all those babies on TV? He feels horribly guilty for feeling this way; she is his baby daughter, after all. He wishes he didn't feel this way. But he does.

This imagery exemplifies the object repetition that was activated in the countertransference. This type of countertransference typically arises with patients who experienced some degree of revulsion from their parents but experienced other, more positive, feelings as well. The negative feelings were so toxic to the patient that they were induced in new situations.

Although this countertransference configuration can be induced at any point in the treatment, it often arises in the first several weeks of the analysis. If the analyst is able to tolerate the feelings, the countertransference evolves quickly, and the analyst shifts into an anaclitic state in which she feels warm and nurturing towards the patient. It is almost as if the patient is testing the analyst to see whether she will be able to stand her at her worst. If so, the patient can move on to other ways of relating, first to the analyst, and then to others in her outside life.

A closely related countertransference – "I'm not the right analyst" – takes a different form in that the patient describes her problems to the analyst, and the analyst quickly concludes that she is not the right analyst for the patient. Sometimes the analyst blames herself, and sometimes blames the patient. In either case, however, the only solution seems to be for the patient to find another analyst.

For instance, a supervisee described an initial consultation she had with a young man. The patient was immediately critical of the analyst's office. It was too dark, he said. "How can you ever expect to help me if there isn't any light in the room?" The criticism, however, did not last long, and the patient quickly moved on to what had brought him there. He described a series of bad relationships, a number of failed efforts to start a career, and chronic problems with money. He ascribed most of his problems to his acne, which was, in fact, quite severe. He had just consulted a crystal healer about his skin. He was certain that his depression would clear up when his skin did. He just needed the analyst to help support him until the crystal worked.

After having reported the session, the supervisee apologetically told me that she probably was not the right therapist for this patient. The reason, she insisted, was purely subjective: she thought the patient was quite bizarre. Although she knew it was unreasonable, the acne really bothered her, as it made the patient difficult to look at. She didn't think she could control her reaction to his hideous appearance. She also had a negative reaction to the idea of the crystal healer. The patient had a right to consult anyone he wanted, of course, but she couldn't condone this kind of bogus mysticism. Besides, she was sure it would lead to a split transference, and she knew that she would be the hated object. She didn't think she could tolerate that so early in the treatment. The only ethical thing to do was to refer the patient to another analyst.

The supervisee's reactions were striking in that they contradicted what I knew about her in a number of ways. First, she was an experienced clinician and had always managed intense negative transference and criticism in the past. Furthermore, she had a number of patients involved with other therapies just as marginal as the crystal healing. And while the issue of acne had never surfaced in our work together, I couldn't quite believe that she would discharge the patient on the basis of a skin condition. I suggested that she try to tolerate her feelings about the patient for a few sessions after which we would reexamine the countertransference.

The patient's stories were remarkably consistent with the fact that nobody wanted to be involved with him for very long. He had no real friends. Even the person who had referred him, one of the supervisee's other patients, said that he found him repulsive. He was fired from a job after one day. A chiropractor from whom he had wanted to get nutritional counseling never had any appointments for him after their second consultation. He hadn't had a date in years.

Viewed from this perspective, the analyst's reactions were completely objective. She, like everyone else, wanted to reject this patient as quickly as possible. While issues like the acne or the crystal healing may have provided the analyst with a subjective framework for her desire to terminate the analysis, they were not the basis of it. The analyst concluded that the patient had induced the same feelings of rejection in her that he had induced in others.

This sort of induction often takes another specific form in which the analyst feels that the patient must be referred to somebody else for diagnostic reasons. The reasons can be limitless: the patient is borderline; she isn't abstinent; she has a dual diagnosis; she requires psychiatric supervision; she is incapable of insight; she is too impulsive to put her feelings into words; she is too fragile to withstand the rigors of analytic treatment; she needs to see a woman or she needs to see a man. The reasons are many, but the conclusion is always the same: the patient must be sent (away) to somebody else.

Of course, any of these reasons might be accurate, and a referral might be the most appropriate action to take in any given case. Furthermore, it is crucial for analysts to acknowledge their areas of professional limitation and to avoid taking on patients whom they are unqualified to treat.

But these kinds of diagnostic evaluations frequently represent intellectualized defenses against powerful impulses to reject the patient – impulses that are a crucial aspect of the patient's repetition compulsion. A failure to study the analyst's seemingly objective diagnostic assessment – and its implications for the treatment – within the overall context of the patient's life story can easily lead the analyst to act on the repetition, rather than analyze it.

In these kinds of cases, the patient induces a rejecting feeling that a parent – usually the primary caretaker – had for the patient as a baby or child. Unlike the disgusting baby induction, the rejection in these cases is more complete, unleavened by loving feelings. Indeed, the parent may never have bonded (or the patient may have perceived the parent as not having bonded) with the child enough to want to keep her. The rejecting feelings are oddly cold, completely unlike the passionate hatred characteristic of the disgusting baby induction. The patient later induces this feeling in other people in her life.

Analyst as depleted parent

Far more common than feelings of rejection by the parent are moments of parental exhaustion and depletion, leading to feelings of helplessness and withdrawal. These feelings are repeated in the object countertransference when the analyst feels overwhelmed by the intensity of the patient's needs. As an example, a colleague described his work with a man who suffered from a relentless, intractable depression. The patient cried nearly every session. He had been a premature baby and had spent his first month in an incubator. His mother, who sounded well meaning and loving but ineffective, said that he had been colicky as a baby. Apart from that, his childhood did not seem to be particularly unusual. While his current life was not terrible, there was a sadness about him in the early years of treatment that nothing seemed to assuage. He experienced a recurrent dream of being surrounded by droves of starving kittens and having nothing to give them. This was exactly the feeling the analyst had towards the patient. Nothing the analyst did seemed to help. He couldn't make the pain go away, even for a few moments. The analyst often fought the impulse to settle back into utter passivity and watch the patient suffer. As much as he liked the patient, the analyst dreaded the sessions, fearing the depth of the patient's despair. The little information that the patient provided about his mother supported the idea that she had felt similarly overwhelmed by the patient's pain.

While the patient's neediness was induced quietly through tears and silence, this type of depleted induction is common with patients who need extensive contact between sessions and/or demand indulgence around lateness, fees, or rescheduling. Some of these patients may induce anger, as well, while others simply create the impression that they are unsootheable, making the analyst feel like the exhausted parent of an ever-crying baby.

Analyst as sexual abuser

Sexual feelings are commonly induced in the analyst, and the meaning of the induction varies, depending on the patient's life story. With patients who have been sexually abused, the induction is often straightforward: the analyst has sexual feelings of an aggressive, non-romantic nature towards the patient. These feelings are frequently incongruent with the content, which is reflective of the fact that the sexual advances were inappropriate for, and thus incongruent with, the patient's developmental needs at the time.

These feelings can also have a strangely dissociated quality. A supervisee described working with a woman who had been abused by an older sister between the ages of 8 and 12. Much of the countertransference comprised warm, caring feelings towards the patient, but occasionally the analyst experienced disconnected, out-of-the-blue impulses to say things like, "Where's the money, honey? Cough up the bucks, babe!" Although the comments were ostensibly about money, the analyst described them as coarse and leering, like a wolf whistle. These dissociated, unpredictable feelings were reminiscent of the crudely objectifying way that the patient's sister had pawed and taunted her as a child. The dissociated quality of the feelings was a result of narcissistic induction within the greater framework of a simple object induction – both the effect and the content of the patient's memory were strongly dissociated from her everyday experience.

The content of incongruent inductions related to sexual impulses is not always overtly sexual. An example is the impulse to make invasive interventions, which commonly occurs with patients who have been sexually abused.

OBJECT COUNTERTRANSFERENCE

This impulse manifests in a number of ways. For example, the analyst might think that she should help the patient to talk about the experience in more detail, ask probing or penetrating questions about it, or make explicit interpretations. More subtly, the analyst may experience the need to make similar interventions on topics that have ostensibly nothing to do with the sexual abuse. What is common to all of them is that the analyst makes interventions that are overly probing, touching things that shouldn't be touched.

A similar problem occurred with a patient who came to see another supervisee for an initial consultation. The patient had been in therapy twice prior to working with the supervisee and was unhappy with both experiences. Both therapists had repeatedly told the patient unsolicited personal information about themselves. One had called the patient between sessions to ask how he was doing even after the patient had told him that he would prefer not to talk to him outside the sessions. The supervisee resolved to keep firm, classical boundaries with this patient. When the patient left the session, however, the supervisee realized that the patient had left his briefcase in the office. Seized with concern that the patient would need it, he rushed out of the office and called out to the patient down the hall by his full name. Immediately afterward, he realized that he had fallen into the same trap of violating the patient, in this case by chasing after the patient and inadvertently breaking confidentiality by using his name. Fortunately, the patient had already left the building prior to the analyst's frenzied pursuit! Over the next several sessions, the patient described how his mother walked around the house stark naked and never allowed him to close his door to his room.

Sexual inductions are not limited to patients who have been sexually abused. Freud (1912) observed that everyone has their own way of being loved, and patients induce the feelings in the analyst that correspond to their own particular needs for love. This concept is illustrated in a case of an induction that was initially experienced by the analyst as incongruent. A supervisee described a passive woman who was underachieving in all areas of her life. She had been in therapy with a male therapist for a number of years before starting treatment with the supervisee. She constantly described comments the previous therapist had made that the analyst found shockingly critical. Most of the time, the analyst felt tenderly towards this woman, as her parents and her previous analyst had treated her cruelly. Sometimes the analyst also had distinctly erotic feelings, however, that included fantasies of humiliating the patient, complete with black leather, spiked heels, and whipping. These feelings were completely incongruent with the content of the sessions, and the analyst had no idea where they came from.

Over time, the patient developed a distinctive pattern in sessions in which she told stories that she ostensibly thought were funny while essentially portraying herself as pathetic. Whenever there was a lull in the session, the patient announced that she had another funny story. The analyst thought these stories were stupid and wanted to tell the patient to stop wasting time – to get to the point. These stories, and the analyst's reaction to them, were the first link between the analyst's sadistic fantasies and the patient's behavior. But it was only after she described her sadomasochistic relationships with her boyfriends, that resembled some of the analyst's fantasies (leather included), that the origin of the sadistic inductions became clear.

Analyst as withholding parent

Patients who have experienced withholding parents often induce a withholding countertransference in the analyst. Withholding inductions can be manifested in how the analyst feels as she responds to the patient on a moment-to-moment basis. These types of inductions can be difficult to identify because many psychoanalytic techniques can appear to be withholding when viewed out of context. How might withholding feelings be experienced? The analyst might feel no desire to talk to the patient, except to reflect questions or to remind the patient that they are working together to get the patient to do the talking. If the analyst works within an interpretive model, she might feel disinclined to interpret, justifying her reluctance by thinking that she does not want to do the work for the patient. If she works within a model that emphasizes emotional communication, she may find herself silent, reluctant to join or to empathize, for the conscious purpose of facilitating the patient's expression of frustration and aggression. Similar manifestations might reflect an unwillingness to compliment the patient, even at moments when praise would be desirable. They may also be reflected in an out-of-character hesitation about arranging a make-up session or a time change.

The issue of analyst as withholding parent was expressed as an acting-out manifestation by a supervisee who had a patient who was extremely reactive to noise. The patient jumped every time the phone rang. The analyst reported that she sympathized with the patient but also felt that it was best for the analysis if the patient had this reaction and verbally expressed his frustration. As it turned out, the patient had put his frustration into words, and had asked the analyst to turn off the phone or at least move it from where she kept it – just a few inches away from the back of the patient's head when he laid on the couch! The analyst could have easily moved it but viewed this as over gratifying the patient. Once the issue was brought to her attention, however, the analyst was able to see a wide range of ways in which she did not want to gratify him, and was able to compare these feelings to interactions the patient described with his parents.

As the above examples illustrate, it is often unclear whether an intervention is a legitimate technique or if an induction has been acted-out and rationalized as a technique. The foremost consideration here is the analyst's feelings towards the patient when she is engaged in behavior that could be viewed as withholding. For example, would the analyst prefer to gratify the patient but decline out of her sense of professional and ethical commitment? Or would she be inclined to withhold even if it were not good technique? If the situation requires generosity towards the patient, does this come naturally to the analyst, or does it require effort?

Analyst as indulgent or controlling parent

The classic reaction to a substance abuser (or any patient with a similar impulse control problem) often grows out of an object induction to be an enabler. A colleague described a young woman with a severe alcohol problem. The patient wept through most of the sessions, inducing the impression that she was an exceptionally fragile person. The analyst often thought she should address this with the patient, but she was afraid it would make the patient feel criticized. Whenever the analyst considered confronting her, the patient would associate to extremely sad moments in her life. The analyst felt protective of the patient and did not want to put undue demands on her by either setting limits in the session or by criticizing her alcohol abuse. No matter how self-destructive the patient's behavior, the analyst feared that she would harm her by suggesting they discuss the matter.

Not surprisingly, the patient's parents also acted with enabling tendencies. The patient had always been temperamental and highly reactive, even as a baby, and they had been protective of her and unwilling to make demands upon her. Although it is unclear whether the parents' behavior was a reaction to the patient's temperament or a cause of it, the analyst's attitude was a repetition of the parents'.

Lest it be concluded that only reluctance to set limits is representative of an object repetition, I hasten to add that the opposite situation, in which the analyst is overly controlling, is equally common. When a patient has had strict or controlling parents, the analyst may find herself wanting to be strict or punitive with the patient. This can take the form of viewing every aspect of the patient's life as a form of impulsivity or acting out, or it can translate into the inclination to be particularly intense in her analytic demands of the patient. For example, the analyst might ask questions in a way that resembles an interrogation rather than an exploration of the patient's feelings. Similarly, she might want the patient to "work harder" in the sessions, or to talk about "productive material." Minor derelictions of the analytic contract are incorrectly interpreted as a resistance, when in fact they are an unconscious attempt to induce a controlling reaction in the analyst.

Analyst as batterer

Controlling inductions are often strongest with passive patients who have a strong propensity to be victimized, such as homeless people or battered spouses. The countertransference scenario with battered patients often follows a predictable sequence. Initially, the analyst, sympathetic with the patient and experiencing a strong desire to help her, is furious with the abusive partner and attempts to mobilize the patient to protect herself. If the patient follows through, all is well and good. But if the patient is ambivalent about standing up to the partner or leaving (as is often the case with battered spouses) the analyst becomes frustrated. The analyst has the impulse to insist that the patient look out for her own welfare. The analyst may become exasperated if the patient doesn't follow her suggestions and consequently may experience the impulse – or even act on the impulse – to make her suggestions more aggressively. She may even go so far as to demand that the patient do what she suggests. As this process continues, the analyst develops the same controlling feelings as the abuser. Although their goals are different, the impulses towards the patient are psychologically equivalent.

Analyst as victim of the child

In most simple object countertransference scenarios, the patient is in the passive role as the object of the analyst's erotic or aggressive feelings. This is a repetition of the fact that there is a power differential between the child and the parents, and the child is the passive object of the parents' impulses. Some children, however, do have more power over their parents than their parents had over them. Some have stronger, more aggressive temperaments than their parents, while others are more ordinary children whose parents did not, for whatever reason, set appropriate limits with them. When this dynamic is repeated in the analysis, the analyst feels on the weak end of the power differential. The patient appears to be in charge, and the analyst feels abused by the patient's behavior. This kind of induction is often completely congruent with the patient's content or behavior, usually around issues such as payment, attendance, or phone contact.

A more specific "abused parent" induction arises with patients who developed hostile, grandiose defenses in reaction to a parent who was grossly weak or ineffective. For example, one male patient's father was physically disabled, and the patient was intimately involved with his care, including bathroom hygiene, from a fairly young age. The patient developed strong feelings of superiority to his father and contempt for his needs. The patient's primary identification was with his mother, whom he viewed as strong and powerful and who also despised his invalid father. This situation was quickly replicated in the transference. The patient was superficially polite and respectful for the first several sessions. But when the analyst explained his cancellation policy, the patient made a denigrating remark about the grubbiness of the analyst's financial needs. The analyst probably experienced this as the father did: he felt ashamed of needing money and afraid the patient would feel that he was an incompetent fraud. The scenario played out in even more detail when the patient went to a female group therapist and constantly talked about how much more brilliant the group therapist was than the analyst. The analyst felt competitive with the group therapist, feeling that he was an object of scorn for both of them.

Analyst as incompetent parent

Finally, we should consider the bad mother induction, what Epstein (1987: 35) called the "bad analyst feeling." With this type of induction, the analyst feels like a bad analyst because the patient is suffering and the analyst can't seem to do anything to resolve it. One patient experienced the world – and my office during the sessions – as a torture chamber. My couch was uncomfortable and hurt her back. Wasn't there anything I could do? I agreed to bring in a mat for the floor. This was somewhat of an improvement, but the dust on my floor was terrible and stirred up her allergies. When smells from a nearby restaurant wafted into the office, she was so nauseated she nearly had to leave. When my phone rang, she seemed to jump out of her skin in alarm. I could soothe her with my verbal interventions, but if they missed the mark even a little, her agony skyrocketed.

There was no doubt in my mind that her suffering was real. I never found her to be either histrionic or manipulative. Nevertheless, it was exasperating to be with her. She was like a colicky baby for whom everything is irritating. Offering milk doesn't help, changing the diaper doesn't help, holding her tight doesn't help (she only arches her back and pushes away), and singing doesn't help. The only thing that might help is to hold her at a particularly exhausting and painful angle, and then only for a few minutes, before this too irritates her and further adjustments are required. This was the repetition in the transference, and the repetition in the countertransference was the feeling of being an overwhelmed, misattuned mother who is frantic because she cannot soothe her baby.

In this example, the patient appears to be passively miserable. In more intense expressions of this dynamic, the patient is more actively miserable. The transference is shaped by the revenge fantasy of victory through defeat (Riek 1941) – the patient will get back at the parent through spectacular failure. In this scenario, the patient initially appears to be helpless and in need of support. The analyst feels warm and nurturing and has the impression that the patient is in the early stages of the anaclitic transference. However, the analyst soon learns that the patient is unable to internalize any of her support. It seems to aggravate the patient – to make her functioning deteriorate further. Nevertheless, the analyst feels increasingly solicitous of the patient's needs, until it appears that the more she tries to help the patient (or simply feels like helping the patient), the worse the patient gets. Unfortunately, abstaining from "helpful" interaction does not make the dynamic go away, and it just gets worse.

Analyst as neglectful parent

In a subtler example, an analyst experienced the impulse to be a different sort of bad mother. One supervisee described a case of a woman who had recently returned to treatment after an absence of several years. The analyst wondered whether she should have tried harder to prevent the patient from leaving, as the years had not been good to her. The patient had left treatment in order to attend nursing school – she had not been able to find the time to do both – and now that she'd graduated, she realized that she hated being a nurse.

The supervisee described the patient as a hardworking woman who had been dedicated to being a good parent above all else. She had married two men, both of whom turned out to be losers who couldn't support her or the children. Her decision to become a nurse was her attempt to remedy the situation, but the demands of being in school had led her to neglect the children's need for supervision and affection on a day-to-day basis. At the time she returned to treatment, the family was a wreck. Her second husband was usually absent and was emotionally abusive when he was present. Both of the children were having a lot of trouble in school, and one of them was involved with drugs.

Despite these problems, the patient was back in treatment and seemed to be solidly engaged. She had quickly taken control of her life when she was previously in treatment, and the analyst had no reason to think that her life wouldn't improve again soon. Nevertheless, I asked the analyst about her primary concern with the patient. She said that she was concerned that the children would not be able to get better unless the patient did something about her husband. Realistically, this may have been correct, and was a legitimate source of concern. Yet it was an interesting answer to my question, for it indicated that the analyst's concern was focused not on the patient herself but on the patient's children. In other words, within the analytic relationship, the patient was not the focus of the analyst's attention in the way that a well-loved baby would be the focus of her mother's attention. Her children had displaced her. In the privacy of her feelings, the analyst neglected the patient, which corresponded closely with the patient's life story, where she later revealed that her mother favored her brothers and sisters over her.

Conditional positive object countertransference

Conditional positive object countertransference recreates a state in which the parents had strong positive feelings for the patient but in a way that did not allow the patient the leeway to develop independently. The following scenarios illustrate conditional positive object countertransference: a boy's mother was delighted with her toddler when he brought back the toys to put in her lap but felt rejected if he asserted his independence and stayed away for too long. The father was proud of him when he was masculine and played soccer but became rejecting when he showed more feminine interests because they aroused the father's fear that he was gay (which was ultimately true). What is important in these scenarios is not that the parent had a negative reaction when the child did something that displeased him – that is inevitable. Rather, what is toxic is the intensity, duration, and unyieldingness of the negative feelings that are experienced as a type of love that is overly conditional, too restrictive and controlling to allow the child to individuate.

During analysis, the analyst has very positive feelings for the patient until she does something wrong. This frequently occurs in relationship to issues around the treatment contract. Early on, the patient is extremely responsible about attendance, punctuality, and paying the fee. On top of that, she talks regularly, speaks of dreams and memories, and shows improvement in her life. She acts like a good patient – repeating the role of a good child who always does her homework and brushes her teeth without being asked. Consequently, the analyst likes her a lot.

At some point the patient begins to change. She comes late, she misses sessions, and she forgets to pay. She obsesses about things that the analyst doesn't think are important. The analyst is disappointed and can't find her former affection for the patient; she is no longer a good patient.

Another example was a patient in the mental health field who started treatment with me with the intention of becoming an analyst. Things went splendidly for a while. The patient studied analysis and had the makings of a terrific analyst, and I couldn't resist the feeling that I had a prodigy and a protégé on my hands. I was delighted. After a few years, however, the patient became critical of analysis – it lasted too long and was too dogmatic. I felt hurt, as though I'd been attacked personally. (On an unconscious level, it may have been true, although the patient consciously professed to like and admire me.) I felt critical of him and was inclined to analyze his shift as resistance and even as a lack of integrity. Eventually, the patient decided that he was really more interested in becoming a cognitive-behavioral therapist and wanted to put his time and his money into that project. By this point, my feelings were no longer affectionate. I read all kinds of nefarious motives into the patient's behavior and even had revenge fantasies in which he realized that he would never get cured unless he stuck, not just with me, but also with analysis. Yet I was also aware that these feelings were way out of proportion. After all, he hadn't done anything wrong – except choose his own path.

This patient's parents had been extremely religious, as the patient himself had been when he was young; he had been well on his way to joining the clergy. In college, however, he had eventually broken with their religion in favor of psychology and had been tremendously disappointed that his parents had been rejecting of him afterward. In the analysis, his decision to become a cognitive-behavioral therapist repeated this dynamic. I experienced the same types of feelings as the parents who rejected him because he asserted his independence of them.

These kinds of situations raise the issue of whether the parent (or analyst) relates to the child/patient narcissistically in that the child's individuality is not respected. What distinguishes this feeling from true narcissism, however, is that the parent recognizes the child's differentiation but doesn't respect it. Thus, it is possible for the parent to be pathologically demanding while still relating within the context of a separate relationship. As we shall see, however, there are situations in which narcissism can occur within the context of a separate relationship, and these can be repeated in the object mode.

Countertransference in which one member of the dyad is narcissistic

An important form of the object mode occurs when either the patient or the analyst relates to the other in the narcissistic mode, and the other does not reciprocate but relates in the object mode instead. The result is a relationship in which the patient and the analyst have different feelings, but one of them does not experience the other as being separate or different. This configuration can repeat two types of pathological object relationships, depending on whether the patient or the analyst relates narcissistically. When the patient relates narcissistically, the analyst relates as an object and experiences the feelings of a non-empathic parent. When the patient relates separately and the analyst relates narcissistically, the analyst experiences the feelings of a narcissistic parent.

We will consider first the case in which the patient relates to the analyst narcissistically. On the surface, she appears to experience the analyst as being just like herself or as an extension of herself. In short, it looks like she experiences a narcissistic transference towards the analyst. However, she does not induce a corresponding narcissistic transference in the analyst. On the contrary, the analyst sees the patient as different or foreign, and in most cases, she is irritated by the patient's assumption (explicit or implicit) that they are the same. She may find the patient infuriatingly self-important, labeling her as narcissistic in the most pejorative sense of the word.

An example occurred with a patient who was going through a period in which religion and spirituality had become extremely important to him. This irritated me intensely, especially when he included me in his spiritual thinking. He said that God had brought us back together after a very difficult period in which he had wanted to leave treatment. This irritated me to no end; I had worked very hard to help him to stay in treatment, and I wasn't inclined to share the credit with God. He said that I must be a very spiritual person – whereas I considered the word to be almost meaningless to me personally. However, in the stridently differentiated state I was in, I would have objected even if it had been true. The crescendo of my feelings of differentness occurred at Easter time, when he warmly wished me a Happy Passover (a holiday I didn't celebrate) after having spent the session talking about how important Easter was to him. I had a strong impulse to tell him that I couldn't care less about Passover or Easter and to please excuse me from any further religious musings.

The situation here is complex. The patient longed for me to share his feelings about spirituality so that I would be a narcissistic object for him. But my feelings were the complete opposite. My hostility towards religion at that point in my life was strong enough to make me think that this was a purely subjective countertransference resistance. On the other hand, I had a number of other quite religious patients who had never aroused this sort of hostility in me. Furthermore, our feelings were different on almost every issue that arose between us. We were as far from a state of narcissistic harmony as I could imagine. The patient later reported that his father had been dismissive of him over religion and spirituality when he was much younger, even though his father was a practicing Christian too. On a deeper level, he also described memories of his mother being coldly non-empathic with his fears, pains, and wishes. My subjective reactions were real but also served as the foundation to which the induction clung. What was repeated in the object mode was the patient's need and longing for narcissistic mirroring and his parents' failure to meet those needs.[8]

In a different configuration, the patient's narcissism is not a form of relating but a form of withdrawal. This is the situation which Spotnitz (1976) describes as the narcissistic defense; the patient's self-absorption serves the purpose of protecting the analyst from her destructive impulses. The patient seems oblivious to the analyst's presence. Whether she is talking or silent, she makes no contact, may ignore the analyst's attempts at contact, and appears to exist as if she were alone in the universe. The analyst may feel as if she were of no more importance to the patient than a piece of furniture. She may be bored, frustrated, and angry that her presence is not just unnoticed but also actively rejected and she may wonder if the patient is really alive or fantasize that the patient is an animal or an alien. I suspect that this sort of induction was the experience that gave rise to Freud's (1917: 423) description of narcissism as "the wall that brings us to a stop," as well as his contention that the narcissistic patient could not be analyzed. Although his conclusion was erroneous, it is emotionally understandable in light of the intensity of neglect that is induced in the analyst by a patient in this sort of narcissistic state.

The countertransference is very different when the patient repeats the experience of trying to relate to the parent as a separate object, and the parent remains narcissistic. One common way for this to be manifested is for the parent to assume that her experience is the same as the child's – the illusion of empathy and attunement. When this is repeated in the analysis, the analyst feels that she is "attuned" to the patient, but the patient is not seeking attunement. For example, the patient wants advice on how to handle a frightening situation. The analyst resonates with the patient's fear but is unresponsive to the patient's wish for advice. More intensely, the analyst identifies so strongly with the patient's fear that she feels panicked — as if the event were happening to her and not to the patient. These examples recreate dynamics in which the parent became so disturbed by the child's feelings that she was unable to provide protective guidance or insulation.

A different scenario plays out when the analyst strives to relate to the patient as a narcissistic extension of herself, which repeats the dynamic of a child being used by a parent to meet the parent's narcissistic needs. This can happen in several ways. The analyst may find herself over invested in the success of the patient's life projects because the patient's success is a reflection of herself. If the patient quits, fails, or succeeds halfheartedly, the analyst is disappointed because she feels like a failure.[9]

In more intense cases, the analyst feels the impulse to mold the patient in accordance with her needs and wants. For example, the patient should change careers, be less impulsive, make up with his parents, come out, go straight, or some other seemingly salubrious project. The idea for a particular type of change may be induced; or the induction may be limited to the general impulse to mold the patient, with the specific project being determined by subjective inclinations in the analyst. Perhaps the most common way for manifestation is for the analyst to have high expectations for the patient: the patient must make progress in the analysis and attain the ideal of analytic health that the analyst's orientation dictates.

The patient may go along with the analyst in order to maintain the analyst's love. Or she may rebel in order to assert her independence. Both reactions recapitulate different original solutions that were available to the child in dealing with a narcissistic parent who put her own needs for the child ahead of the child's needs for herself.

In the most overtly narcissistic scenario, the analyst's wish to control the patient is no longer about the patient's own life; the analyst craves the patient's praise and admiration. She longs for the compliments, the adoration, the feeling that the patient thinks he's the best. In a somewhat perverse version found most frequently among Modern Psychoanalysts, the analyst needs the patient to hate her — not for therapeutic reasons but to validate her ability to resolve resistances to negative transference. Both versions of this scenario repeat the dynamic of the parent who needs the child to worship her — not out of a developmental need — but to shore up her own self-image (Kohut 1971).

All scenarios involving the analyst as narcissistic parent are easily confused with other forms of transference and countertransference. The analyst's desire to get the patient to succeed at a goal of her choice can resemble an anaclitic countertransference in which the analyst feels the impulse to encourage, or even to push, the patient as a good parent might. Furthermore, all analysts must have a strong desire for their patients to make progress in the analysis. It is unlikely that any patient would benefit from the experience without it.

Because the child's experience of dealing with a parent's narcissistic needs is almost universal (albeit to vastly different degrees), these types of narcissistic inductions occur in almost every analysis. At the same time, I suspect there is a higher frequency of subjective countertransference in this particular transference/countertransference configuration than in others. The reason is obvious – the analyst's self-esteem is tied to the patient's progress, whether defined as improvement in her life or as progress in the sessions. Even in the most purely anaclitic countertransference case, the analyst wants the patient to heal, and her need will be frustrated if the patient does not make progress. This tension goes back to the problem of unselfish parental love – an oxymoron if there ever was one. The model parent and the model analyst are able to recognize their narcissistic needs and put them aside, but real parents and analysts can't. Subjective narcissistic needs commingle with anaclitic love at every step of development.

None of these considerations negate the important role that induced narcissistic inductions play in most analyses. An opportunity to work through an important component of the repetition compulsion is lost if the analyst prematurely assumes that the countertransference is subjective rather than viewing it within the context of the patient's life. But in light of the built-in temptation to gratify narcissistic needs through the patient, it is particularly important for the analyst to study both the patient's life story (and her own) to determine the origin of narcissistic needs in the countertransference.

A last idiosyncratic example of simple object countertransference

All of the examples provided thus far have been striking and fairly easy to identify and have fallen into common themes that emerge fairly regularly with a wide variety of patients. Almost all patients, however, induce feelings related to repetitive relationships that are theirs alone. These feelings may be difficult to identify but are nevertheless quite striking once they have been grasped. To illustrate just one example, a supervisee described being afraid of a new patient – an extremely attractive young man. The patient spent most of the sessions crying, while the analyst's primary feeling was fear. I asked if he was afraid that the patient would physically assault him. "No, not that," he said. The patient was much smaller than he was and not the least bit threatening. In fact, the patient had just ended a violent relationship with another man and had been the victim. The patient seemed to be dissociated. We considered the possibility that the analyst's fear was a narcissistic identification with the patient's dissociated fear, but neither one of us was entirely satisfied with this explanation.

The patient had been referred to the analyst by the analyst's other supervisor. He only wanted to stay in treatment for a few months. After that, he was going to move to the Far East to work with a charitable organization. He had lived in a number of different cities over the past several years. Although he did not have any close friends, there had been a number of older men who had taken a strong interest in him over the years and helped him along with his career. The therapist added, almost casually, that the patient met his boyfriends through these older men. I asked if the older men set him up with these boyfriends. No, the boyfriends were initially the older men's boyfriends. The patient would steal them. The patient had told him, in an oblivious tone of voice, that he had lost a lot of important relationships on account of this. The analyst had been equally oblivious to the aggression behind the patient's behavior until he described the patient in the supervisory session.

I warned the analyst to be careful about his relationship with his other supervisor, as this patient had the ability to come between people and make them fight. He said it was already happening. On one hand, he was angry with the supervisor for giving him another low-fee referral. On the other hand, he hadn't told the supervisor he had seen the patient. It was as if he were keeping it secret. The analyst then remarked how incongruous these feelings were. The patient looked very sweet and angelic and was very thin with pale hair. "An angel with fangs," I said. He then associated to Claudia, the child vampire from *Interview with the Vampire* (Rice 1976) – a cold-hearted monster (with good reason) who destroys a relationship between two other vampires.

Finally, the analyst's initial fear of the patient could be seen in context. Although the patient had presented himself as a victim (and may well have been in some contexts), he was also a corrosive person who destroyed other people's relationships and then moved on. (This had already started to happen between the analyst and his supervisor.) Fear had been the analyst's affective reaction to the patient's potential for destructiveness, of which he was already a target.

Inverted object countertransference

In the inverted form of object countertransference, the patient enacts the feelings and behavior of one of her parents (or other significant object in her life) and induces the feelings that she herself experienced in relationship to that object, usually as a child. Anna Freud (1966: 109), who coined the unforgettable term "identification with the aggressor," described the intra-psychic dimensions of this dynamic. In her account, the child defends against the aggression directed at her by the parent through identifying with the parent's behavior and adopting it as her own, turning a passive position into an active position. The interpersonal dimension of this dynamic is that in identifying with the parent, the patient induces the feelings she experienced in relationship to the parent; she recreates her own feelings of intimidation, fear, and anguish in the objects of her aggression.[10]

Typical case examples

A typical example of this occurred with a woman who had originally sought treatment because, as she put it in the first session, she wasn't living up to her potential. I'd expected her to move from this complaint into a list of typical depressive self-attacks, but this was not the case. While she complained vociferously about the world not giving her due, either professionally or in her love life, she criticized herself very little. The target of her criticism was me – everything about me. My comments were obvious, shallow, or inept. My office was small and tacky. My clothes were sloppy and unstylish. She often forgot to come to sessions, and if I called she snickered at the thought that I had been waiting for her. "It's kind of like throwing a party and having nobody come," she laughed. She claimed that the whole experience of therapy was useless and constantly talked about leaving. "Sometimes you do seem very bright," she said, "but maybe you've gone into the wrong field."

My feelings were completely congruent with her complaints. I felt defensive and useless. There was nothing I could do right, and she nearly convinced me I had gone into the wrong field. I felt self-conscious about everything, and I was also extremely resentful. I wanted to scream at her, but was afraid that I would lose her if I ever let her know how I felt. I felt completely tortured when I was with her but completely dependent on her staying in treatment with me. For her to leave would mean that I was a failure, and at times, it felt as if all my self-esteem was connected to how she treated me during the sessions.

This tenacious transference/countertransference configuration went on over several years, due, in part, to my inexperience at the time but also due to the intensity of the aggression she had been subjected to as a child. It took years for the details to come out. Both parents were cold and authoritarian. Her father, a senior law enforcement official, treated his family as his subordinates. Her mother completely supported this situation despite the fact that she and all the children were constantly criticized and ridiculed. There were also occasional episodes of physical abuse in the form of ritualized beatings with a belt. The children were neglected when they weren't being criticized. As a result of this neglect, a friend of the family had also sexually abused her.

An analysis of her relationships revealed a constant alternation between being a victim and a victimizer. In her current relationship she was passive, but in past relationships, she'd been dominant and had also engaged in quasi-sadomasochistic sex. Her treatment of me was similar to the ways she'd experienced her parents. My fear of her abandonment was also a repetition of the fear that she'd experienced at their hands – the feeling that if she didn't measure up, she'd be left bereft and alone.

In a different sort of case, a colleague referred a patient to work with me, specifically because I practiced the orientation the patient was looking for. He told me his personal reasons for coming – he'd struggled with bouts of depression intermittently – but he also wanted to come because of his curiosity about the process. Ordinarily, I expect powerful intellectual defenses in patients who express a strong interest in analytic theory without a strong emotional need for analysis. Not this patient. He was warm, his curiosity seemed emotional rather than intellectual, and for the first half hour of the session, I was delighted to be with him.

However, the session took an unexpected turn. When we were setting up the next session time, I made a mistake about the date – I am notoriously bad at reading calendars – and the patient quickly corrected my mistake. He said this in an accepting, supportive way – caretaking yet profoundly infantilizing at the same time. As he left, he told me how happy he was that he had found somebody who worked within the framework that he'd been seeking and then gave me some helpful advice on fixing the squeak in the waiting room door.

Overtly, there was nothing wrong with the patient's bit of advice. The door did squeak, and there was no reason not to fix it. But again, I felt infantilized by his caretaking comment. Like calendar reading, keeping my immediate environment in clean, working order has never been a task at which I excel. The patient knew where my weaknesses lay. This feeling he induced – that I was a young child in the presence of an all-knowing adult who would be patient with constant, childish mistakes – persisted through several months and appeared to be intimately tied to how his parents had treated him.

Inverted object countertransference in patients who have been sexually abused

The dynamic of inverted object countertransference may take the form of seductive behavior in patients who have been sexually abused. The taboo on intergeneration sexuality having been violated with them as children, they have no respect for it in the analysis. Here, the move from passive to active is expressed when the patient is the initiator of the seduction, and the analyst is the target. These patients can be remarkably tenacious in their demands of the analyst, whether for erotic contact or for other kinds of contact outside the bounds of the analytic contract. Such demands induce a number of characteristic reactions in the analyst. For example, she may feel preyed upon or violated; she may feel aroused and tempted and then feel guilty about these feelings; she may agonize over whether it was her fault – whether she did something wrong to provoke the patient into feeling this way. Finally, she may feel as if she were in great danger from the threat of her colleagues finding out or from legal action.[11] The relationship of these feelings to those of a sexually abused child is obvious.

In making the shift from passive to active through identification with the parent, the analyst usually feels like the passive partner in the relationship. Nevertheless, there are cases where the patient adopts the parent's role but still seems to be passive. In most of these cases, the analyst has the feeling that she is not properly taking care of the patient. The patient may complain about this, overtly or not, or the feeling may be incongruent. Either way, the analyst becomes frantic, feeling that she will let the patient down in some terrible way if she can't alleviate her pain. Whether in her mind or in her behavior, she runs through the case endlessly, desperately trying to find the right way to care for the patient. Coupled with this is a fear that the patient will leave treatment – a fear that is far out of proportion to the real impact this would have on the analyst. The analyst feels her very existence would be threatened in some profound way should the patient leave. She will lose her whole practice. She will be broke. Her failure with the patient will be proof of her utter unworthiness to offer her services and collect fees or even to live her life.

Such are the feelings of a child who feels it is her responsibility to take care of her parent. Impossible emotional demands have been placed upon her – impossible because she is only a child who should be cared for, not a caretaking figure, and impossible because the parent cannot be satisfied. At the same time, she is completely dependent on the parent. If the parent abandons her, her world will fall apart. Her existence depends on taking care of the parent so that the parent can take care of her.

Final thoughts on object countertransference: an idiosyncratic example

In some cases, it can be very difficult to determine whether the analyst is in the emotional position of the parent or the child. Sometimes both seem to be operating simultaneously, or the patient seems to alternate between the two. An analyst once described a patient with whom she consistently felt sexually aroused. She was concerned that it was a subjective response, which was a possibility in light of the fact that she had felt sexually aroused with her patients before. But it was unusual that it was so consistent. Furthermore, a look at the patient's life suggested that other people's sexual feelings towards her were an important issue in her life. For example, the patient's husband was angry with her because she would not have sex with him more often. The patient also had a concurrent relationship with a woman who was also angry that the patient was not having sex with her more often.

At first glance, therefore, the patient seemed to have a pattern of making herself sexually desirable but unavailable and frustrating. However, while the analyst did find her desirable, she was not frustrated with her for her lack of sexual availability. So it wasn't clear how all of this fit together. Was it possible that the analyst would eventually find her sexually frustrating? Another piece of data put a different slant on it. The patient's daughter was angry with her for not spending enough time with her – both when she was little and now that she was grown. In this context, the issue of her sexual unavailability was subsumed in the larger issue of people being angry with her for being unavailable in general. And it turned out that the patient was frustrating to the analyst, in that she left treatment prematurely – complaining about lack of progress – just before the analyst was due out on maternity leave.

The question arises: what role is the patient playing here? Has she taken on the role of depriving mother – giving everyone the impression that she's got the goods, but she's not going to share them? Or did her mother find her to be an alluring but frustrating baby – a baby who never loved her the way she wanted to be loved? Or was that a revenge fantasy? Did she leave because she was angry that the analyst wasn't interested in her, or had she known on some level that the analyst wasn't frustrated by her sexual unavailability and found a more effective way of frustrating her? Was it some combination of these possibilities, or was it something else altogether? In this case, there wasn't enough biographical data in the analysis to confirm any of these possibilities, and the analysis didn't last long enough for the analyst to determine the answer. Would the patient have stayed if the analyst had figured it out? Nobody can tell.

In conclusion, as clear as some cases of object countertransference can be, others remain mysterious. Separate relationships are infinitely variable. Every patient induces unique and complex examples of object countertransference.

8
COUNTERTRANSFERENCE IN PROJECTIVE IDENTIFICATION STATES

Projective identification[1] arises when the patient is unable to tolerate a specific feeling, fantasy, or impulse, expunges it from her emotional experience, and induces it in the analyst. Consequently, the patient no longer feels the original feeling and feels its polar opposite instead. Although the patient has ridded herself of the original feeling, she is incapable of letting it go. She remains deeply connected to it through the relationship with the analyst. The analyst, on the other hand, experiences the projected feeling with an engulfing (although not always conscious) intensity. The patient and analyst's interpersonal relationship plays out the intra-psychic drama of the patient's inability to accept the intolerable feeling as a part of her self-experience or her emotional identity.

At first sight, the projective identification appears to combine elements of narcissistic and object countertransference:

- Like a narcissistic induction, the analyst's feeling is originally the patient's feeling. But unlike a narcissistic induction, the analyst and the patient do not share the same feeling in the moment.
- Like an object induction, the analyst experiences the patient as being different from her. But unlike an object induction, she feels bonded to the patient through the feeling that has been induced, and she experiences a closeness – usually painful – that is almost inexplicable.

These comparisons only partially illuminate the nature and experience of projective identification. The peculiar combination of separateness and unity – the feeling that the patient and the analyst are both involved with their emotional antithesis – is not midway on a continuum between narcissistic and the object modes of relating but rather is a fundamentally different mode of relatedness. More importantly, it is a mode of relatedness that is essentially defensive. It is possible to relate to other people within the narcissistic or the object modes in non-defensive ways.[2] Projective identification, on the other hand, is motivated and shaped exclusively by the need to cope with an intolerable feeling. It usually arises in states of intense over-stimulation as an attempt to maintain a degree of intrapsychic equilibrium when more flexible defenses and modes of relating have failed. I believe it is this desperate, last-resort quality of projective identification that accounts for its intensity and volatility.

The concept of projective identification was formulated by Klein[3] (1946) as an intrapsychic defense and later developed as a concept that bridged the intrapsychic world with the interpersonal world by Bion (1962), Grotstein (1981), Ogden (1982), and others. These theorists have viewed projective identification as an essential component of emotional development – both normal and pathological – and of the analytic relationship. I agree, but with a caveat: Object Relations theorists tend to describe all primitive emotional interactions as well as all induced countertransference in terms of projective identification (and similar schizoid mechanisms). In contrast, I view projective identification as a particular form of emotional induction, both as a type of primitive emotional interaction and as a particular type of countertransference.[4]

Klein (1946) viewed projective identification as a form of splitting, and this can be seen in the lack of complexity in the subjective experience of the countertransference. The feelings are simple and pure, unclouded by subtle emotional shading. What they lack in complexity, they make up for in intensity. The feelings are consuming, flooding, and overwhelming. Projective identification often (but not always) has a life-and-death quality about it that is grossly out of proportion to whatever is being discussed. It is almost impossible for the analyst to avoid being carried away by it, whether or not she is aware of what is happening. Klein viewed projective identification as an infantile attempt to expel unwanted feelings into the mother and a desire to invade her and take control of her from the inside. This often feels literally true; the analyst feels as if she has been invaded and colonized. More so than other forms of countertransference, projective identification can feel foreign, like an infection. At the same time, the countertransference feels connected to something deep in the analyst's being, something very real. It is easy to lose control in these states, easy to say and do things that are unanticipated and later regretted.

Projective identification fosters strong feelings of attraction and repulsion within the analytic relationship. Sometimes, the patient and analyst feel magnetically drawn to each other. This attraction is usually painful (at least for one of them), and they never merge in an undifferentiated way, as they might in narcissistic countertransference. Other times, however, they draw close in a moment of overwhelming conflict, and then the relationship ends. If, for example, the patient's need to expel the feeling is particularly strong, she will project the feeling into the analyst, then reject her and leave the treatment. (If the patient stays in treatment, the analyst usually learns that this is a regular pattern.) Similarly, the analyst may reject the patient, either overtly or covertly, if she cannot tolerate the projected feeling due to her subjective limitations.

The relationship between the analyst's feeling and the patient's feeling is invariant: they are polar opposites. If the analyst feels powerless, the patient feels powerful. If the analyst feels agitated, the patient feels calm. If the analyst feels aggression, the patient feels like a victim. If the analyst feels like she needs the patient, the patient feels that she is a parasite. If the analyst feels wise and competent, the patient feels stupid and helpless.

This polar opposition between the patient's feelings and the analyst's feelings is an important hallmark of projective identification and distinct from the disjunctions that occur in either narcissistic or object countertransference. While the analyst does not experience the same overt feeling as the patient in an incongruent narcissistic countertransference, the analyst's feeling is rarely opposite of the patient's feeling, either in content or intensity. The polar opposition between the analyst's feelings and the patient's feelings can occur in object countertransference. In this case, however, the focus of the analyst's feelings is the patient. In projective identification, on the other hand, the analyst's feelings are about herself and the patient in equal measure.

If the analyst is drawn to the patient, it may feel like the patient fills a void and makes her feel whole in a way that she has never felt before. If the analyst hates the patient, it may feel like the patient is everything the analyst hates in another person – the living antithesis of her values or choices.

Because the essence of projective identification is to feel the opposite feeling as the patient, it is not clear whether it can ever be incongruent in the way that other forms of countertransference can be. The difference and the relationship between the analyst's feeling and the patient's are always visible. It can, however, be extremely subtle, requiring close observation in order to identify.

Projective identifications can occur in different patterns within the analysis. Most of my experience (and that of most of my colleagues and supervisees) has been with projective identification that arises in fairly discrete episodes within a relationship that is dominated by other transference/countertransference configurations. Sometimes, projective identification arises regularly around circumscribed clusters of feelings. In certain borderline and narcissistic patients, it is the dominant mode of relating in the analysis and the dominant form of countertransference. Similarly, there is a variant form of projective identification – the sadomasochistic state – that usually becomes an all-enveloping mode of relating.

Some typical examples

This projective identification occurred in a first session with a patient who had been referred to me early in my career specifically because I was accepting low-fee referrals. She was tall and beautiful, even dazzling. Her clothes were stunning, her voice lovely, and her manner casual and self-assured. (Not exactly what I had been expecting of a low-fee referral.) She immediately told me that she was an interior designer. She specialized in country French interiors because she had excellent furniture contacts in Provence. She was an alcoholic – in recovery – very committed to working the 12 steps. When I asked what she hoped to gain from therapy, she said that her sponsor had recommended it. She thought it would be a good idea because "everyone can stand a little improvement." She had recently broken up with a long-term boyfriend, and although she was over it (the break-up had been all for the best), she still felt that she thought about him too much. Apart from that, there was precious little discussion of any problems that she might have had. She spent most of the session telling me about her good friends, most of whom were famous – and those who weren't she discussed as if they were well-kept secrets, known only to the cognoscenti. She looked a bit askance at my office and made an ever so slightly dismissive remark about the art on the walls. At one point, I asked how the session had been for her. She looked at me directly for the first time since she walked in and told me that I seemed "pleasant enough" and that the fee was certainly reasonable. "Not that you don't deserve more when I can afford it, which I expect will be very soon," she went on to say.

In retrospect (and no doubt to the reader), the patient's condescension, grandiosity, and arrogance came screaming out. But the experience of being in the room with her, under the active influence of the induction, was very different. I was intimidated from the first shake of her exquisite head, the first glimpse of her silk blouse. I immediately felt shabby, unsophisticated, and cheap. My work (as an analyst) felt pedestrian and completely unglamorous in comparison to decorating fantastic apartments and country homes. And she knew all of those famous people that I had only read about. Her problems seemed minor, yet exalted – the romance of being a high-powered alcoholic in recovery. The fact that she was completely broke seemed to be a meaningless blip on a rising graph.

In contrast, my own problems with depression and self-assertiveness (of which I was painfully aware) were utterly banal. Her clothes were better than mine, her friends were better than mine, and her taste was better than mine. Even though her French was worse than mine (something that was obvious from the few phrases she rattled off), there was still something classier about it – something more exotic about the fact that she didn't speak as fluently as I did. I was a working stiff, a boring professional with a tacky office with schlock art on the walls – the kind you sought out if you had a problem like bleeding gums or a plantar wart – but didn't have much money. I assumed that once she got herself on her feet financially, she would drop me immediately and move on to an older, probably famous Upper East Side analyst with a gray beard, an exquisite silk rug, and a complete set of Freud in German. I was filled with envy, competitiveness, and wretched feelings of inferiority.

In every respect, I was the dark side of her gloriously silver moon. Need I add that I was completely miserable by the time the session ended?

This intensity lasted for about four sessions, and then it began to change. I became more comfortable. Although she did not abandon her overtly narcissistic posture, the tone changed considerably and she began a long, slow process of verbalizing layers of self-hatred, most of which were centered (almost word for word) on exactly the same types of feelings that I had experienced in that first session. Gradually, she took back the feelings that had been projected into me and integrated them into her character.

This example shows all of the essential characteristics of projective identification: first, the polar opposition of her feelings and mine; second, the intensity of the countertransference. In this case, the countertransference was clearly congruent with her demeanor, but I must confess that this was not obvious at the time. In fact, I would have said that she was perfectly charming; it wasn't her fault if I was an insecure little schlepper.

Incidentally, the fact that this occurred in a first session is also something that I have found to be typical of projective identification. Indeed, I have seen more examples of projective identifications in the first session (or first few sessions) than in any other part of the treatment. Many patients who do not relate primarily in this mode will do so in the first few sessions. I suspect that the stress of meeting the analyst and beginning the process of describing vulnerable feelings stimulates a defensive regression that accounts for this.

And sometimes the process is so strong it aborts the analysis altogether. This can be seen in another example – again, the first session with a patient who was seeking a low fee. He was very serious and explained at the beginning of the session that before he got into discussing his problems, he wanted to discuss my qualifications. Although this is, in itself, not an unusual (or unreasonable) request, I felt myself freezing up almost immediately. He proceeded to "outline" what he wanted from me. First, of course, my degrees – including the names of the schools, the programs, the specific classes I had taken, and grades – preferably going back to my undergraduate years. Then, he would need recommendations from teachers and supervisors, as well as from current and former patients. Finally, he would want to discuss some of my relevant life experiences (he didn't elaborate on what these might be), and would need to know my favorite novels, philosophers, clinical theoreticians, and political thinkers. After all, he would need to know a little bit about me if he was going to tell me about himself.

All of this proceeded slowly over the course of the session, during which I became increasingly filled with absolute panic. The demands felt absolutely overwhelming, and there was this dread of certainty that I was going to fail and then what?! I made some feeble attempts to explore his requests, but I was crumbling, and I'm sure he knew it. His tone was deadly serious, perfectly calm throughout. The more anxious I got, the more controlled he became. Finally, he looked at me and said, "It seems obvious that I am going to need a very special person to work with me and that you are not it." He got up and decisively left the office. I felt as though I had been crushed and left for trash.

This was the only contact I had with the patient, so I cannot be sure that it was, in fact, projective identification. I knew from the person who had referred him that he was unemployed, depressed, and friendless. Yet even more than in the first example, there had been no discussion of his problems or of what he wanted from the treatment – certainly an unexpected outcome of an initial session with an analyst. Once I could start to think clearly again, my hypothesis was that he had ridded himself of all of his feelings of worthlessness, incompetence, and anxiety by inducing them in me, which allowed him to feel competent and in control. Our exchange bore all the telltale signs. Again, there was the sharp dichotomy between my feeling and the patient's: he was calm, hyper-controlled, and I was consumed with anxiety. Although the issue of discussing qualifications was never the most comfortable of topics for me, what occurred in this session was far beyond my usual range of reactions and went considerably beyond any realistic consequence of failing his test.

Another example occurred about a year and a half into the treatment of an extremely volatile, paranoid woman. She had a long history of starting fights and then being physically hurt. Most of the early months of her treatment were characterized by mutual distrust on both of our parts.

However, after a few months we fell into a more comfortable rhythm, as she settled into talking to me about her life and her problems, and I was quite comfortable listening to her without any striking countertransference reactions. At times she would flare up and become extremely challenging, insisting that I couldn't possibly understand her because she was the child of immigrants from Southern Europe, and I certainly wasn't. But even in the face of these conflicts, the emotional climate in the analysis was rather lukewarm for both of us, which was a productive state of affairs. Things began to shift again as she talked increasingly about how she felt exploited by everyone. It was all give and no take. Nobody ever gave her anything, including me. She frequently told me I was a cheap Jew.

I felt unsympathetic to her feelings of being exploited. It wasn't clear to me who was exploiting her or what they were getting out of it. I suspected that I was having feelings similar to her mother's, whom she described as being chronically unsympathetic.

One day she began the session by telling me that it was high time we did something about the fee. The situation had been going on long enough, and it had to change. At first, I thought that she had finally realized that it was too low and that she was going to raise it. I greedily began to wonder whether it would be doubled to $2 – or even go up to $5! Her agenda, however, was otherwise. She had concluded that the fee was too high. It was time for it to be lowered to zero. After all, we had to take into account that I was in a training program: she was getting the benefit of the treatment and I was getting the benefit of the experience and the credit. That was an equitable exchange, and for me to get paid anything at all was obviously excessive and exploitive. Atypically for her, she wasn't shouting or swearing. Her reasoning was clear and lucid, and her effect was strong yet calm. I felt as if my life force, all of my vital energy, had been tapped with a needle and was being drained off into her. All the while, I was fully aware of her mildly malevolent smile. She was a serene yet determined bloodsucker, and I was fading into oblivion.

It is clear in this case that she induced the feeling that she had been talking about prior to this session – the feeling of being exploited (although exploitation was hardly the word for it). She had attempted to cope with it by talking about it, but when that had not worked (probably because my emotional response to her had not been adequate to her needs), she responded with this projective identification.

Another therapist described a projective identification that took place with a girl who was treated at a school for conduct-disordered teenagers. The girl's home was seriously chaotic; she called it a zoo and referred to her mother and siblings as animals. She was always in some sort of trouble at school and seemed to have some degree of concern about whether she would be able to control herself. The therapist was somewhat concerned about her, but no more for her than the other kids, all of whom were in similar situations.

One day the girl came to her session in a gleeful, exuberant state. She and her sister had just pulled off an unusually serious prank; they had set off the fire sprinklers in the cafeteria. The patient was smiling about it and said that she knew she was going to get caught. The therapist became overwhelmed with anxiety. What's going to happen to you, she asked? The patient told her not to worry. She was already in a "jail school." What else could they do to her? In her more rational mind, the therapist was thinking that something really should be done with this girl because she was completely out of control. But most of her feelings were focused on, "Oh my god, she's going to get in trouble; what am I going to do?" She attempted to get the patient to recognize the seriousness of the situation, but the patient kept laughing and telling her there was nothing to worry about. All of the patient's anxiety was projected into the therapist, while the patient was filled with manic triumph (in the Kleinian sense of the term, not the psychiatric, although this too was considered).

Another example of a projective identification that was less volatile and recurred regularly during a long treatment was of a young man who was preoccupied with dichotomies in all areas of his self-image. He was quite attractive, stylishly dressed and groomed, but he usually looked hunched over and collapsed, like a decrepit child. He had been referred by a friend of his who had seen me speak at a conference, and he had idealized me from the moment he set eyes on me. He saw me as powerful, wise, and compassionate. He wanted me as a role model. He just knew that I lived the kind of life that he did, but he didn't think that I could really be a role model because he was so hopelessly weak, stupid, and selfish that he could never be the way I was.

His words were like a magic spell on me. As he lay on the couch, I had the feeling that he was frail and helpless, the limp husk of a man who was ineffective, incompetent, and lost. And I, on the other hand, felt like a uniquely radiant being: a healing god, a psychoanalytic Apollo. The mere touch of my spirit on this poor waif, and he would spring to life like a desert flower after the rain. All he needed to do to get better was to bask in my presence and all would be well. Despite his talk about how wonderful I was, he also had fantasies that I could barely tolerate his presence and that I sprayed the couch with deodorant after he left the sessions. While I never had exactly those feelings about him, I often thought (with more than a touch of sadism) that his lovers (he infrequently had casual lovers) would think he was completely insane once they got to know him.

In this case, the patient had projected all the good feelings onto me, and he retained all the bad feelings in and about himself. As time when on, he increasingly attributed aggressive, persecutory feelings to me and felt that he was a victim.

Another example of projective identification was described by a supervisee in a case of a male patient who displayed many of the features of the narcissistic personality as described by Kernberg (1985). He was haughty, contemptuous, lacking in empathy, and had a pronounced inability to tolerate dependency feelings. However, as therapy went on, he was increasingly able to discuss feelings of vulnerability. He was even able to understand, on a deeply emotional level, how he resorted to aggression against others when he felt unsafe. After about three years, he revealed that he had been seeing a doctor for about six months about prostate problems. He was rather matter-of-fact about the whole thing, and during the matter-of-fact moments the therapist was equally blasé about the matter. His tone changed, however, after he got the biopsy results back. He laughed cynically and described how the doctor had told him, in an incompetent way, that he had never seen a biopsy like that. There were a number of unusual cells in it, but he didn't know why or what they meant, and he would have to go in for a more invasive test. The therapist was swept with panic. The therapist had the impression that the patient's laughter intensified as the therapist's anxiety rose. He began to speak derisively about a friend he considered to be a weakling. He added that he had told his parents about it, also laughingly, and that they had been terrified.

Here, the patient projected all the fear and the panic about his medical condition into those around him and retained in himself a feeling of denial and manic triumph over weakness and fear.

9

ANACLITIC COUNTERTRANSFERENCE

In anaclitic countertransference, the analyst experiences feelings towards the patient that the patient needs in order to mature. The anaclitic countertransference is induced by the anaclitic transference in which the patient experiences needs for feelings that would enable him to mature. Together they create a transference/countertransference mode that resembles the emotional environment of a well-attuned parent–child relationship. The distinguishing feature of the anaclitic transference is that the patient re-experiences the need for feelings – specific maturational emotional communications – that were lacking or insufficient in his life prior to entering analysis. These needs are usually the same as those he experienced as a child in relationship to the parents or would have experienced with his parents had the relationship been optimal.[1] It is possible that his needs were not met, were met inconsistently, or met with insufficient strength to sustain him through later periods of stress. In any case, the patient re-experiences them in the transference relationship to the analyst. Moreover, he does not manifest defenses against having his needs met. On the contrary, he is ready and eager to have them met by the analyst. It is this last feature that indicates the analyst's feelings are truly anaclitic and not simply subjective nurturing feelings.

The patient may experience the analyst either narcissistically or as a different object. He may be extremely regressed in the transference – going back to the earliest infantile states – but he can also function as an older child, adolescent, or even as an adult child. Conversely, the analyst is never regressed in the anaclitic mode. He experiences the patient as a separate object towards whom he consistently experiences adult, caretaking feelings with a keen sense of the patient's emotional needs at the moment. He is frequently empathic with the patient, but this is not essential. The distinguishing feature of the anaclitic countertransference is that the analyst has the desire and the ability to meet the patient's emotional needs.

This is the opposite emotional situation from the object countertransference in which the analyst's feelings, and the transference/countertransference as a whole, repeats a pathological interaction from the patient's earlier life. The anaclitic mode, therefore, expresses a different form of repetition than what is seen in the object mode and from other forms of countertransference. The patient's contribution is a repetition. He repeats the experience of needing specific emotional communications from a parental figure and attempts to induce the required feelings in a parental figure. The analyst's contribution, on the other hand, is not necessarily a repetition. If the parent responded to the child's neediness with maturational emotional communications, then the analyst's feelings may be a repetition, but if the parent did not, the analyst's desire and ability to meet the patient's emotional needs may be a completely new experience in the patient's life. Practically speaking, it makes no difference whether the analyst's feelings are new or are repetitive. Once the patient successfully induces anaclitic feelings in the analyst, the patient's unmet needs are gratified, and the maturational process restarts. The anaclitic mode begins in the repetition of a need and ends in maturation.[2]

General features of anaclitic countertransference

Anaclitic countertransference comprises feelings that are identical to ordinary parental love. These feelings often feel primitive and unprofessional. And because the proper analytic stance has been associated with neutrality, abstinence, and the image of the cool-hearted surgeon, parental feelings towards patients have often been viewed as non-analytic – something to be outgrown or analyzed away.

Even schools that are removed from classical analytic technique often seem to look for a more sophisticated emotional response to the patient than what is involved in very ordinary parental caretaking. For example, hating the patient feels like a serious analytic issue, whereas wanting to give the patient a lollipop does not.

Furthermore, consideration of these types of feelings has often been tied up with technical issues. Modern Analytic theorists have been concerned that expressing positive feelings too early in the treatment can inhibit the patient from expressing aggression towards the analyst. Relational theorists (e.g., Mitchell 1988) have been concerned that these types of feelings (although they do not use the term anaclitic) infantilize the patient.

Nevertheless, if an analyst can separate the technical issues from the immediate emotional reaction to the patient that constitutes the countertransference, it is obvious that anaclitic countertransference will be a significant component of the analyst's feelings with most patients at some point in their treatment. What makes these feelings potent is not their content, which is often quite ordinary, but that the patient needs them at that particular moment in the treatment.

Occasionally, anaclitic countertransference can be quite dramatic. One of the most striking examples I experienced was with a disorganized schizophrenic man I treated in a state mental hospital. My feelings during the first year or so were as far from anaclitic as could be imagined. He was filthy and drooling all the time. The only thing he seemed to be able to say was, "Gotta cigarette? Gotta cigarette?" He repeated this over and over, sometimes 40 times per session. He started one session by asking me my name, and I was filled with hope that something new was happening. Instead, he looked at me and asked, "Mr. Geltner, can I please have a cigarette?" It was little consolation that his communication had evolved somewhat.

When he wasn't asking for a cigarette, he stared blankly into space or slept. He disgusted me. At times, the only thing interesting about him were his repulsive habits, like his drool. Once, I was intrigued by a glob of spit oozing down his lip, and watched carefully to see whether I could guess the exact moment that it would fall off of his chin and onto his pajamas.

After a year, however, I began to feel more fondly towards him. Once, I looked at his face and decided that he was actually rather cute and began to have fantasies about running my fingers through his greasy hair. He looked at me with bright eyes, and I felt happy to have him in my life.

By this time, he had stopped asking for cigarettes, and he had been silent for several months. After several weeks of feeling warmly towards him, I had one session in which he was particularly silent, almost coy. I had an intense fantasy in which I imagined him being an adult, with his beard and all, but shrunk down to the size of a baby. Then I envisioned myself having breasts and had him nursing and looking up at me with his sweet brown eyes. I was silently lost in this countertransference fantasy for a good chunk of the session when he began to talk. He still didn't say anything coherent, but he babbled softly, like a little baby, in a way that he never had.

As much as I would like to report that this was the beginning of a spectacular cure, the truth is that he was still psychotic when I left the hospital six months later. Nevertheless, this interchange had been important. He became more verbal from that point on, both with me and with the ward. He began to speak sentences that made sense, sometimes five or six in a row. He could form the rudiments of a conversation. This interchange had changed something between us and had left him open to a slightly enlarged range of interpersonal relationships.

Most anaclitic countertransference is a low-key affair – examples such as this notwithstanding. As we shall see, not all anaclitic feelings are positive or loving. But when they are, they tend to feel natural and ordinary, as might be expected, as most parenting is quite ordinary and unspectacular.

Congruence and incongruence

As with all forms of countertransference, anaclitic inductions can be congruent or incongruent. Congruent inductions clearly and obviously correspond to the content of the session. For example, the patient wants advice on how to talk to his wife, and the analyst knows just what to say and wants to tell him. In a slightly less congruent case, the patient may discuss his problems with his wife, without directly asking for advice. The analyst understands that he is not talking to her in the right way and wants to explain how he should talk to her. Or the patient is tearful and agitated after having had a fight at work, and the analyst feels that she just needs to talk to her in a soothing tone of voice to reassure her that this fight is just office politics, not the end of the world. Congruent inductions like this feel completely unremarkable and can create the misleading impression that the feeling is clinically insignificant.

Incongruent inductions, on the other hand, are often noticed by the analyst because they are so out of context with what is occurring in the session. One patient induced a withdrawn, almost bored feeling in me during the first several months of treatment. Then, there was a shift – not in the overt content of the communications, which continued to focus on the details of her everyday life – but in my feelings. I found myself thinking slowly, almost chanting, "I love Rosa Goldenstern [her name]." This feeling continued throughout the rest of the treatment at various intervals for about eight years.

Even more striking are incongruent inductions that are completely at odds with the content. One supervisee described a patient whom I would have found to be thoroughly obnoxious. He was politically belligerent, paranoid, and condescending, and he was genuinely disliked by most everyone in his life – except the analyst. And she loved him. It wasn't because he treated her any differently than he treated everyone else. But she would say, "I know people think he's difficult, but they just don't understand him. He's just like a cranky baby. All you have to do is hold him right, and he'll cuddle right up next to you." It didn't matter that nobody at that point, including the analyst, had found the way to hold him correctly. She was convinced that she would succeed in curing him through her love. Eventually she did, and other people began to love him as well.

Types of anaclitic inductions

Anaclitic object countertransference encompasses a wide variety of feelings – all the feelings a person needs to experience from other people throughout the life cycle. A complete description of all of these feelings would be a fascinating and valuable contribution to our knowledge of emotional development; the following description of anaclitic countertransference includes only the forms that I have seen most frequently.

Roughly speaking, anaclitic inductions can be divided into two main categories: (a) inductions related to nurturing and basic caretaking and (b) inductions related to sexual and aggressive impulses.

Nurturing and caretaking inductions

The instinct to nurture, soothe, and protect a baby is the emotional foundation of parenthood, and the induction of these feelings in the analyst is the paradigmatic example of anaclitic countertransference. Just as MacLean (1990) and Hrdy (1999) assert that as the infant's cry induces the parent's nurturing impulses[3] – both psychologically and physiologically – the anaclitic transference induces the nurturing feelings of the anaclitic countertransference. This is not just an analogy. The process, in both cases, is the same.

This cluster of nurturing feelings can take many different forms, spanning from direct re-enactment of the earliest nurturing feelings, to symbolic expressions of those feelings or to nurturing feelings related to later developmental phases.

Soothing

The most common manifestation of nurturing feelings is the wish to soothe the agitated patient. Agitation is a state of overstimulation. Soothing lowers the patient's level of stimulation, which relieves the distress. When the patient induces the anaclitic impulse to soothe, the analyst becomes acutely aware of the patient's distress and experiences the impulse to alleviate his suffering. One patient came to me in a state of acute panic and agitation over the breakup of a relationship. He was crying uncontrollably and had been for several weeks. While his description of the relationship made it clear that he had many issues to resolve, my immediate emotional response was simply to make him feel better. I had the impulse to say reassuring things to him. I fantasized about taking him in my arms and rocking him gently, murmuring, "Sweet, little pumpkin. Everything will be all right."

The impulse to soothe the patient may be so automatic that the analyst doesn't consciously experience it at all. For example, the analyst may find himself speaking in soft, rhythmic tones, even to the extent of using touches of motherese – the singsong cadence adults throughout the world use when talking to babies (Fernald 1992).

These types of inductions are related to the ways the parent soothes the child in infancy. While these forms of soothing remain important throughout the life span, the parent's repertoire must expand to meet the child's changing emotional and cognitive needs. Clarification and explanation of reality is crucial to helping a verbal child manage his fears and anxieties, as is reminding a child of his strengths, placing his failures in perspective, and giving encouragement, guidance, and instruction. The parent is the first person to teach the child about life in the world, and the importance of this educative role as a form of soothing cannot be underestimated.

These crucial parenting functions are aroused in the anaclitic countertransference when the patient's agitation is due to confusion or misunderstanding. For example, one patient was panicked after having been told by a dermatologist that he had to have a mole removed because it was probably a basal cell carcinoma. The patient had been too frightened to determine what this meant and was convinced that he had a serious cancer. I had the desire to calm him down by explaining exactly what a basal cell was and putting the risk into a more realistic perspective. (In this case, I didn't, primarily because I wasn't confident enough about what I was saying to be comfortable telling him.) Having the desire to coach the anxious patient through ordeals of dating, employment, child rearing – anything, really – can all fall in the category of this type of educative soothing.

One colleague described feelings that she had working with a patient who was a brilliant surgeon but extremely immature in the area of interpersonal relationships. The patient was able to manage her relationships in the operating room but no place else. Around the time the patient started a job at a new hospital, the analyst reported that she frequently felt like she was the mother of a frightened child who was about to enter a new school. The patient asked the analyst to tell her how to manage people so that they would like her, and the analyst was eager to oblige. She would give her the most basic kind of information on social interaction (e.g., reminding her to greet her secretary in the morning) to soothe the patient's frantic social anxiety. Taken into consideration from a purely superficial perspective, their interventions could be classified as "problem solving" or psychoeducation; from a truly psychoanalytic perspective – one that views the intervention within the context of the transference relationship – such interventions represented anaclitic emotional communications.

Feeding

When the patient is not only agitated but also needy, the analyst may feel the impulse to feed him. Occasionally, this is quite concrete, as manifested in the desire to offer the patient something to eat or to drink. One analyst described a patient towards whom she had felt mildly negative for the first six months of treatment. He had been standoffish and arrogant, closed off to the process. One day, however, he was completely overwhelmed by a series of minor life catastrophes, culminating in having been stuck on a train during the time he was supposed to have dinner. He was terribly hungry and terribly distraught in a way that a hungry child can be. The analyst experienced a strong desire to feed him and to take care of him – to make it better.[4]

More symbolically, the analyst may feel the impulse to recommend foods, restaurants, or recipes to the patient. With one patient, who came from a culinarily deprived background (only the most superficial manifestation of the gross deprivation he had experienced in all areas of his life), I often felt the impulse to discuss and recommend various types of goat cheese, olive oil, and vinegar. (I often acted on these impulses, usually to the benefit of the treatment.) Another patient was distressed because a dinner he had put a lot of effort into had not come out well. He had tried to make white asparagus and was miserable that it had been so tough. I gently informed him that the secret was to peel them, and he brightened up immediately.

Part of the reason that food comes up so often in my practice is that it has always been a major source of comfort in my life; expressing my desire to nurture patients through talk of food is an authentic expression of who I am, a crucial element in anaclitic countertransference. While the anaclitic feeling is an induction, in the sense of being stimulated by the patient, the fact that the feeling is not a repetition means that it must be a genuine expression of the analyst's personality. For analysts who are not food obsessed, the anaclitic impulses related to feeding will be manifested differently. One analyst who is particularly knowledgeable about music finds that his desire to share his music with patients serves the same purpose in his practice.

However, the most common way of experiencing the desire to feed is not overtly related to food, rather it is simply the impulse to talk to the patient. Similarly, patients often experience the analyst's words – interpretations, comments, or small talk – as food; they ask the analyst to talk as a way of asking to be fed. In fact, the majority of successful interventions made by analysts of all persuasions probably have nothing to do with their content, rather they work because they are a symbolic meal for the needy, contact-starved patient.

This induction may take the form of the desire to read to the patient. One patient was going through a particularly difficult period after his boyfriend had left him. His career was going nowhere, he was broke, and he had little to look forward to in his life besides AA meetings. I felt very badly for him, but there were many times I simply couldn't think of anything that would help. There would often be an overly long period of five minutes at the end of the session where we both ran out of steam. A supervisor suggested reading to him, and I knew it was the right intervention because I immediately figured out what I wanted to read to him: Yeats' "Crazy Jane" poems. (Why these poems? They spoke to his ambivalence about receiving anal sex from his boyfriend.) He was thrilled with this interaction between us and felt much more vital than he had been in weeks.

Protectiveness

Another cluster of parental feelings originating in infancy is the impulse to protect the child. Parents must protect the child both from dangers in the environment and from the dangers posed by the child's own behavior. These protective feelings form a major component of the anaclitic countertransference.

Protecting the patient from the environment

The impulse to protect the patient from his environment can be powerfully pervasive even with patients who fail to induce any other anaclitic feeling in the analyst. The induction is so common and so basic to the parent's makeup, as well as to the parental aspects of the analyst's makeup, that its absence is more conspicuous than its presence.

One common manifestation is the inclination to take the patient's side in conflicts in which the patient becomes embroiled. Whether the patient has had a fight with a parent, a spouse, or a boss, the analyst in this state automatically feels compassion for the patient and experiences the impulse to protect him against the antagonist. Even if the analyst thinks the patient is in the wrong, he feels as if there were understandable – and exculpatory – reasons for what he did and wishes that the antagonist could see it from his point of view.

An example of this occurred frequently with a woman that I worked with over a number of years. It was very difficult for her to ever express a negative feeling, even though it was clear that she was filled with them. On the other hand, she was scattered and disorganized, which often caused her to forget things in ways that were quite enraging to those around her. In our work, she regularly forgot sessions, arrived absurdly late, bounced checks, and generally created chaos in all areas that touched upon the contract. On this, she was only marginally apologetic and often seemingly entitled. (Eventually it was determined that she suffered from attention deficit disorder, but early on in the treatment, it was all too easy to interpret all this behavior as being purely passive–aggressive.)

I was often enraged, and I was not alone. Her parents, bosses, and particularly her husband had all felt the same way. In the early months of the treatment, we were all united in our opinion (a clear manifestation of a repetitive object induction.) After several months, however, there was a shift in my feelings. I was still angry when she would do these things with me. With anyone else, however, I felt fiercely protective of her. How dare her boss not be more understanding of her coming in late? Didn't he realize how difficult it was for her to get there at all? And as for her husband, I felt that he needed to adopt a new, compassionate attitude immediately. I felt outraged that he yelled at her and humiliated her for what were, after all, trivial mistakes. (The fact that I too got angry with her for equally trivial mistakes felt completely irrelevant to this; clearly, the induction was not, at this point, purely anaclitic, although it evolved into that over time.) I wanted to meet him and yell at him to protect her from his abuse. Thus, she had managed to induce a new feeling in me – a feeling that had been missing in her life since early childhood.

After a few years I was able to have her husband come in, and I worked with him on an individual basis as well. With him, however, there was no lag time in generating a protective feeling from me. When he talked about her, I automatically felt myself taking his side against her and felt the impulse to protect him from her passive aggression. The impulse that I felt to protect him from her (when he was with me) was as strong as the impulse to protect her from him (when I was with her); both sets of feelings were related to the transference, not to the reality.

The anaclitic impulse to protect the patient often appears when the analyst is talking to the supervisor. The analyst may be comfortable saying whatever he thinks or feels about the patient. But as soon as the supervisor makes a comment on the patient's behavior, transference, or dynamics, the analyst responds as if that patient has been attacked and then defends the patient. This recreates a common parental feeling: "I can say whatever I like about my kid, but if anyone else says anything, they're dead!"

Protecting the patient from himself outside the session

The desire to control the patient's behavior (usually known by the unfortunate term "limit setting") is a manifestation of the anaclitic countertransference when it is motivated by the desire to protect the patient (or the patient's interests) – not just to get the patient to behave the way the analyst thinks he should. It arises when the patient is doing something that induces concern in the analyst – usually something in his outside life that would be destructive to himself, to another person, or to the analysis. (Another type of limit-setting induction, related to the patient's behavior in the session, will be discussed below.) A straightforward example comes from a supervisee's work with an alcoholic man. The patient was in a miserable marriage. He hated being at home and drank six to eight beers every night after work. The analyst recommended AA. The patient wasn't interested. He knew that the drinking was probably bad for him, but he liked it, and it made his life tolerable. He didn't want to stop. Although the analyst was frustrated, she wasn't in a hurry. The patient had been doing this for years; she viewed it as an entrenched symptom that would take a long time to resolve. She continued to discuss it with him, but her approach was that she would have to let him come to the decision himself. Her feelings changed dramatically, however, after he told her that he drove home late at night after he had been drinking. When she discussed this in supervision, she said, "Before, I looked at this kind of abstractly; I thought that he should stop, but I didn't have any strong feelings on the matter. But this is really dangerous. He could kill himself!" She told him as much the next session. The intervention was effective; the patient never drove while drunk again. (It did not, however, get him to stop drinking altogether.)

A similar countertransference arose with another supervisee who was working with a patient who said she wanted to find a serious relationship but found it impossible to control her sexual desire. She met men regularly and would go through periods in which she would have sex with four to six different men in a week. This seriously hampered her ability to have a relationship, as she couldn't wait long enough after a date to see somebody a second time. She knew that her lack of control of her sex drive was limiting her to an endless succession of one-night stands but felt completely helpless to control herself. "What can I do," she whined, "I've got to have sex, don't I?" The supervisee at first felt indulgent with the patient. She resonated with the patient's dilemma, recalling her own self-destructive habits. She felt the patient's desperation acutely. This was reminiscent of the mother, who was sweet and understanding, but never provided the patient with the structure she needed to control her spirited temperament.

After a couple of years, however, her feelings changed. The patient had started to meet better men, and knew it, yet she continued to undercut herself at every turn. While she never did anything that was clearly and obviously dangerous, the analyst began to feel that the patient could control herself if she tried. She began to want to tell her it was time to bite the bullet: she had to stop having sex every time she met someone. She fantasized being the patient's mother – telling her how to manage herself on dates – including reminding her to say no. Finally, she felt utterly exasperated with the patient and wanted to order her to stop sleeping around. In short, she developed the feelings that any parent would have for a child who is dearly loved but out of control.

This impulse to order a patient to do something, or not to do something, is the strongest expression of this sort of anaclitic feeling. One analyst described working with a masochistic man who was trying to get ahead in his career but consistently sabotaged himself, especially in the casual and inappropriate way that he dressed to go to interviews. The analyst experienced a strong desire to order him to go out and buy a suit and tie and wear it. Another analyst reported that he ordered a patient, who categorically withheld affection, more out of habit than inclination, to go home and fuck (the analyst's words) his love-starved girlfriend.

Clearly, these kinds of impulses must be carefully studied, especially before using them as the basis of an intervention, as they can have controlling or sadomasochistic meanings rather than anaclitic ones, depending on the transferential context. Nevertheless, the impulse to give the child an order – when it actually is for the child's own good – is an essential component of parenting and one that has a place in the anaclitic mode.

Protecting the patient from their impulses inside the session

The impulse to protect the patient from his impulses within the session – that is to say, within the context of the analytic relationship – can be more difficult to tease out than other protective impulses because the analyst's personal interests often seem to be at stake. When a patient expresses intensely aggressive feelings towards the analyst during a period of negative transference, the analyst may feel very bad or very angry and experience the desire to silence the patient. This self-protective impulse, while understandable, is not anaclitic when the patient is engaged in the analytic task of putting his feelings into words. Should the patient cross the line into abusive behavior, on the other hand, then the analyst's desire to control the patient is indeed anaclitic. While parents must tolerate a lot from the child, the child must not be allowed to abuse them, as this does not help the child learn how to control his sadistic impulses towards his loved ones. The same holds for the analyst and the patient.

Similarly, the analyst's impulse to enforce rules about fees, attendance, and the like can be anaclitic, provided the patient needs these kinds of emotional communications in order to learn how to adapt his behavior to another person's need or to the unfortunate necessity of following hated rules. If the patient does not need these kinds of feelings from the analyst, on the other hand, then they are simply expressions of the analyst's personal requirements (which is unavoidable); if they conflict with the patient's needs, this suggests that the analyst is not the right one for the job.

While we have seen earlier that the impulse to be frustrating can be an expression of a repetitive object induction, it can also be the expression of an anaclitic feeling. This can be seen clearly in a case presented by a supervisee. The patient was a young, attractive man in his early twenties who had been sexually molested by his stepmother shortly before and for a year after he entered puberty. This set into motion a pattern of being desired by older women, who generally used him as a boy toy. For the first couple of years, this pattern held in the analysis; his older female analyst found him to be overwhelmingly attractive. While the induction was congruent with the content in that it paralleled his outside relationships, the patient did not verbalize erotic feelings for the analyst. Although there was never any question of her acting on the impulse, she often described the frustration of being tantalized by him. He was like an exquisitely ripe fruit, perfect for plucking. Of course, she clearly understood the induction – that she was experiencing the stepmother's feelings – yet she still found it painful to be so sorely tempted.

After a number of years, the patient developed an explicit erotic transference to the analyst. He proclaimed his love and attraction to her, his jealousy over her husband, and his anger at the emptiness of the boundaries and rules that kept them separate. The analyst's feelings completely changed. Once the feelings were out in the open, she no longer felt attracted to him. Previously, she had intellectually understood that her desire for him was related to his toxic relationship with his stepmother. Now, her feelings had evolved beyond the induction of the stepmother's feelings and into a true mother's feelings. She felt the impulse to tell him that she would not give in to him even if it weren't prohibited by the analytic boundaries. He had to find somebody his own age, a peer with whom he could be an equal. He would never mature until he realized that she would never, ever return his feelings; those feelings had poisoned him once, and she wouldn't be party to it happening again. Her feelings had moved beyond the repetitive object induction of the early years and into an anaclitic emotional response – a set of feelings the patient needed in order to surmount his repetition.

Loving the patient

The last cluster of nurturing feelings to be considered are those related to loving the patient, and this includes feelings of loving, wanting, enjoying, and admiring.[5] These feelings too originate in early infancy. But just as a parent's love for the child changes as the child grows up, so does the analyst's love for the patient. Loving feelings evolve continuously to match the patient's increasing maturation. The following examples include types of loving feelings that a parent can have for a child throughout the child's lifespan.

Wanting the patient

One of the most basic emotional experiences that a parent must give the child is the feeling of being wanted. In order to do this, the parent must want the child. Many patients, however, did not feel wanted and can induce object inductions in the analyst to reject them. When the analyst finds that he is beginning to want a patient – really want him – and not just in order to analyze him, this aspect of the anaclitic countertransference has developed.

An example is a male patient I worked with for a number of years. The first time I saw him he was perfectly obnoxious. He was sort of an analytic anti-groupie who liked to hang out with analysts and then criticize them. He made insulting remarks about a number of my colleagues to me (I never found out whether he knew that I was involved with them); he sneered at the dust on my bookshelves and overall was insufferably arrogant. Frankly, I hated him. I was torn between hoping that he would reject me and finding some justification for telling him I was not the right analyst.

The next session, however, he was absolutely wonderful. The entitled arrogance was gone, and I felt an intense affection that lasted the duration of the treatment. I looked forward to seeing him, and I wanted him – his stories, his pain, and his humor – almost every session. The induction, which had been a rejecting object countertransference in the first session, quickly evolved into strong anaclitic desire for him. In his case, I had one of the rare experiences of having him validate my feeling. Years after he terminated his therapy, he wrote me a letter and told me that I was the first male in his life who had ever made him feel wanted.

Closely related to this kind of anaclitic wanting of the patient is the analyst's feeling that he is the right analyst for the patient. One supervisee presented to a supervision group the case of a woman who had been severely abused as a child. Her current life was utter chaos: she was bulimic, actively alcoholic, and chronically anxious. As the group discussed the case, most of the other analysts experienced extremely rejecting feelings and were overwhelmed at the thought of treating the woman. These feelings were clearly induced, as they paralleled feelings experienced by many people in the patient's life. The analyst who presented the case, however, was undaunted. She called the patient a sapphire in the mud and said that she would have no trouble polishing her up. She appreciated the patient's talents and charms and was well aware of – but unfazed by – the inevitable difficulties the case would present. Her belief that she and she alone was the right analyst for the patient was only strengthened by the other group member's apprehensions. Clearly, this kind of conviction is identical to a mother's feeling that she is the one true mother for her baby.

Enjoying the patient

Another part of loving a child is enjoying him, and the same is true for loving a patient. The first case of an anaclitic feeling I described – my feelings of delight with the schizophrenic patient – are a vivid example; more muted examples of this feeling are legion. In other examples, I particularly enjoyed listening to the cadence of one woman's voice, as well as her slangy speech, which was unusually authentic and expressive. I just loved hearing stories of another patient who grew up in a small town in Montana during the early 1950s, as well as his intense interest in geology, which is not a subject that easily impassions me. One patient came in beaming over a new pair of shoes, and I felt just like a parent of a gloriously happy toddler. A supervisee once described his intense delight with his patient's career as a violinist. Another was always excited when his actor patient was in a new show. Whether the feeling harkens back to early childhood – like finding delight in a dirty smile – or is the glowing pleasure in the budding individuality of a growing child, the feeling of delight is one that many patients still need.

The feeling of enjoying the patient can be quieter still. One supervisee described a patient who consistently talked about things that were of no interest to him whatsoever. The work did not appear to deepen over time, and the patient seemed to stay on the surface. The analyst found herself bored in the sessions, but she didn't mind. When we explored the patient's outside life, it appeared that he was doing better in all areas: his relationships were better, his career was advancing, and he generally felt less depressed in his life. The analyst wondered, as analysts in this countertransference state often do, if she should be doing something different – something that looked more like real psychoanalysis. Despite the dullness of the sessions, she acknowledged that she rather liked the patient and felt no pressing emotional need to do anything different.

This induction is similar to the feeling parents experience when their children talk or play at something that is neither enchanting nor exhilarating, yet they still find it comfortable and nice to be with them, whether through listening or watching. Not every moment in parenting – or in any other relationship – is filled with excitement and delight. Most are not. Quiet, uneventful love – the ordinary love of everyday life – is part of the foundation that allows deep relationships to endure. Being comfortably and undemandingly bored with a patient gives the patient the experience of being loved and accepted – even when he is not doing anything special (and not gratifying the analyst's needs for stimulation!).[6]

As the child matures and becomes a capable person, delight in the child's being is joined by the pleasure of doing things with the child. This is reflected in anaclitic countertransference states in which the analyst has fantasies about doing things with the patient: taking a trip to Australia, going to a ball game, or just hanging out in a cafe. These fantasies may be incongruent with the material (I imagined skiing with one patient though he never mentioned an interest in skiing), or they may be congruent with fantasies the patient expresses about the analyst. One patient described a fantasy of bringing food over to my house. The two of us cooked a large Italian meal together for my family. It was plain old domestic bliss. In my mind, I was right there with her, chopping the onions and the parsley and smelling the garlic as the butter sang in the frying pan. Another patient loved rock concerts, and I often fantasized going out to hear music with her. (This was clearly an induction: I loathe rock concerts.)

Even when these feelings do not take the form of full-fledged fantasies, the analyst may experience this kind of induction as the desire to talk to the patient about whatever they are talking about, not for the purpose of analyzing the patient, but just for the fun of it. The patient has read a new mystery novel, and the analyst wants to hear all about it. The patient has taken up ballroom dancing, and the analyst is intrigued. The patient complains passionately about the weather, and the analyst wants to bitch too.

All these kinds of thoughts and impulses – too often dismissed as countertransference resistance, collusion, or distraction – can be crucial anaclitic experiences. Even if the patient is able to have these kinds of experiences in his outside life with friends and lovers, he may not have had them with the parent. These feelings represent the parent's appreciation of the child's growing maturity and a willingness to enjoy the child as a growing child, an adolescent, and eventually, as an adult.

Pride and admiration

Pride and admiration are other crucial emotional communications that are essential to maturation, both in the parent–child relationship and in analysis. Although closely related, pride and admiration each relate to somewhat different maturational needs, and present different emotional demands on the analyst.

The analyst experiences the impulse to be proud of the patient for accomplishments that represent steps – whether actual or symbolic – towards maturity. This feeling is analogous to the feeling that a mother feels when her daughter ties her shoes or brushes her teeth by herself for the first time. For example, after a couple of years of analysis, one patient was able to keep his apartment clean on a regular basis. This had been a terrific struggle, as it involved mastering issues of dependency, neediness, and self-control, in addition to accepting the fact that he had an attention disorder that made this sort of thing especially difficult for him. During the period when he was working on this, the patient had experienced lacerating bouts of self-hatred, which were related at times to his mother's feelings about him and to his own introjected anger at her. My feelings on this issue were relatively neutral during this period. At times, I too felt exasperated at his inability, but most of the time I was well aware of the issues that underlay the conflict and felt confident of the outcome.

When he was finally able to tolerate all of these feelings sufficiently enough to actually start cleaning the apartment, he experienced another attack of self-contempt. "This was no real accomplishment," he sneered at himself. "Everybody else can keep their apartment clean. Nobody else needs to go to analysis for two fucking years to learn how to use a broom!"

In a sense, of course, he was right. However, not everyone can keep their apartment clean. I can barely manage this task, and then only some of the time. And it is never grounds for winning the Nobel Prize. What it does represent is the kind of self-care that is a normal and expectable development. And it was for just this reason that I felt proud of him. His accomplishment may not have made him special to anyone but me, but for me he was very special, and his progress made me glow. I told him that many people never manage to keep their room clean and that I thought it was wonderful that he was finally able to keep his apartment in a state such that he could come home and enjoy it. He dropped the self-attack and told me how he was planning to redecorate his living room.

Admiration is related to accomplishments that are a unique expression of the patient's talent, courage, or strength. An important aspect of admiration is that it relates to something that the analyst himself is unable to do. Thus, it corresponds to the positive feeling the parent has for the child when the child surpasses him in some area. It is not, of course, necessary for the analyst to want to be able to do what the patient has done. The crucial features are the analyst's willingness and ability to acknowledge that the patient can do something the analyst cannot and the joy the analyst experiences in the patient's separateness and maturation that this implies.

I experienced this with a 10-year-old boy with post-traumatic stress disorder who I treated at a mental health clinic. The boy's stepfather had become enraged at the boy's mother and had murdered her in front of the boy, and with the same knife, had slashed the boy's abdomen open and left him for dead. The boy had a 12-inch scar on his body, but miraculously he had lived. When he first came to see me, he would break out trembling whenever the phone rang, for fear that it was his stepfather coming to get him. Remarkably, he was able to readjust to life, and in therapy he was able to discuss a wide range of feelings. However, he consistently denied being depressed and claimed that while he was afraid of his stepfather, he didn't feel sad about missing his mother.

After a year, when his case came up for a routine review by the psychiatrist in the clinic, he told the psychiatrist that he was extremely depressed. The psychiatrist offered him antidepressants, which he eagerly accepted. I was completely shocked that he had told the psychiatrist (whom he barely knew!) about his depression but had withheld it from me. When I asked about this, he told me that he didn't think I would have been able to handle hearing about his depression. I would make too big a deal about it.

This was, perhaps, partly a projection but largely true. I probably did feel too narcissistically identified with his depression to be able to hear about it and contain it. I asked if he was disappointed that he had been coming to me for all this time and that I had not been able to help him talk about something so important. He calmly but emotionally said that it had been difficult, but that he benefited in other ways by working with me, and that nobody was perfect.

I was filled with admiration for this boy – for his ability to survive a horrific trauma and go on living, for having the patience to wait until what he felt was the opportune time to ask for the help that he needed, and for being able to value what was in our relationship despite the disappointment he felt. I doubt I would have had the strength to do any of these things under his circumstances. I told him how much I admired him, his eyes filled with tears, and we then went on to play a wonderful game of checkers.

Aggressive anaclitic feelings

Anaclitic countertransference derived from aggressive feelings towards the patient are a complicated phenomenon. While these kinds of feelings are often a crucial component of maturation, they are often feelings that the parent has to contain silently in order for them to be useful for the developing child. Should these feelings be expressed inappropriately – and in many cases any expression of the feelings will be inappropriate – the effect will be toxic.

So why, and in what sense, should aggressive feelings be considered to be anaclitic? The reason, I think, is that these feelings – however potentially destructive they may be if expressed – are analogous to the normal and expectable destructive feelings most parents experience towards their children at some point. The fact that parents experience these feelings towards their child is probably necessary for the child's long-term adaptation to the world. As pleasurable as the fantasy of having a perfectly loving, always well-intentioned, omnipotent parent may be, it is difficult to imagine how such a fabulous creature could prepare a child to live in the world. Even if the parent doesn't have destructive feelings towards him, somebody else certainly will. What makes a parent life affirming and maturational is not whether he has these feelings but how he manages them. Every person must learn to tolerate some degree of hostility from other people, even those who love him. When the parent consciously contains his destructive feelings towards the child, this may immunize the child against the potentially toxic feelings by providing an exposure dilute enough to be healthily absorbed by the child's immature ego.

Furthermore, these feelings may serve as an anchor to genuine, interpersonal reality. As Winnicott (1949) put it, the child who seeks hate must be able to find it, or he will not be able to seek love. As we shall see, many feelings that are potentially destructive to the patient are nevertheless the correct emotional responses to certain maturational milestones; not to experience these feelings would be condescending at best and disempowering at worst.

For both of these reasons, the parent who feels only positive and loving feelings towards the child has deprived the child of the full depth and range of the parent/child relationship. This can be repaired in the analysis, provided the analyst allows himself to feel destructive feelings towards the patient, and contains them in a way that benefits him.

Angry or critical feelings

So many people have suffered intensely from a surfeit of angry or critical feelings from their parents that it is the rare patient who has not received enough negative feelings in his development. Nevertheless, the analyst's experience of angry or critical feelings does provide some patients with clear maturational benefits. These feelings can function positively in a number of different ways in the treatment, depending on the nature of the patient's experience of anger with his parents.

A small number of patients have had parents who were so inhibited in their own angry feelings that they were virtually unable to consciously experience negative feelings towards their child. Whether this was accomplished through hyperrationality, reaction formation, or repression, the child did experience the parent as never having had negative feelings towards him. As a result, the child did not get the experience of the parent being angry and then being not angry; he does not become aware of the normalcy of the ebb and flow in people's feelings. He may not learn that others can be angry with him without hurting him or ending the relationship. Consequently, the child did not develop the emotional sturdiness necessary to maintain relationships with people who experience a wider range of feelings than the parent. And if the parent's lack of anger had been due to the feeling that all aggression is dangerous, the child was likely to have internalized this perspective along with all of the limitations that this imposes on his personality and relationships.

Similarly, the child may know (as he gets older) that certain behaviors should make the parent angry. The parent's lack of anger deprived the relationship of a crucial element of reality. The parent's failure to respond may be experienced as a lack of attunement, emotional absence, or neglect. Should the child want to make the parent angry – an action that helps the child to consolidate a sense of autonomy, power, and interpersonal effectiveness – the parent's lack of reaction leaves the child emotionally isolated and misunderstood.

On the other end of the spectrum, even patients whose parents were abusively angry or critical can derive anaclitic benefit from the analyst's angry feelings. One frequent result of abuse is that the patient is so frightened of evoking anger in others that he becomes passive, compliant, and hyper-vigilant about doing anything that might provoke the analyst. When the analyst does become angry with such a patient – as a realistic, appropriately intense response – it can reassure the patient that they can provoke anger without being abused or threatened. (Besides, of course, being an indication that the patient has become less constricted.)

An example of this occurred with a man I had worked with for a number of years who had almost never asserted himself about anything. A shift came when his financial situation changed for the better, but in the transition, he wanted to pay me on a schedule that was almost impossible for me to keep track of: once every three weeks. I never did understand why this was necessary, but he was as adamant about it as he had ever been about anything. The whole thing annoyed me. However, I did not communicate this to him. He asked me about it directly several times. As I was aware that even minute exposures to irritability left him devastated, I explored his questions rather than answering them – containing the feelings as best I could. Nevertheless, he saw right through me. It did not, however, prevent him from doing what he thought was best for him, and he appeared to be much more secure in making his demands after he realized that I was annoyed but was not going to retaliate. To have been accepting of him without being annoyed would not have had the same effect.

Furthermore, abused patients have also been deprived of the benefits of exposure to modulated aggression, as described above. Once the fear of arousing anger has been neutralized, the analyst's angry feelings can serve the same maturational purpose as with patients whose parents felt ordinary levels of anger towards them.

Competition, jealousy, and envy

Parental competition, jealousy, and envy towards the child are another cluster of feelings that is often toxic or worse. One need only remember how Laius, Oedipus's father, treated Oedipus, to be reminded of this. For example, one patient described his father as a hardworking immigrant, who had come from an extremely impoverished background from a country in the developing world and became a successful scientist working in private industry. Rather than encourage his children, however, he ridiculed them constantly, making clear his feeling that none of them could ever accomplish what he had accomplished because they were neither hardworking enough, intelligent enough, or resilient enough. Not surprisingly, neither the patient nor his sisters had reached anywhere near their potential in their careers. Except for the possibility that it may be best for young children to have an attenuated, contained exposure to all destructive feelings, I have not seen a maturational role for these feelings. (I leave open the possibility that somebody else might find one.)

On the other hand, these feelings do have a maturational role for the adolescent and adult – one that is closely related to admiration. For the parent to feel competitive, jealous, or envious of the child, the child must be a worthy opponent – someone whose talents or accomplishments can provoke jealousy or envy. In other words, the adolescent or adult must be somebody who has surpassed (or threatens to surpass) the parent. This experience is critical to adult individuation – for it means that the patient can become his own person. As with admiration, parental competitiveness and envy are implicit acknowledgements of this accomplishment.

This surfaces regularly with all patients if the analyst works with them long enough. The patient can write the book, sing the song, close the deal, or make the money the analyst always wished that he could, and the analyst is competitive, jealous, or envious. With patients who are not analysts, however, it is often easy for the analyst to see his role as the analyst as superior to anything the patient might do. (Behind every great patient is a great analyst.) The real challenge for analysts involves treating other analysts where the opportunities for these feelings are inescapable. The patient might build her practice quicker, develop more prestigious affiliations, or charge higher fees – all excellent grounds for feeling competitive. But even if these challenges to the analyst's self-esteem are avoided, at some point every patient/analyst will report a clinical situation that he has handled better than the analyst could have done. And the analyst knows it. It is at these moments that the analyst's envy can be most profoundly anaclitic, provided the analyst contains his feeling with true parental grace.

Sadism, contempt, and exploitativeness

If any readers are expecting astute observations or even a flight of sophistry about the value of these feelings in either parenting or analysis, I will disappoint them. I can think of no maturational role for these feelings in the parent/child relationship: they seem to be destructive at all stages of development – although the extent of their destructiveness depends on the individual's vulnerability.

Nevertheless, I am not completely comfortable with this position. This range of feelings is common enough in parents, although their intensity, and the degree to which they dominate the personality and the parent/child relationship, varies considerably. Coming from an evolutionary perspective on human emotions, I am inclined to think that any feelings that occur regularly must have some adaptive value.

However, it is possible that these feelings (like certain types of infanticidal impulses described by Hrdy [1999]) are adaptive for the parent but not for the child. If so, these feelings are only adaptive under special circumstances (e.g., famine in pre-industrial societies), and their presence in a parent/child relationship under ordinary conditions would be evidence of some sort of disorder – immaturity, unresolved emotional trauma, misdirected biologically rooted aggression, or frank mental illness. The only possible positive contribution these feelings might make to ordinary childhood development might be the same one that has been hypothesized earlier: an attenuated exposure to the full range of human feelings may immunize the child against the toxicity of the feelings later in life.

Whatever the origin of these feelings in the parent/child relationship, the feelings are usually manifested in the object countertransference or in certain subjective states. I have never found a case in which I think the feelings served an anaclitic function. I have, however, seen cases in which the emergence of these feelings might be an indication of progress in the analysis. In one case, a supervisee described a patient who had never induced a negative thought or feeling. The analyst was exceedingly careful with him and felt that he was extremely vulnerable. Then, after two years, the analyst had the thought that the patient, who usually presented as an unassuming, modest fellow, was a bit of a pretentious prig. However, this thought did not evolve into a full-blown object countertransference, and may well have been subjective. When he looked at the material, he saw that the patient was showing evidence of greater emotional resilience than he had previously. For example, he described having had open conflicts with others that did not leave him feeling mortified. This progress seemed to be reflected in the analyst's freedom to experience a greater range of feeling with the patient, including feelings that might have been toxic to the patient earlier on in the analysis. However, there was no indication that the analyst's feeling actually led to the patient's greater resilience.

Anaclitic sexual feelings

As with many forms of anaclitic feelings, anaclitic sexual feelings vary, depending on whether they are directed towards the patient as an infant/child or as a maturing adult.

The role of sexual feelings towards young children is complex and poorly understood. As Freud (1905) famously argued, children have sexual feelings, even if these feelings do not take the same form as adult sexuality. What is less understood is what feelings the child's sexual feelings induce in adults. Adults also have sexual feelings towards children, and these feelings are an amalgam of leftover components of infantile sexuality and adult sexuality.

ANACLITIC COUNTERTRANSFERENCE

Many parents, mothers and fathers alike, find babies and older prepubescent children to be alluring and sensual, even though these fantasies usually do not take overtly genital or orgasmic forms. Parents want to inhale their scents, kiss them forever, and gobble them up. Closer to explicit sexuality is the intense sensuality many women experience when nursing.[7] Even when parental sexual fantasies about babies and children do take an overtly sexual form, they are not usually expressed differently than adult genitality. Greenson (1967), for example, described a patient who wanted to lick her young daughter's vagina because it looked like a ripe apricot. While the impact of actual sexual behavior on young children is almost always destructive (in most Western cultures, at least), sexual/sensual feelings help fuel the overtly non-sexual delight that parents feel for their children – the delight that helps the child to feel wanted and loved. Following Kohut and Wolf's (1978) suggestion that sexual feelings between parents are part of the environment that enables the child to associate sexuality with joy, properly contained sexual feelings may form a vital component of the emotional climate that enables the child to feel attractive, sensual, and eventually, sexual.

Unlike parental sexual feelings about babies and children, however, sexual inductions related to the adult patient's childhood often do take an explicitly sexual form in analysis. However, these fantasies often contain a strong element of playful delight, with neither the aggression characteristic of object inductions that repeat earlier sexual abuse, nor the passion of adult sexuality. One analyst, a heterosexual woman, was completely taken with how cute one of her female patients was. The patient once wore a particularly revealing blouse, and the analyst experienced a fantasy of playing with her breasts that had the same quality of delight as a mother stroking a baby's freshly bathed bottom.

Sexual inductions about adult patients as adults, on the other hand, are just like sexual feelings the analyst might have towards anyone else in his life. When sexual feelings arise early in the treatment, especially feelings experienced in the first session, they are most likely object inductions, subjective in origin, or present-anchored.

When they arise later in the treatment, following a period in which other forms of countertransference have predominated and been worked through, they are more likely to be anaclitic reactions. In these cases, they are usually realistic reactions to the patient's growing maturation, his evolution into a sexually attractive adult. Appreciating the patient as a sexual equal – usually in a silent contained manner – serves to reinforce and acknowledge this development in an anaclitic way.

At times, anaclitic sexual feelings of this sort are a response to the patient's potential, rather than his current state. One supervisee discussed a male patient whom she had always found to be neutral or even mildly repellent. She'd never had a sexual feeling about him, despite the fact that he often discussed sex in graphic, but not grotesque, detail. One session, however, she noticed his body more than usual and realized that he was more muscular, more masculine than she had previously realized. She still had a great deal of difficulty integrating this perception with her overall sense of him, which was that he had a submissive, masochistic streak that frequently induced mildly contemptuous feelings towards him in the analyst and in most others in his life. At that point, the sexual feeling was fleeting.

Over the next six months, however, the patient became increasingly assertive and decreasingly masochistic until it became clear that the analyst's sexual feeling had been an early indication of the patient's progress. In this case it was not clear whether the analyst's feelings were merely informational or whether they actually contributed to the patient's maturation. However, it is possible that the analyst's ability to see the patient as an attractive sexual person provided the encouragement the patient needed in order to develop further in this direction.

10

EMOTIONAL COMMUNICATION IN PSYCHOANALYTIC TECHNIQUE

How does analysis cure?[1] Is it through insight and self-understanding or through the relationship – a corrective emotional experience? Is it the interpretations that the patient gets from the analyst, or is it the feelings? Is it cognitive communication, or is it emotional communication?

We must review a few terms before we can approach these questions: interpretation, cognitive communication, and emotional communication. Let's start with interpretation. Interpretation has two different (but related) meanings in psychoanalytic theory, one related to epistemology and the other to the theory of technique.

In psychoanalytic epistemology, an interpretation is an explanation of the meaning and/or origin of some aspect of the patient's mental life – a symptom, behavior, defense, subjective experience, unconscious process, dream, or life history – within the perspective of psychoanalytic theory. It is the analyst's intellectual understanding of something about the patient's mental life – a theoretical construct.

In the theory of technique, an interpretation is an intervention in which the analyst communicates all or part of this explanation to the patient in language that can be understood by, but is at that moment unknown to, the patient's conscious mind. The purpose of an interpretation is to increase the patient's knowledge and understanding of his own mental life – to stimulate insight – and to strengthen the patient's ego (Freud 1940).

Although the technique of interpretation is dependent upon the interpretation as a theoretical construct, it is a separate activity. It is important to maintain the distinction: non-interpretative techniques are always based on interpretations in the epistemological sense, but they do not directly communicate interpretations in language to the patient.

Now let's review the concepts of cognitive communication, emotional communication, and how they are related to language. Cognitive communication conveys many types of information through a consensually agreed upon system of symbols – language – that is experienced and processed as thought. Emotional communication conveys only one type of information – information about the sender's emotions – through non-linguistic channels and is experienced as feeling.

Cognitive communication can name and describe emotions but cannot convey the experience of emotion directly in the way that emotional induction can. The two channels are intertwined in all communications – especially verbal communications – between humans old enough to have acquired language.

In psychoanalytic technique, a cognitive communication is a deliberate communication from the analyst expressed in language and designed to convey meaningful information – knowledge – that will be experienced by the patient as thought.

In contrast, an emotional communication in psychoanalytic technique is a deliberate expression of feeling, by the analyst, through tone, prosody, and the inductive aspects of language, designed to induce a change in the patient's feelings. All psychoanalytic interventions contain emotional communications and most contain cognitive communications as well.

Now we can return to our original question: How does analysis cure? The answer depends, in part, on how the analyst engages the patient – which part of the patient's mind the analyst's interventions address. Freud (1940) didn't consider this question until his last major work, where he argued that the analyst forms a pact with the patient's weakened ego in a struggle against "the enemies, the instinctual demands of the id and the conscientious demands of the super-ego" (173). Why the ego? Presumably because it is the only part of the mind that can distinguish between the past and the present; it is directed towards both the intrapsychic world and the outside world, and what is most relevant to the current discussion, that it is amenable to reason and to the demands of reality. Later theorists (Sterba 1934; Strachey 1934; Greenson 1967) clarified (and this was implicit in Freud [1916]) that the analyst allies himself not with the patient's ego as a whole but with that part of the ego that is healthy, that can cooperate with the analyst's instructions, and that can observe itself like an object – what Greenson (1967) referred to as the reasonable ego.

There is, however, another part of the ego – the part of the patient's mind that participates in the repetitions and transferences, that experiences the world and expresses itself within the emotional logic of the repetitions and transferences. This part of the ego is not oriented towards present reality, cannot cooperate with the analyst, and does not observe itself. This part of the mind can be called the *afflicted* ego.

This is the part of the mind that is the target – the enemy – of the therapeutic alliance as formulated by Freud (1940) and the classical tradition. But other analysts, starting with Ferenczi (1931) and continuing to the present day, have found ways to engage the patient's afflicted ego directly, not as an enemy but as a partner in a different sort of treatment relationship than that described by the classical writers.

However, the analyst must make different types of communications to each of the egos. To the extent that the analyst limits his communications to the reasonable ego, cognitive communications, catalyzed with a limited range of emotional communication (Freud 1916) in the form of interpretations are the primary source of analytic cure. But to the extent the analyst engages the afflicted ego, he must make use of a much wider range of emotional communications coupled with cognitive communications that are not necessarily interpretations.

It is clear from the volume of successful case reports from both traditions that both ways of engaging the patient can work, and both can fail. The question is finding the right approach with each individual patient.

We are now in a position to offer a preliminary answer to the question of how psychoanalysis cures: it cures by providing two distinct, but closely intertwined, types of communication to the two parts of the patient's mind – the reasonable ego and the afflicted ego. First, it provides curative cognitive communications, in the form of interpretations, which serve to enlarge and strengthen the patient's reasonable ego, as Freud (1916) described. Second, it provides emotional communications to the patient's reasonable ego, and also to his afflicted ego – through the medium of the analytic relationship – that catalyze the therapeutic effect of interpretation, meet maturational needs, activate transference, and modify defenses.

Later in the chapter we will define the concepts of the reasonable ego and the afflicted ego more fully. We will describe what it means to address the reasonable ego and the afflicted ego, and we will expand on how cognitive and emotional communications can be combined to form different types of interventions that engage these different aspects of the patient's mind.

But for the moment, let's look at some of these issues more broadly by comparing three different interventions designed to address the same clinical situation, each of which uses a different combination of cognitive and emotional communications to address the patient's reasonable and afflicted egos.

Prior to the session to be described, the patient had appeared to be a timid, usually self-deprecating man who constantly found himself hiding in social situations. He initially ascribed this to a modesty that was inculcated into him when he was young. He was afraid of looking like an arrogant exhibitionist. He was terrified that he would be destroyed – or deeply humiliated – by his parents if he let himself shine in any way. They were also modest and extremely judgmental about the need to keep to yourself. He had been frustrated that he had not gotten much of what he had wanted out of his life – romantically, socially, or professionally. He'd never had a boyfriend, he didn't have many friends, and he felt he could do much more in his work than he had accomplished. He thought – correctly, in the analyst's eyes – that his deferential demeanor had contributed to his lack of success.

But in one session, his way of relating to the analyst has changed somewhat: he cautiously describes fantasies of wanting to stand out more. He'd like to talk more in meetings at work, to put forth some proposals. He'd like to approach men at a health club, and he'd like to call people and make plans. He saw a beautiful leather jacket that would look great with some new jeans he bought – a sharp departure from his usual khakis and pastels. As he describes these thoughts and feelings with the analyst, he sounds very anxious. He tentatively wonders whether the analyst ever experiences these feelings. The analyst asks which would be better – if he did have the same feelings or if he didn't? The patient thinks it would be better if he did, but he can't articulate why.

Obviously, there a number of ways to interpret this situation, but let's suppose that the most relevant interpretation is as follows:[2] the patient's desires (impulses, needs) to show off and to be exhibitionistic have been severely inhibited as a result of his parent's harsh condemnation of these desires and their consequent inability to provide him with the normal narcissistic mirroring he needed to be able to integrate them into his personality. This has led to a repetition characterized by a severe restriction in his ability to pursue his desires in the present. In the analysis, the patient does not allow himself to experience desires and impulses that he had previously suppressed or repressed. However, he is both (a) frightened that the analyst will disapprove; and (b) longing for the analyst to share these feelings so that he will know that they are acceptable and feel the narcissistic reinforcement that was missing from his childhood. Thus, there are elements of both object and narcissistic dimensions of the transference.

The analyst wants to make an intervention based on this understanding of the transference. Three rather different possibilities are described below:

1. *"Perhaps you are anxious because you are afraid I will be as disapproving as your parents were, and you are wondering if it is safe. And maybe you wish that I would share these feelings because then I would clearly be accepting of them and would give you the feeling of sharing them with you that your parents didn't give you as a child."* This intervention, a classical interpretation, is basically a condensed version of the theoretical understanding of the transference. Its therapeutic leverage lies in the cognitive communication that the analyst conveys to the patient's reasonable ego. The interpretation is an observation designed to help the patient understand his feeling, to have insight into the meaning and origin of his anxiety. This cognitive communication is accompanied by an emotional communication that supports it and is designed to help the patient to make use of the cognitive communication. The tone is slightly warm and clearly interested, and it conveys mild empathy that the patient is saddled with this problem. Nevertheless, the emotional communication is not an emotional response to the feelings the patient has for an analyst. It is designed to gently shift

the patient's attention away from his actual feelings about the analyst and to observe and understand them in light of his past experience and the analyst's interpretation.

2. *"It sounds like it's really hard for you to take the risk of telling me about these feelings. I can imagine that you might be afraid that I'd react the way your parents did – attacking or humiliating you for having feelings and desires that are completely natural and healthy. They didn't understand that, and made you feel bad about stuff that was actually really good. It would have felt so much better if only they had those feelings, too."* In this intervention – an empathic interpretation[3] informed by Self Psychology – both the cognitive and the emotional communications are viewed as being equally important. The cognitive communication, which is essentially the same message as the first intervention, is designed to convey self-understanding and insight to the patient and is addressed to the reasonable ego. However, the language is closer to the patient's experience, and the emotional communication that accompanies it is more intense than in the first intervention. It is designed to do more than support the interpretation. The words, and even more the tone, are more explicitly empathic with the pain the patient feels and felt and are addressed to the afflicted ego. The emotional communication is a direct response to the patient's current feelings about the analyst. As a whole, the intervention encourages him to view his current feelings in light of the past, but it also provides an experience of being emotionally understood in the present in a way that the patient did not get from his parents.

3. *"Of course I have those feelings. Why, sometimes all I want to do is show off – sound smart, be seductive, and wear cool clothes. It's really scary. You never know how people will react, but sometimes there is just nothing more wonderful than showing people your stuff – going after the world and getting it. That jacket sounds really great. Where did you see it? What kind of leather is it? It sounds like it would make a fabulous outfit."* In contrast to the first two interventions, this one is not designed to help the patient to observe or understand his feelings in light of the past. No communication is made to the reasonable ego. Rather, the analyst works to provide the afflicted ego in the present with the emotional experience that he did not have with his parents. Whereas the second intervention conveyed empathic understanding of the patient's feeling, this intervention explicitly reflects and amplifies the patient's nascent extroversion. The self-disclosure is designed to give the patient the feeling that he is with a twin, who meets a developmental need and solidifies his sense of self. He provides direct narcissistic mirroring and validation, which encourages the patient not just to accept his feelings but to embrace and enjoy them. He is trying to help the patient experience and tolerate higher levels of excitement and joy – positive affect – in his impulses than he has ever known. The emotional communication is the primary source of therapeutic leverage in this intervention, and the

cognitive communication supports and amplifies it. Both the cognitive and the emotional communications are addressed to the afflicted ego.

Although each one of these three interventions is based on approximately the same interpretation of the case, each uses a different combination of cognitive and emotional communication, and each addresses the patient's reasonable and afflicted ego in different ways.

We will go into greater depth about how these combinations should be conceptualized and what aspects of the patient's experience they are designed to engage. But for the moment, let's make a basic observation: there is a fundamental difference between classical interpretations, which address the reasonable ego primarily through cognitive communication, and other types of interventions (including other types of interpretations) that address the afflicted ego primarily through emotional communication. When the cognitive communication is of primary therapeutic importance, the analyst emotionally positions himself outside of the transference – outside of the way the patient emotionally experiences him; his communications take the form of observations about the transference. He attempts to modify the patient's repetitions by helping him understand them. In interventions in which the emotional communication is granted equal or greater importance, on the other hand, the analyst positions himself inside the transference – on the basis of the way the patient experiences him, and the analyst's communication directly engages with the feelings that characterize the repetition. The analyst attempts to modify the patient's repetitions by using his own feelings to change the patient's feelings.

Repetitions and interventions

A brief review: repetitions are stable, ongoing patterns of feeling and behavior that are rooted in the past – frozen emotional moments that lack the fluid reactivity to the actual external world that characterizes present-oriented moments. A person in the grip of a repetition feels and acts as if he were living in the past, even if he is consciously aware that he is not. Repetitions persist in the face of changes in the environment.

The goal of clinical psychoanalysis is to loosen the grip of involuntary repetitions on the patient's feelings and behavior (Spotnitz 1976).[4] This frees him to experience new feelings and to develop new ways of relating, based on his needs, desires, and a more pragmatic understanding of the world in the present. And this, in turn, enables him to get more of what he wants out of his life, which is the reason most people seek analysis.

Loosening repetitions may involve any or all of the following: making the unconscious conscious; establishing ego dominance over the id; resolving the Oedipus conflict; working through the depressive position; introjecting whole objects; overcoming splitting; learning to love without fear of destroying the other; developing a stable sense of self; learning to hate constructively; enjoying a robust subjectivity; understanding one's impact on others; having insight; feeling all feelings; resolving the narcissistic defense; developing a realistic sense of self and other; separation and individuation; accepting the reality principle; recognizing the subjectivity of the other; integrating disparate self-states; understanding one's desire; and any number of other salubrious intrapsychic or interpersonal developments. But in the end, the main issue comes down to enabling the patient to move out of the shadows of the past so that he can act and react in the context of the present, based on current goals and desires.

Relatively superficial repetitions can sometimes be loosened by cognitive awareness of the irrationality of the thought processes that accompany the repetition, as in cognitive therapy. More deeply entrenched repetitions must first be activated in the treatment in the form of transference, to which the analyst responds with interventions that address the intrapsychic and interpersonal dimensions of the repetition within the context of the analytic relationship.

Cognitive and emotional communications as components of interventions

An intervention is a communication, from the analyst, designed to loosen a repetition that has been activated, in the psychoanalytic relationship, in the form of transference. Thus, an intervention is always based on analysis of the transference.[5] It would be tempting to say that interventions are done consciously and deliberately, were it not for the fact that so many interventions can seem thoughtless and spontaneous. So it is more accurate to say that anything that the analyst would have said or done deliberately, if he had the presence of mind to formulate it consciously, should qualify as an intervention. An intervention, like most human communications, is comprised of one or two components: an emotional communication, with or without a cognitive communication.

Cognitive communication in psychoanalysis conveys many types of information – ideas, requests, descriptions, questions and descriptions of the analyst's emotional state – through language. When successful, it makes unconscious elements of the patient's experience known to his consciousness, contributes to the patient's intellectual understanding of himself or some aspect of the world around him, and strengthens the ego. For example, if the analyst makes an interpretation of a patient's fear of snakes as a displacement of his fear of his sexuality, the analyst conveys his intellectual understanding of the patient's fear for the purpose of making him conscious of its meaning.

The cognitive component of an intervention can be operationally conceptualized as what the analyst says. In the discussion that follows, the terms "language" and "the words" will be used synonymously with cognitive communication.

Emotional communication conveys information about the analyst's emotional state, in relationship to the patient, in the form of feelings. When effective, it induces a change in the patient's emotional state. The emotional component of an intervention can be operationally conceptualized as how the analyst says what he does – the feelings that accompany the cognitive communication. In the discussion that follows, the term "the feelings" will be used synonymously with "emotional communication."

Let's consider the relationship of the cognitive communication and the emotional communication using the interpretation about the patient's fear of snakes described above. If the analyst's interpretation of the patient's fear of snakes is made in a warm tone, it might communicate that the analyst feels sympathetic empathy with the patient's state of fearfulness, or it might communicate an acceptance of the patient's sexuality that the patient himself does not feel. On the other hand, if the interpretation is made in a cold tone, this might communicate that the analyst is disappointed by the patient's fear or is contemptuous of it. In all cases, the emotional communications will have a significant – usually overriding – impact on how the patient understands and experiences the cognitive component of the interpretation.

An emotional communication may be reinforced by congruent cognitive communications that express the same feelings in words. It may be attenuated or contradicted by incongruent cognitive communications that express different feelings, or the cognitive communication may convey something completely different from the emotional communication. Most often, the emotional communication is not expressed explicitly in the analyst's language – the cognitive communication – but implicitly through the non-linguistic channels that accompany the language. Even when a feeling is directly expressed in words, such as, "our work together is very important to me," in an intervention, the words alone cannot fully convey the emotional communication without congruent communications expressed through non-linguistic channels.

An emotional communication is characterized by three features:

1. a specific feeling
2. a specific relational mode
3. a specific intensity.

The *specific feeling* – or combination of feelings – is what gives the primary emotional tone to the emotional communication. It might be interest, anger, depression, fear, anguish, anxiety, tenderness, or any feeling that the person can experience.

The *relational mode* of an emotional communication is the global way in which the analyst relates to the patient, in terms of the degree of differentiation between them and the role he plays in the patient's mind. The relational mode provides the relational context in which the specific feeling will be expressed. Let's briefly review the different relational modes in the context of interventions that make explicit emotional communications.[6]

Narcissistic emotional communications convey that the analyst experiences or views the patient as being similar to, or the same as, merged with, or a twin of the patient. Examples of narcissistic communications are illustrated below:

- *"I can understand how that was very difficult for you."* (Expressed in a warm, empathic tone that still maintains the boundary between patient and analyst.)
- *"It must have been fantastic to be with such a hot guy."* (Expressed in a tone that conveys a strong sense of sharing the feeling of excitement.)
- *"I would have wanted to kill the son of a bitch, too!"* (Expressed in a tone that assumes that they share, or would share, the same feeling in the same intensity.)

Object emotional communications convey that the analyst experiences the patient as a separate, differentiated object in the context of the repetition of a pathological interpersonal relationship as illustrated in the following examples:

- *"It makes me angry that you haven't brought the check."* (Expressed with just a hint of anger in the tone but still basically accepting.)
- *"When you lecture me like that, I think you treat me the same way your mother treated you."* (Expressed with a clear feeling that the analyst doesn't like how he is being treated.)
- *"Maybe you are just stupid."* (Expressed with contempt.)

Analytic emotional communications express caring, nurturance, or an attempt to fulfill an unmet dependency need in the context of a differentiated relationship. For instance, as described below:

- *"Maybe I should talk for a while. Let me read this poem to you."* (Expressed in soothing tones, and the analyst does read the poem.)
- *"You need to stop drinking so much at parties! You will never meet a decent man if you keep it up like that."* (Expressed in a firm, caring tone.)
- *"I really admire how you handled things with your boyfriend."* (Expressed in a tone that suggests that the analyst not only admires what the patient did but also the sense that the patient did it better than he could have.)

A specific feeling will have a different impact and meaning when expressed in the context of different relational modes. For example, a hateful feeling will be experienced by the patient one way if he is the target of the analyst's hate (an object emotional communication) and another way if it is expressed as a feeling the analyst and the patient both share towards a third party (a narcissistic emotional communication). For this reason, relational mode is part of the essential description and definition of the total emotional communication, and is, at times, seemingly more important than the specific feeling.

Specific intensity is the third characteristic of an emotional communication. Each emotional communication has a distinct intensity, whether it is expressed overtly or implicitly. The intensity relates to the level of stimulation at which the emotion is being conveyed. The intensity plays a significant role in the impact of the emotional communication. It may change the meaning of the emotional communication and will certainly have an effect on how the patient makes use of the emotional communication.

Functions of cognitive and emotional communications

Functions of cognitive communications

Cognitive communications serve two primary functions in interventions:

1. conveying the analyst's understanding of the patient through interpretations;
2. supporting and clarifying emotional communications.

Perhaps the most prominent function of cognitive communication in psychoanalytic technique is its role in interpretation. Through interpretation, the analyst communicates his intellectual understanding of an aspect of the patient's intrapsychic or interpersonal world to him. The function of interpretation has been variously described: to make the unconscious conscious; to strengthen the ego in relation to the id; to reintegrate the patient's personality; and to catalyze insight and self-awareness – all of which are viewed as being responsible for the therapeutic action of psychoanalysis.

Interpretation was the first psychoanalytic technique, and more classically oriented analysts still argue that interpretation is the only genuine psychoanalytic technique. As we shall see, even classical interpretations are not purely cognitive communications. All verbal interpretations are accompanied by a specific type of emotional communication. However, the emotional communication serves a supportive role in interpretation; the cognitive communication is viewed as being the primary source of the interpretation's therapeutic impact.

In addition to its role in interpretation, cognitive communications also play an important role in non-interpretative psychoanalytic interventions in which they clarify and enhance the impact of emotional communications. In some types of interventions, the cognitive and the emotional communications are viewed as having an equal role in the intervention's therapeutic impact; in other types, the cognitive communication is a supportive role in the intervention.

Functions of emotional communications

Emotional communication serves four primary therapeutic functions within psychoanalytic treatment:

EMOTIONAL COMMUNICATION IN TECHNIQUE

1. activating the repetitions/transferences in the treatment;
2. meeting unmet maturational needs;
3. resolving specific types of defenses/resistances against experiencing and verbalizing feelings;
4. demonstrating the patient's emotional impact on the analyst.

Let's look at each of these specific functions in turn.

1. *Activating repetitions.* Freud's (1912) idea, that the analyst should be a blank screen to the patient, led to the notion that transference will spontaneously develop if the analyst provides a neutral environment in which he does not contribute his own personality. This creates a sort of Petri dish in which the patient's repetitions will bloom, without distortion, in a way that allows both the patient and the analyst to observe them. It was a brilliant idea, but it doesn't always work. Some patients will spontaneously develop a transference in a neutral emotional environment, while others will not. This is largely because the classical analytic stance of interested-but-largely-cool-neutrality is too foreign to the patient's emotional life history to be emotionally meaningful. For example, a patient with an extremely critical mother might be unable to form a maternal transference with an analyst who seems too neutral. The transference might only unfold if the analyst communicates something that the patient could experience as critical. Similarly, a highly emotional patient who is very expressive and experiences frequent mood shifts, might not be able to develop a narcissistic transference if the analyst is too stable, quiet, and reserved. Finally, a patient with strong anaclitic needs may be unable to develop an anaclitic transference with a neutral analyst who does not communicate nurturing feelings. But these transferences may become activated if the analyst makes emotional communications that resonate with a relevant aspect of the patient's repetition. Thus, the analyst might have to express mildly critical feelings to activate the object repetition in the woman who had a critical mother. Similarly, he might need to communicate caretaking feelings in the case of the patient who has strong anaclitic needs.

   In a more complex situation, which would only arise after a number of years, a patient may have spontaneously established a strong transference in which productive work was done, but had not ameliorated problematic areas in his life that were not related to the repetition that underlay that transference. Occasionally, it is possible to activate the other repetition by making relevant emotional communications. For example, suppose a patient had developed an object transference related to his critical mother and had worked through a number of issues related to this repetition. However, he might continue to have problems rooted in an anaclitic repetition that hadn't yet been activated by the analysis. Although he might no longer experience all women as being critical, he might continue to suffer from unmet dependency needs. Providing emotional communications that arouse the patient's dependency needs in the analysis might serve to bring that repetition into the analytic relationship in the form of anaclitic transference.

Some patients will not need emotional communications for either of these two purposes.[7] They have either found an analyst who actually resembles some aspect of the original environment enough to attach to them, or they experience the analyst as being sufficiently compelling through transferential distortion.

Or they may require emotional communications that serve the opposite function, at least in part. For example, a patient in a state of object transference or negative narcissistic transference may experience the analyst as being so consistent with his life history that he feels the need to flee treatment. In this case, the analyst might have to make strikingly warm communications to counteract the patient's "dread to repeat," in Ornstein's (1974: 231) beautiful phrase.

These types of cases notwithstanding, emotional communications can serve a crucial function in activating repetitions more effectively than a sort of one-size-fits-all neutral stance. However, it is important to note that emotional communications used in this way are not in themselves curative. They can create the emotional intensity necessary to allow a cure to take place, but they are only the beginning of the process, not the end.

2. *Meeting maturational needs.* This function is based on the idea that a central problem in most repetitions is that the patient did not experience the emotional communications from the parent(s) that he needed in order to grow and mature; consequently, the analyst must provide these still-needed emotional communications in order to restart the stalled maturational process.

The difference between a cognitive communication and an emotional communication is particularly clear in the case of maturational needs. A cognitive communication, related to maturational needs, will be an explanation of what was missing in the patient's development. For example, the analyst might tell the patient that the he seems to want the analyst to soothe him. The emotional communication, in contrast, can provide the soothing, thereby meeting the unmet need. As Balint (1968) put it, instead of a description of an object relation, the analyst provides an object relation.

Two basic types of maturational needs can be met through emotional communications: narcissistic needs and anaclitic needs.

Narcissistic needs include all needs related to merger, symbiosis, mirroring, twinship, and empathic attunement. The key feature common to all narcissistic needs is that the patient must feel that the analyst is similar to, the same as, an extension of, or merged with him, all of which can serve to stabilize, strengthen, or consolidate the patient's sense of self.

For example, the patient may be able to integrate his fearfulness of success into his self-experience and hence be less threatened by his fears. This is possible if the analyst communicates that he too is afraid of success in a way that the patient accepts being similar to his own experience. Narcissistic maturational needs are met through emotional communications that are expressed through the narcissistic relational mode.

Anaclitic needs, on the other hand, are related to dependency needs in relationship to a differentiated object. These are the needs related to soothing, nurturing, loving, appreciating, and all the other functions that the parent(s) serves in his capacity as a separate object. For example, the anxious patient might be soothed by the analyst reassuring him and speaking to him in a calming, loving tone of voice. Or the out-of-control patient might be helped to attain impulse control by limit-setting interventions. Anaclitic maturational needs are met through emotional communications in the differentiated anaclitic relational mode.

3. *Resolving specific types of defenses/resistances against experiencing and verbalizing feelings.* Certain defense/resistance configurations, particularly those involving self-hatred or introverted object aggression (the narcissistic defense), can be difficult to loosen without specific emotional communications that irritate the patient enough to overcome his deep-seated inhibition against experiencing and expressing aggression towards a valued other person (Spotnitz 1976). For example, in order to help the depressed patient both experience and express rageful disappointment with the progress of the analysis, the analyst blames himself for the patient's lack of progress in a way that provokes the patient to overcome his defense/resistance against experiencing and verbalizing anger.

4. *Demonstrating the patient's impact on the analyst.* An emotional communication can be used to demonstrate the patient's impact on the analyst. The purpose is to heighten the patient's awareness of how behavior affects other people, whether desirably or undesirably. For example, the analyst might express the frustration that he feels if every comment he makes is dismissed by the patient. Likewise, the analyst might express that he feels interested or intrigued by what the patient has expressed if indeed this is the effect that the patient actually has on him. Emotional communications made for this purpose are usually expressed explicitly in language – for example, "I'm feeling frustrated" – and are accompanied by a congruent affect.

Supporting and catalyzing the impact of an interpretation

Emotional communication serves another function that is a secondary, but still essential, source of therapeutic action – supporting and catalyzing the impact of interpretations. In a classical interpretation, the primary source of therapeutic action is the information conveyed by the interpretation. However, interpretations are inevitably accompanied by emotional communication, which can catalyze, neutralize, or counteract the therapeutic effect of the interpretation. When an emotional communication is curative, the patient has a greater ability to absorb and make use of the interpretation. When an emotional communication is neither curative nor toxic, the patient may understand and agree with the interpretation, but the impact is often superficial. When the emotional communication is toxic, the interpretation usually has no impact or is experienced as an attack. Occasionally, a patient can make use of an accurate interpretation despite a toxic emotional communication, but this is rare and does not usually have the same benefit as an interpretation created by a curative emotional communication.

Emotional communication and interventions

Targets of intervention: the afflicted ego and the reasonable ego

The patient is the target of the intervention, of course, but the patient can experience both his own internal experience and external reality – including the analyst's interventions – from two radically different perspectives: from the part of his mind that participates in the repetition and/or the part of his mind that observes it. Let's consider a patient who had extremely critical parents and developed a repetition of experiencing nearly everything anyone says to him as critical. If his wife asks him to pick up some groceries, he feels he is being criticized for not getting them earlier. If his boss compliments his work, he feels he is being criticized for all the work that the boss has not complimented. If someone steps on his toe in the subway, he feels it is a criticism for not watching his feet. He alternates between being hurt by the perceived criticisms and feeling rebelliously angry.

Much of the time, the patient knows that he exaggerates and that he expects and finds criticism where none is intended. He knows that people cannot possibly be as critical as he expects them to be, and he can jokingly make predictions about the terrible things that he thinks people will say about him and about what he will feel. He knows that these feelings are the long shadow of his early childhood in which it often seemed to be literally true that he could do nothing right.

But when he is in the grip of feeling criticized, he is engulfed by it and cannot think his way out of it. He experiences the feelings full on. With his wife, he alternates between being hurt and exploding with anger. At work, he just feels hurt and withdrawn. When he is under a lot of stress, for whatever reason, he can't step back and observe it. He relives the past in the present – sometimes knowing it is unreal, and at other times without the slightest sense that it is exaggerated.

One part of his mind can observe his repetition, while another part participates in it. The experiences are different, both cognitively and emotionally.

The different perspectives can be conceptualized as the experiences of two different aspects of his mind: the afflicted ego and the reasonable ego.

The afflicted ego[8] is the medium and the motor of the repetition – the part of the patient's mind that actively creates, maintains, and participates in the repetition. It experiences the specific feelings, through the relational mode, that define the repetition. It was shaped by the intrapsychic and interpersonal circumstances in which the repetition was formed and comprises the feelings, fantasies, memories, and defenses that make up the repetition. It views the present world and reacts to it through the template of this earlier time. It is the aspect of the mind that recreates the past through the mechanisms that have been previously discussed – distortion of the present; attraction towards people and situations reminiscent of the past; and emotional induction. Objective countertransference is a product of the afflicted ego, and the afflicted ego relates to the world and experiences the world in all relational modes except the present-anchored.

The afflicted ego is rational within the context of the original interpersonal and intrapsychic circumstances in which the repetition arose, but may be irrational (or non-rational) in the context of the present. For example, a patient who was constantly criticized as a child might experience all comments about him as critical. This may be untrue in the present, but makes sense to the extent that the patient's afflicted ego is still living in the past.

The afflicted ego is partly conscious and partly unconscious. In both cases, it functions compulsively and involuntarily. All patients have an afflicted ego because everyone engages in repetitions that are, to some extent, maladaptive. However, it is sometimes difficult to access the afflicted ego in patients who have strong reality-oriented defenses or defenses that work extremely well in the present.

The reasonable ego (Greenson 1967) is the part of the mind that is oriented to the reality of the present and is rational in the context of the present. It experiences the repetition as irrational and it has (or can develop through psychoanalysis) the capacity to stand outside of and consciously observe the repetition. It can experience some degree of emotional and cognitive distance from the feelings and the relational mode that define the repetition. In the case of the patient who was criticized as a child, the reasonable ego would be the part of his mind that is able to step back and recognize that not everything people say to him is critical. The reasonable ego is more conscious and preconscious than unconscious. Depending on its strength, it can exert a degree of conscious control over the experience and/or the behavior that characterizes the repetition.

The reasonable ego has another function that is relevant to psychoanalytic technique: the ability to make use of insight and self-awareness to control and master the repetitions emanating from the afflicted ego.

Feelings can also be induced by the reasonable ego, but they are not grounded in repetitions. Inductions emanating from the reasonable ego are the unverbalized dimensions of the patient's here-and-now feelings. Inductions from the reasonable ego are most fruitfully viewed as moments of present-anchored relating. They may contain mildly narcissistic or anaclitic moments. These are not rooted in unmet developmental needs but rather in the ways in which narcissistic and anaclitic experiences are part of the fabric of mature present-anchored functioning.

All patients, except (perhaps) those in certain severe psychotic states, have a reasonable ego. However, it varies both in the degree to which its ability to self-observe is developed and in its strength in relationship to the afflicted ego. These two qualities are not necessarily related. Some patients have a reasonable ego that is well developed in self-observation but weak in relationship to the afflicted ego. Some patients are aware of the disparity between what they experience in the repetition and the reality of the present – and may even have insight into why this occurs – but this awareness does not enable them to overcome the repetition. Consider a patient with a snake phobia that has its roots in a fear of sexuality. Sometimes, it is possible that the patient has a reasonable ego that is able to observe and understand the origin of the phobia, but for this to have no effect on his ability to control the feelings associated with the phobia. His reasonable ego is weak in relationship to the afflicted ego. On the other hand, some patients have a reasonable ego that is strong in relationship to the afflicted ego but not well developed in its ability to self-observe. Such a patient might have no awareness of why he is afraid of snakes but can use insight into its meaning to dramatically change his experience of the fear and to strengthen his ability to control it. Finally, there are some patients who have a high degree of self-observation and a reasonable ego that can exert considerable control over the afflicted ego.[9]

The distinction between the afflicted ego and the reasonable ego is not absolute; there is always a degree of interpenetration between the two. It is rare for the afflicted ego to be completely without any measure of self-observation, and the reasonable ego is never fully rooted in the here-and-now. They should be viewed as metaphors, not sharply defined entities.[10] Nevertheless, they do describe a duality in human experience. At any given moment in time, one of the egos might be the dominant mode of conscious experience or both may be functioning simultaneously.

These concepts highlight the complexity of the patient's experience – including the different ways the patient might experience the same intervention – depending on which aspect of the mind is dominant at that point in the treatment. For example, an interpretation addressed to the reasonable ego might be experienced as critical, rejecting, or alien if the patient's afflicted ego is foremost in his relationship to the analyst. Conversely, a non-rational emotional communication to the afflicted ego may be experienced as crazy, mocking, or ridiculous at times when the patient's reasonable ego is dominant.

Communications to the different egos engage the repetition differently. Communications to the reasonable ego are always about the repetition. They

EMOTIONAL COMMUNICATION IN TECHNIQUE

are observations made at a distance from the immediate experience of the repetition and address the repetition from the outside. Communications to the afflicted ego, on the other hand, engage the repetition directly, and have their impact within the emotional logic of the repetition.

It might first appear that cognitive communications are made primarily to the reasonable ego and emotional communications to the afflicted ego, but this is not exactly correct. Both cognitive and emotional communications can be made to both egos, but again, they function differently in each case.

Cognitive communications to the reasonable ego tend to be rational and reality oriented. They may communicate information about the afflicted ego, the analyst's understanding of the patient's feelings or life story, and/or the analyst's perceptions or feelings, instructions, suggestions, or requests. These communications are straightforward and intended to be understood literally. Some examples of cognitive communications to the reasonable ego would include the following statements:

> "You seem to have felt some anger towards your father."
>
> "I sometimes feel anxious when you talk about your mother; do you have any idea why that might occur?"
>
> "Please tell me more about that."

Cognitive interventions to the afflicted ego, on the other hand, are grounded in the logic of the repetition. They may sound rational, but they may also sound irrational (or non-rational) in the context of the present reality because they address the part of the mind that is still living in the period in which the repetition was formed. They do not convey information as much as they communicate that the analyst understands the patient's emotional logic. If they sound paradoxical, it is because they are attempts to communicate with the thinking and feeling processes of the afflicted ego on its own terms, which may be contradictory to what the patient wants and feels in his reasonable ego. Examples of cognitive communications to the afflicted ego include the following statements:

> "Why would you want to go on a diet? You might starve to death."
>
> "Of course you would want your daughter to worship you; isn't that what children are for?'
>
> "I should probably be treating you for free; only my selfishness prevents it."

Notice that cognitive communications to the afflicted ego are based on an interpretation and can be said to contain interpretative content. For example, let's consider the first example. The comment, "You might starve to death," is based on the interpretation that the patient believes that he will starve to death. The intervention puts the patient's feeling into words but not in a way that is designed to help the patient examine the feeling at a distance. Furthermore, the first part of the intervention, "Why would you want to go on a diet?" conveys that the analyst agrees that the patient's perception is right – within the emotional logic of the repetition – something very different than a simple explanation of the patient's feelings.

Emotional communications to the reasonable ego cover a limited range of feelings: empathic sympathy for the pain that the repetition causes the patient; empathic sympathy for real-life stresses the patient experiences; and support and solidarity with the patient's present-oriented goal of mastering the repetition or dealing with real-life issues. These types of emotional communications do not directly engage the feelings that make up the repetition. For example, if the analyst expresses empathy with the criticized patient's reasonable ego, he expresses understanding of the pain involved in having to cope with this irrational reaction to everyone and the limitations this places upon him.

The relational mode of the emotional communication to the reasonable ego may be mildly anaclitic or narcissistic, or it may be present-anchored. In any event, it is not derived from the feelings that make up the repetition. They are derived from the analyst's feelings towards the patient as an adult – albeit an adult that is enduring the pain of the repetition.

In contrast, emotional communications to the afflicted ego can cover the entire spectrum of human feelings, at all intensities, and may be made in all relational modes. If the analyst expresses empathy with the criticized patient's afflicted ego, it is empathy with the pain and injustice of being criticized as a real here-and-now experience, not with the pain of being burdened with this irrational reaction. Because the patient's afflicted ego experiences the world within the confines of the repetition, emotional communications to the afflicted ego make use of feelings that make sense within the repetition. These communications may appear to be irrational, unrealistic, or exaggerated by the standards of the present.

Types of interventions

There are two basic types of interventions: expressive and containment. Expressive interventions include all non-silent communications in which the analyst overtly says something to the patient. Expressive interventions combine emotional communication with cognitive communication. Containment is a silent intervention in which the analyst consciously experiences a feeling but does not deliberately express it verbally or through any overt non-verbal channel (Bion 1963).[11] Containment interventions are composed solely of emotional communication.

EMOTIONAL COMMUNICATION IN TECHNIQUE

Expressive interventions

Unlike containment, expressive interventions have two components: a cognitive communication and an emotional communication.

As in all verbal communications, the cognitive and the emotional communications are intertwined in expressive interventions. They may convey complementary meanings, different meanings, or contradictory meanings. When they convey complementary meanings, they may support and reinforce each other. When they convey different meanings, two communications may be made simultaneously. And when they convey contradictory meanings, they tend to subvert each other.

In some interventions, the cognitive and the emotional communications both address the same ego. However, each can simultaneously address a different ego – a different part of the patient's mind. Different types of interventions can be classified according to the way the cognitive and emotional communications combine to address the patient. There are three possible combinations:

1. Cognitive and emotional communications both address the reasonable ego.
2. Cognitive communication addresses the reasonable ego; the emotional communication addresses the afflicted ego.
3. Cognitive and emotional communications both address the afflicted ego.

Let's look at a few brief examples of each combination to see how different types of interventions can be formulated.

Cognitive and emotional communications both address the reasonable ego. This is the structure of the classical interpretation – the original psychoanalytic intervention. The cognitive communication conveys the analyst's understanding of some aspect of the patient's intrapsychic or interpersonal experience. This might be the nature of a defense or an impulse, a description of a self-state, the relationship of a current symptom to earlier events in his life, or any other feature of the patient's emotional life. The emotional communication is designed to support and help the patient understand and make use of the cognitive communication and is usually mildly empathic or sympathetic with a low intensity. The purpose of a classical interpretation is to stimulate insight, self-understanding, and self-awareness in the patient, thereby strengthening the reasonable ego over the afflicted ego. Examples of these types of interpretations are listed below:

> "The banana in the dream represents your father's penis."
>
> "The fact that you did not realize that I was pregnant suggests that you have been denying something very important about me."
>
> "You feel like you disintegrate when you feel envy."

The information the analyst conveys in the cognitive communication is considered to be the source of the interpretation's therapeutic leverage. This type of intervention can also meet a narrow range of maturational needs related to anaclitic needs for teaching and guidance in self-awareness. The emotional communication supports and reinforces the cognitive communication; nevertheless, the interpretation usually fails if the emotional communication is not curative.

Cognitive communication addresses the reasonable ego; the emotional communication addresses the afflicted ego. This type of intervention is designed to address both egos equally, thus providing interpretations or other sorts of interpretative communications to the reasonable ego, coupled with an emotional communication to the afflicted ego. The cognitive and the emotional components are viewed as being equally important. Their purpose is to strengthen the reasonable ego and the patient's self-awareness while simultaneously meeting maturational needs. One example would be a cognitive description of a feeling combined with a strongly empathic emotional communication expressed both in the words and in the tone. For example, the analyst might say, "I get the sense that you want to kill your husband when he doesn't listen to you. It's enraging to be ignored like that!" This would be delivered in a tone that conveys the intensity of the anger and the murderous wish to demonstrate that the analyst would feel the same feeling and approves of it. Other examples of this type of intervention are described below:

> *"That must have been very shaming for you."* (Delivered with deliberate warmth and empathy for the part of the patient's mind that feels the shame, even if it is excessive or irrational by the standards of the reasonable ego.)
>
> *"You feel like if you don't make money you could actually starve to death."* (Delivered in a tone that mirrors the patient's anxiety about not having enough money and his determination to avoid starvation and also accepts the feeling as realistic in the context of the patient's worldview.)

In these examples, the cognitive and the emotional communications are largely congruent and address basically the same feelings – and hence the same repetition – with each ego.

However, an intervention can also target two different repetitions simultaneously: the emotional communication addressed to the afflicted ego targets one repetition, and cognitive communication addresses another in the reasonable ego. This is used primarily when the content of the session is incongruent with the induction, which suggests that the repetition activated in the afflicted ego is strongly unconscious and split off from the patient's conscious experience. Here, the reasonable ego is unable to observe the afflicted ego or the repetition.

For example, the patient complains about his wife's temper, which the analyst understands to be a repetition related to his mother. However, this repetition has never been active in the treatment relationship. It is not part of the transference, and the analyst has not experienced any inductions related to that repetition. The induction he does experience is a desire to protect and soothe the patient, which he understands to be an anaclitic countertransference induced by the patient's unmet anaclitic needs – an anaclitic transference. According to this analysis, the patient has verbalized one group of feelings but induced a different group of feelings. The analyst decides to interpret the patient's feelings about his wife in connection with his mother, but his emotional communication is protective and soothing. Thus, his cognitive communication addresses the reasonable ego, while his emotional communication addresses the afflicted ego and the unconscious transference that underlies the content of the session. No effort is made, in this sort of intervention, to make the patient aware of or understand the nature of the transference. The curative leverage is usually seen to lie in the emotional communication, with the cognitive communication serving primarily to keep the patient consciously engaged in the relationship while absorbing the emotional communication.

Cognitive and emotional communications both address the afflicted ego. This type of intervention is addressed solely to the afflicted ego. It is intended to override the reasonable ego's objections to the afflicted ego's irrationality and communicate with the afflicted ego on its own terms. Although these interventions do not always sound irrational, they are always grounded in the emotional reality of the repetition and the conditions under which it was formed, not the conditions of present-day reality. The cognitive communication primarily serves to support and highlight the emotional communication. The intervention is designed to activate repetitions, to meet maturational needs, or to unblock defended feelings. Although the patient may develop insight or self-awareness as a result of this type of intervention, this is considered to be the result of the intervention, but not the source of its therapeutic action. Here are a few examples:

"That was an impressive accomplishment." (Delivered in a tone of deep admiration and/or pride.)

"You are wise not to speak in class; people might become envious of you." (Delivered in a tone that reflects the patient's own fear and endorses his conclusion that the fear is a legitimate reason to be silent, viewed from within the perspective of the repetition, of course.)

"I'm a pretty stupid analyst. It's no wonder you aren't making any progress." (Delivered in a mildly provocative, matter-of-fact tone designed to agree with the patient's feeling that the analyst is stupid and designed to help the patient to be more critical of the analyst.)

Containment

Expressive interventions can be used to address the transference whenever the patient can understand, absorb, or in some other way make use of an overt communication — cognitive or emotional, direct or indirect — about the transference. However, expressive interventions always risk disrupting defenses before the patient is able to tolerate the feelings connected with the transference, which can lead to excessive and unmanageable levels of anxiety, anger, depression, or sexual stimulation. The fragility of the defenses, connected with the transference active at the moment, usually determines whether the patient will be able to make use of an expressive intervention. The more fragile the defenses, the less likely it is that the patient will be able to make use of an expressive intervention.

For example, suppose the patient says that he hasn't paid his friend some money that he owes him, and the analyst has the distinct sense that he is not paying because he is angry at the friend. Then the analyst remembers that the patient is late in paying him; he hypothesizes that the patient is angry at him in the same way he is angry at his friend. However, the analyst knows that the patient is strongly defended against any direct expression of anger at the analyst and tends to attack himself when the analyst has made any reference to the possibility. For this reason, he thinks that he will disrupt the patient's defenses if he makes any reference, explicit or implicit, to the possibility that the patient is angry at him.

Containment is used when the patient cannot tolerate any verbal reference, cognitive or emotional, to a feeling that has been induced in the analyst. In containment, the analyst experiences a countertransference feeling consciously, but does not express the feeling to the patient, directly or indirectly. For example, an analyst who contains feelings of irritation at the patient does not convey the irritation through words, tone, or allusions. Containment operates purely through silence.

When the analyst successfully contains an objective countertransference feeling, the patient and the analyst are attuned. The patient's message has gotten through to the analyst, and the analyst's silence conveys a subtle emotional communication to the patient that could not have occurred had the analyst not experienced the contained feeling. It is an induction from the analyst to the patient that he has received the feeling but is not acting upon it. When the patient needs containment, and the analyst provides it, they repeat an old feeling, but the interaction leads to a different outcome than what the patient usually experiences when he induces that feeling. For example, suppose the patient's repetition is to induce the intense anxiety he feels in those around him, which usually leads them to defend against it by telling him what to do. For the analyst to contain the anxiety, without repeating the typical behavior, is a completely new interaction that may allow the patient to verbalize and tolerate the anxiety himself, and it may provide the opportunity for the patient to have a new type of interpersonal interaction than the one that usually arises when he is anxious.

Most of the emphasis in this book and throughout the literature on technique is on expressive interventions. Nevertheless, containment is one of the most profoundly curative factors in psychoanalysis. The analyst's ability to feel the patient's inductions, to hear the seductive song of the repetition – and remain unwilling to respond in kind, is an experience the patient will have with few other people in his life.

Although containment is a silent intervention, it doesn't require silence to work. Containment can work in the background while the analyst makes an expressive intervention that conveys a cognitive communication or an emotional communication that is different than the feeling being contained. Indeed, expressive interventions are almost always layered upon a contained feeling, except in the rare situation where the analyst communicates his feelings undiluted, in language, to the patient.

Consider the following situation: the patient has a two-part repetition related to men. She gets sexually exploited when she seeks help from men, and she gets involved with rageful men who terrify her. Both parts are derived, fairly obviously, from interactions with her father: he was seductive with her when he was helpful and aggressively abusive when he was angry.

The patient tearfully tells the analyst that she has a problem with her landlord, who has threatened her with eviction. On a cognitive level, the analyst thinks that she needs to understand the intensity of her fear of the landlord in the context of her relationship with her father and wants to interpret this to her. However, he also feels the pull of the other side of the repetition: he's sexually aroused by her tears and her appeals for help. One part of the repetition is active with the landlord, and the other part is active with the analyst. In addition, he has a non-sexualized feeling to instruct and protect her – an anaclitic feeling induced by the need for protection that was unmet by the father. He thinks that any reference to the sexual repetition between them, at this point, would be traumatic for her. In this case, he makes the interpretation about her landlord and her father, being supportive and sympathetic in his expressed emotional communication, while carefully containing the sexual feelings. Thus, this intervention has three components: a cognitive intervention – an interpretation addressed to the reasonable ego; an expressed but indirect anaclitic emotional communication addressed to part of her afflicted ego; and a contained feeling of sexual arousal, which was rooted in an induction from a different aspect of her afflicted ego.

Would the intervention be equally effective if the analyst did not, for subjective reasons, experience the sexual feelings – if the patient attempted to induce them, and the analyst was not receptive? Of course, we can never know for sure, but I suspect not. For the analyst to feel the sexual feelings and not act upon them is a different interpersonal interaction and a different communication than if he was unresponsive because he had not experienced them at all. In the former case, he is emotionally attuned to the patient; in the latter case, he is not.

In general, containment interventions are less risky than expressive interventions. Nevertheless, no intervention is risk-free. Some patients are not sensitive to the subtlety of containment, and some analysts cannot consciously use containment to induce strong enough feelings that patients can consistently feel. In either of these situations, containment can cause the patient to feel emotionally unheard or abandoned, and the analyst is forced to rely on expressive interventions. Similarly, containment can cause a patient to feel that the analyst is unresponsive if he needs an expressive intervention, and the analyst provides only containment.

Characteristics of curative emotional communications

Having considered the functions that emotional communication plays in the analytic process, let's move on to an examination of the general characteristics of curative emotional communications. More simply put: what feelings does the patient need to receive from the analyst to loosen the repetitions? Unfortunately, neither the particular feelings, nor a particular type of emotional climate[12] can be prescribed in advance because this is completely dependent upon the individual patient's needs. One patient might need a neutral overall environment, peppered with warm supportive moments, while another might need a warm, supportive environment, punctuated by coldness or even frank hostility. Any combination is possible. In general, however, one can say that the analytic relationship should be similar enough to the original interaction to be compelling but different enough to be curative.[13]

Let's unpack this dictum. The first part is based on the idea that the repetitions cannot be activated in the treatment with curative intensity without some degree of real similarity between the analytic relationship and a relevant aspect of the patient's original emotional environment. When this similarity is missing, nothing much happens in the analysis. The patient and the analyst are like a couple on a blind date with no chemistry. There's no juice, no draw, no passion. If the absence is obvious from the start, the patient may leave. If he does stay, the relationship may or may not be pleasant, but the experience tends to be superficial and intellectualized. Because the emotional forces that drive the patient's repetitions aren't mobilized, his relationship with the analyst stays cut off from the main currents of his emotional life. Consequently, the analyst often has no particular feelings about the patient beyond professional concern – a necessary, but far from sufficient, component of the work.

The second part is more obvious. If the analysis is not different enough from the original environment, if it is nothing more than a similar and compelling repetition, no cure takes place. At best, the analysis is more of the same – another in the ongoing series of painful, frustrating repetitions. At worst, the analytic repetition, which can be as potent as the original relationship with the parents, is malignant – re-traumatizing the patient and driving him into even more painful patterns of relating than those he brought to the analysis. It is for these reasons that emotional communications will be different enough, from the original interactions, in a way that either meets maturational needs or resolves certain defensive patterns.

Specific characteristics of curative emotional communications

Now that we have considered the most general features of a curative emotional environment, let's consider the qualities of particular curative emotional communications. I have found that a curative emotional communication is characterized by the following features:

- a response to an active transference;
- based on an accurate understanding of the specific feeling and the relational mode that characterize the transference;
- communicates a specific feeling, in a specific relational mode, at a specific intensity that activates a repetition, meets a maturational need, or unblocks specific defensive patterns.[14]

Let's consider each characteristic of a curative emotional communication, in turn.

A curative emotional communication addresses an active transference. A curative emotional communication is a response to a transference that is active, in the moment, in the analytic relationship.[15] In other words, the analyst does not simply provide particular emotional communications because they are generally curative but rather because they are in response to how the patient is experiencing him, as a partner in the repetition, in the moment. If, for example, the active transference is narcissistic, the patient experiences the analyst as being like him, a part of him, or fused with him in some way. If the active transference is anaclitic, the patient experiences the analyst as someone who can meet his dependency needs.

How do you identify an active transference? It is easiest when the content of the session – what the patient says and does – is congruent with the countertransference, in the sense that both convey essentially the same message. For example, the patient may describe countless instances of people who hate him; the countertransference would be congruent if the analyst feels the same way. This suggests that the patient's repetition of inducing people to hate him is active in the transference, at that moment. A curative emotional communication would be a response to this transference.

Things are more complex when the countertransference is incongruent with the content. Suppose the patient describes countless examples of people who hate him, while the analyst feels only loving feelings towards him. What is going on here? There are two possibilities. The first is that the dimension of the transference that is inducing the loving feelings is unconscious, and the patient has strong defenses against consciously experiencing the feelings associated with it. The other, of course, is that the analyst is experiencing a subjective countertransference – an idiosyncratic, personal reaction that has nothing to do with the patient. (Maybe the analyst is attracted to people that most people hate, or the analyst is simply out of touch with who the patient really is.)

However, I suggest that in the absence of clear and convincing evidence that the countertransference is subjective, the countertransference – and not the content of the session – is the more reliable guide to the active transference. Thus, the analyst's first hypothesis should be that the incongruent countertransference is a product of the unconscious transference. In the example of the analyst who loves the patient whom everyone else hates, the analyst's first hypothesis should be the repetition that the patient describes in his outside life: an object repetition of inducing people to hate him is not active in the transference. Rather, an anaclitic transference is active – one that is incongruent with the content – and the curative emotional communication must address this transference. Given this, even if the curative emotional communication must address the unconscious transference, the analyst must remember that there are strong defenses against this transference. Consequently, the emotional communication should probably not be too direct or it will require containment.

Now, let's consider some more complex cases, putting all of these ideas together. In this first case, the patient complains bitterly about everyone in his life but never directly to the person who disappoints him, which is consistent with the fact that he has never expressed complaints to the analyst about his performance either. In a new development, however, he is complaining, ever so tentatively, to the analyst, who he feels has let him down. The analyst feels attacked, defensive, and enraged. This countertransference is directly congruent with the content of the session – the patient's intense complaints about others. It is also largely congruent with the patient's complaint towards the analyst. Moreover, the countertransference feeling of being attacked is far more intense than the patient's direct complaints, which suggests that the patient isn't complaining nearly as intensely as he needs to. Therefore, the analyst's first hypothesis is that the active transference – the issue of the moment – is a negative object transference rooted in the patient's anger at the analyst.

Still, the analyst isn't entirely sure about the hypothesis and considers a different one that has worked in the past: the patient is in an anaclitic transference and needs to be soothed. He makes an anaclitic intervention, trying to soothe the patient, by telling him how difficult and frustrating the work of analysis can be. The patient momentarily stops complaining but sounds slightly more aggravated. Then, the analyst makes an emotional communication attuned to the patient's need to express more anger. Within the context of a negative object transference, he says, "I must be doing a pretty poor job for you to continue to feel so frustrated," blaming himself for the patient's lack of progress, and thus making himself an attractive target for the patient's aggression. The patient's rage begins to flow. Despite the analyst's initial hesitation, the active relevant transference was congruent with the countertransference.

Now, on to a similar case but one with a twist. This patient also complains bitterly about everyone in his life – except for the analyst. In fact, he has never complained about the analyst, nor does the analyst feel attacked. Instead, he agrees with most of the patient's complaints. What, then, is a therapeutically relevant transference in this instance?

Here, we will consider three of the most likely possibilities, keeping in mind that there are more.

First, the patient feels that the analyst implicitly agrees with him, sees his point of view, and is strengthened by the feeling that the analyst understands him. He really isn't angry at the analyst in the transference, even if he is angry at the rest of the world. In this case, we would have a narcissistic transference. This possibility is supported by the countertransference where the analyst is in agreement with the patient.

Second, the situation is the same as in the first case. Again, the patient is bitterly angry with the analyst, but has stronger defenses (resistances) against expressing this to the analyst, so he expresses it in a displaced way towards others. This, again, would be object transference. There is nothing in the countertransference to support this hypothesis. This is not definitive; the patient's defenses may be so strong that the patient does not allow him even to induce the feeling.

Third, the patient is deeply agitated and seeks to be soothed by the analyst. He's not angry with the analyst, but he doesn't need to have his worldview reflected, either. This would an anaclitic transference. This hypothesis is supported by the fact that the analyst has often soothed the patient in the past. This time, however, the analyst does not feel like soothing the patient.

Thus, we have three hypotheses, based on three repetitions the analyst has identified in the patient's life. He initially makes an intervention based on the second hypothesis – that the patient is actually very angry with the analyst – and again blames himself for the patient's lack of progress. But this time, the patient just seems confused by it. Next, the analyst makes an intervention based on the anaclitic hypothesis and attempts to soothe the patient's anger. The patient, however, is unmoved by the analyst's soft talking. "Yes, yes," he says impatiently, "but the fact is that the situation is an outrage." Finally, our bungling analyst (maybe he's having a bad day) goes back to the countertransference, makes an intervention based on the first hypothesis – that the transference is narcissistic – and intervenes by expressing explicit agreement with the patient's complaints. The patient says, "Thank you; at least someone gets it!" and the level of tension noticeably lowers.

This response suggests that the first hypothesis was correct: the countertransference, which was narcissistic, was congruent with the active transference, which was also narcissistic. Although the anaclitic and object repetitions were active in the patient's life, they were not active in the analysis at that moment; emotional communications based on these repetitions did not have a curative impact. It is possible that addressing them through the cognitive communication – in the form of an interpretation – might have some intellectual impact on the patient, but this would be less likely to have a profound emotional impact. The narcissistic transference is emotionally meaningful at this point in the analysis; consequently, this is where the analyst's emotional leverage lies.

In both of these cases, what I have suggested should be the first hypothesis – that countertransference is the most likely indicator of the transference – is correct. Alas, the analysis isn't always so straightforward, and the first hypothesis is not always correct. In light of this, let's look at another situation. Like the second case, the patient complains about everyone except the analyst, and the analyst agrees with the patient, but, like the first case, the analyst does feel attacked. Focusing on the countertransference, the analyst decides to go with the first hypothesis: based on the countertransference, the therapeutically relevant transference is the anger towards the analyst. He intervenes as he did in the first case: he criticizes himself for the patient's lack of progress to encourage the patient to attack him. This time, however, the patient feels misunderstood and begins to criticize himself – holding himself responsible for his own lack of progress.

What happened? The analyst, in this case, went with his first hypothesis – the countertransference was a product of the unconscious transference – and formulated his emotional communication as a reaction to that transference. And he may have been right. However, he did not sufficiently take into account that his feeling of being attacked was partially incongruent with the content. After all, the patient did not say, or even explicitly hint, that he was angry at the analyst. This suggests that defenses were operating and that the patient might not be able to work with this emotional communication directly, even if its motivating theory was correct. This was confirmed when the patient responded to the analyst's invitation to attack him by attacking himself instead, which suggests that the narcissistic defense was operating. Anger at the analyst is there, but the patient is not ready to express it.

However, once the analyst realizes his mistake, he decides to contain his feeling of being attacked. He refrains from making any reference to the patient's anger towards him. Instead, he makes an intervention related to the narcissistic dimensions of the communication by explicitly agreeing with the patient's anger. This intervention makes the patient feel understood and strengthened.

This third case has two active transferences: narcissistic and object. The narcissistic transference is not defended, while the object transference is heavily defended. Both transferences, however, must be addressed – the narcissistic transference through an expressive intervention and the object transference through containment.

A curative emotional communication is derived from an accurate understanding of the specific feeling and the relational mode that characterizes the transference. A transference, like all emotional moments, is composed of a specific feeling and a specific relational mode. To understand the transference is to understand both of its essential dimensions. Let's return to our example of the bitterly complaining man who feels that his analyst agrees with his anger. To address this transference, the analyst must first understand the nature of the patient's anger, that is, the specific quality of his feelings. Is it righteous anger or helpless anger? Does it grow out of entitled disappointment or hopeless disappointment? Is he angry because others are not like him, because they are like him, or for some other reason altogether? His anger may contain just one particular shade, or it may be a combination. But whatever it is, the analyst must understand it in its specificity.

Similarly – and equally important – the analyst must understand the specific relational mode through which the patient experiences him. The interventions will be experienced differently if the patient experiences the analyst as being like himself, as opposed to being different. And within the spectrum of experiencing the analyst as being like himself, does the patient experience him as being similar to, merged with, or part of him or just sharing his feelings empathically? If the analyst is like him, does he like the analyst the way he likes himself or hate the analyst the way he hates himself?

A curative emotional communication is based on an understanding of the transference in detail, not just in general, because patients experience specific feelings, not general feelings. And as we shall see, the specific aspects of the transference must be targeted with equally specific communications from the analyst to loosen the repetition.

A curative emotional communication communicates a specific feeling, in a specific relational mode, at a specific intensity that activates a repetition, meets a maturational need or unblocks specific defensive patterns. In order to be effective, an intervention must be therapeutically attuned to the patient's transference, which means it must be attuned to both the feeling and the relational mode. To be attuned to the patient's countertransference means that the specific feeling the analyst communicates is one that the patient needs to experience from the analyst and is communicated in a relational mode that the patient can use and understand at that particular point in the treatment.

Attunement, however, does not mean that the specific feeling or the relational mode should be the same as the transference. Sometimes they should be, but sometimes they must be different. Unfortunately, there is no way of knowing in advance. For example, let's go back to the case about the bitterly complaining man who experiences an object transference and needs to verbalize his anger directly to the analyst. The analyst's intervention must be made through the relational mode that allows the patient to get angry with him, as a separate object. If the analyst communicates that he is the same as the patient, this may not allow the patient to feel separate enough from the analyst to be able to express aggression towards him, which is crucial to him at this point. And if the analyst relates as a caretaking anaclitic object, then he is not the disappointing object of the patient's transference – the disappointing object he needs to attack in order to overcome this repetition.

Simultaneously, the analyst's intervention must communicate a specific feeling that allows the patient to express his anger. If the analyst appears too nice, the patient may feel that it is unreasonable to attack him. If he appears too fragile, the patient may be afraid of attacking him for fear of harming him. If he appears too neutral, the patient may be unable to express anger because the encounter isn't similar enough to be compelling and lacks emotional reality. And if he appears too aggressive or too retaliatory, the patient may be inhibited for fear that the analyst will hurt him. The analyst, therefore, must communicate a specific cluster of feelings: that he is a reasonable target for the patient's anger; that he will not be harmed by the anger; that he cares; and that he will not retaliate.

This description might sound like an ideal emotional communication to allow anyone to express anger. But it's not. First, let's consider the relational mode: not all patients need to express anger towards a separate object. Some need to express anger to a mirror image of themselves – a negative narcissistic transference – to deflect their self-attack away from themselves. Others cannot tolerate the anger at all and need to expel it into the other person through a projective identification.

Next, let's consider the specific feeling that the analyst communicates. Some patients need to feel that the analyst is retaliatory so that they can have the experience of challenging a dangerous, hostile object. Others might need the analyst to be nice: their transference is rooted in anger at a nice object, and they need to be able to express the anger, despite the object's niceness.

In theory, almost any combination of feelings and relational mode is possible. In practice, the analyst must find a specific combination that the individual patient needs at the particular point where the transference is active in the analysis. And as noted earlier, this emotional communication will have to be both similar enough to the original interaction to be compelling but different enough to be curative. Greater detail than this cannot be specified in advance.

It is possible – even probable – that more than one combination of feeling and relational mode will meet one of the three possible functions of an emotional communication at any given point in time. However, a communication that is not attuned to the specific dimension of the transference that the analyst is attempting to address will be unlikely to have the intended impact[16] because it is actually addressing a different aspect of the transference or a different transference.

Misattunement

What happens when the emotional communication is not attuned to the patient's need, in either the specific feeling or the relational mode? It varies considerably. In non-interpretive interventions, mild emotional misattunement may leave the patient feeling misunderstood; the intervention can feel irrelevant to what he has been saying or experiencing. When the intervention is an interpretation, and the emotional attunement is only a little off, the intervention may feel (and be) helpful, but the experience tends to be abstract and intellectual. The interpretation doesn't sink in on the emotional level in a way that loosens the repetition. This is often at the root of the patient's complaint: "I understand what I do, but it doesn't help me to change it."

When the attunement is further off, the emotional intensity of the transference often increases, as if the patient is talking louder in response to not being heard. For example, a patient in a narcissistic transference characterized by feeling the analyst is his twin might become more insistent on seeing the analyst as being just like him. When this occurs, the patient is frequently described as being more "resistant." Resistance often increases when the analyst has not provided the curative emotional communication, which aggravates the patient's desperation to get the response he is seeking. On the other hand, sometimes the intensity of the transference diminishes, and the patient emotionally withdraws. The lack of attuned response from the analyst causes the patient to relinquish a measure of investment in the analytic relationship because the analyst has become too dissimilar to be compelling, or the frustration of not getting through has become too high to be tolerated.

Furthermore, emotional communications that are misattuned to the curative relational mode often stimulate some of the following typical reactions.

Narcissistic misattunement

When the patient needs a narcissistic emotional communication, and does not receive it, he commonly feels either narcissistically depleted or insulted. When depleted, the patient may become depressed and withdrawn or more self-absorbed in a disconnected, exhausted way. Sometimes, the patient's communication becomes confused; his thinking becomes fragmented and dissociation or depersonalization may arise (Kohut & Wolf 1978).

Narcissistic rage, on the other hand, is a frequent reaction when the patient feels insulted by the lack of narcissistic attunement. In its mildest form, the patient withdraws in an arrogant way and makes a point of insisting – in complete contrast to his previous transferential strivings – on his difference from the analyst. When narcissistic rage is more intense, the patient can become openly indignant, contemptuous, attacking, or emotionally abusive.

Interpretations that are not narcissistically attuned to the patient, or whose content disrupts the narcissistic transference, are often experienced as attacks.

The patient may become paranoid, or feel that the analyst simply doesn't understand him in a global way.

Object misattunement

When the patient needs an object response from the analyst and doesn't get it, the most typical response is an intensification of the transference that continues until the analyst responds in kind. Furthermore, the transference may become more rigid and stereotypical in his transferential position. For instance, suppose the patient feels that the analyst is cold and needs to fully experience and express anger at a cold object in order to loosen the repetition. If the analyst responds with an interpretation framed in an empathic, narcissistic mode – "It must be really hard for you to feel that I'm so cold and uncaring" – it is possible that the patient will become more insistent with his complaints about the analyst, even as the analyst is doing the opposite. Furthermore, if the patient specifically needs a response that will help him to express anger towards the analyst as a separate object and does not get it, he is likely to lapse into a self-attacking state and become filled with self-hatred. These types of situations often provide the analyst with an impressive demonstration of the tenacity of the patient's repetition because the patient's response to what the analyst hopes will be a "different enough" emotional communication is to become more entrenched in the object repetition.

Anaclitic misattunement

When the patient needs an anaclitic response and doesn't receive it, the effects are similar to the depletion reaction in narcissistic states (as described above). Further, if the patient feels more deprived and hopeless, he may lose his initiative and motivation to get better, ultimately causing him to withdraw from life. When the patient receives a narcissistic communication, instead of an anaclitic one, he may feel understood but still feel hopeless about getting what he needs. If he receives an object communication, he may be greatly hurt by the analyst's lack of responsiveness. He may become passive and feel helpless. Occasionally, a patient will become angry or enraged at the analyst when his anaclitic needs are not met, but this is not usually characterized by arrogance or contempt, as it is in narcissistic rage. Rather, it is more of a cranky, crying anger, not a cool pseudo-detached hauteur more typical of narcissistic injury.

Projective identification misattunement

It is never therapeutic for the analyst to respond to a projective identification with another one, and the curative emotional response is never, to my knowledge, in the projective identification relational mode. However, if the analyst is not receptive to or able to contain a projective identification, the patient is, like in object states, liable to increase the intensity of the transference. For example, if the patient needs the analyst to feel weak while he feels strong, the patient is liable to relate in ways that further increase his feeling of strength and the analyst's feeling of weakness. Or if the analyst's lack of responsiveness is too far off, the patient is liable to withdraw in more dramatic ways or even to leave the analysis altogether.

The impact is worst when the emotional communication is not just misattuned, but actually toxic, which is to say that they are the same as or worse than the emotional communication in the patient's early environment. These communications usually reinforce the repetition or re-traumatize the patient.

These are only the most common patient reactions to the wrong emotional communication, and I have discussed them only in relationship to the relational mode. Nevertheless, the possibility that the emotional communication is not curatively attuned to the patient should be considered under the following circumstances: when the intervention is not working as planned; when the transference intensifies; or when an intervention seems to fall completely flat. Of course, there are other reasons that any of these situations can arise, including the possibility that the cognitive communication is wrong, but the misattunement of the emotional communication is one of the most important reasons that an intervention fails. When the analysis is progressing, on the other hand, the emotional attunement is almost certainly correct.

The relationship of the objective countertransference to the curative emotional communication

We have discussed the characteristics of the curative emotional communication. But what is its relationship to the objective countertransference – the feelings that are induced in the analyst as a function of the patient's transference (Spotnitz 1985)? These feelings arise spontaneously and represent the part of the analyst's feelings about the patient that are clinically relevant to the transference. Properly understood, they allow the analyst access to aspects of the patient's emotional life that he is unable to put into words. The objective countertransference is an important part of the clinical picture: the clearest manifestation of unconscious and/or involuntary dimensions of the patient's relationship to the analyst. Is the curative emotional communication based on objective countertransference?

We can start with a general statement: the objective countertransference always forms a part of a curative emotional communication, but it does not always form the basis of an expressive emotional communication[17] – what the analyst actually says to the patient. Sometimes, expressing the objective countertransference itself is curative. More often, it must be modified in order to be curative, and sometimes it is toxic, and the curative feeling is completely different in all its characteristics. When any expression of the countertransference would be toxic, the analyst must contain the feeling, in which case the contained countertransference forms the silent background of the total emotional communication.

Thus, the objective countertransference is strongly linked to the curative emotional communication, but it is not identical with it. But while there is no direct formula for determining the curative emotional communication on the basis of the objective countertransference, a careful analysis of the objective countertransference and the content of the sessions, combined with the analyst's understanding of the patient's repetitions, guide the analyst to finding the curative feeling.

General features of the curative emotional communication

We have previously described the curative emotional environment as being similar enough to the original interaction to be compelling, but different enough to be curative. How does objective countertransference fit in with this framework?

Its role in the first part of the dictum – similar enough to be compelling – is straightforward: when the patient induces an objective countertransference and the analyst feels it, the past is recreated in the here-and-now of the analytic relationship, and the similarity to the original environment is palpable enough to be compelling. Although it isn't the only potentially similar element in the relationship – the analyst's real resemblance to either the patient (or his original objects) also plays a role here – its presence virtually ensures that analysis contains the potential to develop the intensity necessary to engage the patient on a deeply emotional basis.

The role of objective countertransference in the second part of the formulation – different enough to be curative – is more complex. At first glance, it would appear to be an unpromising source of different enough emotional communication because objective countertransference is, by definition, a repetition of a past interpersonal relationship and/or self-state. Although this is sometimes true, the analyst must keep in mind that objective countertransference is only one component of the total emotional environment in the analysis. Whether the objective countertransference feeling has the potential, in and of itself, to be curative depends on the larger context of the rest of the analytic relationship. A straightforward repetition can be curative in the context of some emotional environments but repetitive in others.

For example, suppose the patient had a childhood pattern: he made mistakes, his father would yell at him, and the patient became angry, but he was incapable of expressing this to his father. In the analysis, the patient forgets to pay the analyst, and the analyst feels furious and disappointed. The analyst's anger might be a curative expressive communication if the overall emotional environment of the analysis enables the patient to express his anger at the analyst. However, this would probably be a purely repetitive feeling – possibly even a toxic one – if (for whatever reason)[18] the patient was unable to express his anger.

In a slightly different vein, the countertransference may repeat some aspect of the original experience but not all of it: the difference determines how the feeling functions in the analysis. For example, a narcissistic countertransference is always a repetition of the patient's self-experience, but it is not always a repetition of the interpersonal relationship in which the self-experience took place. Suppose the patient feels a deep sadness, and induces this feeling, narcissistically, in the analyst. It is possible that the patient never had a relationship with anyone who could relate to him – share his experience – in this way. Consequently, he was deprived of a crucial developmental experience of being understood in an intimate way. In this case, the emergence of the narcissistic countertransference, in the treatment, is not a repetition; it is a new interpersonal experience, even though it is a repetition of an old self-experience. In this case, the feelings experienced in the narcissistic countertransference might be different enough to be curative.

On the other hand, suppose the feelings in the objective countertransference were a repetition of an interpersonal relationship, as well as a repetition of the patient's self-state: the parent had a strong proclivity to experience the child's self-states – in a pathological way – that immobilized both of them and kept the child mired in painful self-absorption. Here, the countertransference feelings might not be different enough to be curative.

When is an objective countertransference toxic? I have suggested that the objective countertransference is always a part of the total curative emotional communication if only – and this is frequently the case – in the form of silent containment. But there may be exceptions to this general rule. Some patients are so sensitive that they appear to be unable to work productively with an analyst who experiences any toxic feelings towards them, no matter how carefully the feelings are contained. (Of course, the patient may respond badly because the analyst has not adequately contained the toxic feelings.) Such patients need to work with an analyst who doesn't experience the repetitive feelings at all and feels only the different enough feelings. While this is frustrating for the analyst, it is excruciating for the patient; the patient must find an analyst who is insensitive to the feelings he habitually induces and receptive to feelings that few people have ever experienced towards him. I know of one case in which the patient induced strong negative feelings – that he was stupid and irritating – in almost every person he encountered (including me). This was reflected in decades of failed analysis with at least four different analysts. (I was not one of them, although I certainly would have been had I been given the opportunity.) Finally, late in life, he found an analyst who felt nothing but love for him; the change, over the course of just two years, was astonishing. When this occurs, the missing feelings are usually anaclitic; the patient has basically suffered from a lack of love in his life.

However, there are other patients who need an analyst who can feel negative feelings towards them – whether narcissistic or object – and cannot make progress without it.

Most patients can work productively with an analyst who experiences potentially toxic objective countertransference towards them, provided it is contained properly. But this raises the question: when is the expression of the countertransference toxic? This happens in two basic situations:

Situation 1: While expressing the countertransference, it repeats the original emotional environment, in a way that reinforces the repetition, rather than loosening it. This is a state of pathological attunement. In this situation, the emotional communication is not different enough to be curative.

Situation 2: Expressing the countertransference disrupts the patient's defenses against the relational dynamic and/or the feelings that have induced the countertransference. For example, suppose the patient calmly discusses a medical problem while the analyst feels swamped with anxiety about it. This suggests that patient has a strong defense against experiencing the anxiety. In some cases, the analyst can make an expressive intervention that expresses the anxiety in a way that will be curative. But in other cases, any expression of the anxiety will disrupt the patient's defenses: this may cause the defense to become more entrenched; worse, it may break down the defense, leaving the patient overwhelmed with anxiety that he is unable to tolerate.

The risk of toxicity can change over the course of the analysis. Emotional communications that might be toxic early on may be less so, or even curative, after different aspects of the repetitions are loosened, and the patient grows stronger. Spotnitz (1976: 47) went so far as to argue that the deliberate communication of potentially toxic feelings – *the toxoid response* – should be used to determine whether the patient is ready to terminate. In theory, this sounds like a good idea, but I've never had a patient with whom I felt confident enough to try it, and I suspect that most patients would require an analysis considerably longer than the average human lifespan, in order to reach that point. (But perhaps I'm overly cautious.)

Specific features of the curative emotional communication

As was described earlier in this book, a curative emotional communication communicates a specific feeling, within a specific relational mode, which is therapeutically attuned to the patient's need at that specific point in the transference. Similarly, an objective countertransference is also characterized by a specific feeling, relational mode, and intensity. When we consider whether the objective countertransference will be curative, we need to examine it along each of the three aforementioned dimensions. There are four possible outcomes as to how the curative emotional communication will be:

1. the same as the objective countertransference – unmodified, except perhaps, for its intensity;
2. similar to the objective countertransference but modified so significantly in its intensity that it seems to be a different feeling;
3. based on the objective countertransference but modified either in its specific feeling or relational mode;
4. completely different from the objective countertransference – both in the specific feeling and the relational mode – but one that is usually related and thus deducible from it.

We will examine each of these possibilities in turn:

The objective countertransference is the curative emotional communication. Sometimes, the objective countertransference feeling itself is the curative emotional communication in the sense that the analyst can communicate the induced feeling (implicitly or explicitly), and this feeling will be curative for the patient. For example, the patient tells the analyst that he got a job that is particularly hard to get; the analyst feels admiration towards the patient, and this is the curative emotional communication. The intensity of the feeling may have to be modified slightly. Perhaps the patient is now in a position to absorb more admiration than previously, but still less than the analyst actually feels; this is usually not significant enough to change the feeling.

Here's a narcissistic example: the patient describes a fight with his boyfriend. He complains that the boyfriend ran up a bunch of bills on the credit card for clothes, even though he had just lost his job, and the patient is supporting him with great difficulty. The patient voices some rage at the boyfriend but defensively seems to minimize its intensity through sympathetic rationalizations for the boyfriend's behavior. The analyst senses that he is not allowing himself the full intensity of his anger, so the analyst directly communicates the induction: "If he were my boyfriend, I'd scream my head off until he returned every last pair of socks!" This is the narcissistic communication that the patient needs in order to fully feel and express his anger.

Much less often, an unmodified object induction will be the curative emotional communication. For example, the analyst knows from the patient's own stories that the patient has a history of taking advantage of his friends – despite his seemingly gregarious and innocent demeanor. One day, the patient casually asks the analyst whether he can borrow one of his books, and the analyst feels a sudden irritation with the patient's presumptuousness. The analyst asks, with evident irritation, "Why should I loan you one of my books? I know your history of taking care of things." The patient, who until then had been polite to the point of obsequiousness, pours out a stream of hate at the analyst's lack of trust and generosity. The communication has facilitated the verbalization of previously defended aggression that he previously acted out passive–aggressively through his irresponsible behavior.

However, these types of situations involving object inductions are rare; more commonly, object inductions spontaneously repeat the past in a non-curative and possibly traumatic way.

Furthermore, we can't forget that analytic and narcissistic inductions are not always the curative emotional communication, even when they are induced. Let's return to the patient with the spendthrift boyfriend. The induced feeling was rage at the boyfriend – a narcissistic countertransference that formed the basis of a narcissistic emotional communication. However, it's possible that what the patient needed was an anaclitic communication: help in deciding how to handle the boyfriend or even a command telling him to stop giving the boyfriend access to his credit cards.

The curative emotional communication is based on the objective countertransference, but the intensity must be modified significantly – enough so that it seems like a different feeling. In these cases, the analyst feels the specific feeling that needs to be communicated to the patient, but the intensity must be modified significantly in order for the patient to be able to make use of it. This usually occurs when the countertransference is strongly incongruent with the intensity of the content.

Let's return again to the patient with the spendthrift boyfriend. But this time, the patient is neither complaining about the boyfriend nor complaining minimally, while the analyst is feeling so angry that he really wants to kill him. However, after he says, "If he were my boyfriend, I'd scream my head off," the patient defends the boyfriend or becomes anxious about getting cancer. This suggests that the emotional communication has been too intense and has activated the patient's defenses. In this case, the curative emotional communication might be something like: "Some people find it a little stressful when they are the primary provider, and their partners do not fully appreciate what that means," delivered in a confident tone with just a hint of anger largely overshadowed by sympathetic empathy. This is a diluted feeling that is on the same emotional spectrum as the first communication, but so much less intense, that it seems like a different feeling altogether.

Or the induced feeling may have to be intensified. Let's take the same scenario as above: the patient minimizes his anger towards the boyfriend, and the analyst is only very mildly annoyed – much like the patient. In this case, it is possible that the patient needs the analyst to model more intense anger at the boyfriend to help him feel that getting really angry is acceptable.

The curative emotional communication contains a specific feeling from the countertransference but is expressed in a different relational mode than the analyst experienced it. Sometimes, the curative emotional communication is not the countertransference itself but is derived from the same specific feeling; however, it must be expressed in a different relational mode than the one in which it was induced.

A common situation occurs when the analyst experiences a feeling – usually negative – in the object mode, but the patient needs the feeling communicated back to him in the narcissistic mode. For example, the patient drones on in a low tone of voice that induces boredom, depletion, and fatigue. The analyst hates it. His mind wanders, he wants to sleep, and he finds it impossible to stay on track listening to the patient. The analyst does not just feel miserable; he feels that the patient is making him miserable. His first thought is that the patient's drone is passive aggression – a deliberate (although probably unconscious) withholding of life-sustaining stimulation. Consequently, the analyst feels attacked by the patient and irritated at him for boring him.

How do we understand this situation? The most likely possibility is that this is a repetition of the parent's feeling. Perhaps the patient expressed his depression as crankiness when he was a child. This may have induced depressed feelings in the father, but he didn't recognize them as an empathic resonance with the child's depressed feelings. Instead, he experienced them as an attack on his own sense of well-being. Thus, he experienced the depression in the wrong relational mode and misunderstood the child's attempt to communicate his depression. Out of irritation, he told the child to stop complaining and ruining everyone's good time, which caused the patient to tone down his complaints and adopt the monotone. This formed the basis for a repetition in which the patient continued to strive for a narcissistic emotional communication but continually induced the parents' feeling instead. Other people experienced the patient's depressed feelings in the object mode – as an attack upon their own good moods – leaving the patient to cope with his depression in isolation and secondarily with feeling criticized for being boring.

What then is the curative emotional communication? The analyst knows that many people have told the patient that he is boring, passive–aggressive, and withholding, and this has always hurt him deeply. So, the analyst is certain that communicating the irritation would be repetitive but not curative. It occurred to him that the transference would look different if he experiences the depression in the countertransference, in the narcissistic mode. Then, he breaks through to the patient's self-experience. Nobody before had communicated empathic understanding of the pain of the patient's depleted depression; nobody even recognized that the patient was communicating his depression by making them feel bored. This suggests that the analyst should try a narcissistic emotional communication based on the patient's depression. This might mean silently containing the depression and communicating an occasional grunt of agreement with the patient's despair. Or the analyst might say, "You know, sometimes life just feels so hard and mean and boring – it's hard to even keep your head up," saturating his comment with a forlorn, exhausted tone. In this way, the analyst communicates the specific feeling in the countertransference – the feeling of boredom – but in a different relational mode than the one in which he originally experienced it.

In the scenario given, the analyst's misunderstanding of the relational mode of the bored/depressed feeling was rooted in a repetition. Sometimes, however, the analyst experiences the correct specific feeling[19] in a non-curative relational mode for subjective reasons. For example, the analyst might have a low tolerance for boredom and a propensity to experience anyone who bores him as a threat to his well-being.

The analyst might also misunderstand the relational mode for theoretical reasons. For example, he has trained himself to see all interpersonal exchanges as taking place in the object or present-anchored modes; consequently, he consistently misunderstands narcissistic inductions. Similarly, an analyst might be trained to understand all countertransference narcissistically, in which case he would have a propensity to misunderstand object inductions. In either case, it is difficult to find the curative emotional communication when the relational mode is misunderstood.

Situations in which the analyst experiences the right specific feeling in the countertransference, but must change the relational mode, occur fairly often. However, not all specific feelings can be transposed from one relational mode into the other.

The curative emotional communication is completely different than the induction, in both the specific feeling and the relational mode. These are the cases in which the curative emotional communication is completely different from induced countertransference.

Let's look at an obvious example: the patient has forgotten to bring the check, and the analyst's first reaction is impatience and anger. "Why can't that patient be more responsible," he thinks. "Why does he make me wait for my money? Why can't he take care of anything himself?"

The patient has recounted many stories like this: he forgets things, and people become harsh with him. So the analyst's reaction is obviously a repetition. The analyst also remembers the patient's reactions to being criticized: he feels hurt and withdraws. Or he gets angry in return, but the anger doesn't free him up either. Nothing ever changes.

With this in mind, the analyst cannot see any rationale for communicating the countertransference. He doesn't think that changing the intensity will make any difference; irritation just seems to be the wrong feeling to communicate, at least in the object mode.

He then considers changing the relational mode. Is it possible that experiencing the irritation in the narcissistic mode, instead, will yield the curative emotional communication? Thus, the analyst imagines what it would be like if he was angry with himself instead of at the patient and thinks that the patient might be angry with himself for not bringing the check.

This is a definite possibility and might lead to a narcissistic emotional communication, which might be something like: "It's frustrating to forget things, isn't it? It makes you so angry at yourself." Or, "I know just what it's like. I always forget to bring checks and pay people. They get so angry. It's so upsetting!"

But what if the analyst doesn't think that will work either? In this case, he needs to consider changing the specific feeling and the relational mode. The only mode left is the anaclitic mode. From this perspective, the patient may need help in figuring out how to remember things. For example, the analyst might ask one of the following questions: "It seems like it's hard for you to remember this kind of thing; is there a better way we can handle this?" "Would you prefer to mail me the check?" "Is there anything that might help you remember?" "Would you like to leave some checks here, and I will keep them in my desk. You don't have to worry about remembering them, and you won't fill them out until the end of each month?" In this case, the curative feeling would be almost the opposite of the induced feeling – both in feeling and in relational mode.

Now, let's look at the scenario in reverse. Again, the patient forgets the check, but this time the analyst has what he initially takes to be an anaclitic feeling. He wants to help the patient to learn how to remember. However, he has tried a number of times and it's never worked. And he recalls that the patient's parents are always very "helpful" with him. What appears to be anaclitic may actually be an object transference, in which the analyst is feeling the parent's feelings.

He tries to imagine feeling the desire to help the patient in the narcissistic mode, and this doesn't translate. There is no way to experience this feeling in the narcissistic mode. Consequently, he tries a narcissistic communication, as above: "It's so frustrating to forget things like checks." But he's also tried this in the past and it has never worked before. So he moves on.

Finally, he considers the possibility that both the patient's confused and apologetic demeanor and the seemingly anaclitic countertransference they induce are expressions of a defense: beneath the defense, the patient is expressing passive–aggressive defiance or hatred towards the analyst by forgetting the check, or he is sadomasochistically provoking the analyst. The analyst considers an expressive intervention in the object mode, designed to help the patient to express his defiance or sadomasochism, openly. If so, the curative emotional communication might be: "What the hell is wrong with you? Can't you remember anything at all?" This would be the curative emotional communication – if and only if – it helped the patient to experience and verbalize the hatred that he had actually been feeling. As in the first case, the curative feeling is the opposite of the induction, both in specific feeling and in the relational mode.

Situations in which the curative emotional communication is different from the induction, in both specific feeling and relational mode, can involve all transference/countertransference configurations. In my experience, however, it occurs most often in object transference/countertransference configurations. When this is the case, the curative emotional communication is narcissistic or anaclitic.

Another situation in which the curative emotional communication may be completely different from the countertransference occurs when the countertransference is strongly incongruent with the content. This situation suggests that the patient's conscious experience is strongly defended against the unconscious transference that is inducing the countertransference. In these cases, the analyst should usually contain the induced feeling, while making an emotional communication related purely to the content.

For example, consider a case in which the patient is describing her daughter's sleep problems. The baby has been up crying, many nights in a row, and the analyst is filled with fantasies of tossing babies in the air and letting them smash on the sidewalk. The aggressive fantasies about babies are probably a narcissistic countertransference related to the unconscious content of the patient's communication. However, they are strongly incongruent with her effect and her conscious experience. She describes only love for her child – feeling sad that the baby is so upset. She also feels helpless and asks the analyst how she should handle the situation. While her concern is certainly genuine, there appears to be a defense operating against experiencing the aggression that she feels towards her baby, a hypothesis that would explain the analyst's fantasies. However, the analyst thinks that any reference to the aggression would disrupt the patient's defenses. Instead, he makes suggestions about coping with the baby's crying. Thus, he contains the aggressive feelings, which are related to the unconscious narcissistic transference, and he formulates an anaclitic expressive communication that is related primarily to the patient's conscious experience – and is completely different from the induction.

Auto-induction: stimulating the curative feeling when it has not been induced

Situations in which the curative feeling is completely different from the induction are often the most difficult to work with because the analyst does not immediately feel the emotional communication that the patient needs. Where does the analyst find the needed feelings? The objective countertransference cannot be relied upon to provide all the feelings the patient may need to experience from the analyst. Some patients do (eventually!) manage to induce all the feelings that they need to experience in order to loosen their repetitions. But this is rare. In order to provide the "different enough to be curative" dimension of curative emotional experience, the analyst must often summon the needed feelings within himself through a process of auto-induction. The analyst may have to actively and deliberately place himself in the patient's emotional position, the parent's position, or in the position of an ideal parent to the child and then imagine himself experiencing the feeling. Because the needed feeling will be completely different from the objective countertransference, it may feel foreign, inauthentic, or abstract. And it may not come immediately. Sometimes it takes years.

For example, one analyst developed an intensely negative object countertransference to a new patient after the first several sessions. She was initially interested in the patient because he was involved in a profession that intrigued her, and he had been referred by another patient, whom she had deeply enjoyed. But she was soon disappointed in him. She found him intensely irritating – but for no particular reason. The patient was profoundly depressed yet superficially agreeable. The analyst found him to be obsequious and she hated him with a disdain that was far outside her usual range of feeling.

The induction was clearly objective. Numerous employers had rejected the patient, and over time, all of his friends had abandoned him. The analyst hypothesized that the patient had developed a superficial false self to cover the memories of two parents who both loathed him and to avoid being loathed in the present. But try as he might, he was unable to escape the repetition. The analyst had a strong sense that the patient needed a loving communication but just didn't feel it. During the first couple of years, the most loving thing she could do was to contain her loathing while forcing herself to treat him nicely – but not overly so. She reminded herself that the parents hated the patient and tried to imagine loving the patient as a baby. Although this felt inauthentic, she noticed small changes in the treatment that suggested that this approach would work. After two years, during which time the analyst was nearly silent and struggling with her feelings, the patient occasionally reported feeling better, and the analyst occasionally felt that she enjoyed him. Slowly, these two feelings amplified each other as the analyst began to feel loving feelings that felt more genuine.

In this case, the curative feeling differed in every way from the objective countertransference. The analyst was able to make different-enough emotional communications but only after the she had intellectually determined what the patient needed and then auto-induced the needed feelings. However, it was, in a sense, the opposite of the countertransference, and in that way, the countertransference guided the analyst to it.

Situations that require auto-induction are obviously the hardest to manage and require the most imagination and capacity for emotional self-control. The patient who has pitilessly demeaned the analyst for years may need the analyst to empathize with his inability to feel understood by the analyst. Or the patient, whom the analyst cherishes and adores, may need the analyst to insult him so that he can release long-held, self-directed rage. It may take a long time for the analyst to realize this and even longer before he can feel the feeling with sufficient intensity to communicate it to the patient. Nevertheless, I have found that the analyst can usually auto-induce the feeling, provided he can identify what the patient needs, and then overcome his own resistances to experiencing and communicating it.

Although I favor viewing this as a necessary method of working through for both the patient and the analyst, I'm not sure whether it should actually be viewed as one of the intrinsic inefficiencies in analytic practice. What I do know is that it is inevitable. When the patient needs some form of the feeling that he induces in the analyst, and the analyst allows himself to use the feeling, the progress of the analysis feels smooth, natural, and spontaneous. But when the patient needs a feeling that he does not induce in the analyst, the analysis can feel stalemated, even when the analyst knows what that feeling is.

This doesn't mean that the analysis is, in fact, stalemated. The apparent lack of progress may mean that the patient isn't ready to experience the needed feeling. Moreover, the struggle to find the needed feeling can be valuable because the patient often knows, on some level, that the analyst has struggled to give him what he emotionally needs. Alas, not every patient will feel this way. Some may have been ready for the feeling earlier and may just feel frustrated that the analyst took such a long time to come around to it. It would be ideal if we had some way of consistently referring patients to the analysts who will have the right feelings for them. Without such a plan, there is nothing to be done about the problem. The analyst can't communicate a feeling that he doesn't have. At some point, both the patient and the analyst must come to terms with the analyst's limitations in this area.

On a more cheerful note, I am consistently surprised by how frequently so many analysts, each with the limitations imposed by his own subjectivity, are able to find the needed feelings for so many of their patients.

Summary: finding the curative emotional communication

There is, alas, no formulation for finding the curative emotional communication. No amount of information or understanding of the patient can provide the answer with certainty, and every analyst will encounter idiosyncratic cases in which he seems to stumble upon the right feeling by accident. Nevertheless, the various ways that the curative emotional communication can be related to the countertransference defines the range of the most likely possibilities. In the vast majority of the cases, the curative expressive intervention will be related, in some way, to either the induction or the content of the session. So the list of ways that the induction can be related to the induction can serve as a sort of decision tree that allows analysts to consider the various possibilities in an organized fashion. With this in mind, the analyst should consider four factors.

First, consider whether the objective countertransference itself – either as he experiences it or with its intensity modified in some way – is the curative emotional communication. In this case, the analyst communicates the same specific feeling that he experiences in the same relational mode that he experiences. This situation usually occurs when the countertransference is either anaclitic or narcissistic, and it is the easiest situation to work with because the analyst does not need to engage in auto-induction.

Next, consider whether the countertransference requires a significant change in intensity. In this situation, the analyst, again, has the right specific feeling and the right relational mode, but the intensity is either too high or too low. If too high, it tends to disrupt the patient if the emotional communication is made directly. If it is not intense enough, the emotional communication may not have any impact on the patient. As above, emotional communications in this category tend to be analytic or narcissistic. Changing the intensity of the emotional communication requires a degree of emotional imagination by the analyst, but this is not usually difficult to achieve.

Then, consider whether the analyst is feeling approximately the right specific feeling but in the wrong relational mode. In this case, the analyst should attempt to feel the same feeling he already has but in a different relational mode. For example, if he feels fear in the narcissistic mode, he should attempt to experience the fear in the object mode. If this seems to clarify the situation, then the emotional communication should probably be made in a different relational mode than the patient had induced. This situation can occur with countertransference in all relational modes but occurs most often when the induction is in the object mode, or when the transference and the countertransference are in different modes. Usually, the patient's history will show a pattern of feeling consistently misunderstood, within many relationships, in which he consistently receives the opposite feeling to what he expects and wants.

Cases in which the analyst must change the relational mode of the feeling do require more mental effort by the analyst, but they are often accompanied by a moment of sudden recognition. Once the feeling is experienced in a different relational mode, the clinical encounter is completely changed but often makes much more sense.

Finally, consider whether the patient needs an emotional communication that is completely different than the countertransference, in both specific feeling and relational mode, while the objective countertransference itself is contained. For example, if the countertransference is in the object mode, the analyst might want to consider what he might feel in the other modes. This situation occurs most often when the transference/countertransference is in the object mode and when the transference and countertransference are in different modes. In these cases, the curative emotional communication is completely different from the countertransference, but it is usually related to it in a fairly logical manner.

11
NARCISSISTIC EMOTIONAL COMMUNICATIONS

A narcissistic emotional communication conveys that the analyst shares the patient's feelings – that in some way she is like, similar to, the same as, or merged with the patient. A narcissistic emotional communication is communicated through, and intended to be experienced within, the narcissistic relational mode. The specific feelings the analyst communicates are the same as or are closely analogous to some aspect of the patient's specific feelings in the moment. If the patient is afraid, angry, sad, or outraged, the analyst communicates that in some way she either empathically understands, shares, or agrees with the patient's feeling herself.

Narcissistic emotional communication spans the whole spectrum of the narcissistic relational mode. Less intense communication, addressed to the reasonable ego, conveys the analyst's empathic understanding of the patient's feelings in the context of clearly differentiated ego boundaries. For example, if the patient expresses cynicism, the analyst might convey that she empathically understands the patient's cynicism. A simple verbal or visual nod and a sense of understanding might be sufficient to convey this. Or the analyst might say, "Sometimes it can feel like everyone is in it for themselves."

More intense narcissistic communication, on the other hand, addresses the afflicted ego and goes beyond empathic understanding to convey emotional agreement with the patient or a concrete sense of unity, twinship, or merger. In this case, if the patient expresses cynicism, the analyst might communicate that she too is cynical, in the same way as the patient: "Yes, you are absolutely right. Nobody is honest about what they are looking for." Notice that the analyst no longer simply understands the patient's feeling here, she also shares it.

Narcissistic emotional communication is needed when the therapeutically relevant transference is grounded in a problem with the patient's self-experience. There are two basic types of problems related to self-experience: in the first type, the patient is in a state of narcissistic depletion that results in a weak or unconsolidated sense of self-cohesion or self-esteem or a generalized narcissistic vulnerability (Kohut 1971; Spotnitz 1976). This vulnerability requires emotional communication that makes the patient feel that the analyst is like her or similar to her in ways that are syntonic. This communication is immediately stabilizing, and the patient usually finds them to be soothing, comforting, or supportive.

In the second type of problem, the patient is in a state of pathological self-absorption and/or self-hatred, such as melancholic depression as described by Freud (1917) or the narcissistic defense described by Spotnitz (1976), both of which are grounded in introverted aggression. These states require emotional communication that makes the patient feel that the analyst is like her in ways that are dystonic. This enables the patient to turn his self-directed aggression away from herself and towards the analyst. These interventions are initially destabilizing – in a controlled way – and subsequently stabilizing. The patient experiences them before the discharge of aggression as irritating and provocative and after the discharge of aggression as relieving and liberating.

Narcissistic emotional communication only works when the patient is in a state of narcissistic relatedness to the analyst. This means that the narcissistic transference must be in place before the analyst makes the emotional communication. Or the emotional communication must be powerful enough to induce the narcissistic relational mode in the patient.

Specific types of narcissistic emotional communications

Interpretation

Interpretations are designed to stimulate insight, self-awareness, or self-understanding. The defining component of all interpretations is an explanation of some aspect of the patient's self-state – a feeling, an impulse, a defense, a dream, or a memory – to the patient's reasonable ego. Some examples include the following dialogue from the analyst: "You get deeply injured when someone doesn't appreciate your talent." Or "It is comforting to you when you and I have the same opinion about something but painful when we don't." The accuracy of the cognitive component and its relevance to the clinically relevant transference are crucial to the success of an interpretation.

Interpretations can be combined with narcissistic emotional communications. There are two types of interpretation, differentiated by the type of emotional communication: the classical interpretation and the affective interpretation.

The classical interpretation combines the cognitive communication with a narcissistic emotional communication to the patient's reasonable ego. The range of feelings that can be communicated to the reasonable ego is limited to empathy with the patient's adult pain at having to cope with and manage the repetition. The classical interpretation is designed to help the patient to observe the repetition. Therefore, the analyst does not directly engage the feelings that characterize the repetition.

The affective interpretation, on the other hand, combines the interpretive explanation with a narcissistic emotional communication to the afflicted ego. The affective interpretation is not only designed to help the patient to observe the repetition but also to engage the feelings that characterize the repetition and meet the unmet maturational need that underlies the repetition. The range of feelings that can be communicated to the afflicted ego is broader, and the emotional communication can be more intense than in the classical interpretation.

Let's look at a simple example of an interpretation in both the classical and the affective versions, considering first the classical. The analyst notices, based on his countertransference and the content of the sessions, that the patient becomes confused whenever she touches on a topic that involves anger. The patient is vaguely aware of being confused, but would not identify it as such, and seems unaware of the possible link between confusion and anger. The transference state is not very intense, but the analyst has the sense that the patient generally feels understood by the analyst. The analyst makes the following interpretation: "It seems like you get confused when a situation that might make you angry is brought up." Both the words and the feelings are addressed to the reasonable ego. The interpretation is delivered in a mildly empathic and sympathetic tone. The interpretation is formulated and communicated such that it is clearly an observation by the analyst about the patient, not a shared experience. The cognitive component explains something about the patient's self-experience, while the emotional communication conveys empathy with his plight in having to cope with this repetition but not with the feelings that motivate the repetition.

The analyst has several immediate goals: (1) to make the patient more aware of his confused feelings; (2) to make the patient aware of the possible link between confusion and anger; (3) to give the patient words for his feelings, thereby assimilating them into his ego. The effect of all of this is to strengthen the reasonable ego, with the idea that eventually understanding the whole process will loosen its grip on her and help her to maintain more consistent adult functioning. The classical interpretation always carries with it the implicit but subtle suggestion that the feelings connected to the afflicted ego are both unrealistic and immature.

An affective interpretation conveys essentially the same cognitive content but is formulated and expressed in a way that gets closer – is more "experience-near," (in Kohut's striking phrase) to the confusion and the anxiety. To facilitate this, the analyst might universalize the interpretation by putting it in the third person with the tone implicitly conveying a strong sense of first-hand understanding of the problem, with a hint of the confusion and the anxiety laced into the tone and the prosody. "It gets confusing, especially when anger might be involved." Or the analyst might use the same tone but stay in the second person but again in a way that universalizes the observation, making it less about the particular patient and more about the human condition, which implicitly includes the analyst. "You get confused, especially when the situation involves anger. That's understandable."

The analyst is still making an observation about the patient's experience but from the perspective of someone who shares the experience. The patient is no longer alone with his feelings. This meets the developmental need for shared emotionality with another person who is similar to the patient. The accuracy of the interpretation enhances the patient's feelings of being emotionally understood as well, but the affective interpretation does not convey the idea that the feelings connected with the repetition are unrealistic or immature. Rather, they are viewed as being understandable within the context in which they are experienced.

Thus, the effect of the two types of interventions is quite different, and therefore they serve different functions within the treatment.

In my experience, the classical interpretation rarely works to actually cure problems with self-experience because it does not meet the maturational need that underlies the repetition.[1] Furthermore, classical interpretations of self-states carry the substantial risk that the patient will feel that the interpretation is experience distant (Kohut 1971), which is to say that the interpretation sounds harsh and foreign, even if it is accurate, or that the patient feels that the analyst recognizes and describes the feeling but neither shares nor understands it firsthand. Although the patient may hear the analyst's empathy with his frustration with the repetition, she doesn't receive – and consequently doesn't experience – empathy with the feelings that characterize the repetition itself. Either situation can disrupt the narcissistic transference because the patient no longer feels that the analyst is similar to her. This can lead to rage, despair, or withdrawal. Attempts to interpret self-experience from an even more neutral emotional communication invariably fail for just this reason: they convey a feeling that the analyst is commenting from a position of difference rather than sameness, and the interpretation is usually experienced as a criticism.

This is not to say that classical interpretations of self-states are necessarily useless or damaging. I have found that they can effectively enable the patient to control herself, and to feel better in general, especially with patients who have a reasonable ego that is both strong and strongly split off from the afflicted ego. These patients tend to be unwilling or unable to consciously feel the intensity of the feelings connected with the repetition itself. Such patients are often reality oriented and view themselves as rational, in the sense of being unswayed by and free from the influence of emotions; they view the feelings connected with the afflicted ego to be irrational and unworthy of serious attention. They tend to react to narcissistic injuries with anger or an irritable depression rather than a passive depression, fragmentation, or withdrawal. After they acknowledge the feelings, they feel more in control. This type of patient might say: "Oh yes, I guess I got depressed because they didn't recognize that I am the Messiah," acknowledging his grandiosity – from a distance – while mocking it at the same time. The patient does not allow herself to feel the pain as acutely as the analyst suspects that she does, and the patient has no interest in doing so. These patients prefer to control the feelings rather than feel them and have little interest in integrating them into the rest of their personality. In these cases, the classical interpretation enables the patient to label, observe, and control the feelings in an abstract, intellectual way that is similar to the effect of cognitive therapy.

While this may sound antithetical to "deep" analytic work, the enhanced ability to intellectualize can still be profoundly relieving. Some of these patients move on to experience the feelings more fully and allow the unmet maturational needs to emerge in the treatment. But others won't. It is important to remember that not everyone seeks, nor takes away, the same experience from psychoanalytic therapy.

The affective interpretation, on the other hand, has the capacity to actually meet some of the unmet maturational needs in the context of the analytic relationship, which allows a qualitative change in the patient's experience of the repetition. In theory, the affective interpretation can enable the patient to mature in a way that the classical interpretation does not. However, the choice here is only partly up to the analyst. The patient must be willing and able to allow the afflicted ego to become activated in relationship to the analyst, and she must be willing and able to allow the analyst to become something to her other than a trusted, competent professional. Even if the analyst is emotionally open to this, not every patient is able or willing to do it.

Let's consider the effects of the two types of interpretation in terms of one particular problem: ego weakness rooted in unmet narcissistic needs for admiration. For example, the patient feels sad and deflated. She then mentions that she made a proposal at work that was greeted with lukewarm acceptance rather than thunderous applause. When asked, she says that her feeling is unconnected with the event. After all, she understands that it's unreasonable to expect that her ideas will actually be met with applause. Maybe it wasn't even a good idea, she says. Nobody should get praise for bad ideas.

The situation is straightforward: the patient craved praise and appreciation but received little. Consequently, she feels narcissistically injured. However, she has little acceptance or appreciation of either her needs or the injury. In addition, it has triggered a degree of self-attack. Her rational ego is strong enough to see the external reality of the situation correctly, but it is not strong enough to master the feelings of the afflicted ego. This is clear from the countertransference. Despite the patient's conscious attempts to minimize the pain, the analyst feels strongly empathic with her. He feels the strength of her craving for admiration and the pain of not receiving it. This suggests that the patient's afflicted ego is activated in the transference.

Interpreting her feeling of deflation as a result of the disappointment, or interpreting her attempts to rationalize the disappointment, would probably accentuate the patient's feeling that her wish for applause is unreasonable or childish. This is because these feelings are childish if they are viewed through the eyes of the rational, adult ego. The act of naming a narcissistic need, without a strongly empathic communication, can make the patient feel there is something wrong with having the need. Thus, a classical interpretation might inadvertently increase the patient's self-attack.

An affective interpretation is more likely to be effective in this case. The analyst might say, "Who doesn't feel miserable when their ideas don't get the recognition they feel they deserve. Doesn't everyone want applause when they think they have come up with something great? Maybe it's not a reasonable expectation, but who cares? It hurts not to get recognition." When the analyst can communicate enough empathy with the patient's afflicted ego – the part of her that feels disappointed – she becomes more aware of, and also more accepting of, her craving for admiration as a result.

Suppose the patient had had more tolerance for the feeling, even if she didn't accord it any particular respect, and she had become angry rather than depressed. For example, she had come in and said. "You know, I'm so pissed. I presented this idea at the sales meeting, and they just fucking sat there, like a bunch of idiots. But I don't know what I expected. A medal or something?" And the patient laughs as she says this last line.

In this case, the analyst doesn't feel particularly pained by the story, which suggests that the patient's afflicted ego is not strongly activated in the transference. But he does think the patient spoke more truly than her apparent sarcasm allowed when she said that she expected a medal for her presentation. He thinks the patient is strong enough to consider that she really did want more admiration but has no interest in actually feeling the craving and the hurt more than just recognizing it. Here, the analyst might make the following statement with a touch of humor. "Why shouldn't they give you a medal? Don't you really like getting medals for your ideas?" In this case, adding too much empathy to the blend might humiliate the patient or lead her to defend against it by protesting that that kind of response is for wimps.

Other risks of interpretations

Only those feelings that are to some extent compatible with, or syntonic with, the patient's sense of self can be safely interpreted. Or to put the same idea differently, only those feelings that are not heavily defended can be safely interpreted. Interpretation of feelings that are heavily defended or dystonic tend to be experienced as attacks that disrupt the narcissistic transference, stimulate rage or withdrawal, and cause the patient to feel misunderstood. Consider again the example of the confused patient: the patient's confusion can be safely interpreted only if the confusion is to some extent compatible with her sense of self. This does not mean that she has to like the idea of being confused, but it cannot be interpreted safely if the idea of being confused is strongly dystonic to her sense of self, i.e., if she views being confused as being a serious weakness – a flaw in her being. If so, the patient is liable to experience the interpretation as an attack on her sense of self.

Similarly, interpretations of defenses themselves lead to narcissistic injuries for as long as the defenses are necessary to the patient's stability. It is only after the patient has come to view the defense as dystonic, and the feelings underlying the defense as somewhat compatible with her sense of self, that the defense can be readily interpreted.

Use of the narcissistic countertransference in formulating interpretations

The narcissistic countertransference offers the analyst almost direct access to what the patient is feeling and thus can serve as the basis for interpretations. But it must not be forgotten that the analyst is often (usually!) capable of consciously experiencing feelings the patient is not conscious of or defended against. Thus, the fact that the analyst feels the material in the countertransference does not mean that it can be safely used in an interpretation. Furthermore, the analyst's reluctance to make direct use of the material in an interpretation is often itself an induction – an indication that the patient is not ready to openly deal with the feelings in a self-reflective manner.

Interpretation usually works best in low-intensity states that are dominated by uncomplicated empathy. In these cases, the feelings that the analyst experiences are usually only lightly defended, and the patient can often benefit from having them interpreted with the analyst's empathic support. But the further the feelings in the countertransference are from the patient's immediate experience, the more they are likely to be dystonic or defended. For example, if the analyst feels strongly dissociated while the patient is talking about some seemingly unimportant event in his everyday life, it is more likely that the feelings of dissociation, and the feelings underlying the dissociation, are strongly defended.

In high-intensity transference/countertransference states with blurred ego boundaries, interpretations tend to remind the patient of the analyst's separateness and disrupt the transference.[2] (An exception to this principle will be discussed below.) In these cases, the analyst usually experiences feelings in the countertransference that cannot be safely interpreted, requiring the analyst to contain them or make use of a less direct type of intervention.

Furthermore, the therapeutic impact of the cognitive communication tends to be greatest in low-intensity narcissistic states where there is little or no blurring of ego boundaries. Its impact decreases as the blurring increases. Effective interventions in blurry states primarily depend upon the correct emotional communication, rather than on the degree of insight, awareness, or verbal structure that they bring to the patient.

Sometimes a state with blurred ego boundaries can provide an opportunity to interpret material that is somewhat incompatible with the patient's sense of self or that is more strongly defended. The fact that the analyst shares the patient's experience in a deeper, less differentiated way than simple empathy can intensify the power of the emotional communication, preventing the cognitive communication from disrupting the transference. But there's a limit as to how far this can go. If the content of the interpretation is deeply incompatible with the patient's sense of self, it is likely to inflict narcissistic injury – no matter how blurry the boundaries.

The considerations we have discussed so far relate to interpretations combined with syntonic emotional communications. But can interpretations be made with dystonic emotional communications? Interpretations that disrupt the narcissistic transference readily make the patient angry, thereby supplying the irritating element for a dystonic communication. Furthermore, an emotional communication can be empathic without being sympathetic, which again can combine with an interpretation to create a dystonic intervention.

However, I think that a dystonic interpretation puts the patient in a bind: the anger that is mobilized serves the purpose of bringing the patient out of the self-absorbed state, but it also leaves her less inclined to accept the interpretation. Conversely, accepting the interpretation makes it more difficult to maintain the anger. The cognitive and the emotional communications tend to work at cross purposes. Nevertheless, these interventions do work sometimes, reversing the patient's flow of anger and providing insight at the same time.

When I was in training as a Modern Analyst, it was a basic assumption – almost an article of faith – that interpretations of narcissistic states were inevitably experienced as narcissistic injuries and should be avoided at all costs. One instructor – in other ways brilliant – went so far as to say, "It is easier to prove that interpretations of pre-oedipal states are damaging than it is to prove that the earth revolves around the sun."

Since then I have learned, as analysts from other schools have long known, that interpretation of these states can be very effective but only when accompanied by a narcissistic emotional communication. Furthermore, there are some patients for whom the Modern Analytic dictum is absolutely right. These patients experience all interpretations as a disruption of the narcissistic transference or as an attack, no matter how carefully they are crafted. These patients respond only to the non-interpretative emotional communication directed at the afflicted ego that will be considered next.

Psychological reflection

In all forms of psychological reflection, the emotional communication is the main source of therapeutic leverage. In passive psychological reflection – Rogerian reflection – the analyst reflects the patient's conscious experience exactly as the patient expresses it. In active psychological reflection – joining and mirroring – the analyst expresses active agreement or identification with the patient's experience, either conscious or unconscious. Some of these techniques combine straightforward interpretative content in the cognitive dimension of the communication. Others interpret only obliquely or communicate no interpretive content.

Rogerian reflection

The Rogerian reflection (developed by Carl Rogers, and used by almost everybody) is the simplest reflective technique: the cognitive component repeats whatever the patient has said, in almost exactly the same words the patient has used. If the patient says, "I hate my father," the analyst responds with, "You hate your father." The emotional component, however, reflects only a touch of the specific feelings the patient has expressed, mixed in with the warm, sympathetic, understanding feeling characteristic of uncomplicated empathy.

The tone may be modulated for specific therapeutic purposes. If the patient is agitated by the intensity of his feelings, the analyst may use a less intense tone than the patient's to lower his level of stimulation. If the patient is inhibited in experiencing the full intensity of his feelings, the analyst might intensify his tone to help the patient get better access to his effect. But for the most part, the Rogerian reflection is a passive form of psychological reflection in which the analyst only communicates back to the patient what he has heard.

This technique communicates that the analyst has heard and accepts the patient's feelings and does not evaluate them from an alien or differentiated perspective. They do not target the patient's specific feelings so much as they are an emotional communication to the patient's general relational mode. (I have yet to determine whether this type of intervention is addressed to the reasonable or the afflicted ego and don't find the distinction useful here, as I'm not sure that it helps the analyst to refine the way she thinks about or formulates the intervention.) Rogerian reflection seems to work best in states of low-intensity narcissistic transference/countertransference in which the analyst's dominant countertransference is uncomplicated empathy: the patient experiences the analyst as being similar to herself but separate. She is primarily self-focused, with little interest in the particulars of the analyst's separate existence but without significant blurring of ego boundaries. The patient is validated by the analyst's reflective presence, but she does not actually feel merged with or connected with her. Similarly, the analyst feels that she understands the patient but does not feel merged or twinned with her.

These techniques definitely do not work for everyone, even in states of mild narcissistic transference/countertransference. Some patients experience them as the epitome of therapeutic cliché and feel demeaned by them, no matter how genuine the emotional communication. Nevertheless, I am always surprised how often these techniques do work – making the patient feel understood while stabilizing and calming her at the same time.

Joining and mirroring

Joining and mirroring are forms of psychological reflection in which the analyst makes active and explicit use of her own experience to communicate that she is like the patient in specific ways. Where the Rogerian reflection communicates acceptance and understanding of the patient from the position of empathy, joining and mirroring communicate full-blooded solidarity with the patient's thoughts and feelings. Unlike interpretations, they do not address the repetition; rather, they directly target the thoughts and feelings that make up the repetition.

Joining and mirroring are essentially emotional communications to the afflicted ego. Sometimes they can be made without any significant cognitive communication. But when they do include a cognitive communication, it too addresses the afflicted ego. The cognitive communication may sound irrational, reflecting as it does the experience of the afflicted ego. But even when it sounds rational, it reflects the rationality of the repetition – the reason it developed and its emotional adaptive value to the patient – and not the rationality of the here-and-now, reality-oriented reasonable ego.

Joining. In narcissistic joining,[3] the emotional communication conveys that the analyst implicitly shares the patient's feelings in a concrete, specific way; if there is a cognitive communication, it explicitly conveys the analyst's intellectual agreement with the patient's thoughts and feelings. Because both types of communication reflect the patient's thoughts and feelings, successful joining rarely sounds foreign to the patient. It tends to enhance the narcissistic transference rather than disrupt it.

Consider a very simple example. The patient comes from a heavy rainstorm and says, "The weather is just horrible today!" The analyst responds, "It sure is – absolutely disgusting!" The analyst does not, as in Rogerian mirroring, reflect the patient's feelings and thoughts; she straightforwardly agrees with them.

The primary function of a join is to provide an emotional communication directly to the afflicted ego. The cognitive communication also addresses the afflicted ego, serving to deliver, enhance, and fine-tune the emotional communication. While it may increase the patient's cognitive understanding of his feelings, like an interpretation, this is always a secondary purpose of the intervention.

Joining works across the full range of narcissistic states. In low-intensity states, with no blurring of ego boundaries, the join communicates that the analyst is like the patient in a differentiated way. In high-intensity states, with mild to extreme blurring of boundaries, the join communicates that the analyst is like the patient in less differentiated ways, such as states of twinship or even merger.

Although all forms of narcissistic joining express the analyst's sameness with the patient, the analyst's joins can be syntonic or dystonic. We will consider syntonic joining first.

Syntonic joining is used when the patient is in a narcissistic transference characterized by a weak sense of self. It is especially useful with a particular type of weakness: the inability to fully experience a particular feeling – or feelings in general – without validation by another person who shares the feeling. For example, the patient has nascent or inconsistent feelings of being happy, arrogant, or sexually excited and is unable to fully sustain them unless the analyst reflects them. Or the patient is loudly insistent on a particular feeling because she is searching for another person to reflect back its correctness and thereby validate it. The analyst is able to validate them by virtue of being similar to, the same as, or merged with the patient. Furthermore, the transference must be positive in the sense that the analyst is experienced as being like the patient in ways that the patient basically finds acceptable to her sense of self. Only then can the patient use the analyst to fully embrace and sustain the feeling.

A syntonic join not only conveys that the analyst empathically understands the patient, but it also conveys that the patient is right to feel and think as she does, and implicitly, that the analyst shares her relational mode and her specific feelings and/or thoughts. A successful syntonic join slips past the intellectual defenses erected by the reasonable ego to directly engage the afflicted ego, allowing the patient to discuss and embrace feelings that might ordinarily be dismissed as unrealistic or immature.

Joining meets developmental needs for narcissistic attunement in a way that interpretations cannot. It does not help the patient to understand the type of emotional experience she craves as much as it is the experience the patient needs.

As with all joining, syntonic joining can be used across a wide range of narcissistic states. It tends to enhance the narcissistic transference in general, and it has a special affinity for self-directed narcissistic transferences in which ego boundaries are blurred to some degree. (It can be more difficult to use when the analyst is in a strongly self-directed narcissistic countertransference because the analyst easily loses enough awareness of the patient to agree with her.) It is particularly useful with patients who are intolerant of interpretation because they tend to experience it as critical or damaging to their defenses.

Some patients can benefit from both interpretive and joining interventions, but the two interventions are usually not interchangeable. Each provides a different type of emotional experience. Although the cognitive component of a syntonic join may lead to insight or self-awareness, this is always a secondary benefit.

Syntonic joining is less effective when the patient has a strong need to understand his dynamics intellectually, when she needs a more dilute, differentiated narcissistic communication, or when she needs her reasonable ego to be engaged in order to feel understood.

Attempts to use this type of joining in object or anaclitic states may be experienced as ineffective, inauthentic, invasive, or just plain stupid. Rather than feeling that the analyst understands her deeply, the patient may feel she is being manipulated or patronized.

The mechanics of syntonic joining look deceptively simple: the analyst just emotionally agrees with the patient. Let's first look at joining the conscious thoughts and feelings. In a tone of shrewd knowingness, the patient says, "You've got to be careful when you start a new job. Employers always try to screw you." The analyst responds in the same tone. "If you aren't clear on your boundaries right from the start, they'll walk all over you."

Or if the patient says wistfully, "I had the most perfectly caring mother in the world." "Yes, she was truly an angel," the analyst responds in an equally wistful tone.

When the transference is analyst directed, the analyst may bring herself explicitly into the intervention with comments like, "I think that you're right about that." If the transference is more self-directed, the analyst might speak more impersonally, in the tone of universal authority, echoing the patient's thoughts and feelings: "Yes, it's true that . . . " or, "Isn't it always like that!"

What is far more complicated than simply agreeing with the patient is deciding which aspect of the patient's communication to join. Syntonic joining was originally formulated[4] as a particular approach to working with resistance, which is defined as a defense operating in the context of a transference: the idea is that defenses are an expression of a weakness in the ego; joining defenses strengthens the ego until the need for the defense is outgrown. For example, if a patient says that it's dangerous to leave his house, this feeling would be viewed as a resistance/defense against some thought, feeling, fantasy, or memory. The analyst would join the resistance by telling the patient that he was right to avoid going outside. It is indeed dangerous. Often this would make the patient feel more comfortable, stronger, and eventually able to give up the need for the defense.

While this is true, it is often difficult, and not always useful, to distinguish defenses from other parts of the patient's mind, such as impulses, fantasies, inhibitions, feelings, and memories. All feelings can serve defensive functions at some moments; all can be defended against by other feelings at other times. Joining strengthens the patient's sense of self when applied to almost any feeling, whether it is functioning defensively – if it is the right feeling to join.

What is the right feeling to join? Generally, the feeling that needs to be joined is the one that will stabilize or strengthen the sense of self. This may be a defense, or it may be a conscious feeling or impulse that the patient is unable to comfortably sustain on his own. It could also be a preconscious feeling or one side of a set of ambivalent feelings, that the patient is uncomfortable experiencing consciously. Finally, it could be a completely unconscious feeling. In any case, a successful join must always be based on an accurate interpretation of the transference/countertransference configuration at the moment – essentially the same interpretation that would be given to the patient if the analyst were interpreting instead of joining.

Now let's look at how a join interacts with the type of ego weakness it's designed to address: the patient says bitterly, "My life sucks. It really does. I can't stand it. And every time I talk to my god damned mother about it, she tries to cheer me up – tells me to think positive."

The analyst knows, from previous experience, that if she contradicts the patient, the patient either becomes more quietly despairing and withdraws or more argumentative, so she joins the patient.

"Yeah," the analyst says. "Your life really does suck."

"I mean," says the patient, "I live in a shitty apartment with a ridiculous rent. I hate my job. I've got no future, and it's January, and I hate the fucking snow."

"Yep," says the analyst, "it's really horrible. And you haven't even mentioned your worthless boyfriend."

The patient laughs, her mood obviously lighter, brighter. "You're right. I forgot all about that stupid son-of-a-bitch!"

What has transpired here? First, we notice that the patient has expressed her feeling with significant intensity. The problem is not that she can't feel this feeling but rather that she can't sustain it without insisting upon it. The insistence betrays the instability of her emotional situation.

The interpretation of this situation is that the patient does not have the ego strength to experience her feeling of hating her life on her own. She is almost shouting (and will shout, if provoked by contradiction) for a validating response from someone who understands her and agrees with her. She needs to be in the presence of a person who sees and feels things the way she does. This is the narcissistic attunement that she was seeking, unsuccessfully, from her mother – the attunement her mother apparently cannot provide when her mood gets too dark.

Understanding why she feels the way she does is not what this patient needs. Rather, she needs the experience of being related to in a specific way. The analyst's cognitive and emotional agreement validates her. Her mood improves, partly because she no longer has to fight to prove her point. The outside world is no longer totally against her. She feels that she is in the company of a like-minded other who's mirroring communications strengthen her ability to sustain her feelings.

Now let's look at an example that works primarily through questions:

"My husband has a new complaint," the patient says dully.

"Again? What's his problem this time?" (The tone mirrors but slightly intensifies the patient's, expressing weariness with the ongoing conflict.)

"Something completely new. I don't enliven him enough when he is depressed."

"How are you supposed to enliven him?" (This time, the tone mirrors her non-comprehension and exasperation at his complaint.)

"That's just the thing! He goes to his shrink, he comes back with a new accusation, and I'm supposed to understand it!"

"How could you possibly understand it?" (Mirrors and somewhat intensifies her defiant hopelessness about the issue.)

"I never get him, I just never get him! He tells me this stuff like I'm supposed to read his mind. But I guess I could ask him what he means. You know, ask him for some examples, couldn't I?"

"Why not?" (Mirrors and expresses agreement with her attempt to find a solution to the problem.)

Notice that the analyst's cognitive communications add almost nothing to what the patient is saying. The analyst is working primarily with questions that don't challenge the patient's feelings or perspective. Each question is asked in a way that is implicitly grounded in the patient's emotional logic and shared by the analyst.

The overall effect of successful syntonic joining is to stabilize the patient's sense of self. Once this is accomplished, the patient is often able to consider the situation from different angles and becomes able to experience different feelings. Total agreement with the patient's perspective usually leads to increased flexibility. In the first example, having her worldview joined might allow the patient to have other feelings about her life, such as happiness or contentment. In the second example, joining might eventually allow the patient to consider what her husband is saying to her from a less purely defensive position. In both examples, the patient's feelings were fully conscious, right out in the open.

Now, let's look at how the syntonic joining can be used to help a patient to expand her emotional range to include feelings that she might be less aware of, less comfortable with, or ambivalent about expressing.

The patient's father is ill, near death, and the patient has great expectations. He needs the inheritance. He's broke, wants to buy a house with his boyfriend, and doesn't think he will ever make enough money to do so. The patient loves his father deeply, but every now and then he has images of having tons of money and being able to do whatever he wants for the first time in his life. Furthermore, the patient is dimly aware that his father has been pretty stingy with him and hasn't been truly accepting of his sexuality. The analyst starts to wish that the father would hurry up and die so that the patient can get the money. The analyst also thinks that he might raise the patient's fee then and feels guilty about these thoughts.

NARCISSISTIC EMOTIONAL COMMUNICATIONS

The content of the session – the ambivalence about his desire for his father's money – is overtly about a relationship to a different person, an object repetition. But the countertransference suggests that patient and analyst are relating in the narcissistic mode. Thus, the transference repetition is grounded in the patient's self-experience: he has trouble fully accepting his feelings of greed and aggression. However, he does not have a strong defense against them: he can let the thoughts in, but he's not comfortable with them. He's on the edge of being able to integrate these feelings but not quite there. He sounds fuzzy, tentative, and awkward.

The patient says, rather timidly, that the thought has occurred to him that he might be able to buy the house he wants sooner than he thinks if his father dies, but that's a terrible way to think, isn't it? The analyst says that on the contrary, it's a perfectly practical way to think. Doesn't everybody think about the money they will inherit when somebody dies? The patient relaxes and agrees. Maybe he will be able to start looking really soon, he adds. Maybe right after the funeral, says the analyst. The patient chuckles and adds, "Why wait, he's as good as dead anyway. Maybe I could start looking right away."[5]

In this example, the analyst's comments pick up and extend, ever so slightly, the patient's conscious thoughts and feelings. And his emotional communication says loud and clear that he thinks it is just fine that the patient is thinking about his father's money. Implicitly, he would feel exactly the same way. The patient's feelings are validated, which strengthens his sense of self. Given that the patient has reported few experiences like this with his parents, the intervention has probably served the purpose of meeting a developmental need to have his greedy feelings reflected and accepted by someone who shares them.

If the analyst thought the patient could tolerate going a little further in this same direction, he might add something a little stronger. "After all, he hasn't exactly been generous with you. And he hasn't been particularly accepting of you being gay. Hell, you might say he owes you the house." This would contain more interpretive content but with a much stronger narcissistic emotional communication than if these impulses had simply been interpreted empathically.

However, this last intervention would run a higher risk of making the patient feel misunderstood and attacked, as an interpretation might do. Although joining can work with much more heavily defended material than interpretation, there is still a limit beyond which even a join will disrupt the narcissistic transference. If the feeling the analyst is trying to join is deeply incompatible with the patient's sense of self, the intervention is likely to fail. Indeed, when a join miscarries in this way, the result can be even more jarring than an interpretation.

When this occurs, it means that the analyst may be joining the wrong dimension of the patient's experience. If, for example, the patient's greed and his slightly veiled death wish towards his father were heavily defended, this would mean that these feelings are intolerable and potentially destabilizing. In this case, the analyst needs to join the defenses against accepting and embracing these feelings. Once this is accomplished, the patient is usually in a stronger position to reconsider them. Consider the following example:

"You know, every now and then the thought comes into my mind that I could get the money for a house when my father dies. But I hate it. I chase it away!"

"Why," asks the analyst?

"Because the most important thing for me is to become self-sufficient, not rely on my father."

"Yes, waiting for money could weaken you," says the analyst in a tone expressing total agreement with the patient's reasoning and feelings.

"Exactly! Besides, I keep saying that I want to be independent of my father. Wanting to get money from him ties me more deeply to him. Although I guess if he's dead, I'm not really going to be attached to him."

This is an example of how the analyst's agreement and solidarity with the patient's defenses serves to reinforce them. One possible result of this approach is that the patient, feeling understood and strengthened by the analyst's agreement, will be able to allow other, previously defended feelings into his consciousness – probably including the desire for the inheritance. In the long term, this is the most likely outcome.

But it is also possible that the patient, feeling understood, will also feel confirmed in his decision not to think about using his inheritance without having allowed himself to experience the defended feelings. However, he will probably be more at peace with himself about the issue. Thus, his sense of self will have been strengthened but possibly at the expense of some degree of emotional freedom. Often times this is temporary; sometimes it's not.

If it's not temporary, an analyst can legitimately consider whether the repetition has been loosened. The outcome depends on which one the analyst is looking at: the repetition related to the more general weakness of the patient's sense of self, leading to the inner turmoil and self-doubt, has been loosened; the one related to defending against his feelings of greed and his death wish towards his father has not.

What does this mean? It must be acknowledged that solidifying the patient's sense of self in this way does not always lead to the increase in emotional freedom that analytic theory posits as a goal of treatment. This may have occurred because joining in this way was not the ideal way of approaching this situation. It is possible that a different approach would have better expanded the patient's emotional freedom.

In general, the goal of stabilizing the patient's sense of self is more important, in both the short term and the long term, than enabling the patient to feel that particular set of feelings. Furthermore, it is possible that the patient has a degree of choice, whether conscious or unconscious, about how far she is willing and/or able to stretch herself to experience feelings that are incompatible to her sense of self. At some point, everyone stops expanding and settles with the way they are at the time. The analytic ideal of being able to say and feel everything always has its individual limits. Nothing works all the time, and sometimes it's difficult to know whether the issue is a problem with the analyst's skill or an expression of the patient's will.

Thus far, we have discussed joining conscious and pre-conscious feelings that are congruent with the content. And what of more deeply unconscious feelings based on more profoundly incongruent inductions? Occasionally, these can be successfully joined. When this happens, the analyst makes a comment that relates to what she hypothesizes the patient is feeling but has nothing to do with the content of the patient's communication. One analyst described a patient who was talking about a seemingly superficial conflict with her boyfriend. The discussion involved something about how they were going to divide the housework, and the patient had asserted herself more than usual. Both she and the analyst were pleased with her progress. As they concluded the discussion the analyst said, "And remember, your vagina is your house. You have to keep it safe," at which point they locked eyes, smiled, and nodded heads in synchrony.

The analyst was flabbergasted. The intervention had been completely spontaneous. She had no idea why she had done it. But after she said it, she sensed a profound oneness between them. It was clear to me that the patient had felt understood on a deep, primitive level, even though the analyst had no idea what she had understood. The patient had a history of sexual abuse, which she had previously discussed. This may have had been unconsciously linked to the discussion with the boyfriend about the housework. The analyst's intervention seemed to be received as though she was agreeing with the measures that she was taking to protect herself from sexual attack.

I've heard of similar interventions being formulated and delivered deliberately, based on incongruent countertransference feelings. When they work, the results are impressive, as if the analyst has found a way to talk directly to the patient's unconscious wishes and impulses, bypassing the defenses that surround the issue in question. Occasionally I have been successful in this type of intervention, but most of my attempts have failed miserably. The patients either ignored me or reacted as if I were talking nonsense. I eventually stopped trying because I suspect that I lack whatever skill is necessary to make this kind of intervention work consistently. And I suspect that I am not alone. Addressing the unconscious directly requires a special type of talent.

In these examples, the analyst worked with specific feelings that were problematic for the patient. However, joining can also be used to work with the patient's need for narcissistic relatedness as a whole. In this case, the analyst might agree with whatever the patient's perceptions are, whether the patient is conflicted about it. For example, the patient says that it is hot. The analyst agrees that it's sweltering. The patient goes on to complain about a political event that enraged him. The analyst agrees it's disgusting. Then the patient complains about his wife. The analyst concurs that wives are like that. And so on. In this situation, the analyst's comments actively reflect that patient's experience as a whole. Joining would be used when the patient needs his sense of self to be reinforced as a whole, as opposed to a specific feeling here and there.

Syntonic joining can meet unmet developmental needs for the type of narcissistic attunement that allows the patient to generate affect, positive or negative. For example, a patient says blandly that he would like to take a trip. The analyst feels excited and begins to think of all the wonderful things there are to do in the world. He replies, with just a touch more enthusiasm than the patient, "Where would you like to go?" The patient brightens up a little. He'd like to go to London. The analyst asks more questions, making comments that subtly tune up the excitement to the level that he thinks the patient aspires to but cannot reach on his own. The emotional communication conveys that the analyst shares the patient's excitement, feels that it is a good idea, and gives the patient permission to embrace the fantasies and fully enjoy them. These exchanges are similar to aspects of the development of positive affect between parent and infant (Stern 1985; Schore 1994).

Joining can reflect the patient's ambitions, goals, and grandiosity – reinforcing the developmental process described by Kohut (1971) – but it's not limited to that. A wide range of feelings can be joined, provided the patient is in a state of narcissistic transference in which he can tolerate a strong narcissistic bond with the analyst. In these cases, the effect will be to enhance the patient's degree of comfort with his feelings and the solidity of her sense of self. It is a far more powerful way of relating to the patient than through an empathically informed interpretation.

Syntonic joining is particularly useful for communicating that the analyst accepts, understands, and implicitly shares feelings that the patient may feel are shameful, crazy, and weird, helping her to accept thoughts and feelings that are mild to moderately incompatible with her sense of self or defended against. For example, a patient says guiltily that she felt like strangling her baby after having been kept up half the night. The analyst responds, "I'm surprised you didn't feel that way after five minutes." If successful, the patient feels less guilty about her aggression towards her child, and more able to experience these feelings and elaborate on them with the analyst.

When the patient is in a narcissistic transference and induces a narcissistic countertransference, the analyst usually feels the same feelings as the patient, and it is relatively easy to agree with the patient. As in the case of interpretation, the analyst must be careful not to assume that everything that she feels can be the basis of an intervention. It is always possible that the analyst is comfortable feeling something that is alien to the patient's sense of self, and that will disrupt the narcissistic transference. The risk is far lower than with interpretation, but it is still very much there.

Syntonic joining is more difficult when the patient does not induce the feelings that need to be joined. Indeed, in this very common type of repetition, the patient induces the opposite feelings to those that need to be joined. She needs emotional and cognitive agreement, but instead she induces emotional and cognitive disagreement. This might be an object induction, or it might be an induction of the self-hating part of the patient's mind. Whatever the reason, the analyst experiences the desire to confront, dispute, or modify in some more benign way the patient's feelings or perception of reality. Often, the analyst has the desire to say almost anything to the patient except what the patient needs to hear, either because she doesn't feel like agreeing with the patient or because the feeling that the patient needs the analyst to validate is so illogical, unrealistic, or brutal that the analyst loathes the idea of communicating it. For example, the patient who felt guilty about wanting to strangle her child needed the analyst to validate that feeling. When the patient induces the same feeling, it's easy. When she doesn't, it can seem completely impossible.

This is when intentional, intellectually driven empathy is required to auto-induce the feeling. Once the analyst understands what feeling the patient needs, why she needs it from a biographical and dynamic perspective, how it will be experienced in the context of the narcissistic transference/counter-transference relationship, and what function it will serve in the patient's current self-state, it is usually possible for the analyst to actually experience the required feeling. This may take time – sometimes a very long time – a period that is part of the working-through process for both the patient and the analyst. But the wait and the work are well worth it. The impact on the patient can be quite powerful.

All too often, joining is viewed (both by partisans and its critics) as a form of reverse psychology, like the paradoxical interventions developed by the family therapists, rather than as a form of emotional communication. This is partly because the effects of a join sometimes appear to be paradoxical, in the sense that the patient does the opposite of what the analyst suggests. For example, the analyst tells the patient that she is right to be frightened, and the patient becomes more courageous. If he tells her she should be angry with her mother, and she becomes more understanding.

Of course, this doesn't always happen. We must remember that sometimes a join will strengthen the patient's sense of self without changing her feelings. But even when the patient experiences the opposite extreme of feeling after a join, the paradoxical effect is only superficial. The change is due to the patient feeling more comfortable with the feeling in question, more accepting of it, and having a stronger sense of self. Once her sense of self is stronger, she becomes more capable of experiencing other feelings. This is why he changed her emotional position – not because the analyst has performed emotional judo on her.[6]

It is true that the cognitive component of a syntonic join, like all techniques, can sometimes work without the corresponding emotional communication. This usually occurs when the patient's narcissistic transference is so strong that it completely distorts her experience of the analyst. More often, a join without the correct emotional communication sounds mechanical and is experienced as fake.

What makes syntonic joining work deeply and curatively is the emotional communication that goes with the cognitive communication – the genuine feeling that the analyst conveys that she does in fact agree with the patient's perception and implicitly shares the same feeling as the patient. This frees the patient, in Kohut and Wolf's (1978) words, of the burden of unshared emotionality. The patient is no longer alone with her feelings. She is with another person who is similar to her, and this eases the burden of even the most painful feelings.

When the emotional communication accurately meets the patient's narcissistic needs, the patient usually experiences a profound sense of relief and comfort. This is sometimes coupled with a feeling of surprise, especially when the analyst agrees with something that the patient feels or thinks is usually considered to be illogical or unrealistic.

The true emotional flavor of a successful join is difficult to convey, not only in writing but also verbally if it is heard outside the experience of the patient's feelings – the narcissistic transference. Outside of this context, a join can sound contrived, illogical, or insincere.

Analysts who are unfamiliar with syntonic joining often wonder whether it is really a form of collusion with the patient's pathology. In other words, does joining simply enable a patient to remain in the repetition, thereby preventing her from making the changes she claims to want?

This is a legitimate concern, and it does seem logical: why would agreeing with the patient lead to change?

The reason may be that the patient's attachment to the repetition is almost always reinforced by feeling alone, isolated, and misunderstood, while the experience of feeling understood to the degree produced by a successful syntonic join is so powerfully maturational that it almost automatically leads to a change in the patient's subjective experience of the problem and a reduction in her feeling of isolation. Feeling understood usually strengthens and stabilizes the patient's sense of self: this allows her to experience a greater range of feelings and to consider alternative perspectives on her situation. This is not to say that she immediately becomes less attached to either the feelings or the defenses that comprise the repetition. But she does become less invested in the need to defend and protect her point of view. This tends to lead to greater emotional and behavioral flexibility.

Furthermore, it is probable that the patient knows, in some part of her reasonable ego, that the repetition, no matter how understandable in the context of her afflicted ego and its experience of her life history, is to some degree self-destructive in the context of her current circumstances. Once her afflicted ego feels understood, her reasonable ego can reassert itself more effectively in the present.

Whatever the reason, syntonic joins do not tend to lead the patient to become more rigidly entrenched in the pathology. This sometimes seems to happen on a short-term basis, with the patient saying something to the effect of: "I knew I was right! At last someone agrees with me! I'm sticking to my guns!" Over time, however, the patient usually becomes less entrenched in the pathology, not more. This might take time, but it is the usual course of things.

But not always. I don't think I have ever seen a syntonic join actually make a patient worse, but it doesn't always lead to the desired change. No technique, no approach to communicating with the patient, works consistently in the expectable manner in every instance. An intervention can always be experienced differently than the analyst intends it. The analyst must be alert to the possibility that this, like any intervention, will backfire.

Dystonic joining. Dystonic narcissistic joining[7] is a powerful emotional communication used exclusively to reverse unstable, dystonic states of pathological self-absorption and self-directed aggression. Before considering dystonic joining in detail, let's first review the structure of the states of pathological self-absorption. These states arise when the patient has developed a pattern of experiencing aggression or rage at another person that she is unable to discharge outward and instead attacks herself. The self-attack may take the form of depression or low self-esteem, confusion, psychosis, masochistic or self-defeating behavior, psychosomatic illness,[8] or conversion reactions, or anything similar. The patient's aggression is directed towards herself for any (or all) of three reasons:

1. The aggression is originally the patient's own aggression. The patient is angry at a disappointing other person (object) to whom she had related in a partially narcissistic way; this person (object) has been introjected into her identify. Consequently, the patient rages at herself as a way of attacking the introjected other person. This is the state of melancholic depression (Freud 1917).
2. The aggression is originally another person's – a person who has been aggressive or abusive to the patient. This abusive object has been introjected into her identity. The aggressive introject continues to attack the patient through self-attack. This type of situation has been described extensively by Klein (1946).
3. The aggression is originally the patient's own. The patient is enraged but afraid her rage will destroy the other person; consequently, she attacks herself to avoid harming the other person. This is the state of the narcissistic defense (Spotnitz 1976).

In all three scenarios, aggression that should be expressed outward has become directed towards the patient herself, leading the patient into a narcissistic self-absorbed state that is defensive in nature, i.e., unrelated to narcissistic needs of normal development. Typically, this dynamic becomes the general pattern for the patient's expression of aggression.[9]

This pattern is always painful for the patient and always involves a restriction in her emotional life. However, it is often a stable, syntonic dynamic that is deeply embedded in the patient's character. At these times, the analyst might need to join the patient in ways that do not superficially appear to be syntonic. For example, the patient might say, "I know that my work schedule is killing me, but my boyfriend says that he needs more money for clothes, so I don't see what else I can do." The analyst, neither seduced by the logic nor induced to agree with the patient, asks questions that imply that there might be alternatives or that the boyfriend's demands are excessive, unreasonable, or abusive. The patient, however, gets threatened and anxious and only hardens in her insistence on the need to sacrifice herself to meet her boyfriend's needs. The analyst begins to feel that she's right; regardless of how it looks, she really doesn't have any choice at this point. She really does have to sacrifice herself. So the analyst says, "Yes, you're stuck. You have to keep working hard. It's terrible." At this point, the patient feels calmed and understood, even if still rather miserable. The analyst has made a syntonic join.

These types of syntonic joins calm the patient in the moment. But over time, they tend to destabilize the dynamic. The patient becomes increasingly uncomfortable with the repetition, and the analyst senses that the patient is striving to be free of it and to hate others rather than herself. Sometimes further syntonic joins, adapted to the patient's changing degree of comfort towards the pattern of self-attack, help the patient progress to the point of expressing her outward aggression. For example, the analyst might ask the same questions that initially made the patient anxious, indirectly suggesting that the boyfriend is unreasonable and that the patient is being victimized. In the countertransference, the analyst usually remains empathic with and sympathetic to the patient's dilemma, and these feelings fuel the syntonic joins.

But things may not evolve in this way. Another possibility is that the patient strains to reverse the self-attack but always comes back to it, at ever higher degrees of intensity. Using the same example, the patient begins to agree that her boyfriend's demands are impossible. Besides his demands for money, he doesn't do anything else in the house. She does feel like a slave. The analyst asks why she doesn't tell him to get a job and do some of the work around the house. "I can't," she says. "He loves me; I'm his girlfriend. But it makes me feel like kind of a loser," she says bitterly. The analyst can almost taste the patient releasing her attack against the world. But it always flies back at herself. The pattern of self-attack is now dystonic, but the patient still cannot free herself of it.

In the countertransference, the analyst now feels critical of her, either for the same reasons she attacks herself or because she attacks herself. The analyst's feelings are the same, either in direct content or through analogy, as the patient's feelings about herself – the feelings characteristic of a sadistic superego, a critical introject, or some such structure. The analyst is empathic, but not sympathetic. This suggests that the patient is in a narcissistic transference in which she experiences the analyst in the same way she experiences the part of herself that attacks herself, as one aspect of her afflicted ego.[10] This is the time when a dystonic join might be helpful.

The analyst asks whether she has an objection to being a loser. The patient laughs a bit nervously.

"Well, nobody likes a loser," she says.

"Actually, your boyfriend seems to like a loser. Or at least, he's willing to put up with one. After all, he gets money for clothes, he doesn't do a thing around the house. Who wouldn't?"

Another laugh from the patient, more noticeably miserable from than before, but with a hint of irritability in it.

"So what does that mean?" she asks, "I'm supposed to just keep giving him everything and work my ass off for him; is that what you're saying?"

"Yes," says the analyst firmly. "That's what losers are for, isn't it?"

At this point the patient's rage begins to flow, attacking the analyst for calling her a loser, for not helping her to stand up to her son-of-a-bitch boyfriend, for telling her she's supposed to sacrifice her life so that she can be loved by that stupid, exploitive fucker. (In real time this exchange might take place over a single session, or it might require weeks or months of work, with lots of down time in between.)

In a dystonic join, therefore, the analyst uses the negative feelings towards the patient to agree with patient's negative feelings about herself, for the purpose of stimulating the patient to attack the analyst instead of herself. By giving expression to these feelings in a carefully modulated way, the join externalizes that part of the patient's mind – the attacking part of the afflicted ego – onto the analyst and simultaneously mobilizes a rebellion against it. The intervention transforms a self-directed transference into an analyst-directed transference. The result of a successful dystonic join is to pull the patient out of the self-absorbed, self-attacking state and into a more differentiated state in which she expresses anger towards the analyst, experiencing her either as a narcissistic object, a critical twin, or a hated separate object.

Dystonic joins are difficult to make. They are specifically designed to help patients who manage anger towards others (whether experienced as narcissistic objects or separate objects) by directing against themselves. They must be made just at the point when anger is at or just below the surface of their consciousness, ripe to come out but still held in check to the extent that the analyst is certain that the patient will not be able to discharge it without this assistance. But if they are made before the patient is ready, they make the problem worse, not better. Almost any outcome other than the patient counter-attacking the analyst is problematic (keeping in mind that multiple interventions may be required over time to get the desired effect). A patient who is not yet able to discharge aggression will become more depressed and more tightly entrenched in the defensive self-absorption.

Furthermore, an angry response in and of itself does not indicate that the intervention was successful. Patients who are readily able to discharge rage at the analyst do not benefit from this type of intervention. Similarly, a sadomasochistic transference/countertransference configuration can be mistaken for a negative narcissistic configuration, in which case dystonic joining will simply perpetuate the sadomasochistic repetition.

These considerations highlight that dystonic joining is a particular form of emotional communication that is useful only in a particular form of transference. Attempts to use it for other purposes generally fail, often spectacularly.

These interventions are most effective when based on an induction in which the analyst experiences the feelings of the part of the patient's mind that is engaged in criticizing and attacking herself. In other words, the analyst feels aggressive towards or critical of the patient. These feelings have to be genuine. If the analyst makes a dystonic join that she doesn't mean, the patient may feel (at best) that the analyst isn't serious, or (at worst) that she is being toyed with.

Many analysts have trouble allowing themselves to give voice to (or even to experience) the intensely negative feelings that are used in dystonic joining.[11] It is often felt – quite understandably – that the feelings communicated in these joins are exactly those that are maintaining the repetition as is. It is profoundly counterintuitive to expect that agreeing with the patient in ways that are most painful for her will have any sort of curative impact.

On the other hand, it can also be extremely tempting to join the patient's attack on herself. After all, the patient, by inducing this intense narcissistic induction, is begging for it, albeit involuntarily. And it can be exhilarating to have license to express feelings that are usually confined to private, sadistic fantasies or behind-the-back jokes. The intervention can even be further rationalized by the idea that it is good for the patient to know what effect she has on another person when she behaves like that.[12]

Thus, the analyst must steer a delicate course between allowing herself to experience the full measure of the feelings and not enjoying them too much. It is usually a bad idea to make a dystonic join when the analyst is feeling only negative feelings towards the patient. These emotional communications work best when the negative feelings are embedded in a backdrop that includes positive feelings and high levels of emotional and professional commitment towards the patient. The raw induction, therefore, almost never serves as a good basis for the intervention. Dystonic joins made spontaneously, without regard to the total emotional communication, are usually destructive.

Dystonic joins were, in a sense, the signature intervention of Modern Psychoanalytic technique. This is not because they were ever the most common Modern Analytic intervention but because they illustrate more clearly than any other intervention how negative emotional communication can have a curative impact. Although using these sorts of interventions was an important part of my training, I rarely use them. I have found that containing the negative feelings often leads to the same effect, with less risk. But it does take longer. Furthermore, there are situations in which a dystonic join will reach the patient when no other form of emotional communication will, and for these moments, it is indispensable.

Mirroring

Like joining, mirroring is an active form of psychological reflection in which the analyst experiences the same feelings as the patient and then expresses the same thoughts or feelings as the patient. It differs from joining in that the analyst does not simply agree with the patient's perception; the analyst goes further and expresses the feeling as her own, taking full responsibility for it, with or without specific reference to her similarity to the patient. The underlying message of joining is *"You're right. I agree with you."* In contrast, the underlying message of mirroring is *"Me too, I'm just like you."*

Although mirroring can be used in differentiated narcissistic states, it is most effective when the patient is either in an extroverted narcissistic transference in which she experiences the analyst as a twin, with or without blurred ego boundaries, or in self-directed introverted narcissistic transference in which there are blurred ego boundaries creating a feeling of merger. On the countertransference side, the analyst must experience the same feelings as the patient, both towards herself and towards the world and must also view the patient as a twin. Even more so than in joining, the feelings must be genuine. While there is always a risk that the patient will feel mocked by mirroring this reaction is almost guaranteed if the feelings are fake.

As with joining, mirroring can be syntonic or dystonic. We will consider syntonic mirroring first.

Syntonic mirroring. In syntonic mirroring, the analyst expresses feelings that are consistent or syntonic with the patient's sense of self. Like syntonic joining, the emotional communication is intended to validate and strengthen the patient's sense of self. However, the analyst is more explicit that he feels the same way the patient does. The patient sheepishly mentions that he is afraid of flying. The analyst responds, "Ugh, flying. Scares me to death." Or the patient says he feels isolated at the office because he's so much smarter than everyone else. The analyst responds, every bit as haughty as the patient, "I know what you mean. Most of the analysts I meet are absolute dumbshits. I'm just luckier than you because I don't have to see them every day." The patient complains that her boyfriend leaves his socks all over the place, and the analyst chimes back, "Don't you just hate it when they do that!" As with syntonic joining, both the cognitive and the emotional communications are addressed to the afflicted ego but with even more emphasis on the emotional communication that conveys the sameness of patient and analyst. They are two peas in a pod, united in nourishing harmony.

Mirroring (again more than joining) usually reflects the patient's tone, speech rhythms, and vocabulary as well. This must be done with subtlety and real feeling; otherwise the patient is liable to feel manipulated, demeaned, or mocked through sarcastic imitation. When done correctly, however, it is both stabilizing and validating, and the impact on the patient's sense of self is powerful.

Mirroring can work with discrete moments and feelings, but it is often most powerful when the analyst mirrors the patient's whole mode of thinking, feeling, and relating. This can be done deliberately. What is fascinating about mirroring, however, is how often it develops spontaneously and preconsciously out of the narcissistic transference/countertransference.

The patient and analyst often move in synchrony when they are in states of twinship or merger. The analyst's voice automatically tends to fall into the same cadences as the patient's. The analyst has similar interests, similar reactions, and similar curiosities as the patient. They may have similar weaknesses as well. For example, the patient loses the check, while the analyst loses the bill, and nobody is upset because they understand each other. Patient and analyst seem to hum along in perfect attunement. These moments of syntonic mirroring can be intensely intimate and satisfying.

On the other hand, they can be extremely unpleasant as well. Take the analyst who finds that she is unable to formulate a clear sentence when she is with a patient who can't collect his thoughts or the analyst whose voice begins to tremble in harmony with the patient's freely expressed anxiety as examples.

A kind of spontaneous mirroring often occurs when the analyst is in a state of symmetrical narcissistic countertransference. For example, in cases where the patient and the analyst each become the object of an identical paranoid suspicion of each other, each can begin to relate to the other as if they were a threat to be managed and avoided.

Strictly speaking, this sort of unplanned, unconscious mirroring is an acting-in rather than an intervention. This isn't to say that it can't be deeply curative, but it also may not be. A patient in the twinship or merger transference frequently requires the analyst to engage in this sort of mirroring, at least initially, in order for the environment to be similar enough to be compelling. But what the analyst doesn't immediately know is whether the spontaneous mirroring will also be different enough to be curative. If the patient is experiencing the narcissistic transference because her narcissistic needs were not adequately met in childhood, then she needs them to be met now, and the spontaneous mirroring will be a curative emotional communication. On the other hand, it is also possible that the narcissistic transference and its accompanying countertransference are a repetition of an earlier interpersonal relationship and that what is needed now is a different sort of emotional communication.

For example, a supervisee described a patient who felt completely helpless and induced similar feelings in the analyst. The patient and the analyst both feel helpless, and the analyst fumbles around just as much as the patient in an effort to understand what is going on. It is possible that the emotional communication the patient needs is an anaclitic one, requiring the analyst to pull herself out of the induced hopelessness and into the role of active parental caretaker to the helpless patient.

When mirroring that is supposed to be syntonic misfires, the results can be disastrous. I once did an initial session with a teenager who was paranoid and threatening in a covert sort of way. He described a number of situations in which he said that he had to be very careful because he might get in trouble. He then asked me to tell the psychiatrist, who he was supposed to see after me, that I didn't think he had anything wrong with him and that he didn't need to see him. I told him that I too had to be very careful about what I said to the psychiatrist because I was afraid that I might get in trouble. I was attempting to mirror his paranoia. Furthermore, this was not really a fabrication because I actually did have to be careful about what I said to the psychiatrist, and so it seemed, in my inexperienced state, that this was also genuine. In any case, the intervention had the effect of inflaming him. "Hell, if you can't do anything around here without getting in trouble, then what do I need you for?" he shouted and stormed out, slamming the door. I had inadvertently made a dystonic mirror, which prematurely released an uncontrolled outburst of aggression.

Dystonic mirroring. Like dystonic joining, the purpose of dystonic mirroring is to reverse a state of pathological self-absorption created by self-hatred or self-directed aggression. And the purpose of both types of dystonic emotional communications is to draw the patient's aggression away from herself and towards the analyst. However, they are applicable to slightly different types of narcissistic transference/countertransference configurations in which the analyst experiences different aspects of the patient's feelings.

In dystonic joining, the analyst experiences the feelings of the part of the patient's mind that is critical or hateful towards the patient, such as a sadistic superego. The purpose of the intervention is to both externalize the self-attacking part and to stimulate a rebellion against its tyrannical hold on the patient's functioning. In mirroring, on the other hand, the analyst experiences the patient's feelings of being attacked and criticized. When she communicates to the patient that she is just like her, she is attempting to draw the fury of the attacking part of the patient's mind towards her for being as deficient as the patient's own ego.

I once worked with an eight-year-old girl who constantly criticized herself. For example, she would color in a drawing and then attack herself for making a bad drawing, calling herself stupid. I felt extremely stupid as I witnessed this because her drawings were actually much better than anything I could do, and I didn't seem to be much of an analyst for her either, as none of her problems seemed to be getting any better. I mirrored her by also coloring a drawing and doing the same thing she did – attacking myself for making a bad drawing and calling myself stupid. In other words, I was just like her – except maybe a little worse. Over a period of a couple of sessions, she began to tell me that I was even more stupid than she was, and that her drawings were better than mine. I felt just terrible when she did this. Her criticisms really hurt. But it was worth it; this eventually led to a lowering of her anxiety and getting along better with her mother.

Dystonic mirroring, like dystonic joining, is a complex intervention to use. It is important that the analyst genuinely feels the negative feeling that the patient is attacking and also accepts the feeling. For example, if the analyst is mirroring the patient's feeling of incompetence, the analyst must be able to tolerate the feeling of incompetence without becoming swept away in self-attack herself, either as a result of her own feelings or after having been criticized by the patient. In other words, the analyst's message must be "Yes, it's true, I'm incompetent. Feel free to attack me, but as far as I am concerned, I don't object to being incompetent and I will not crumble under your attack."

This is important for a number of reasons. First, and perhaps the most basic, the analyst must not allow herself to be genuinely harmed by the patient. She owes it to herself, to her other patients, and to the people in her life to practice in a way that preserves her emotional and physical health.

Second, the patient cannot safely release the rage that is bound up in self-attack unless she is sure that the analyst will not be harmed by it. The whole function of one form of self-attack – the narcissistic defense – is to protect the object. Thus, if the object can be harmed, then helping the patient to direct the rage outward may work in the short term, but it will leave the patient feeling horribly guilty and convince her that she is genuinely dangerous and must keep her aggression directed inward.

Third, even those patients who would not be immediately harmed by hurting the analyst are liable to be harmed in the long term by learning from the analyst that it is acceptable to hurt other people with their aggression. While there is a measure of truth in this – all people hurt each other to some extent and must learn to tolerate it – devastating other people with whom they are involved is another matter altogether.

Fourth, the patient may lose confidence in the analytic process as a whole if she can't withstand the emotions that she has unleashed. The analytic relationship is a partnership, and the analyst must be the driver. It is acceptable for the patient to take over from time to time but not at a moment as intense as this. The patient is liable to leave the analyst in disgust, or stay in treatment out of pity, and neither of these options will do either of them any good.

For all of these reasons, the analyst must be in a strong state of self-acceptance and self-resilience to weather the storm that may be unleashed by a successful dystonic mirror.

Finally, there is one more way in which dystonic mirroring is related to the patient's well-being. By feeling, expressing, and accepting the feelings that the patient so strongly objects to, the analyst conveys that the feeling, however contemptible it may be, has its place in the spectrum of human emotions, and this usually allows the patient to integrate it into her own personality in a different way than before. This last function of dystonic mirroring overlaps into a closely related type of intervention – modeling – which will be discussed in greater detail below.

Modeling

In modeling, the analyst makes use of a specific narcissistic transference/countertransference configuration to modify the patient's defenses against experiencing a feeling that she has not previously allowed herself to feel. The analyst does this by demonstrating that it is acceptable to experience and express a feeling that is strongly inimical to the reasonable ego.

In order for this to be successful, the patient must be in a state of mild merger or strong twinship with the analyst, usually with some blurring of ego boundaries. Furthermore, it must be an idealizing transference, or at least a strongly positive transference. In the countertransference, the analyst has access to the feeling that the patient does not allow herself to feel. Under these conditions, the analyst expresses the feeling as her own – taking full responsibility for it – in the expectation that this will enable the patient to emulate the analyst and experience it for herself. The intervention conveys the message *"I can experience and express this feeling; why shouldn't you?"* When this works, the patient feels that she can allow herself to feel the feeling because the idealized analyst feels it. The intervention expands the patient's emotional freedom into realms of feelings that she had not previously been able to experience.

Successful modeling is always a syntonic emotional communication. It is not clear whether the distinction between the afflicted ego and the reasonable ego is helpful in understanding the therapeutic action of this intervention. It is addressed to the afflicted ego, but when it is successful, the reasonable ego becomes much more flexible. While this is true of all interventions addressed to the afflicted ego, it is more immediately obvious with modeling. A patient may feel deeply understood or liberated after a successful join or mirror but not understand why. The communication has completely bypassed the reasonable ego. This doesn't happen with modeling. The cognitive communication in modeling is straightforward, and it doesn't have even a superficially paradoxical effect. Although modeling is used to work with feelings that are objectionable to the reasonable ego, it does so from the perspective that the reasonable ego's attitude towards them is just plain wrong. For example, the analyst might cheerfully observe that it can be great fun thinking about slashing somebody's face, as though this were the most obvious idea in the world. The purpose is to help the patient to accept, and eventually embrace, these sadistic fantasies. If the intervention is successful, the patient will know this: *"If it's okay for the analyst to feel it, it's okay for me, too."*

Let's look at a simple example of modeling and then move on to different variations.

The patient is extremely inhibited about expressing any annoyance or aggression towards her mother, who is subtly undercutting and condescending towards her most of the time. The patient describes telling her mother about a new man that she is dating, and the mother starts her usually litany of questions: Where's he from? How much money does he make? Why is he single? Or if he's divorced, what happened? He's not Jewish? Did he pay for the date? And on, and on. The patient says her mother has her best interests at heart. Nevertheless, she also knows that this set of questions always leads her to doubt herself, cut out of the relationship, and remain single.

When the patient first described these interactions to the analyst, the analyst was suspicious of the mother's motives but didn't have a particularly strong emotional reaction. But as time went on she began feeling enraged at the mother, which she hypothesized was the patient's mounting rage and resentment.

"That's quite a list of questions," says the analyst in a tone of mild exasperation.

"What do you mean?" asks the patient. There is a little anxiety in her voice, but also a quickening interest.

"I mean I would find them kind of pushy."

"Really?" The patient laughs.

"Yes, really."

It is important that when a feeling is strongly defended, the analyst models a degree of feeling just one degree more intense than where the patient is. In this example, the analyst described her feeling about the mother as "kind of pushy," rather than "really intrusive," or "outrageously controlling" because she was concerned that if she were too far ahead of the patient, it would put too much pressure on the defense and disrupt the narcissistic transference.

If the analyst thought this was as far as the patient could go, she would leave it. However, if she thought the patient was ready to experience a more intense level of feeling, she might add to the conversation like this:

"I would want to tell her to be quiet and let me handle it. (Or stronger still, I'd want to tell her to shut the fuck up!) But then, I don't like people questioning my choices."

"Even if it's for your own good?" the patient asks, a bit astonished but clearly intrigued.

"Especially if it's for my own good!" (This last comment models not just criticism of the mother but bright-eyed stubborn independence.)

The intervention is based on the hypothesis that the analyst feels the way she does because of a narcissistic induction from the patient. Thus, the analyst offers herself as an example of how the patient might express herself, a model of how she might open herself up to feelings that she has previously objected to.

In this example of modeling, the analyst speaks only for herself. She does not directly suggest that the patient might, can, or should feel the same way she does. Indeed, she keeps emphasizing that it is she – and not the patient – who has these feelings. This allows the patient to maintain her distance from them. If she is ready to embrace them, she can. However, the modeling may not instantly allow the patient to have the defended feeling. She might remain intrigued with the analyst, studying her from an emotional distance, thinking "Oh! She's so aggressive!" in worshipful tones, before allowing herself to feel the feeling as her own.

On the other hand, let's suppose the analyst has misread the situation completely; the patient isn't ready to experience this feeling on any level, even through the analyst. Or the analyst isn't really feeling the patient's feeling; it's a subjective response. In this case, having the analyst own the feeling as her own allows the patient to reject it, perhaps viewing the analyst as a bad person for thinking that way.[13]

As was mentioned above, it is important that modeling be only slightly ahead of the patient's level of comfort when working with a strongly defended feeling. If the analyst is too far ahead of the patient, the patient experiences the analyst's feelings as foreign to her, disrupting the narcissistic transference and making it impossible to absorb the analyst's communication.

Properly titrated, however, modeling can help the extremely inhibited patient move first into socially acceptable feelings that were nevertheless unacceptable to the patient's defenses. It can also help the patient integrate feelings that are not usually socially or morally acceptable – murderous fantasies, greediness, pettiness, arrogance, grandiosity, or strong sexuality. One patient was uncomfortable with his overall level of aggression and irritability. He described aggressive feelings but only at a fraction of the intensity that he felt them. I sensed that he could tolerate hearing much stronger feelings but was unable to get there on his own. I decided to make a significant leap in intensity with him. Once he said he was annoyed because a teenager ran past him and knocked his briefcase down in the subway. I told him I would have wanted to cut the little fucker's head off, and he roared with laughter. After a number of similar interventions, he moved into a state of being much more aware of and less frightened of the enraged, sadistic feelings he experienced.

In a different variation of modeling, the analyst instructs or suggests to the patient thoughts, feelings, or fantasies that he might experience. In this way, the analyst more explicitly gives the patient permission to have these feelings, with the understanding that the analyst shares them and approves of them. This is useful for when the patient is more likely to respond directly to the analyst's ideas, without having to experience them first through the analyst. It is also more likely to work when there is a state of mild merger, rather than a twinship. In this case, the analyst's comments can be experienced as though they are a part of the patient's mind, a benign introject, or superego.

For example, one female patient was struggling to allow herself to experience sexual feelings for a woman. She rather hesitantly described her, focusing on her clothes, her hair, and her graceful walk. The analyst herself felt aroused listening to this, which she hypothesized were the patient's feelings, but the patient seemed at a distance from them – not quite able to own them.

The analyst said gently, but nonchalantly, "She sounds really hot."

The patient relaxed and sighed slightly. "Yes, she is. I wonder if I'm attracted to her? I mean, she's a woman."

"Why wouldn't you be attracted to a woman like that?"

"Yes," the patient said more confidently. "I guess I am. You know, I can actually imagine myself making love with her."

"That sounds exciting."

Similarly, a man described his feelings about being in a class where everyone was more advanced than he was. That was just fine with him. He really was there to learn. He didn't need to compete. He was ready to just submerge himself in it and see what came of it.

The analyst asked him matter-of-factly, "Don't you want to be the smartest person in the class?"

"Why, yes, of course," said the patient.

"So why don't you do it. Why don't you just go in there and show them all how smart you are."

"I think I will." The patient beamed.

Containment

Thus far we have considered expressive forms of narcissistic emotional communication. Now let's consider containment.

First, we should recall that in containment, the analyst consciously experiences a feeling or range of feelings without deliberately communicating these feelings towards the patient either overtly or covertly. Containment is used when the patient cannot tolerate any overt expression of, or reference to, the feeling in question. Although containment is in itself a silent intervention, it can be used with silence, as the analyst quietly listens to the patient, quietly sits with a silent patient, or combines it with an expressive intervention that communicates a different feeling than the one being contained.[14]

Containment can be an effective narcissistic emotional communication across the whole range of the narcissistic relational mode. However, it serves two rather different functions, depending on the intensity of the narcissistic state. In the least intense narcissistic transference states, in which there is no blurring of ego boundaries and the patient is consciously aware of and able to tolerate her feeling state without any significant defenses, containment can help the patient feel understood without intruding upon the patient's experience or in some other way disrupting the narcissistic transference. For example, suppose the patient talks openly about his anguish over his daughter's illness while the analyst feels the patient's anguish empathically: some patients need no intervention beyond silent containment to feel deeply understood in a curative way. On the other hand, other patients will experience the analyst's silence as non-responsiveness, no matter how much feeling she contains. These patients require more expressive communication from the analyst in order to feel that they are empathically attuned to them.

Once the patient experiences some degree of defense in relationship to the feeling, containment serves the more complex function helping the patient to integrate the feeling though the analyst's unspoken willingness to tolerate, accept, or metabolize[15] (Bion 1962; Ogden 1979) the feeling. Because there is always a degree of fluidity or openness between ego boundaries in the narcissistic relational mode – even when there is not frank blurring of boundaries – the analyst's ability to tolerate the feeling is induced back to the patient. Through the cycle of reciprocal induction, the patient gives her pain to the analyst, and the analyst gives her strength to the patient. The experience is a nonverbal form of modeling. The interpersonal dynamic of induction and containment creates a way station for the patient between needing to defend against the feeling and being able to accept the feeling as a note in her own emotional spectrum.

This function of narcissistic containment is especially important with incongruent countertransference. For example, let's first consider a mildly incongruent example (described earlier): the patient describes an upcoming medical procedure without apparent anxiety, while the analyst experiences considerable anxiety about the procedure as she listens to the patient. The anxiety the analyst feels is understood as being the anxiety that the patient is defending against. The analyst's ability to contain the anxiety may enable the patient to consciously experience it and eventually verbalize it; or it may serve to help the patient tolerate it even if she does not verbalize it. While the analyst might be silent during this containment process, she might also contain while she overtly mirrors the way the patient is overtly coping with the anxiety. For example, she might discuss the upcoming procedure on a purely rational basis, agreeing that there is nothing to worry about, emphasizing the high degree of statistical safety. In doing so, she actively reflects the patient's denial of any anxiety about the issue, effectively resonating with both parts of the patient's experience – the anxiety and the defense.

The analyst might choose to initially contain the feeling, eventually using the countertransference as the basis for an expressive intervention, once she decides the patient is ready to deal with it more consciously. Certainly, the prejudice in almost all schools of analysis has been towards eventually helping the patient to put everything into words. On the other hand, I have observed that containment frequently leads to resolution of the problem, even if not verbalized by the patient or the analyst. This is especially true of deeply incongruent inductions, such as the intense anxiety that I described in relationship to a patient's anxiety that superficially correlated with his thoughts about learning to cook. In review, the patient was learning to cook. When he discussed his progress, I was regularly overwhelmed by almost intolerable levels of anxiety focused on my sense of intellectual adequacy that seemed unrelated to the topic of cooking and required tremendous self-control to contain. It was extremely difficult to think about anything besides the anxiety when this occurred. When this phase of the treatment resolved, the patient had learned to cook and seemed in general to be more confident, or related, and more emotionally complex. However, the anxiety itself was never verbalized, nor did I find any allusion to it in the content of the sessions.

It is moments like this that the term "metabolize" seems most appropriate, as does the concept of the holding environment. For it is not in the quiet moments of blissful sleep and cooing that the parent has difficulty holding the infant but rather in the moments of intense anxiety, fear, and frustration that it is difficult hold the infant's experience, to stay the course and remain calm in the face of the infant's emotional storms. Incongruent bouts of anxiety such as those I have described seem to be split off, encapsulated bits of raw, unmetabolized experience that the patient has managed to keep segregated from his consciousness. Split-off swaths of experiences are communicated through induction. When the analyst can contain them and induce her ability to tolerate them back to the patient, the experience becomes reintegrated into the patient's emotional life often without any conscious awareness on her part. These are the moments in which emotional communication takes place silently, beneath the surface of the interaction, that reveals the full extent of the curative power of the narcissistic mode and the value of containment.

Conversely, when these feelings are not contained or when the analyst experiences a defense (or resistance) against experiencing the induction full on, the analyst frequently sees chaotic despair, irritability, or disorganization in the patient that has no apparent relationship to what they are talking about. When cases like this are presented in supervision, and the analyst becomes able to consciously experience the previously uncontained feelings, the patient often stabilizes immediately, without any other change in intervention except for the re-establishment of emotional attunement that results from the ability to successfully contain intense, incongruent feelings.

Whether the containment needs to be accompanied by silence or by an expressive intervention depends on the patient's degree of vulnerability to the analyst and her need for verbal communication from the analyst. Some patients relating in the narcissistic mode are injured by almost any verbal communication from the analyst. These patients often require long periods of silent containment. This situation is fairly common among schizophrenic and schizotypal patients and certain post-traumatic stress patients. Most other patients need some form of verbal communication, in addition to containment. Failure to talk to these patients results in frustration, rage, and the experience of being neglected by the analyst.

Multiple transferences might be active in the analysis. Thus, one transference might be unconscious and related to a strong incongruent induced feeling, while the other transference might be congruent with the content. In this case, the analyst might need to make an expressive intervention related to the content and contain the other induced feeling. For example, it is very common for a patient to induce anxiety that is incongruent with the rest of her communications. However, it is disruptive for the patient if the analyst makes any expressive intervention related to the anxiety. Thus, the analyst must limit expressive interventions to the content of the session, not the induction.

Once the analyst realizes that containment can be an effective form of emotional communication on its own, without an expressive intervention or in combination with an expressive intervention that is unrelated to the contained feeling, she often experiences a much greater sense of freedom in relationship to her ability to relate to the patient. She realizes that she can work indirectly with the content, engaging whatever form of communication is necessary with the patient, without worrying that she is colluding or in some other way not doing her job.

12

TECHNIQUES OF OBJECT EMOTIONAL COMMUNICATIONS

In emotional communications in the object mode, the analyst communicates a specific feeling that (a) repeats a feeling from a pathological interpersonal relationship from the patient's past and (b) is expressed in and through a differentiated mode of relatedness in which the patient and the analyst are more or less separate.[1]

Emotional communications in the object mode, which we will refer to as object emotional communications, differ significantly from communications in the narcissistic, anaclitic, and projective identification modes. These latter communications in the other modes can serve the following purposes:

- make the environment similar enough to be compelling;
- resolve specific types of defenses/resistances;
- meet maturational needs for emotional communications that were missing or insufficient in development.

Object communications, on the other hand, only serve the first two purposes. Raw and unprocessed, they always tend to perpetuate repetitions. Formulated strategically, they can be used to resolve specific types of defenses. But because they are rooted in pathological interpersonal interactions, they are never analogues of normal maturational emotional communications and can never meet unmet needs for maturational communications. Consequently, they have a smaller range of therapeutic action. They can be used for three distinct purposes:

- to facilitate the patient's understanding of and insight into his effect on the analyst and thus on other people in general;
- to create an emotional environment that is similar enough to be compelling to facilitate the development of the transference;
- to actively recreate the original pathological interpersonal relationship within a controlled level of intensity that allows patients to (a) consciously experience and tolerate feelings that they were unable to experience in the original relationship; and (b) to express feelings to the analyst that they were unable to express to the original object.

Occasionally, these experiences allow the normal developmental process to restart, especially when the intervention serves the last function. More frequently, they lower the intensity and the frequency of the feelings associated with the repetition, which allows patients to have more conscious awareness and control over their reactions and behavior and enable them to be receptive to other types of emotional communications – usually anaclitic – that met the emotional needs that were unmet in the pathological interactions that formed the object repetition.

Furthermore, the range of techniques that make use of object communications is smaller than that of narcissistic communications. This is not because differentiated communications are any less important in emotional development but because they are a more complex relational mode than either the narcissistic or the anaclitic modes. Unfortunately, this doesn't mean that object communications are less difficult to use. On the contrary, it is much more complicated to make successful object communications than narcissistic or anaclitic communications. Object transference is rooted in pathogenic interactions, which can be conscious or unconscious and overt or covert, whereas object emotional communications are almost always made in the context of the patient experiencing the analyst in the context of repeating an interaction that was originally pathogenic. Even the mildest object interventions carry some risk of retraumatizing the patient and reinforcing the repetition. For this reason, it is dangerous to use them spontaneously. They should always be formulated with specific goals in mind.[2]

Furthermore, there is little room for error; they must be made with precision in order to work effectively and avoid retraumatization. While it is always important for the analyst to constantly monitor the impact of his interventions, it is even more important with object communications. If the analyst suspects that the intervention is harming the patient by leading to an increase in self-hate, depression, withdrawal, psychotic thinking, or dissociation, it is imperative that he change tack immediately. This usually involves shifting to a narcissistic or anaclitic emotional communication.

Interpretation

The goal of all interpretations is to create intra-psychic and/or interpersonal change through insight. Although insight is most powerful and effective when the feelings associated with the insight are experienced simultaneously (or in close proximity), the cognitive understanding conveyed by the interpretation is its defining feature.

Object transference was the original focus of psychoanalysis, and object transference interpretations designed to stimulate insight into the transference were the original psychoanalytic technique. These interpretations comprise a cognitive communication and an emotional communication, both addressed to the reasonable ego. The cognitive communication describes or explains the feelings and behavior of the patient's afflicted ego. The emotional communication usually communicates support for the patient's struggle to master the problem, and it is communicated in either the anaclitic or the narcissistic mode.[3]

In other words, the emotional communication in a classical interpretation is not an object communication but rather a narcissistic communication or an anaclitic communication. Although the patient is relating in the object mode, the emotional communication is designed to induce a shift in his mode of relatedness, a counter-induction, to either (a) the narcissistic mode, specifically the low-intensity empathic state in which ego boundaries remain clear and the patient feels understood by the analyst or (b) the anaclitic mode, in which the analyst is experienced as the parent whose instruction and wisdom help the child to understand himself. Either type of emotional communication (depending on the state the patient is in) can facilitate the patient's emotional ability to accept and make use of cognitive dimensions of the intervention. Object interpretations succeed when the analyst induces a shift in the mode of relatedness and tend to fail (or are less powerful) when he doesn't. When the counter-induction does not take place, the interpretation is likely to be experienced as an attack or a criticism of the patient's feeling or level of emotional maturity or as an empty, intellectual point.

If the object transference is intense and the afflicted ego strongly dominates the patient's experience, a narcissistic or anaclitic emotional communication will seldom be powerful enough to induce a shift in the patient's relational mode. At these times, interpretations generally fail.

What about the object emotional communication itself – the feeling that is congruent with the object transference and repeats the feelings of the original pathological relationship? Can it serve as the emotional communication in a classical interpretation? Only rarely. Communicating these feelings tends to activate the patient's afflicted ego and its desire to repeat the original relationship with the analyst. This leads the patient to further experience the analyst as the original object, not as an ally in the working relationship in the present. And this works against the reasonable ego's efforts to step back, observe the transference, and make use of the interpretation.

There are exceptions, however. It can sometimes be useful to describe the induced feelings, without affect (this might be viewed as a form of self-disclosure) as an element in the interpretation, while still conveying a mildly empathic/supportive emotional communication. This combination can make the interpretation more compelling and convincing. For example, the analyst might interpret that by going to work late, and arriving late to sessions, a patient is repeating a relationship that he had with his mother that made him seem inept and lead to her being critical. Adding a non-affective communication of the induced feeling, the analyst might say: "And even I begin to feel critical too, just like your mother did."

Notice that this intervention communicates information *about* the induced object countertransference but not the induced feeling itself. It is not an emotional communication. It is addressed to the reasonable ego, not the afflicted ego. It is not designed to engage or further activate the feelings that are driving the repetition but rather to allow the patient to observe the effect of his behavior on others and relate it to the interpretation.

Occasionally, the analyst might describe the countertransference feelings and include a highly diluted communication of the feelings with affect. This is done for the purpose of demonstrating the reality of the analyst's feelings to the reasonable ego. For example, if the patient typically experiences the analyst as supportive and empathic, he might have trouble believing that the analyst actually does experience the more problematic object feelings. In this case, the emotional communication is addressed to the reasonable ego, not to the afflicted ego. However, this moment has to be carefully chosen and only used with a patient who can tolerate it.

I have found that this last type of intervention is most effective in inverted object configurations, in which the analyst experiences the feelings that the patient had as a child, and the patient acts and experiences the feelings like the parent. Even expressing the feeling *with* affect can also be useful in this context, especially when the transference is extremely intense, and the patient strongly repeats the parent's behavior in relationship to the analyst. Communicating the object countertransference, with affect, and addressing it to the reasonable ego can make the patient vividly aware of his impact on the analyst and its relationship to his past.

For example, the patient is critical of the analyst's small mistakes, like forgetting some minor detail about his life or not cashing his checks quickly enough. This repeats a pattern the patient had with his father in which his father was relentlessly critical of him for ordinary human failings. Increasingly, the patient uses the same contemptuous, critical tone with the analyst that his father used with him. This has the same effect on the analyst as it did on the patient: the analyst feels like he can't do anything right, and he's reluctant to say anything at all for fear of the inevitable attack. The analyst eventually says, "You treat me just like you father treated you. I can imagine how you felt, but I really can't stand it. I'm afraid to say anything at all." This immediately pulls the patient out of the repetition and into a reflective mode, curious at how deeply he has internalized his hated father.

Risks of object interpretations

The primary risk in making all interpretations, not just interpretations of the object mode, is that they can disrupt the patient's defenses by making him aware of feelings, memories, or defenses that he is not ready to deal with on a cognitive level. The fact that the analyst understands the transference and the countertransference in the object mode does not mean the patient is ready or able to work with it openly. Furthermore, he might need other experiences in the object mode that an interpretation cannot facilitate, and usually prevents, such as verbalizing feelings towards the analyst that he felt with the original object but was not able verbalize at the time.

Communication of the object countertransference – without interpretation – to stimulate insight, self-understanding, or awareness of interpersonal impact

In the non-interpretative communication of the object countertransference, the analyst discloses the countertransference without the additional cognitive explanation that characterizes an interpretation. It can have a number of related but distinct goals: it can stimulate genetic insight by helping the patient to make connections between the interaction with the analyst and with his other relationships, whether in the past or present. It can stimulate self-awareness by helping the patient recognize what he is currently feeling when he learns what the analyst is feeling, and it can enhance his understanding of his interpersonal impact by helping him to see the emotional impact he has on the analyst.

The analyst can communicate the feeling with or without affect. When it is done without affect, its effect is similar to an interpretation, particularly when delivered with an empathic/supportive emotional communication. For example, the patient says that he went out drinking a few nights earlier and passed out in a bar, only to be awakened at last call and nudged out onto the street by the bartender. The analyst is horrified and wants to berate him. The analyst might say: "I'm having the feeling that I want to be very critical of you. Really give you a piece of my mind." However, the analyst does not convey the criticism through his tone or phrasing. The cognitive communication clearly describes the analyst's feeling, but fused it with an empathic/supportive emotional communication. Or if the analyst wants to move in a more interpretative direction, he might add: "I wonder if this is how your father felt when you made mistakes?" Or "Has anyone else ever had those kinds of feelings towards you before?"

This type of intervention may have some advantages over an interpretation. First, describing the countertransference carries less authority than making an interpretation. The patient may feel less pressured to accept it as fact out of compliance or submissiveness or less pressured to reject it out of defiance or oppositionalism. Furthermore, it can't really be wrong, in the way an interpretation can, because it is just the analyst's feelings, not a statement about the patient – at least when it is done in good faith. Provided the analyst does not insist that the patient is responsible for the feeling (even though he privately hypothesizes that he is), communicating the countertransference without interpretation can allow the patient a lot of room to explore the situation. He can more easily reject it in the event that he is not ready or able to consciously work with it, and/or if analyst's feeling really isn't an induction and has nothing to do with him. This type of communication is often used to initiate a discussion of what is occurring emotionally between the patient and the analyst in the moment.

This intervention is sometimes useful when the analyst doesn't understand what is happening. In these cases, the analyst really does not have an interpretation in mind and hopes that communicating these feelings to the patient will help the patient say something that will clarify the situation. This is especially true when the countertransference is incongruent with the content.

However, it is important to remember that communicating the object countertransference, even without the affect, is always risky. Patients who are very sensitive can be easily injured by this approach if the dynamic is a powerful one and they are not yet strong enough to deal with it directly.

If the analyst wants to draw the patient's attention to the idea that his feeling is related to what the patient is doing, he might tell the patient what he is feeling and ask him if he has any idea why that might be. For example, he might say, "I'm feeling kind of bored/anxious/angry/annoyed etc.; can you help me understand why I might be feeling that way?"

While I have occasionally used this formulation, I have strong reservations about it. It is difficult for me to believe that most patients would hear this without also hearing the strong implication that it's their fault the analyst is feeling how he is. While I certainly think that the patient usually causes the countertransference – this whole book is based on that idea – I do not think that the patient is responsible for this in any ordinary sense of the word. Induction is almost always an unconscious, involuntary process over which the patient has little or no conscious control. For this reason, I'm reluctant to say anything that might suggest that the countertransference is in any way the patient's fault. Furthermore, this intervention would seem to carry a high risk of disrupting the patient's defenses.

I sometimes recommend this intervention when the patient is either conscious or preconscious of the analyst's feeling and understands on some level that he has caused it. On the other hand, it can be assaultive if the feeling is grossly incongruent with the content, if the feeling is unconscious, or if the patient is strongly defended against acknowledging the dynamic that is creating the induction. However, analysts I know and respect tell me they find this to be a safe and effective intervention, and some consistently rely on it. Bollas (1983) has described using it effectively, so I suppose it depends, as do all techniques, on the analyst's degree of comfort with it and his ability to communicate effectively with it.

What about communicating the object countertransference – with congruent affect – for the purpose of stimulating insight, self-awareness, or understanding of the patient's impact on others? Although some analysts report that doing so can be a particularly effective way of helping the patient to appreciate his impact on others, this is seldom effective and always risky in my experience.[4] It can sometimes be useful if the affect is strongly diluted, particularly if it is mixed with a degree of playfulness or gentle sarcasm, but the latter emotional blend is already far from the original affect. And most of the time, communicating object feelings with affect intensifies the object transference in ways that make it impossible for the patient to observe himself. Other goals can be achieved with affect-laden object communications, but in my experience, insight is not one of them.

Non-interpretative object emotional communications with affect for purposes other than stimulating insight or self-awareness

Although I have touched on ways in which an object emotion communication with affect can be useful in combination with an interpretation, it can also be used for non-interpretative, non-insight oriented purposes as well. However, they are complex and risky, and in my opinion, must be used with extreme care.

First, we should consider the goal of using these kinds of communications. Some analysts seem to think that good things are bound to happen if they are authentic in their responses to the patient, provided they are fundamentally committed to the patient's well-being. They anticipate that the patient may have strongly negative reactions to this, and they plan to deal with these reactions honestly and directly.

I don't doubt that this sometimes works, and when both patient and analyst are committed to working out the relationship no matter how each one might feel, the results can be impressive. At the same time, the failures can be disastrous. The idea of communicating these feelings based solely on faith in the therapeutic value of authentic emotional communications does not make sense to me. Neither emotional honesty nor authenticity is intrinsically therapeutic. The object feelings that were originally toxic to the patient were probably authentic as well. If a patient suffered from being hated by his mother, there is little reason to doubt that her hatred was genuine. Whether any particular emotional communication is toxic or therapeutic depends on the patient's response to it, as determined by his past history and its place in the context of the current relationship, not on whether it is authentic. For that reason, I use object communications that utilize intense affect only in a targeted, goal-oriented way, never relying on authenticity and commitment alone to do the work.

So what specific goals can be accomplished with affect-laden object emotional communications?

First, they can make the emotional environment similar enough to be compelling. This aspect of the emotional environment usually develops spontaneously when the analyst blunders into a mild enactment that is consciously unnoticed by either patient or analyst, provided the patient and the analyst are minimally attuned in this area.

However, there are cases in which the analyst must show himself to be similar enough to the original objects for the patient to be able to attach and take him seriously as an emotional object. This can be done implicitly or explicitly. In an explicit example, the patient and the analyst may have the following exchange:

"You're just like all therapists – money-hungry parasites who claim they're doing it for your own good."

"That's about the size of it. Don't fool yourself for a minute that I'm anything but rapacious," the analyst replies.

"That's what I like about you: you're honest. Not like that last little hypocrite I saw."

Here, the analyst's comments explicitly express support and agreement with the patient's perceptions. Initially, these interventions are experienced as primarily syntonic; they confirm the patient's worldview, allowing him to feel that he is in familiar, albeit unpleasant, territory.

In other cases, the analyst may need to express the object countertransference implicitly through the way he relates to the patient. For example, a patient who grew up with parents who were silent and withholding might need a cold withholding emotional environment in analysis in order to attach. In these cases, it is extremely unlikely that the patient will be able to verbalize this request – he is probably not even aware of it – and the analyst does not make his attitude explicit. He just relates in a way that is cold and remote. Exactly how similar the analyst needs to be to the parents may vary. Some patients will need the analyst to be a near copy of the parent, while others will need just a taste of the original situation from time to time.

This type of intervention that involves verbalizing feelings or behaving in ways that clearly perpetuate a pathological interpersonal relationship on a temporary basis, which can actually last a long time, can be very difficult for many analysts (including myself). Furthermore, this type of intervention carries a high risk of retraumatization if used with the wrong patient or in the wrong way.

On the other hand, some patients do need them and may shop around until they get them. While I would never recommend that an analyst use an intervention that makes him extremely uncomfortable, it is usually better for the patient if the analyst isn't too comfortable with this type of arrangement. It's also better for the patient if the analyst is doing this purposefully rather than doing it unconsciously. Patients who need this particular kind of emotional environment are difficult to treat, and not every analyst will be successful with them.

Similar to the patients who need the analyst to actually repeat specific pathological aspects of the their early emotional environment are those who can't trust the analyst's sincerity unless he expresses a wider range of feeling towards them than the empathic/supportive and/or neutral communications that are the foundation of most analysts' stock in trade.[5] Some patients consistently experience this emotional environment as phony or insincere – mere professional pap. This attitude might be due to having had particularly frank parents, supportive/empathic parents who were experienced as insincere, or parents who had a taste for relationships with a higher than average degree of conflict. Let's go back to the earlier example of a patient who describes blacking out in a bar, which induces critical feelings in the analyst. One patient might respond best to the analyst saying: "I feel like being really critical of you," expressed with neutrality or even a little warmth. On the other hand, a superficially similar patient might respond better to the same line delivered with anger or even a bit of contempt. However, the closer the analyst's communication gets to being a straight repetition, the riskier this type of intervention becomes – at least for the purpose of making the patient feel that the analyst is being genuine with him.

But there is another, usually more important goal that can be achieved with affect-laden object communications: to help the patient to (a) (re)experience, with full intensity, feelings that were defended in the context of the original relationship; and (b) tell the analyst what he was unable to say to the original person in the pathogenic interaction. Their feelings are usually intensely negative – resentment, hatred, Oedipal rebellion, rebellion against victimization, or revenge against a separate object that abused or mistreated the patient. Less commonly, sexual feelings and desires may be at play in these sorts of repetitions. These feelings may have been defended for any of the following reasons:

- The original person in the pathogenic interaction communicated to the patient, either overtly or covertly, that expressions of anger, disappointment, or frustration would not be tolerated.
- The patient feared harming the person who was the target of his rage.
- The patient feared abandonment if he expressed those feelings.
- The patient feared other types of physical or emotional revenge.
- The patient feared that expressing the sexual feelings would lead to actual sexual relations with the object.

Thus, the repetition is shaped by a constellation of three elements: intense negative or sexual feelings; the defenses against these feelings; and the fears that motivate these defenses.

This repetition does not always come into the analytic relationship as an object transference in which the analyst is the target of these defended feelings. It is not uncommon for the patient to experience the repetition in relation to someone besides the analyst while relating to the analyst in the narcissistic mode. For example, the patient experiences strongly defended rage towards his father, and the analyst also feels rage towards the father. In these cases, the analyst can often help the patient by modeling the hatred or rage or other types of narcissistic emotional communications.

But when the analyst is the target of the repetition in an object transference, the repetition can be extremely difficult to loosen. It tends to be strongly resistant to interpretations. Although the patient may quickly understand the situation, he is still unable to feel or express the feelings. Part of the problem is the nature of the repetition itself: its essential feature is a strongly defended negative feeling. Moreover, two factors in the analyst's interactions with the patient often reinforce the problem.

The first is that the analyst may communicate, usually inadvertently, that he cannot or will not tolerate being the object of the patient's feelings. This may be an induction – a repetition of the original object's communications to the patient – or it may be due to subjective issues in the analyst. Whatever the origin of this communication, the analyst needs to understand it, work with it, and over time, control it.

The second factor is that the analyst's behavior is often not realistically hurtful or offensive enough to justify the intense negative feelings in the eyes of the patient's reasonable ego. Consequently, defenses emanating from the reasonable ego, such as the patient's conscious thought that his feelings are unrealistic, reinforce defenses within the afflicted ego to prevent the experience and/or expression of the defended feelings. Sympathetic or empathic communications, which may be crucial to working with the patient at other times, make things worse when this transference is active. Even a cool, neutral stance may not be aversive enough to overcome it.

A really strong unplanned enactment in which the analyst repeats the original object's behavior and emotional communications sometimes does the trick, particularly in cases where the analyst verbalizes feelings that the original object communicated only non-verbally. For example, the analyst actually says something critical directly to the patient, instead of shaking his head wearily as the patient's mother did.

Enactments of this sort are probably the most frequent way this type of repetition gets loosened, provided the analyst has his wits about him to quickly move out of the enactment and into an emotional position in which the analyst is receptive to the patient's reaction. Spontaneous enactments feel genuine to both the patient and the analyst, which can make them particularly powerful. This is wonderful when they are successfully negotiated but quite destructive when they are not.

In addition to the problems with enactments that I mentioned earlier, there are other reasons why they cannot be relied upon exclusively to loosen these types of repetitions. One reason is that enactments are spontaneous and unpredictable. Consequently, the needed enactment may not develop, in which case the needed object communication will not be made, and the transference does not get addressed on an emotional level. Another reason is that the needed enactment may occur, but without sufficient intensity to enable the patient to express the defended feelings or without sufficient differences from the original communication to be curative.

Object joining

The technique of object joining was formulated specifically to address these kinds of repetitions. In object joining, the analyst accepts and agrees with the patient's perceptions of him as true, making no effort to challenge, contradict, or correct them. Nor does he interpret them. The only change he might make would be to agree with them in a slightly exaggerated way. If there is a conflict between the reasonable ego's perceptions and the afflicted ego's perceptions, the analyst's cognitive communication supports the afflicted ego's perceptions. The emotional communication is derived from the object countertransference, or when this is not induced, by the auto-induction of the needed feeling. The cognitive and the emotional communications are addressed to the patient's afflicted ego and to the reasonable ego.

Unlike a spontaneous enactment, the emotional communication is planned, and its intensity is carefully titrated in a way that is designed to (a) overcome the patient's tendency to cling to the "realistic" perception of the analyst that prevents him from fully experiencing him as the pathological object of the original relationship and (b) framed in a way that facilitates the patient's ability to express these feelings.

For these reasons, the emotional communication in object joining is usually dystonic, irritating, or provocative.

Once this occurs, the analyst adopts an attitude of being open to hearing whatever the patient says, making no effort to defend himself or to dispute the patient's points, while still remaining dystonic enough to keep the patient's verbalization of the defended feelings going as long as is needed.

In a sense, the analyst provokes a fight for the purpose of losing it. He relates in a way that is designed to minimize any guilt these attacks might normally arouse in the patient. The patient is helped to feel justified and comfortable with his aggression, to view it as a valid response to the analyst and a valued part of his character.

An important clarification: I have said that the analyst's emotional communication is irritating and provocative. However, it must be emphasized that the analyst provokes solely for the purpose of releasing the expression of object-directed aggressive feelings that are already present within the patient's transferential experience of the analyst but constrained by defenses. The analyst does not provoke purely for the purpose of arousing anger that is not consistent with the transference. The analyst must have a specific reason for using the intervention in a particular situation, not a general rationale such as the idea that it's good for patients to be able to express anger towards the analyst.

As with dystonic narcissistic joining and mirroring, these emotional communications are not analogues of any sort of emotional communication that would ordinarily be required in the course of normal development. Rather, they are specialized emotional communications that are designed to unblock the heavily defended feelings that underlie the type of repetition that has been described.

Furthermore, this type of intervention is not useful for the patient who already expresses his aggressive object-directed feelings freely. For example, it is not used with borderline, bipolar, or narcissistic patients who tend to express aggression in a disinhibited or uncontrolled manner. It is reserved almost exclusively for those who are inhibited in this area (with the exception of a situation that will be discussed further on).

Types of object joining

There are two forms of object joining: explicit and implicit. In the explicit form, the analyst's cognitive communication explicitly endorses the patient's perceptions of him, while the emotional communication combines narcissistic and object elements with low-intensity affect. In implicit object joining, the cognitive communication does not openly support the patient's perspective, but it does relate in a way that is aggravatingly consistent with the patient's experience of him and communicates an unmixed object communication with strong, clear affect.

Let's look at explicit joining first. In the most straightforward type of object join, the analyst agrees with the patient's perceptions of him as the patient has articulated them, adding nothing to their content but doing so in an unapologetic tone that is seemingly oblivious or indifferent to the patient's reaction. For example, the patient tentatively complains about the analyst. The analyst feels severely criticized, far in excess of what the patient is saying. He hypothesizes that the patient is defended against expressing the full measure of his rage. He uses an object join to help the patient to verbalize these more intense feelings of frustration and aggression.

This can be seen in the following example, in which the patient starts the interchange with a mild complaint about the analyst's policy about paying for missed sessions.

"I understand that you have to make a living and that you can't do this if you see people for free, but somehow I feel that it isn't quite right that I have to pay for a session even if I give you plenty of notice that I'm going to be out ahead of time."

"You are correct," says the analyst. "It isn't quite right. In fact, I'd go further: it's not fair at all."

"If it's not fair, then why do you do it?"

"Why might I do it?," replies the analyst, reflecting the patient's question. (This question is designed partly to explore the patient's thoughts on the matter but also to mildly frustrate that patient, to further facilitate the patient's expression of frustration and aggression.

"You tell me," says the patient, at this point clearly angry. "Because you are greedy?"

"Yes, that's what people say about me," the analyst says blithely. "That I'm greedy. Some people even say I'm rapacious."

"How can you say that so casually?"

"It's about time you start to see me for what I am," the analyst replies.

"Well I think you're disgusting," the patient says, with real rage.

In this case, the patient was able to verbalize a relatively strong criticism but was unable to reach the even more powerful rage that underlies it. The object join used the patient's complaint as a starting point, combined with an irritating and provocative emotional communication, to help the patient to fully feel and verbally communicate these intense feelings of frustration and aggression.

The emotional communication in this type of join is complex, in that it contains both narcissistic and object elements. The analyst agrees with the patient's perception completely, which provides an element of narcissistic resonance with the patient, strengthening his sense of self and his confidence in his experience. On the other hand, the perception that the analyst agrees with is a negative experience of the analyst himself, experienced by the patient in the object mode. Thus, the analyst agrees with the patient against himself.

Furthermore, the affect is relatively dilute and not directly related to the object countertransference. In the above example, the analyst agrees that he is greedy, but he does not really act that way. It is more as if he were dispassionately observing his worst features and pointing them out to the patient. He voices a degree of detached sympathy with the patient's plight, but he is unwilling to do anything about it.

In the case example above, the patient was able to express a clear complaint about the analyst that the analyst then used as his basis of intervention. More frequently, however, the patient will be far from expressing that much aggression directly; that is the crux of the problem. The analyst may feel the aggression in the countertransference. Less frequently, he may hypothesize that even more heavily defended aggression – defended so heavily that the patient is incapable of inducing it even in an incongruent way – is at the root of the repetition.[6] In these cases, the analyst may join the patient's unstated perceptions by verbalizing them for him. Initially, this looks much like an interpretation, except that the analyst states the patient's feeling as a fact about the analyst, not as an observation about the patient. This gives the patient permission to feel and express the feeling, and it provides an initial verbal framework for him as well.

For example, the analyst is a few minutes late for the session, and the patient is uncharacteristically quiet. The analyst thinks the patient's silence is hostile – he feels reproached, and associates those feelings to memories of being reprimanded. The patient has told him that he falls silent, almost speechless, when he is angry. However, the analyst was never aware of the patient being angry with the analyst before this. The analyst's goal is to help the patient to verbalize the object-directed anger that he hypothesizes the patient is feeling.

The analyst begins by pointing out his tardiness while pointedly not apologizing for it; to do so could potentially take the edge off of the patient's anger. The patient remains silent.

"Well," the analyst says, "that was pretty irresponsible of me – to keep you waiting like that."

"I didn't say that," the patient responds. (The patient sounds annoyed, but could also be feeling criticized and defensive; this could be a reaction to the analyst stimulating his defenses by giving words to the patient's feeling. If his reaction continues in this vein, the analyst should probably change his line of intervention. Or it could be that the patient's annoyance has been displaced away from the analyst's tardiness and on to this comment. If this is the case, then there is no problem. The analyst decides it's the latter and moves on.)

The analyst replies: "Of course you didn't. I did. Facts are facts, aren't they?"

In reality, if this were the first time the analyst did something that made the patient angry in this way, the interchange would probably end at this point. The more intense moments of expressing anger towards the analyst as object usually have to be built up slowly. But in this case, similar interchanges have previously taken place, thus some preliminary work has been done, and the analyst works to develop the intensity.

"Yes, they are," says the patient. "But that's about the only area in which you are irresponsible. Anyone can be late once in a while." (The patient is still restricting his anger but has uttered the word irresponsible more boldly than before.)

"That's the only area that you've had the good fortune to see," says the analyst. But I actually have lots of areas of irresponsibility."

"Really?"

"Haven't I ever lost any of your checks?" the analyst says in a deliberately casual tone.

"You lose checks!?" Now the patient is genuinely shocked.

"I sure do. And you know what's worse? I don't even offer to pay the stop payment fee. I just ask patients to write me a new one."

"You really are irresponsible!" The patient is no longer protecting the analyst and is allowing her anger free expression.

A similar series of object joins may be appropriate when the patient is not – or feels that he is not – making progress in the analysis and wants to blame the analyst but is too inhibited to do so.[7] Working with this transference engages the more general repetition of inhibiting object-directed anger, and the attendant restrictions in the patient's character that this entails.

"I feel like I'm not getting better. Nothing is changing."

"Why haven't I helped you more?"

"Why would it be your fault?"

"Isn't it my job to help you? Isn't that why you are coming?"

"Yes, but it's my fault if I don't get better."

"Why is that? You do your part. You come regularly. You talk. You pay me for the sessions – a rather high fee, I might add. Shouldn't I be held responsible for something here?"

The first time this intervention is used, the exchange will probably end there. However, it may develop over time.

The patient begins the interchange by complaining about his life again.

"I can't shake the feeling that I'm not helping you," the analyst responds.

"I didn't say that."

"I know you didn't. I did. You are not getting better, and it's my job to help you do better in your life. You are being very generous with me – letting me off the hook rather easily."

The patient giggles nervously. "Really? You know I do sometimes feel like I'm paying a lot of money to just come here and complain."

"I'm supposed to be doing something besides helping you complain, aren't I?"

As in other cases, the next exchange might take place in the next session, or it could take an extended period of time However, it is likely to develop, if the analyst has responded to the transference correctly.

"I'm beginning to think you are right about not helping me."

"Really?"

"Yes. I do come, I do talk, and I certainly pay, and things just aren't getting better."

"Yes, I see your point. You definitely sound like someone who is not being helped."

"You say that as if it's a big joke. But it's not! This is my life, you know. And I sacrifice a lot to come here, and for you to talk about it so flippantly is really enraging! I want to be doing better, and I want you to start doing your job!"

Analysts unfamiliar with this type of intervention often ask: What do you do next – after you have helped the patient say that you are not doing your job, at full volume? Doesn't it undermine the analysis? Why would anyone stay in treatment after having reached that conclusion?

It must be remembered that the patient is being helped to verbalize feelings he experienced before the intervention was made. (The somewhat revolting but still useful analogy to describe this intervention is that it is like lancing a boil.) Most often, the patient knows he is making progress when he feels the relief of being able to express these feelings, and this deep, "unthought known" (in Bollas' [1987] pithy phrase) overshadows the complaints that are explicit in the content of the patient's communications.

The patient may feel two contradictory feelings at once: a deep sense of release and acceptance and a really horrible interpersonal conflict. I recall, in my own analysis, the profound shift in my experience that occurred after a burst of rage like this. I wanted to stay in treatment but was having trouble reconciling it to the apparent irrationality of what my analyst and I had said to each other.

There is, however, a risk of the patient leaving treatment in a rage if this sort of intervention is badly timed or ill chosen. (However, it's worth remembering that the patients are also liable to leave if they are not helped to verbalize their frustration and dissatisfaction with the analyst. This may be just as destructive for the patient – sometimes even more so – but less unpleasant for the analyst.) Furthermore, if the patient is not able to respond to the analyst's comments with corresponding aggression over time, the intervention risks reinforcing the repetition.

As is the case for all of the dystonic emotional communications aimed at the afflicted ego, the object join is a powerful communication that, in the vast majority of cases, must be used carefully, precisely, and infrequently. And in order for the intervention to work, the analyst must, in addition to agreeing with the patient's perception of him and providing sufficient provocation to facilitate the expression of the aggression, the analyst must also provide the patient with some reassurances:

- he will not be harmed by the patient's rage;
- he will not abandon the patient if he feels these feelings or verbalizes them;
- he will not take revenge in any way on the patient for communicating these feelings.

Now let's consider implicit object joining. Here, the analyst does not overtly agree with the patient's perception of him, so instead plays out the role assigned to him in the transference. This usually involves verbalizing the object countertransference or, if need be, the auto-induced object feeling, with sufficient affect to provoke the patient into responding to him. The emotional communication is addressed to both the afflicted ego, which is confirmed in its experience, and the reasonable ego, which is temporarily neutralized by the object communication.

As in explicit object joining, the feelings that the analyst helps the patient to verbalize are usually strongly negative feelings such as rage, rebellion, or contempt. The emotional release facilitated by the implicit object join is extremely powerful, often stronger than what is aroused by explicit joining. While this is not always the case, the analyst must be prepared to receive and embrace the full strength of the patient's defended feelings if he is to make a successful implicit object join.

Let's look at a straightforward example. The patient has a history of cowering before authority, afraid to ask for anything, based on a relationship with a tyrannical and withholding father. The patient has lived out his life asking for as little as possible, grabbing crumbs for himself here and there, when he won't be noticed, and speaking quietly at all times. Although he has voiced many feelings with the analyst, he has also maintained his quiet, respectful manner in his requests – or rather his lack of requests – towards the analyst.

At the point in the treatment under discussion, the patient uncharacteristically asks to reschedule an appointment a few weeks in the future. The analyst feels uncharacteristically annoyed, all out of proportion to what is being requested, and concludes that he is feeling the father's feelings. Deciding the moment is ripe, he gives voice to the object countertransference through an implicit join.

"I don't know about that," he says irritably, "can't you manage to come at the usual time?"

"I can't, actually. I have to see a specialist, and that's the only time he could give me."

"Yes, but it's extremely inconvenient for me to reschedule. Why should I go out of my way?" The analyst is sounding deliberately selfish and self-absorbed.

"What do you mean, 'why should you go out of your way'? I've been coming for three years, and I've never asked for anything similar, and I'm not even asking to cancel, just to reschedule."

The patient's anger is rising, and if this was the first time such an interchange occurred, the analyst might stop it there – often with the analyst complimenting the patient (immediately or at the end of the session) for his assertiveness. Let's assume, however, that the analyst thinks the patient is even angrier than he sounds, and that he can reach it if pushed a little further.

"That may be, but that doesn't make it any less inconvenient for me right now. How should I feel anyway, about you changing your time with me just to go to another doctor? You're supposed to be here at that time."

"I can't believe what an asshole you are! I can't believe how rigid you are! And I can't believe how selfish you are! I'm supposed to compromise my health so that I can be here with you every week?! You'll be lucky if I ever come back here!"

How does this sort of exchange end? Sometimes, the analyst is just quiet or says something quiet and reasonable. Or the analyst might make an explicit comment that takes him out of the object role and into a more anaclitic stance, such as: "You're right, and that's exactly how selfish assholes should be talked to." When intervention is successful, the patient understands, either consciously or unconsciously, what has transpired.

Differences between object joining and dystonic narcissistic joining

Object joining and dystonic narcissistic joining are so similar, both in their formulation and their effect, that they can seem to be identical. In both cases (a) the patient suffers from greatly inhibited aggression and aggression turned against his self and (b) the analyst makes provocative and irritating communications to the patient that are designed to help the patient to discharge his aggression away from himself and towards the analyst.

Although the outward procedures are the same, it is worth differentiating the two interventions because what is happening, both intrapsychically for the patient and interpersonally between the patient and the analyst, is different in the two situations.

In dystonic narcissistic joining, the analyst gives voice to the patient's feelings about himself, whereas in object joining the analyst gives voice to the feelings of a separate object whose experience of the patient is different from the patient's experience of himself. Granted, it can be difficult to differentiate between these two states, in part because the patient's feelings about himself in the narcissistic state might be an introject of what was originally someone else's feelings about him. However, once another person's feelings become integrated into the patient's mind, it functions differently from when it is experienced as coming from the other person. The dystonic narcissistic join enables the patient to relieve his self-hatred by transforming it into hatred of a differentiated other person. The object join enables the patient to express hatred that is already linked to a differentiated other person.

Risks of object joining

Object joining, whether explicit or implicit, is a powerful intervention, but it can create serious problems when it doesn't work. The most important risk is hurting or retraumatizing the patient with the object communication. Keep in mind that the raw object communications are nearly identical to the toxic emotional communications that originally formed the repetition that is active in the transference. The analyst must be confident that the patient will be able to respond to the provocation with appropriate aggression or assertiveness.

Although the process usually takes a number of small interchanges before the patient can express the defended feelings directly, the analyst needs to be sure that process is moving in the right direction. Generally, there are indications that this is happening. For example, the analyst may feel the patient's anger rising more directly in the session, the patient may report becoming more expressive in other areas outside the analysis (often without the patient even being aware of this), or there may be material in dreams, associations, or parapraxis that show an increase of flexibility, outward directed aggression, or expressiveness.

Similarly, any evidence to the contrary suggests that the analyst is on the wrong path. This might include increased self-attack by the patient, increased inhibitions outside the session, or a general feeling of emotional withdrawal. These signs suggest that the intervention may potentially retraumatize the patient.

Unfortunately, the analyst usually gets both types of information, as the patient wavers back and forth between reinforcing the defenses and overcoming them, and there are few guidelines except experience and good supervision.

The explicit form of object joining is less risky because the affective component of the emotional communication is less intense, because the analyst has already presented himself as being in the wrong, and because he is clearly inviting the patient to attack him. Of course, the patient must still mobilize enough aggression to express, but there is less danger of the patient feeling attacked than there is in the implicit join. On the other hand, there is a greater danger that the patient will feel that the analyst isn't serious, that the analyst is toying with him, or that he is mocking his feelings.

Explicit joining certainly isn't for every patient (nor is it for every analyst), and it lacks the spontaneity and authenticity of an enactment or a properly delivered implicit join. Even if the intervention seems to work, it can feel artificial or contrived.

The implicit join never feels contrived. And, when it is done properly, it feels completely serious. All of which compounds its riskiness. The patient must be ready and able to respond to it, or it will be a traumatic repetition and nothing more. If the analyst senses that the intervention is failing, it is imperative that he change tack immediately. This means moving out of the object position and taking full responsibility for the interchange, either attacking himself or apologizing. The analyst must make it clear that the problem is his, and he must do this in a sympathetic and empathic way.

A potential problem with both types of object joining is that the patient may be unable to forgive the analyst even though the intervention seemed to work. Sometimes the insult is just too great, and the patient is too disappointed, even if the immediate goal of the intervention has been met. Sometimes the situation can be salvaged by appealing to the value of working things through, by pointing out the progress the patient has made in being able to say what he said to the analyst, or if all else fails, by begging for forgiveness. But sometimes nothing works and the patient leaves.

Analysts usually don't like this resolution. They feel terrible and they fear – with good reason – that the patient will say terrible things about them. But it isn't necessarily bad for the patient. While it's appealing to think that things work out for the best when you stay and work them out, not everything can be resolved with words. Some patients have to act out the rage and rebellion that they felt towards the original object by angrily rejecting the analyst in order to really master it.[8] And if the analyst has actually done something to warrant such treatment – well, so much the better; the patient can leave feeling confident that he is reality oriented and has good cause. While I wouldn't plan an ending like this, it's important to recognize that the consequences of our mistakes are not necessarily our patient's failures.

Nevertheless, for this and all the other reasons discussed, it's best to use these interventions with extreme caution – if at all. Many analysts are extremely uncomfortable with this type of intervention and would never consider it. That's understandable, and there's usually another way of approaching the problem. Personally, I rarely use explicit joining, but I do find it to be a valuable form of emotional communication. In contrast, I have only occasionally used an implicit join. Despite the fact that it usually worked quite well, I would be reluctant to use it again. My level of discomfort, compounded by the risk of failure, is too high, and I would almost always try to find another way of working with transference. But it isn't always possible, and I think that sometimes I could get better results with an implicit object join. Both forms of object joining are valid and effective forms of therapeutic emotional communication for those analysts who are skilled with them and for those patients who need them. But whether an analyst uses them or not, it is important to understand what their purpose is and how they function because they illustrate important points about human emotional communication and how the full range of feelings can be harnessed in the service of emotional growth.

Containment

The containment of object inductions is a crucial emotional interchange that occurs at some point in almost every analysis. For some patients, object inductions are a rare event, and the emergence of object inductions is often a surprise to the analyst in work with patients whose repetitions are primarily in the narcissistic or anaclitic modes. This development almost always indicates progress because it suggests that the patient's maturational needs have been met (at least to some extent) and that they are now working in the analysis on some of the interpersonal issues that occurred secondarily to the frustration of these needs. For example, patients who suffered a deprivation of dependency needs often induce a withholding response in others, and this often arises in the analysis after their dependency needs have been met in the analysis. While these patients occasionally need object emotional communications at these times, containment usually resolves these transitions.

For patients whose repetitions are primarily in the object mode, however, object containment is by far and away the most important intervention the analyst makes. Although some of these patients eventually require expressive object emotional communications, such as joins, most need a long period of containment before these interventions can be used. Furthermore, containment alone is usually enough to loosen even strongly entrenched object repetitions.

In fact, most of what the analyst does with these patients is to experience and contain the extremely negative object countertransference that these patients induce. The analyst resists the almost unbearable temptation – really a sort of invitation – to reject, attack, humiliate, neglect, exploit, or seduce the patient, just to name a few of the most likely possibilities. The analyst, often alone among the people with whom the patient is involved, feels these feelings intensely – undiluted and undefended – but does not act on them. This is the source of therapeutic leverage.

The patient feels a degree of acceptance and commitment in object containment that is qualitatively different from not communicating these feelings because the analyst just doesn't feel them. While that too can be a powerful, curative experience, it does means that the object induction has not been activated in the treatment, and is not really comparable to what happens in object containment, which is a different interpersonal experience. Neither experience is better, nor is it a matter of choice. Neither the analyst nor the patient can control which repetitions become active in the transference. The important point is that the analyst understands what is happening in both situations and is able to work accordingly.

When patients induce strong object inductions, analysts often feel a strong temptation to reject them – whether through referral to a different analyst or to a different form of treatment – ostensibly because the analyst doesn't have the right feelings towards the patient, lacks empathy, or doesn't think it's ethical to work with a patient for whom he has such negative feelings. This is often formulated in terms of professional responsibility. While any of these are reasonable responses if the analyst cannot or does not want to shoulder the emotional stress of enduring these feelings with any particular patient,[9] it is wrong as a theoretical position unless the analyst is certain that he will be unable or unwilling to control himself. Almost inevitably, allowing the patient to induce these negative object feelings without acting on them has a profoundly positive effect on the patient that significantly loosens the repetitions with other people in his life. When the patient is able to concentrate on the object induction in the transference and move it out of the repetitions in his life, his relationships with others almost always improve. It is as if the illness has been encapsulated, leaving the patient free to live differently in other spheres.

Some analysts have the idea that containing these feelings is somehow disingenuous, or that in some way, they are a disservice to their patients by not helping them to know their impact on another person. On the contrary, I think that this is a powerful act of love, the willingness to endure terrible feelings out of a commitment to helping the patient outgrow the need to induce them. And I have found that these inductions change over time, provided the analyst is patient and willing to wait. Object inductions regularly evolve into anaclitic or narcissistic inductions over time.

Silent containment and containment combined with other forms of emotional communication

Containment is always a silent intervention, but this does not mean that the analyst is usually silent when he contains. However, there are times when this is the case. For example, one analyst described an intense dislike for a paranoid patient who spent his sessions fulminating against hippies and leftists. He couldn't stand his tone of voice, he loathed the contempt that oozed from the patient every time he used the word "hippie," and he had heard the tirade so many times that he could anticipate every word. Furthermore, the patient seemed to be stuck in a historical time frame that was completely out of joint. He was far too young to have ever actually met a hippie. There were subjective elements to the analyst's feelings. He had been a bit of a hippie himself and considered himself a refugee from the Sixties. However, it also appeared that everyone the patient came in contact with felt the same way. He had no friends, and most people fled as soon as they got to know him. The analyst often felt as if the patient was torturing him with his jeremiads.

The patient initiated no interaction during the sessions and responded to everything the analyst said with either a quick, "Yes, yes" or simply ignored him. It was all the analyst could do to keep himself from throwing the patient out. He was afraid to say too much for fear that his hate would leak out. The analyst limited his communication to a few neutral, object-oriented questions[10] per session. The patient came religiously for years before the analyst's feelings changed.

The only situations in which there would be more silence than this are very exceptional patients who can't tolerate any verbal communication from the analyst. There was an additional emotional communication in addition to the contained object countertransference: the analyst tolerated the patient because he remembered that nobody else could. So the object induction was girded by anaclitic commitment, as it always must be. So the object induction was received in the context of anaclitic commitment, as it always must be. Furthermore, the analyst's neutral questions provided a form of anaclitic emotional communication. But it was a very restricted form – just the minimal but crucial amount necessary to keep the treatment going.

The analyst never felt any clear sympathy for the patient while in the sessions until years into the treatment. On a moment-by-moment basis, his feelings were completely negative. This was as close to pure object containment as it gets.

But this is rare. More often, the object inductions are contained in the background while the analyst expresses narcissistic or anaclitic communications. These may not be particularly intense, they may feel superficial, and they may require significant effort (through auto induction) to express in a way that sounds and feels genuine. They may be coupled with various types of questions or with mild interpretations that are designed more to keep the patient consciously engaged in the treatment while the work of containment proceeds. And in cases where the analyst does make object emotional communications, the period of prior containment creates the degree of safety and attachment that enables the patient to weather the storm.

13

TECHNIQUES OF EMOTIONAL COMMUNICATION WITH PROJECTIVE IDENTIFICATION

The projective identification mode[1] is often the most difficult mode to work with, and repetitions based in projective identifications also tend to be the most difficult to loosen. As I argued earlier, other modes may reflect pathological relationships that include defenses, but they also involve ways of relating that are not essentially defensive. A person can experience another person as either being similar to or differentiated from herself, without this automatically involving a defense. Projective identification, on the other hand, is essentially defensive; it arises exclusively as an attempt to use an interpersonal relationship to maintain intrapsychic equilibrium. Consequently, any attempt to loosen a repetition grounded in projective identification immediately involves modifying a defense against experiencing a feeling the patient is especially desperate to avoid experiencing. The afflicted ego is usually strongly dominant in projective identification states and quite unreceptive to anything that doesn't confirm its worldview. Unlike narcissistic repetitions, however, confirming its worldview doesn't usually loosen its hold.

In many cases, repetitions involving projective identifications loosen as a byproduct of meeting the patient's narcissistic needs during periods of narcissistic transference. The analytic strategy, therefore, is often a matter of helping the patient – and the analyst – to endure the analytic relationship during the periods when the projective identification mode is active but expecting most direct therapeutic interchanges to take place at other points in the treatment.

Nevertheless, several types of emotional communications do, at times, have a therapeutic impact when the patient is actually in the projective identification mode. In contrast with the narcissistic, object, or anaclitic modes, however, the analyst never deliberately makes an emotional communication in the projective identification mode to a patient. Responding to a projective identification with a projective identification almost always results in a disruptive intensification of the transference, and in the short term, a tightening of the repetition – an enactment. Furthermore, these enactments tend to be more intense than enactments in the narcissistic or object modes. While they sometimes work to the benefit of the analysis, they may also be disastrous more frequently in this mode than in the other modes.

Challenging as they are, repetitions grounded in projective identification can sometimes be loosened directly, and curative emotional communication is critical to the process. Let's consider how to loosen these types of repetitions, what types of emotional communications can be of value in this process, and what dilemmas and risks arise in work with projective identification.

Silent interventions

Up to this point, I have described only one type of silent containment. Recall that in containment the analyst silently allows herself to fully experience the induced feeling without overtly communicating it to the patient. The effect of successful containment is varied, depending on the relational mode of the contained feeling. In the narcissistic mode, the analyst's containment can be seen to silently model the feeling for the patient, demonstrating that the patient will be able to tolerate the induced feeling because the analyst has shown her that it is possible. Similarly, the analyst's willingness to contain the feeling can also be seen as digesting or metabolizing the feeling for the patient, making it easier for the patient to tolerate it. Finally, containing the feeling and tolerating it silently often communicates to the patient that her communication has been heard, even if the analyst never says anything overt about it.

Containment functions differently in object inductions. While it silently communicates to the patient that her message has been heard, it also communicates that the analyst will not act on the induced feelings – that she acknowledges the repetition while abstaining from perpetuating it. Given that most people in the patient's life unreflectively and spontaneously react to the patient in a way that is consistent with the repetition, containment of object inductions can be a powerful experience for loosening the repetition.

Containment of induced projective identifications is sometimes similar to containment with narcissistic inductions. As with narcissistic inductions, the analyst's ability to contain the induced feeling can also serve to model or to metabolize it for the patient.[2] For example, the patient describes how strongly he asserts himself, no matter the circumstances. He constantly talks about how important it is to him for everyone to know where he stands and not to let anyone push him around. As he discusses this, the analyst thinks about how infrequently she asserts herself, how she accommodates everyone and allows everyone to walk all over her. The difference in their feelings is the polar opposition that is the hallmark of projective identification. The patient has projected his compliance – his impulse to allow himself to be dominated – into the analyst, and the analyst has accepted it. The analyst's silent containment of these feelings, her willingness to tolerate the feeling without resorting to a defense – either interpersonal or intrapsychic – can serve to

TECHNIQUE WITH PROJECTIVE IDENTIFICATION

make it possible for the patient to reintegrate it into his own mind. By accepting the feeling, she demonstrates to the patient that the feeling is not necessarily toxic – that it can be part of human experience and need not be expelled. It is silent modeling. When it works, the patient will, over time, begin to feel impulses to accommodate and also concomitant feelings of weakness and fear that underlie the defense.

However, containment does not always work in this way with projective identification. Because the function of projective identification is to keep the projected feeling out of the patient's sense of self, the contained feeling does not flow back towards the patient as consistently as it does in the narcissistic mode. Rather, the induced projection can remain settled within the analyst's experience in such a way that its expulsion from the patient's intrapsychic state remains unchanged. When this occurs, containment may work to stabilize the defense by accepting it, but the containment does not loosen it; the patient may remain in a stable state of projective identification.

This can be useful. When the analyst contains the projective identification, the patient may resort to it less outside the treatment, concentrating and isolating the repetition within the analysis, which is almost always a good thing. Furthermore, in most cases, it helps to keep the patient attached to and engaged in the analytic relationship, allowing the analyst to make more directly therapeutic types of emotional communications when the patient is in a more accessible relational mode.

Another type of silent intervention that can sometimes loosen the hold of projective identification – silent refusal – is nearly the opposite of containment. In silent refusal, the analyst allows herself to feel the projected feeling – the feeling that is the polar opposite of the patient's feeling – but works to experience it as something that is foreign to her identity. In contrast with containment, she does not internally join the patient or agree with the patient's perceptions. The analyst does not accept the role in the relationship that the patient has assigned to her through the projection. Instead, she rejects the feeling, while still maintaining awareness of it.

For example, if the patient induces feelings of worthlessness and powerlessness in the analyst, she stays aware of the feeling but forces herself to maintain a sense of value and effectiveness. If the patient induces grandiosity and elation, she forces herself to feel resolutely honest and realistic about her sense of self. In other words, the analyst refuses to fully accept the induction as a feeling that belongs to her or to allow her subjectivity to be used to maintain the patient's intrapsychic equilibrium. The goal is to silently force the patient to take back the feeling that has been projectively identified.

Although silent refusal is a silent intervention, it is more risky than containment. It works best when the patient is on the cusp of being able to relinquish the need for the projective identification. If the patient still needs the defense to maintain her emotional equilibrium, the analyst's silent refusal can be experienced as an attack; the patient may respond by increasing the intensity of the projection, in a counter-effort to force the analyst to accept the projected feeling. This can easily lead to enactments.

On the other hand, both types of silent intervention run the risk of being too subtle for the patient to experience and can be experienced as a lack of emotional responsiveness. In these cases, the patient may again increase the intensity of the projective identification.

Both types of silent interventions work best when the projective identification is active in the analytic relationship but are not the overt focus of the analytic work. Suppose the patient expresses feelings of timidity and fear and induces feelings of courage and fearlessness in the analyst. The silent interventions are more likely to be effective when the patient discusses feeling timid in some other part of her life, such as work or outside relationships, rather than when she actually compares herself to the analyst. In the latter case, the analyst usually must make some sort of an expressive intervention.

Both silent interventions – containment and silent refusal – are usually the most effective forms of emotional communication in working with projective identification and less potentially disruptive than the expressive interventions. They tend to maintain the analytic relationship at workable levels of intensity. This allows the patient to change at her own rate and helps her to develop a maximum level of trust in the analyst. Furthermore, the analyst's unwillingness to act on the induced feelings tends to interrupt the more overt aspects of the patient's repetition, allowing for the different enough to be curative dimension to be experienced by the patient.

Both types of silent interventions can be very difficult for the analyst to tolerate emotionally. All countertransference – except some of the positive narcissistic states and many of the anaclitic states – can be painful to experience, but few states are as urgent as projective identification. The analyst can usually remember that she has to tolerate the other states, but projective identification often arouses a feeling of rebellion and a desire to expel the psychic intrusion. It can be easier to bear when in a state of silent refusal than in containment. However, the temptation always exists to make the refusal verbal, to want to tell the patient, clearly and definitely, that she's got it all wrong. The intensity of the feelings often seems intolerable, especially when it must be endured for long periods of time.

Nevertheless, it's often worth it. When the analyst can bear the pain of the silent interventions, the work of loosening the projective identification can often proceed silently and slowly. Containment is especially useful in the early stages of treatment when the similar enough to be compelling aspects of the relationship are at the fore. When the analyst feels that the patient might be able to tolerate a bit more, she can shift her internal state to one of silent refusal, thereby adjusting the emotional communication without overtly disrupting the flow of the sessions.

Expressive interventions

Interpretation

The therapeutic aspect of classical interpretation with projective identification is, as with the other relational modes, a cognitive communication that conveys the analyst's intellectual understanding to the patient's reasonable ego, combined with an emotional communication that supports and catalyzes the interpretation. Classical interpretations can sometimes be beneficial with some aspects of projective identification, provided that the patient's reasonable ego is strong enough and present enough in the analytic relationship for the analyst to communicate. This is not always the case because projective identification often leads to a strong dominance of the afflicted ego, and it tends to color every aspect of the patient's experience and perception of the analyst. But when the patient's reasonable ego has some measure of control over the afflicted ego, and especially when the patient knows that the feelings or the behavior associated with the projective identification are problematic, an interpretation can sometimes calm the patient, provide her with some distance from the intensity of her feelings, and help her to differentiate her feelings from reality. Under these conditions, interpretations can be effective, whether or not the analyst is the overt target of the projective identification.

However, the interpretation will often be incomplete; it will describe one aspect of the repetition but not the whole process. Or the interpretation will have to proceed in steps. For example, suppose the patient projects his feelings of weakness and then becomes angry and contemptuous of the person to whom he has projected his weakness. "You seem to get riled up by other people's weakness," combined with a mild narcissistic emotional communication, can help the patient to become aware of the intensity of and the reason for his reaction. Notice that in this phase of the interpretation, no mention is made of the idea that the weakness that angers him is his own feeling, which has been projected onto the other person – only that the weakness upsets or angers him. Sometimes, the interpretative process can proceed further and it can be suggested to the patient who has trouble experiencing his own feelings of weakness. But sometimes not. Sometimes the first phase is as far as the patient can go.

Will this loosen the repetition? In some ways, it will. This approach to projective identification can help the patient control himself and reach a point where the projective identification interferes less in his life. This can be very beneficial to the patient. On the other hand, this will infrequently lead to true maturation, in which the need to expel the intolerable feeling and experience it as residing in the other person significantly lessens and the patient develops the ability to accept the projected feeling as a part of his experience.

Thus, the effect of successful interpretations of projective identifications can be somewhat superficial. But this is not a reason to avoid it. Projective identifications can create serious problems in the patient's life, and it is not always possible to loosen them. Anything that helps to control them is usually beneficial though.

Furthermore, the effect of the interpretation can sometimes be extended with a stronger narcissistic emotional communication after the interpretation has helped the patient to recognize that he has problems with the projected feelings. Consider the previous example in which the patient is able to recognize and accept that he has trouble dealing with other people's weakness. The analyst might follow this up with a narcissistic emotional communication such as, "It can be really enraging to be around weak people." If the patient felt understood by this, it would indicate that the patient has shifted into the narcissistic mode in the transference. Further along the process, the analyst might be able to use narcissistic modeling to help the patient experience and tolerate the feelings of weakness. Thus, classical interpretation to the reasonable ego followed by narcissistic emotional communication to the afflicted ego would loosen the repetition.

Non-interpretative emotional communications

Verbal refusal: contradicting the patient's projection

Two forms of emotional communication addressed to the afflicted ego sometimes work with projective identification. The goal of each is to convert the projective identification state into a narcissistic transference by inducing a shift in relational mode in the patient. The first is a variation on silent refusal, except that it is not silent. The analyst briefly allows herself to experience the feeling but does not absorb it as she would in containment. Rather, she consciously attempts to not feel it as a part of herself. She rejects it: she uses both her feelings and her thoughts to diminish the hold that the feeling has on her, as if to send it back to the patient – without metabolizing it for the patient. And this return is not silent. The analyst's comments implicitly or explicitly contest the patient's experience of the analyst. The intervention is the opposite of a join. The purpose is to force the patient to take back the projected feeling. This rarely results in the patient being able to feel it and tolerate it directly; rather, it may serve to cause the patient to move into a narcissistic, or less commonly, an object mode of relating – both of which are easier to influence than projective identification.

For example, a patient comes to a first session and the analyst immediately feels intimidated. Although the patient seems to be polite, she is strangely lacking in pain or anguish. Her interest in getting help, although rooted in a very real problem – her lover has left her – seems detached and intellectual. She says that she wants to understand what happened, but she doesn't seem terribly upset about it. She has an extremely successful career in the entertainment business, and she makes a few mildly disparaging remarks about therapists. For example, she thinks the person who referred her to the analyst – her brother's analyst – is a simpleton. She doesn't think much of her brother either. The analyst feels combative. He wants to ask: "Why on earth would you accept a referral from a person you think is a simpleton, anyway?" He notices that he is on the edge of being out of control. He is feeling increasingly defensive and envious of the patient's wealth and her position in the world. He has fantasies of her being driven around in a big limo (in fact, she's rich, but not that rich) and sending underlings out to get cappuccino with demanding specifications about milk and sugar.

He hypothesizes that the patient is coping with the pain of losing her lover by making herself feel strong and him weak. He thinks that if he allows her to undermine him he will be despised and dumped. With effort, he doesn't rise to her provocations and maintains a cool stance throughout. At the end of the session, the analyst states his fee, and the patient replies:

"That's an awful lot for a therapist, isn't it?"

"Oh, I don't know," the analyst replies, unruffled. "It seems just about right to me."

"Don't you ever reduce it?"

"Yes, for schoolteachers and social workers, not executives in the movie business."

"Do you have any idea how much I lost in the market this year?"

The analyst hadn't expected his last turn so early: the patient actually placed herself in the victim position, and in a roundabout way, verbalized feeling vulnerable and exploited – a feeling that had been central to her relationship with her lover (although the analyst didn't know this until later on). It seemed as though the patient was on the verge of feeling the projected feeling. However, the patient's behavior was still more bullying and manipulative than hurt or vulnerable; the analyst decides not to respond to the vulnerability and maintain the tough stance:

"I'm sure you'll manage," he says coolly.

In the next session, the patient was generally softer and more able to tolerate vulnerability. In this example, the analyst's refusal to accept the projection of weakness helped to loosen the projective identification directly. However, this could not have occurred so quickly unless the patient had been on the cusp of being able to relinquish the need for projective identification.

Now let's look at a case in which the patient projects the feelings of strength and aggression and keeps the feelings of weakness. The patient criticizes herself for being too passive in relationships with men. She never asks for anything and is never able to get anything except to garner the crumbs that fall to her. The analyst feels distinctly empowered listening to her patient. The analyst thinks about how she asks for things from her husband and from her father. It's easy for her: she asks and she gets – not like this poor wretch on her couch. She considers this feeling silently for several months. Eventually, she realizes that this perspective isn't exactly true. She does ask for things from her husband, but this took years, and it still doesn't come naturally. In fact, it's pretty difficult for her to get the things she wants without an internal struggle. She's more similar, in some ways, to the patient than she feels when she listens to the patient. She realizes that she has been induced with the patient's projection into her as a powerful, marvelously confident woman, which supports and contrasts with the patient's feeling that she is a helpless little mouse. The analyst recognizes that this is a projective identification and bides her time until the appropriate moment.

The moment occurs when the patient actually discusses a fantasy about the analyst, and her envy begins to break through.

"I tried to talk to my boyfriend last night about washing the dishes sometimes. I really tried to stand up for myself. But he just laughed at me. He even said, 'Oh, did your therapist start giving you self-assertiveness training?' She sighs. "I bet you don't have problems like that. I bet you snap your fingers and your husband stands to," she says, with more bitterness than admiration.

"I wish," the analyst says with a light laugh. "Actually, I've been trying to get him to sometimes, just sometimes, leave me enough milk for my coffee in the morning. But does he?"

"You mean you have trouble getting what you want out of him?" The hint of bitterness has turned to anger.

"That's a charitable way of describing it."

"Why is that?"

"Men are difficult, self-absorbed creatures. It's pretty difficult for most women to get anything out of them. And I'm a woman – no doubt about that." The analyst clearly contradicts the patient's projection matter-of-factly but without self-hatred.

"How are you going to help me to be more assertive if you can't do it yourself? I thought that you were such a big, strong woman. And now it turns out that you are as weak as me."

"Well, suppose that is true. Then what?"

"It's pretty fucked up; that's what it is!" The patient says this with real anger – not her typical whiny resentment.

In this case, the emotional communication completely undid the projective identification, inducing a change in the patient's relational mode to a negative narcissistic transference. At this point, the analyst's emotional communications functioned more like negative narcissistic mirroring: the analyst verbalizes the parts of the patient's self-experience that the patient hates the most to drain the patient's self-hatred away from herself and towards the analyst.

This type of emotional communication might also induce a positive narcissistic transference in the patient. In this case, the patient would feel comforted and affirmed by the analyst's communication that she too had trouble getting what she needed from a man. She might see herself as being less alone and gradually able to become more assertive as a result of positive narcissistic mirroring.

The second form of emotional communication that can be used with projective identification might be viewed as a variant of narcissistic modeling (see Chapter 11) and is based on the same principle – the analyst's ability to experience, tolerate, and express the projected feeling can enable the patient to integrate the feeling as a part of her personality. In both cases, the analyst models the projected feeling itself, which she embraces and metabolizes for the patient, and then offers it back to her as an acceptable aspect of human emotional experience.

Consider a case of a patient who had a florid narcissistic personality. He worshiped success and despised mediocrity that he equated with failure. He thought of himself as a very special person who was on the verge of a mighty breakthrough that would bring him fabulous wealth. He saw an analyst whom he admired and charged a similarly fabulously high fee. But he couldn't or wouldn't (it was difficult to say which) pay it after a while and asked for a referral to an analyst that he could afford. When he met the analyst who would see him for a fee that he could/would pay, he was already convinced that he was inferior, at best. He began treatment by lauding the enormously skilled but unattainable first analyst and remarked on the new analyst's less impressive office. Over the next several sessions, he described his plans for success, his specialness, and his unusual circumstances, all the while becoming increasingly deprecating towards the analyst. He commented that the analyst must be a beginner or he must have had some other reason – not a good one – for not having a large practice and needing to charge a low fee. He didn't seem as charismatic as the first analyst. He hadn't hit the ground running like the first one did. What was it like, he asked, to be getting referrals from somebody who was more expensive than he was. Wasn't it humiliating?

"Why not at all," the analyst replied. "In fact, it works out quite well for me."

"Really?" the patient asked, aghast at the analyst's response.

"Of course," the analyst said brightly. "That other analyst writes and talks and has to sound special all the time, whereas I don't have to do anything at all and business just flows right to me because I work for less. He does the hard work of making himself known, building a big reputation, and generally being successful, and I get whatever he can't take. It's perfect."

"But they really wanted to see him, not you."

"Yes, but they end up coming to me anyway, and that's good enough for me. I'm a scavenger. Maybe the lion gets the best cuts, but the hyena never goes hungry either!" The analyst says this with deliberate glee, making it clear to the patient that as far as he is concerned, there's no shame – and everything to gain – in living off the leftovers.

The choice of metaphor – comparing patients to food – is also designed to mirror the way in which the patient has objectified the analyst. Just as the patient only sees the analyst as someone who can't get the goods, the analyst communicates that he sees the patient as the only goods he can get.

In other words, the analyst accepts the patient's premise, which is partially true, that he is not as successful as the first analyst but rejects the humiliation and the shame that the patient attaches to this position. He may be second rate, he may be mediocre, but he's happy anyway. The analyst models accepting the feeling that the patient rejects and projects. Thus, he offers it back to the patient as an acceptable and respectable feeling to experience.

When successful, however, the short-term effect is different than it is when the analyst engages in straightforward narcissistic modeling. In the narcissistic transference, the patient may initially be a bit shocked at the analyst's acceptance of a dystonic feeling, but he is quickly exhilarated when the analyst embraces a feeling that has pained her.

In the case of projective identification, however, the initial effect is strongly dystonic and confusing. The patient may be appalled that the analyst's attitude towards the projected feelings is so different from her own. Remember, she has projectively identified the feeling because she cannot tolerate it. The analyst's communication is a direct challenge to the patient's system of intrapsychic stability. To see the analyst not only tolerate but also embrace it is to have her emotional world turned upside down. The patient might object, wondering – silently or aloud – what (the hell) is wrong with the analyst? How could she possibly feel that way? Her first response might be that the analyst is simply crazy.

When the intervention is successful, however, it initiates a shift in the relational mode from projective identification to narcissistic, and the intervention then begins to function in the same way as narcissistic modeling. Sometimes, this will be overt. The patient might say,

"I feel like a loser, just like you are, but it doesn't seem to bother you. Why not?"

"Why should it bother me? What is wrong with being a loser? Everybody is a loser sometimes – except maybe Dr. X." The analyst laughs at this last comment with clear irony, implying that he knows that this is not true.

"But it just seems wrong. Shouldn't you hate yourself for being a loser?"

"If you need to hate yourself, then yes. But if not, I just don't see the point. Why not enjoy all your feelings? Isn't it fun to watch a movie with a loser in it when you identify with him, like in an old Woody Allen movie?"

On the other hand, the action may be covert. The analyst finds that the patient resorts to projective identification less frequently, talks in a looser, more intimate way, and shifts into the narcissistic mode more unobtrusively. The analyst finds that she is now responsive to more typical narcissistic interventions.

Risks of expressive emotional communications with projective identification

The primary risk in all expressive interventions in the projective identification mode is essentially the same as the risk in silent interventions: the intervention will present too strong a challenge to the patient's need for the defense, and the intervention has the effect of prematurely disrupting the defense.

The best possible outcome in this situation is that the patient intensifies the projective identification, without leaving the treatment. This can allow the analyst to go back to a position of containment and wait for the treatment to restabilize. Sometimes, however, the intensification of the projective identification will lead the patient to leave the treatment.

Another possibility is that the transference will be transformed into a negative object transference that becomes too intense for the patient to tolerate. Here again, this can lead to the patient ending treatment.

Finally, there is the possibility that the patient's defensive structure will deteriorate in other ways, and she will appear to be more psychotic in her way of relating or in her overall use of defense.[3] For example, the patient might become more openly paranoid or develop strange or odd ideas. In these cases, it is important that she go to a much less stimulating, more emotionally supportive environment, usually with a lot of syntonic, narcissistic joining. The goal here is to stabilize the patient's intrapsychic functioning and the treatment relationship, not to immediately loosen any repetitions.

For all of these reasons, expressive emotional communications that directly address projective identification should be used with great caution. Patients who frequently relate in the projective identification mode can be very frustrating for the analyst because of the sheer tenacity of their need for this defensive structure combined with the intensity of the countertransference they induce. But it can help to keep in mind that the degree of stress that the analyst experiences in working with them is an indication of the underlying fragility of their intrapsychic equilibrium. As many difficulties as projective identification can create for patients and those around them, it nevertheless can protect them from being overwhelmed with intolerable feelings and from slipping into psychotic-like states.

14

ANACLITIC EMOTIONAL COMMUNICATIONS

This chapter will be somewhat different from the other chapters on technique because the major examples of anaclitic emotional communications were integrated into the chapter on anaclitic countertransference. For this reason, this chapter will focus on general properties of anaclitic emotional communications, and a number of specific issues that come up in relationship to them.

Introduction

In anaclitic emotional communication, the analyst communicates a feeling, as a differentiated object, that the patient needs in order to complete the developmental process – to mature. The needed feeling may have been missing from the patient's life history; it may have been present but insufficiently intense to meet his developmental needs; or the patient may need to re-experience a feeling that he had sufficiently experienced in the past in order to heal from the effects of a later trauma.

Anaclitic emotional communication was an essential component of Freud's (1940) theory of technique – the first type of emotional communication to be used deliberately in psychoanalysis. Although he viewed interpretation as the feature of psychoanalytic technique that differentiated it from the other psychotherapies, he also argued that it had to be accompanied by (what is defined here as) a specific range of emotional communications: the analyst takes a serious interest in the patient, relates to him with sympathetic understanding (Freud 1913), and soothes and encourages him in his efforts to overcome his resistances (1940). The analyst also provides an "after education" (1917: 451) in which the analyst corrects some of the mistakes the patient's parents made with the patient, taking – to a limited degree – an explicitly parental role.

These interventions, which are not interpretations, help the patient to persevere in the analytic process and to accept and make use of the interpretations. In terms of the theoretical framework that I have presented, these aspects of Freud's technique may be described as anaclitic emotional communications.

The emotional communications that Freud (1940) advocated are directed to the patient as an adult, struggling with the pain of the neurosis and the difficulty of overcoming it. Although there is a regressive, childlike element to the positive transference and to the adult patient's feelings of dependency on the analyst, Freud never directly engaged the patient's more profound transferential regression on an emotional level. Rather, he worked to assist the patient, as an adult, to observe this regression. When Freud (1917) writes that the analyst and the patient's weakened ego form a party together against the id and the superego, it is clear that the weakened ego that Freud forms his alliance with is the part of the ego that observes the repetition, not the part that participates in it. In terms of the framework that has been presented here, Freud addressed his anaclitic emotional communications to the patient's reasonable ego.

Anaclitic emotional communication is more powerful when it is addressed to the afflicted ego. The origin of this technique can be found in Ferenczi (1931), and to a more limited extent in Balint (1952, 1968). Later, Winnicott (1965) made extensive use of this type of emotional communication, focused on anaclitic needs related to earliest infantile development, conceptualized in terms of the "holding environment" (47). Sechehaye (1951) also made extensive use of it in her concept of "symbolic realization." Spotnitz (1985) explicitly formulated the concept of the anaclitic transference and of anaclitic interventions.

In addition, I suspect that many analysts throughout psychoanalytic history have made significant use of anaclitic emotional communications to the afflicted ego but were reluctant to discuss it openly, or viewed it as part of the art but not the science of psychoanalysis.

Although Freud made explicit use of a narrow range of anaclitic emotional communications, he used them sparingly. He warned against providing too much gratification in the transference-relationship, arguing that "spoiling" the patient reduced his motivation to overcome his problems (1919: 164). He wrote, "the patient must be left with unfulfilled wishes in abundance" (Freud 1919: 164).

Furthermore, the form that Ferenczi's last experiments, with what might be considered anaclitic emotional communication, took – such that even a commentator as sympathetic as Balint (1968) viewed them as seriously flawed – and Freud's stern condemnation of them (Gay 1988), no doubt had a chilling effect on the psychoanalytic mainstream. The prejudice against this form of emotional communication was reinforced by theorists such as Strachey (1934), whose focus on the importance of emotional neutrality in the treatment was more extreme than Freud's. Although Eissler's (1953: 104) renaming of non-interpretive interventions as "parameters" created a place – albeit a second-class place – for these (and other) types of interventions within psychoanalytic technique for patients who were viewed as being unanalyzable (at least in that moment), the deliberate use of feelings to meet developmental needs was viewed as unorthodox until the beginning of the 1990s. And in spite of the great changes that have occurred in psychoanalysis since then, I have the impression that many contemporary analysts, even from schools that make extensive use of emotional communication, tend to shy away from interventions that are overtly nurturing.

The structure and function of anaclitic emotional communications

Anaclitic emotional communications are made within the differentiated mode of relatedness: the analyst and the patient experience each other as separate and different. However, the patient may not be consciously aware of the analyst as a separate and distinct object. In states of deep, anaclitic regression, the patient experiences the analyst, like the infant experiences the parent, more like the air that he breathes (Balint 1968) than as a separate presence. The analyst, however, is aware of the patient as being separate and distinct from himself. For example, the patient might be completely absorbed in telling the analyst about his week in such a way that he doesn't appear to acknowledge the analyst's presence or subjectivity. However, he still requires the analyst's presence, and he derives tremendous benefit from the analyst's attentive listening.

The patient and the analyst experience different feelings, but their different feelings are closely related to each other. If, for example, the patient feels anxious, the analyst feels like soothing the patient's anxiety. If the patient feels hungry, the analyst feels like feeding him. If the patient feels out of control, or simply is out of control, the analyst feels like controlling him and preventing him from hurting himself.

The anaclitic mode of relatedness involves a revival of the dependency needs in his relationship to the analyst – needs that were insufficiently met in his original relationship with his parents. Thus, the anaclitic transference is, in part, a repetition and creates the similar enough to be compelling dimension of the analytic relationship. However, the analyst's communications are usually a new experience or occasionally they are a repetition of an experience that is needed again.

Anaclitic emotional communications primarily serve two planned functions within the treatment. First, they can make the analytic environment similar enough to be curative, thereby activating an anaclitic transference. Many patients cannot tolerate an emotional environment that is too neutral and won't engage in the treatment unless the analyst provides some degree of anaclitic emotional communication – right from the first session – that resembles nurturing elements of their childhood or offers the feelings that they were missing but are ready to receive. More importantly, over the long term, anaclitic emotional communications meet unmet maturational needs, allowing the normal developmental process to restart.

Much less frequently, anaclitic emotional communications unblock pathological defensive patterns, such as introverted aggression and the narcissistic defense or similar but less entrenched defenses such as inhibited aggression. In cases like this, the analyst makes an anaclitic communication; soon thereafter, the patient responds with an outburst of aggression indicating a strongly negative object transference. This seems to come out of nowhere, tends to be self-limiting, and usually disappears as quickly as it arose. The analyst may be confused by this turn of events because it is so different from the typical response to an anaclitic communication. In these cases, it seems that the patient only feels safe to express the negativity after having been assured that the analyst is sufficiently different from the original object to be able to withstand it. It is also possible that receiving the anaclitic emotional communication from the analyst first makes the patient aware that these types of communications were missing from the original relationship and this gives rise to rage, which he expresses to the analyst in a momentary shift to an object transference. These moments are almost invariably progressive, but they cannot be planned because this dynamic is not predictable in any individual case.

Anaclitic relatedness in development and in analysis

Anaclitic emotional communications are, along with the healthy narcissistic emotional communications, the basic emotional elements required for normal emotional development. Together, anaclitic and narcissistic emotional communications encompass every feeling the developing child needs to experience from a parent.

What is the difference? A brief review: in anaclitic needs, the child requires a communication from the parent that is essentially different from the feeling the child experiences. The needed feelings are rooted both in nurturing responses to the child's more purely biological needs, such as hunger, as well as the more psychological needs to be loved and adored, to be structured and protected, to be instructed and guided – the whole range of needs related to being dependent on the parent.

Narcissistic needs, on the other hand, require a communication from the parents that is essentially the same as the child's feeling and reflects this feeling back to the child, although it may differ in intensity. Such a response indicates that the parent understands, shares, or is in some way a part of the child's experience. It is an experience of shared emotionality (Kohut & Wolf 1978).

Let's compare an example of each type of need in childhood, considering an anaclitic need first.

The need for food is both biological and psychological: the baby requires food for its biological survival, but getting nutrition is not enough. The infant needs to be fed in the context of a dependency relationship characterized by love and nurturance. This dimension is an anaclitic need. When the child cries from hunger, the anaclitic emotional communication from the mother makes the child feel that she can and will do what is required to alleviate his distress because she loves him.

In this archetypal anaclitic exchange, the infant and the parent communicate through a differentiated mode of relatedness: they experience and relate to each other as different and separate from each other. The child experiences hunger, and the parent experiences the desire to feed and comfort.

In contrast, the infant's need to share a laugh with the parent is a narcissistic need: when the infant laughs and seeks his mother's eyes, he seeks to share the moment, to see his high spirits reflected in the mother's expression. The attuned mother, in turn, seeks out the infant's eyes and shares the laugh (Stern 1985; Schore 1994). The infant needs the feeling that the mother understands his state and essentially feels the same way. They gaze at each other as their laughter intensifies through their shared emotional experience. This does not mean that the parent always reflects exactly the same feeling. It may, for instance, differ in intensity or in some other detail that does not change the essential sameness of the communication. They are communicating through the narcissistic mode of relatedness. They experience each other as being similar, the same as, or connected to each other.

But what, it might be asked, is the role of empathy in anaclitic emotional communication? Doesn't the mother want to feed the baby because she feels his pain? Isn't there an overlap between the differentiated and the narcissistic modes in this type of relatedness?

Yes, there is an overlap. The mother provides a correctly differentiated response on the basis of an empathic understanding that is a product of narcissistic relatedness. Thus, there is often (but not always) an element of sameness of feeling as a component, or at the base of, an anaclitic emotional communication. But the anaclitic response to the child's needs is more complex than empathy alone: the mother must do more than feel the child's needs and feelings; she must also understand the feeling required to meet the need at the moment. It is not enough to know that the baby is hungry and distressed and to communicate this understanding back to him; she must also know to feed him, know how to feed him, and know (on whatever level) that she is meeting his need, not simply eliminating her own distress caused by hearing a crying, hungry baby. Most importantly, she must communicate a nurturing feeling of love and a wish to soothe – a cluster of feelings that is a reaction to, but fundamentally different from, the child's feeling.

Similarly, if the child is anxious and overwhelmed, he needs somebody to understand more than his anxiety. He needs a communication from a parent that is calm, controlled, and soothing – a different feeling from the one he feels.

At times, the difference between simple empathy and anaclitic communications is subtle, but it is not trivial. The experience of receiving a needed feeling that is different from one's own feeling – on the basis of having one's own feeling understood – is fundamentally different from the experience of having one's own feeling understood, shared, and reflected. They are different ways of relating. One experience does not substitute for the other, either in development or in analysis. How would the baby fare if the mother only felt empathy with his hunger but had no impulse to feed him? Conversely, how would he fare if she understood his expansive joy but felt the desire to feed him instead of sharing his laughter. In both cases, it is not just the specific feeling communicated that would be wrong, it is how the parent relates to the infant and behaves towards him, based on the relational mode in which she experiences him, that is misunderstood and misattuned.

Both anaclitic and narcissistic emotional communications are necessary at different moments, based on different needs. The same is true in analysis: there are different types of emotional communication and each has its own time and place.

Differences between anaclitic emotional communications in development and in the psychoanalytic relationship

Anaclitic emotional interactions in psychoanalysis resemble those in development but are far more limited and transpire in a different relational context than in development: an anaclitic emotional communication in psychoanalysis is the expression of a feeling, explicitly or implicitly, through verbal communication, silent induction, or facial expression. Only rarely is an anaclitic emotional communication embedded in some other type of action or behavior. And even when it is, the action is designed to clarify and amplify the emotional communication; it is not an end in and of itself.[1]

Anaclitic emotional communication in normal development is experienced within the context of the child's emotional and physical immaturity and his actual dependence on the parent for his emotional and physical needs. Consequently, parental anaclitic emotional communications are often bound up with care-taking behavior. For example, a mother's desire to nurse when her baby cries from hunger infuses the feed with feeling, both for the mother and the infant. The anaclitic feeling is not symbolic of nursing; rather, it is a crucial ingredient of successful nursing.[2] In a loving environment, there will also be many anaclitic communications not directly connected to the satisfaction of purely physical needs, such as taking delight in the child.[3] But in general, anaclitic emotional communications in childhood are part of the warp and the weft of caretaking behavior.

The patient's relationship to the analyst is different. The patient is physically mature and does not need the analyst to meet his actual dependency needs. (Similarly, if the patient is a child, the responsibility for the child's actual dependency needs lies with the parent, not the analyst.) Thus the analyst does not assume the responsibility for the patient's life that a parent would. Rather than actual dependency, what occurs in analysis is a repetition and a regression. Within this regression, the patient induces analytic feelings in the analyst and is also receptive to having these met in a way that is symbolic of, but not the same as, having actual dependency needs met.

For example, when the analyst experiences the anaclitic feeling to feed the patient, he will rarely actually feed the patient. Instead, he will make some sort of symbolic communication, such as telling a story, recommending a restaurant or a recipe, or just talking to the patient. Even if he does actually feed the patient – by giving him a sandwich, for example – he does not satisfy the patient's need in the same way the mother does in nursing because the patient does not actually depend on him for his food and comfort, even if the patient is hungry. The sandwich will be symbolic of, but not the same as, the nursing experience.

What makes getting a sandwich special in analysis and therefore different from getting a sandwich at a diner? When properly attuned and delivered, the sandwich is a symbolic communication that is experienced by the patient in the context of the anaclitic transference. The transference imbues the analyst's emotional communications with curative impact and differentiates them from ordinary gratifications.

Analysts who reject these types of interventions as non-analytic often misunderstand this aspect of anaclitic emotional communication. All psychoanalytic interventions – interpretive and non-interpretive, cognitive and emotional – depend on the state of the transference in which the patient experiences them for their curative impact. The analyst's communications are curative because they are made in the context of a particular relationship at a particular point in time. If not, patients could experience psychoanalytic cure by reading interpretations in books or listening to pre-recorded emotional communications. While these activities can be helpful, for most patients they don't compare with the impact of real, interactive human relatedness.

Interpretations as anaclitic emotional communications

Interpretation serves two primary functions: The first, which is shared with a number of other techniques, is to help the patient put into words experience that is unconscious or preconscious, unformulated or unmentalized (whether for defensive or developmental reasons), or in any way unthought, unsaid, or unarticulated. Freud (1923) suggested that material from the id can enter the ego by being put into words, and thus interpretation helps to build and strengthen the reasonable ego by enlarging the range of experience that can be experienced and expressed in language. It gives the patient the "words to say it" (Cardinal 1983) and the words to think it.

The second function, which is unique to interpretation, is to educate the patient's reasonable ego about the functioning and experience of his afflicted ego – his wishes and impulses, his dreams and his fantasies, his superego and his memories – in order to strengthen the reasonable ego in relationship to his repetitions and his out-of-conscious-control feeling states.

Both functions of interpretation have developmental antecedents that serve anaclitic functions. The child's need for interactions that foster his cognitive development is part and parcel of his overall dependency needs. The parents, through their words, first shepherd the child from the world of unmixed emotional communication of the preverbal period to the weave of emotional and cognitive communication that characterizes mature human speech, and in doing so, nurture the development of the reasonable ego. Furthermore, they are the first to cultivate the child's sense of self-awareness and self-understanding.

Similarly, interpretation fosters the development of the reasonable ego in the patient, and if accompanied by a properly attuned anaclitic emotional communication, can meet an anaclitic need in the transference that catalyzes the patient's ability to make use of the interpretation. In classical interpretations, the emotional communication addresses the reasonable ego. In affective interpretations, the emotional communication addresses the afflicted ego. The two types of interpretation function differently and involve different ways of relating, and will usually affect how the interpretation will be experienced by the patient.

Classical interpretations with anaclitic emotional communications

In a classical interpretation, both the cognitive communication and the emotional communication address the reasonable ego. The cognitive communication is the intellectual content of the interpretation, while the emotional communication is mildly anaclitic, mildly narcissistic, or present-anchored. It can be hard to differentiate between the three types of emotional communication, as they are very similar at the lower levels of intensity. Nevertheless, there are differences: the analyst's feeling is more caretaking and nurturing in the anaclitic communication, more purely empathic and understanding in the narcissistic communication, and more purely observational in the present-anchored communication.

Classical interpretations involving anaclitic emotional communications tend to be most useful in three situations. The first is when the patient's reasonable ego is dominant in the analytic relationship for non-defensive reasons. This usually occurs when the patient experiences feelings linked to a repetition and is consciously aware of these feelings, either completely or in part, at an intensity low enough to allow him to observe the repetition with a relatively high degree of detachment.

While there is transference active in the treatment at this moment – there always is – it is not the dominant element in the patient's relationship to the analyst in the sense that the relationship is not shaped primarily by a repetition. But there is an affective attachment or relatedness to the analyst – often a strong one, usually of a mildly anaclitic or narcissistic character – that emanates primarily from the reasonable ego. The feelings of anaclitic dependency or narcissistic identification that the patient experiences in these attachments are reminiscent of and grow out of their childhood prototypes (as all adult feelings do), but unlike transference, they are not repetitive and involuntary, bound tightly by the inflexible patterns rooted in childhood. They are primarily adult level experiences – the here-and-now feelings and needs that one adult can have for another adult. The patient usually experiences the analyst as a trusted ally in these attachments.

I suspect that this is precisely the type of attachment that Greenson (1960) sought to foster on the basis of his concept of the working alliance. It is during these times the patient's interest in self-understanding is often high and he is able to make use of the information conveyed by the interpretations in a way that is not self-attacking. The cognitive communication contained in the interpretation strengthens the patient's reasonable ego. This creates an emotional structure that enables the patient to stay attached to the adult present while observing and experiencing the feelings in the repetition more strongly and directly, with a low risk of either becoming overwhelmed or defensive. Mild anaclitic emotional communications to the reasonable ego help the patient to absorb the sometimes distressing self-awareness by conveying the analyst's acceptance and respect for the patient's adult struggle with the repetitions, thus providing a crucial element of interpersonal support.

For example, one woman was in this type of low intensity transference in which I was the focus of her repetitions through most of five years of analysis. At one point, she experienced an increased level of conflict with her girlfriend, with whom she previously had an unusually cooperative and loving relationship. During one of these periods, her girlfriend had become quite angry with her for reasons that she didn't understand at all. I saw this as a repetition of a childhood pattern of her father becoming sporadically angry with her. She had discussed the memories of her father many times before. This was the first time that the feelings were alive and real again in an active repetition in her current life, but she was unable to see the similarity. I could feel her confusion and distress as she discussed her girlfriend's behavior, as well as her mild dependency on me at that moment. I interpreted the similarities between her current situation and her childhood relationship with her father. I combined this cognitive communication with a distinct but low-intensity tone designed to soothe her anxiety. Although she was initially reluctant to consider the similarity – she objected to the idea that her girlfriend was in any way like her father – I gently pushed her to consider it in a soothing tone, and she became more able to recognize the similarities.

This is an example of a classical interpretation in which the analyst was not the target of the repetition. However, classical interpretations can also be used when the analyst is the target of the repetition, provided that the reasonable ego is dominant in the relationship at that moment, as can be seen in the case of a patient who was extremely angry with an analyst who was unwilling to change a date on an insurance form. The patient was typically in a state in which his reasonable ego was dominant, but the analyst's refusal triggered a full-blown object transference in which the patient's reasonable ego was neither dominant nor accessible. The patient felt that the analyst was deliberately withholding and was callous. No expressive intervention worked during this period. The analyst was left to contain and explore as the patient verbalized his relentlessly negative feelings. This went on for a couple of months, after which the patient returned to the more typical state in which his reasonable ego was dominant. He was able to see the intensity of his negative feeling but was left with the nagging feeling that the analyst had been unfair and hostile. The analyst gently interpreted that when the analyst was not able to give the patient what he wanted, he immediately felt that the analyst wanted to hurt him. She said this in a tone that made clear, to the adult side of him, that she didn't want to hurt him. The patient was able to see the repetition clearly as a pattern in his life for the first time. The emotional communication helped the patient differentiate between his negative perception of the analyst in his object transference fantasies and the actual analyst who was talking to him. The emotional communication served to reinforce the information that was conveyed in the interpretation.

Classical interpretations can be very helpful for the rather specific situation in which the patient (a) tends to get overwhelmed by the repetition and is easily overstimulated within the repetition and (b) has a reasonable ego that is weak in the sense that it does not have consistent control over the afflicted ego but is readily mobilized and is able to regain control with the benefit of outside interpersonal assistance that leads to self-awareness. These types of patients are sometimes confusing because they respond extremely well to more purely emotional communications to the afflicted ego when they are not overwhelmed. But when they are, they really need interpretation to re-stabilize them. Sometimes an affective interpretation (see below) will work better, but at other times, a classical interpretation, which clearly reinforces their adult sense of self, is more effective. In these patients, the self-understanding provided by interpretation is often experienced as extremely soothing and binding. It is remarkable how quickly the interpretation can bring them out of a state of real emotional chaos. The mild anaclitic emotional communication helps them to make use of the interpretation, but it is important to do so in a way that affirms their adulthood – and does not foster the regression – and thus supports the most mature dimensions of their personalities.

Classical interpretations combined with anaclitic emotional communications – or rather, as we will see, an intervention that looks just like it – can also be useful with patients who have strongly intellectualized or rational defenses. The nature of the intellectual defense is to attach to an overly rationalized interpretation of reality as a means of defending against clusters of painful or conflictual feelings. For this reason, this defensive structure can resemble the reasonable ego and can superficially appear to be reality oriented. But it is actually shaped by the logic of the repetition of which it is an expression.

When it is activated in the treatment, the afflicted ego is dominant in the relationship to the analyst, not the reasonable ego. When the analyst relates to the patient in this state, he is not helping the patient to observe the repetition, as he would if he were addressing the reasonable ego; rather, he is relating to him within the repetition. In a sense, offering the patient in this transference state an interpretation is a form of joining intervention.[4]

Nevertheless, the interpretation looks and sounds exactly like a classical interpretation. The mild anaclitic emotional communication, which should be a soothing tone attuned to the patient's anxiety about experiencing the feelings he is defended against, will help the patient make use of the interpretation. However, the emotional communication must be subtle. If it is too strong, it runs the risk of infantilizing the patient and undermining the intellectual defense.

In light of the fact that it looks and sounds just like a classical interpretation, it might be asked: what is the difference? The primary function of the true classical interpretation is to provide insight, while the primary function of the interpretation in this situation is to strengthen the patient's intellectual defenses until he is strong enough to experience the feelings more directly. The intellectual interpretation does not really integrate the feelings into the ego and the person's identity, in the truly curative manner of a classical interpretation; rather, it reinforces the boundary between the intolerable affect emanating from the lost provinces and conscious experience. The intervention will usually help the patient to feel more in control, but unlike a classical interpretation, it does not directly help him to integrate defended feelings into his personality. More purely emotional communications, usually narcissistic mirroring, will often be necessary to help the patient to more fully tolerate the feelings against which the intellectual defenses were erected.

Although patients in these three types of states tend to respond to classical (or classical-like) interpretations, I have found that it is not easy to predict which patients will respond to interpretations – particularly classical interpretations. It is not uncommon for patients who seem like they are in one of these states – particularly the first, in which there seems to be a transference emanating primarily from the reasonable ego – to not respond or respond poorly to classical interpretations. Conversely, patients who don't seem to be in any of these states sometimes respond extremely well to classical interpretation.

The anaclitic affective interpretation

In the affective interpretation, the cognitive communication – the content of the interpretation – addresses the observing ego, while the anaclitic emotional component addresses the afflicted ego. In contrast with the classical interpretation, the emotional communication is as important to the effectiveness of the intervention as the content of the interpretation; it does not play a purely supportive or catalytic role. The affective interpretation addresses the patient simultaneously as an adult and as a child: the cognitive content of the interpretation strengthens the reasonable ego, while the anaclitic emotional communication provides the patient with a needed feeling.

The emotional communication in the affective interpretation is stronger, much less subtle than in the classical interpretation. Whereas the classical interpretation is designed to maintain and support the patient's adult ego by contacting only the reasonable ego, the affective interpretation is designed to activate and meet the unmet dependency needs within the regressed, afflicted ego. While the interventions can resemble each other, the quality of the relatedness and interaction that they work within and engender are very different.

The transference state in which affective interpretations are effective is fairly common, and this type of intervention has a wide range of therapeutic action. A strong anaclitic emotional communication makes interpretations usable that might otherwise be experienced as injurious or assaultive if communicated in a more neutral manner. The emotional communication is what conveys that the analyst is not criticizing the patient. This is particularly true of interpretations of defenses – especially those operating outside of the transference: the anaclitic tone communicates that the analyst appreciates the defense protects the patient and appreciates that it is motivated by the underlying vulnerability. Without the emotional communication, the interpretation is more likely to be experienced as a critique of the patient's functioning or behavior. Similarly, genetic interpretations that link the patient's current feelings to past situations are more likely to be experienced as supportive, rather than critical or shaming, when the patient feels the analyst's emotional communication meets the underlying need for nurturance in the context of dependency. Finally, transference interpretations of all sorts – whether about impulses, wishes, defenses, or memories – can often be made more accessible when coupled with a strong anaclitic emotional communication.

The affective interpretation usually works best when the patient is in a strong state of anaclitic transference but is able to access the reasonable ego, to the extent of being able to observe and reflect upon the feelings in the repetition, and is interested in understanding some aspect of the situation more intellectually. Conversely, affective interpretations are less effective when the afflicted ego is so strongly dominant that the patient is unable to experience the analyst at all outside of the transference. For example, the patient discusses a conflict with his girlfriend that clearly repeats a conflict with his mother; he is also in an anaclitic transference in which he craves comfort and soothing from the analyst. An affective interpretation about the similarities between his feelings about his mother and his girlfriend could be very helpful if he is curious about the origin of dynamics in his relationship to the girlfriend or if he tends to feel more in control or supported with this type of self-understanding. However, if his primary need at that moment is to be comforted, the interpretation itself would most likely be distracting from what he needs emotionally at that moment and would interfere with his ability to make use of the soothing.

In this case, an anaclitic emotional communication without interpretative content might be more helpful.

Furthermore, interpretations about the patient's anaclitic fantasies about the analyst tend to work well with anaclitic emotional communications when the analyst also experiences the fantasy. For example, if the analyst wants to interpret that the patient wishes the analyst were omnipotent and would always know how to take care of her – especially if the analyst also wishes that he could be that kind of perfect, all-powerful parent for the patient – he would layer the interpretation with the feelings that express his wish. Indeed, the analyst might use the same tone that he would use if he was saying, "I wish I could always do that for you, always know what's best for you and always be there for you." And while he is making the related communication, he understands that this is what the patient wants from him.

Of course, the analyst might also actually say the part about wishing that he could provide this for the patient, without the interpretation. But that would be an undiluted emotional communication to the patient's afflicted ego, which is a different sort of intervention altogether. The choice could depend on whether the analyst thinks it is more important for the patient to understand his wish towards the analyst, or to actually feel the emotional strength of the analyst's wish towards him or both.

Anaclitic emotional communications, the reality ego, and use of the couch

The couch is, alas, controversial these days. For a long time, some analysts have argued that certain patients, especially schizophrenics and borderlines, needed to be able to see the analyst and that this served a developmental need for these patients. More recently, a number of theorists and infant researchers have argued the infant's ability to see the mother's face and interact with her directly (Schore 1994; Beebe *et al.* 2005), and engage in mutual gaze interactions, are crucial developmental experiences, or in the framework presented here, anaclitic needs. From this perspective, the use of the couch deprives the adult patient of the opportunity to relive – and if necessary, to repair – these early experiences in the context of the transference.

The infant research supporting this position is rich, and to a certain degree, convincing. And from clinical experience, I would agree that facial interaction[5] with the analyst can, for some patients, be a crucial channel of anaclitic emotional communication. Some patients panic or dissociate if they do not maintain face-to-face contact with the analyst; others are unable to establish an emotional relationship with the analyst when they use the couch. And still others find the experience of visual contact with the analyst to be a crucial curative dimension of their treatment. Obviously, these patients shouldn't use the couch.

As important as visual interactions may be, I think these theorists seriously underplay the importance of audio-vocal contact in development. And in clinical practice, they ignore how the couch can enhance the emotional impact of verbal communication in analysis. It has often been suggested that the couch facilitates the development of the transference. Although some patients do require emotional communication through visual channels to attach to the analyst, for others the visual contact reinforces the reality of the current situation and thus the dominance of the reasonable ego in relationship to the analyst. Conversely, the lack of visual contact, combined with emotional communication conveyed through the sound of the analyst's voice (or silence), can have a regressive effect, activating and intensifying the transference and engaging the patient's afflicted ego. Because the afflicted ego is reactive and responsive to a much wider range of emotional communication than the reasonable ego, the use of the couch in these cases increases the therapeutic leverage of the analyst's vocal emotional communications.

In the simplest terms, using the couch can help the patient be less responsive to the current reality and more responsive to the analyst's emotional communications.

This is true for all emotional communications. The couch can help the patient forget the realistic facts of their differences and separateness and become absorbed in the narcissistic transference and the analyst's narcissistic emotional communications. And it can help the patient forget that the analyst isn't really the parent of his past and react at full intensity to an object emotional communication that voices the parents' pathogenic feelings towards the patient.

The couch is equally helpful with anaclitic emotional communications because patients are often embarrassed or humiliated by the dependency feelings that are activated in the anaclitic transference. Of course, these are not the only types of feelings that the patient can find humiliating. Even in our supposedly uninhibited times, many patients are often extremely reluctant to express sexual desire for the analyst or even sexual desire that is not directed at the analyst. The couch can help in this situation as well. But for patients with strong, well-developed reality egos, anaclitic needs can be particularly difficult to bring into the treatment. This may be partly out of a concern that they will be reawakened only to be re-frustrated (Ornstein 1974). But even more than in the case of some of the other types of transference, the patient is all too aware that his needs are out of step with the reality of the situation. In these cases, the couch can help the patient's reasonable ego to relax – to forget that he and the analyst are both adults – and encourage him to allow the anaclitic needs to rise to the surface of his consciousness.

By increasing the intensity of the transference, the couch also helps this kind of patient to respond to anaclitic communications. For example, the patient mentions that he had a birthday; the analyst senses that he wants to tell the analyst what he got. There are two ways he could do so: in the emotional position of an adult who takes pleasure in his gifts – and perhaps ironically plays at being a child; or in the regressed emotional position of a child, who is dying to tell a parent how great his gifts are. The fact that the patient is on the couch can allow the more childlike feelings to bloom. The analyst can ask simpler questions: "How big is it? What color is it? Is the leather really smooth?" And he can often use a muted variant of the slowed down, exaggerated tones usually reserved for young children, without insulting the patient. What might feel condescending when sitting up can feel natural when lying down and being out of sight.

When the analyst faces the patient, he must be mindful of respecting the patient's adult self – the reasonable ego – while still making contact with the emotional edge of the transference – the afflicted ego. While the analyst must still attend to this with the patient lying down, the couch opens a wider window on the afflicted ego, allowing the patient's repetitions a much stronger presence in the relationship.

Furthermore, reducing and simplifying the amount of visual stimulation emanating from the analyst tends to amplify the importance of his verbal communications in the patient's mind. It allows the analyst to pay less attention to his facial expression while shaping his verbal communications with greater precision.

This is not to say that the couch is necessary to develop a transference, or that it always develops a transference of optimal intensity. Some patients develop sufficiently intense transferences while sitting up, some develop overly intense transferences while lying down, and for others it makes no difference either way.

Some have argued that the use of the couch somehow makes the experience less real, more contrived, or less genuine. This argument goes against all of my personal and professional experience. As a patient, the couch has made my analytic experience far more emotionally powerful than it ever was in treatments in which I was sitting up. There is simply no comparison, and I can't imagine that any sort of eye contact would do anything but dilute it. And in my professional practice, I have found that there is no general difference between the level of intensity with patients lying down or sitting up. A few patients don't do well on the couch and have developed great emotional intensity sitting up, while most do much more powerful emotional work on the couch.

The couch has become associated with the restricted style of communication prescribed by certain (but not all) classical American Freudians and I've heard the same horror stories everyone else has: patients lying on the couch in stony, cold isolation while the analyst sits silently behind them, saying nothing, for years on end. But to the extent that this experience is not what the patient needs – and it occasionally is – these stories represent an incompetent use of the couch, not an indictment. While it is true that the couch allows more use of silence than sitting up – something that can be extremely valuable – it can also facilitate a greater range of talking by the analyst. To exclude the couch purely on the theoretic grounds that it deprives the patient of the opportunity to meet one set of developmental needs is a serious technical error that can deprive them of the opportunity to meet a far greater range of developmental needs through more intense verbal interactions. It's not for everyone, but for those who can make use of it – in my experience, the majority of the patients that I have worked with and supervised – the benefits in terms of enhancing the degree and intensity of emotional communication in the treatment are profound.

Talking about the day

A particularly important form of anaclitic emotional communication occurs when the analyst feels a combination of interest, tenderness, affection, and concern for the patient and infuses these feelings throughout the session, regardless of the content discussed. The patient may be happy or sad. He may be introspective and reflective, discussing his intrapsychic or interpersonal functioning acumen and insight, but more often, he is completely extrospective, recounting details of his day or talking about other people with nary a hint of self-awareness. The analyst sticks close to the content, asking questions, making comments, laughing, or sighing as he sees fit, while making no effort to direct the patient's attention to any sort of latent content beyond the surface or to refocus the patient on his feelings – in short, to "deepen" the analysis.

The sessions may appear to be filled with trivia. Supervisees sheepishly describe what goes on between them: the patient talks about TV, complains about washing the dishes, reports infinite details about meals that he has eaten, quibbles with his spouse, or gives accounts of office politics.

Judging from the content, no analysis is taking place; the patient and the analyst are just talking. If the patient is in a good mood, they appear to be enjoying each other's company. If the patient is in a bad mood, the analyst's presence comforts him, and the analyst feels sympathetic and concerned. In this case, the analyst also feels empathic with the patient's pain, but what he communicates is more the sympathy than the empathy – the focus more directly on how the patient feels, rather than the analyst's understanding of how the patient feels.

The therapeutic action of the interaction lies in equal measure in the analyst's interest and affection – more often love – for the patient. The experience of being loved and paid attention to in this way can meet a major maturational need for these exact feelings. In these moments, there is no pressure on the patient to perform in any way. He doesn't have to do the work of analysis, be insightful, look at himself, and perhaps most importantly, he doesn't have to keep the analyst entertained or engaged. These are moments of everyday unconditional love and acceptance – not the unconditional love in the face of stark revelations about one's character, evil impulses, or bad behavior, but the unconditional love involved with just being with a person who is playing a parental role in the interaction.

This seems like a simple experience, and perhaps it is. Again, it might be asked, how is this any different from getting the same feelings from a friend or romantic partner? In part, the answer again goes back to the fact that the interaction takes place in the context of the anaclitic transference; the transference amplifies the importance and impact of the analyst's communication of love, affection, and interest.

Furthermore, the patient may not have friends or a romantic partner who will give him this attention, and even those patients who do often do not get enough of these types of interactions in their lives. Their parents may have been too busy to give the patient enough of these moments.[6] It is also possible that the parents' own needs, rooted in their own repetitions, for the child to behave or relate in a particular way made it impossible for them to supply the child with enough of these moments. When these moments were not sufficiently plentiful or intense in childhood, the patient's ability to induce them from others as an adult can be severely impaired. The analyst is often the only person in the patient's life who is consistently able to give the patient these feelings.

This kind of diffuse anaclitic attention is particularly important with patients who experience anaclitic depression in the transference. These patients are often extremely depressed and consumed with feelings of hopelessness, powerlessness, and insignificance. In contrast with other types of depression, there is usually little or no irritability, and the patient may appear to have lost all will to live or any hope that things can ever change for him. They tend to be non-demanding while remaining firmly attached to the analyst. Although they generally feel comforted in the presence of the analyst, there is often an inconsolable air about them, as if there is nothing that the analyst can do that will alleviate their suffering. And in the short term, this is true. Although they do seem to respond to the analyst's anaclitic caring, they are like a starving concentration camp victim when presented with a big meal; they can only take in a little or they will get sick. Interpretations usually go nowhere with these patients, and while they often induce strong narcissistic countertransferences, they rarely translate into curative emotional communications. Rather, the analyst's ability to remain interested, loving, and gentle with the patient – usually expressed through the tone of questions and comments – is what eventually brings these patients back to life. The process may take years (usually at least two years and often quite a bit more) but I have found that the anaclitic attention – the parental-like willingness to remain committed to the patient no matter how hopeless it all seems – is the crucial element. When the analyst can endure it, the patient usually responds.

The primary obstacle to success in these situations is the analyst's unwillingness to embrace the idea that in expressing loving attention to the patient, he is not only doing the best that he can do, but he is also doing exactly what the situation requires.

Risks of anaclitic emotional communication

I have found that anaclitic emotional communication has a wide scope of action, much wider than even Spotnitz (1983) suggested and that it has more forms than most of the other contemporary schools have conceptualized. For example, theorists such as (Stern 1985) have emphasized issues of emotional attunement, the development of positive affect, and the use of facial communication in treatment. While I think that all of these are important and would be included within the concept of anaclitic emotional communication[7] (although I have noted my disagreement with the universal value of eye contact), anaclitic emotional communications should not be limited to these types of interactions.

In my experience, most patients benefit from – and need – a significant degree of anaclitic emotional communication in order to reach their full potential.

However, there is a danger that the analyst, impressed and inspired by the power of anaclitic emotional communication and feeling (overly) liberated from the need to "act like an analyst," becomes so enamored of it that he uses it to the exclusion of all other types of emotional communication and all types of other interventions. As powerful as it can be, few patients are cured with anaclitic emotional communication alone. While object emotional communications and those related to projective identification are typically used less often than anaclitic communications, narcissistic emotional communications are used just as much and to omit these from the treatment would deprive many patients of crucial emotional interactions. Furthermore, many patients need interpretations, which can be combined with anaclitic emotional communication, but cannot be omitted from the treatment altogether.

The risk of pathological dependency

A common concern about anaclitic emotional communications is that they will stimulate and reinforce an unhealthy degree of dependency on the analyst. Freud (1919) first argued that the analyst should not give the patient so much in the analysis that he no longer needs to seek gratification in his life. In theory, this concern seems well founded and reasonable.

In practice, however, I have not seen it have this effect. This is probably because the anaclitic needs that arise in analysis are not adult needs; they are rooted in earlier stages of development. For this reason, they are neither readily nor optimally satisfied in adult relationships, nor, for most patients, do they substitute for adult emotional needs. Although romantic relationships and friendships usually satisfy unmet anaclitic needs to some degree – sometimes to a very large degree – this is a fringe benefit of a well-functioning adult relationship, not its main focus; adult relationships usually go awry unless they are anchored primarily in adult needs and desires, not anaclitic needs.

While it might be argued, as even Spotnitz did at one point, that the analysis should enable the patient to meet these sorts of needs from people outside the analysis, this seems to overlook the possibility that many of these needs – particularly the most primitive ones – are most efficiently and accurately met by the analyst. To force patients to seek this gratification outside the analysis is to artificially slow down their development in the interest of maintaining a particular vision of analytic cure.

Nevertheless, it might be objected, even though anaclitic needs are not adult needs, it is possible that the patient may regress in the analysis to the point that he prefers the satisfaction of childhood anaclitic needs to the exclusion of adult needs outside the analysis.

This is a possibility, and must be kept in mind, but in my experience, the most frequent scenario is that as a patient's anaclitic needs are gratified in the analysis, they become more able and motivated to seek what they desire in the world. The combination of an anaclitic relationship in the transference and the increasing pursuit of adult-oriented life goals occur simultaneously. If some patients appear to be exclusively focused on their analytic needs in analysis for a period of time, this is usually because they can't pursue their adult desires until the anaclitic needs have been met.

Once these needs have been met and they have been set back on the path of maturation, few patients will settle for childhood satisfaction alone when the gratifications of adulthood can finally be reached. However, it must be acknowledged that this can sometimes take so long that it will test anyone's confidence in the process.

There are, as always, exceptions. Just as some children are more attached than others to the needs and satisfactions of childhood, and might prefer to remain children if given the choice, some patients have trouble relinquishing the satisfactions of anaclitic emotional communication and are reluctant to seek out adult satisfactions.[8] However, the solution in these cases is not to eschew anaclitic emotional communication but to augment the gratifying types of anaclitic emotional communication with others that encourage – and sometimes actively push – these patients away from the analytic nest and towards the world of adult gratifications at the rate that they are able to do so.

Finally, there are patients who lead successful and gratifying adult lives but seem to need anaclitic emotional communication, possibly on a lifelong basis, either to maintain and progress in their adult lives or simply because they feel much better when they get it. While this may not be ideal in terms of expense or from the ideological perspective that argues that everyone can and should eventually grow up and become emotionally independent, it might be the best we can do from a clinical point of view. Some might argue that it would be better to terminate the analysis and see whether the patient can reach his full potential outside the analytic relationship, while others would counter that it's best not to disrupt a treatment that is working. It is worth considering, however, that many medical conditions require lifelong treatment, and nobody argues that they should be discontinued simply because they don't cure the problem. It might be useful to view very long-term, or even lifelong, analysis in the same way, provided, of course, that the patient wants to do it.

This must be differentiated, of course, for situations in which the analyst fosters, whether out of his own subjective needs or as the unconscious impact of an induction, a degree of dependency that infantilizes or cripples the patient throughout the rest of his life. When this occurs, the emotional communications are obviously not anaclitic, although they might feel that way to both the patient and the analyst, but they are actually object emotional communication or projective identification. In the short term, it can sometimes be difficult to determine when this is happening. It is possible that a case that is going well might seem, to everyone involved, to be at risk of developing a pathological dependency. Some patients do seem to need a period of intense emotional dependency on the analyst, to the exclusion of others in their outside life.

Over time, however, the course of a truly anaclitic transference and one that is pathologically dependent should emerge with increasing clarity, even if the degree of apparent dependency in the sessions remains unchanged. The patient in the anaclitic transference should be making progress in his outside life in areas that he was unable to do before treatment. The patient who was never able to harness his energies in his career makes professional progress. The patient who was unable to find a lover is dating or has begun an ongoing relationship. The patient who was unable to assert himself is asking for things, either with strangers or in an intimate relationship. In other words, the patient should be seen to be changing outside the analysis, even if he does not seem to be moving inside the analysis. At the beginning of this process, the progress might be extremely subtle, but over time it should be more palpable. Furthermore, the analyst should experience pleasure in the countertransference about the patient's outside accomplishments. When, after a period of time – and unfortunately it is impossible to say how long this should be – there is no evidence that this progress is occurring, the analyst must seriously consider the possibility of a pathological dependency.

The effect of badly attuned anaclitic emotional communications

In general, anaclitic emotional communications that are mistimed or misattuned are less risky than other forms of emotional communication. However, there are several situations in which emotional communications that appear to be anaclitic can have a detrimental impact on the patient. One situation arises in cases of introverted aggression. In the case of the narcissistic defense, for example, the patient protects the other person – the analyst (in the transference) – and directs his aggression towards himself, either in the form of depression or low self-esteem, thought disorder, increased anxiety, or emotional withdrawal. In this case, the patient's most important need is to stop the flow of aggression towards the self and redirect it outwardly towards the analyst. To overcome the patient's extreme reluctance, the analyst must transform himself into a more easily attackable target by making himself strongly aversive or offensive to the patient, as described in the sections on ego dystonic mirroring or joining. In these situations, interventions that appear to be anaclitic because they are nurturing, gentle, or soothing can have the effect of making the patient inhibit his aggression and attack himself even more intensely.

In my experience, these situations are rare – much rarer than the Modern Analytic literature would suggest. Spotniz's (1985) work was based on work with schizophrenic and schizotypal patients,[9] and while I would agree with the importance of caution in making anaclitic emotional communications with these patients, I have not seen this type of reaction very often with other types of patients.

There is usually more risk in withholding anaclitic emotional communications than in providing them. Furthermore, many patients will not dare to express disappointment or anger towards the analyst unless they feel loved by the analyst. The fear of the analyst retaliating and not accepting them because of their anger is usually more powerful than the fear of damaging the analyst. But the fear of damaging the analyst is nevertheless real, and the analyst must be cognizant of it.

The issue here, as in all cases, is that the analyst must observe the effect of his emotional communications and not just assume that they are therapeutic because they feel right. If the analyst makes a seemingly anaclitic emotional communication, and the patient responds with increased depression, withdrawal, or any other negative reaction, then the analyst must consider the possibility that the emotional communication has been misattuned. Furthermore, there will usually be an increase in negative feelings and frustration in the countertransference in these situations. It is only by carefully examining the impact of the interventions, in terms of the patient's reaction, the content of the associations, and the analyst's feelings, that the analyst can navigate his way towards the curative feeling.

This is not always easy to determine, and many patients will initially respond poorly to an emotional communication but then respond better after their initial negative reaction has been explored. For example, one patient responded poorly to the analyst's admiration of one of her accomplishments because she assumed that the analyst was ingenuine: he was "just saying that because he had to." It was only after this was explored, and the analyst made his admiring feelings more explicit still, that the patient believed him and felt positive feelings in relationship to the intervention.

Regression as a consequence of anaclitic communication

A more frequent danger is that the anaclitic emotional communications will provoke a severe regression. In these cases, the patient, having received a taste of having old unmet needs suddenly met, regresses very quickly to a demanding and angry infantile state. This type of reaction occurs most frequently with borderline patients. Unfortunately, these situations are difficult to predict,[10] and when this happens early on in the treatment, both the analyst and the patient become quickly overwhelmed. Sometimes a dramatic shift to a limit-setting approach, with a strong focus on strengthening the reasonable ego with reality-oriented interpretations can help, but at other times the treatment can't be salvaged.

Similarly, there is the danger that the patient will interpret the anaclitic emotional communications as a form of sexual seduction. This again does not occur frequently – indeed, I would call it a sub-type of the case in which the patient regresses severely. However, this tends to be more predictable. The patient is often seductive with the analyst – overtly sexual in ordinary demeanor – or early in the treatment discusses how others have been seductive or sexually predatory in a way that feels stimulating in the session. There is often a history of sexual abuse, which is revealed very quickly. And the analyst usually experiences noticeable anxiety in the countertransference. Clearly, the analyst should avoid anaclitic emotional communications with these types of patients until and/or unless the analyst feels quite certain that the patient won't experience them in a seductive or sexualized way.

Self-disclosures and anaclitic emotional communications

The issues raised by self-disclosure by the analyst are complex and are riddled with questions that are as much ethical and philosophical as they are technical, and these latter issues will be touched on only briefly. But from a more purely clinical point of view, we should begin with the idea that self-disclosure is not a single technique, but rather it serves a number of distinct functions within the psychoanalytic relationship.

Before we begin, it is worth keeping in mind that all emotional communications are self-disclosures. Every time the analyst expresses a feeling, whether implicitly or explicitly, through tone and prosody or in direct language, he is engaging in a form of self-disclosure – a communication of his feelings in relationship to the patient.

At this point, however, we will only be discussing self-disclosures that are made specifically in words, in which the analyst explicitly tells the patient something about himself – his feelings, thoughts, character, or life story.

Self-disclosure, like all communications, has both an emotional and a cognitive component. The cognitive component is the actual information about the analyst that is revealed to the patient: whether the analyst is a parent, whether he is straight or gay, whether he suffers from anxiety or revels in self-confidence. The emotional component, on the other hand, communicates how the analyst is trying to relate to the patient and being experienced by him. As usual, the relational modes in which the analyst communicates and the patient experiences the communication profoundly influence the impact of the disclosure.

Let's look at a number of different functions that a self-disclosure can serve, in modes other than the anaclitic mode of relatedness. (This list is by no means exhaustive.)

Self-disclosures in the narcissistic mode

In positive, narcissistic transference states, self-disclosures can express a narcissistic commonality, twinship, or merger with the patient or convey empathic understanding. For example, "I was fired too. I felt as humiliated as you," or "I loved that movie, too!" In this mode of relatedness, the communications validate the patient's feelings, reinforce his sense of self, and help him feel less alone with his feeling. They can also meet unmet developmental, narcissistic needs. (Syntonic mirroring)

Again, in a positive narcissistic transference state, a self-disclosure can help the patient experience previously intolerable feelings and/or integrate them into his sense of self. For example, "If somebody had said that to me, I would be mad as hell at them. But then, I'm an ornery son of a bitch." Or "I got a prize like that once. Yeah, I know it seems like just a silly little award, but I felt like I had just won the Nobel, the Oscar, and the Legion of Honor all rolled into one. Shit, I was high for a month." (Modeling)

In negative, narcissistic transference states, a self-disclosure can help the patient direct self-hatred towards the analyst. For example: "You think that was humiliating? Why, I did something even worse once, and I was actually fired. The boss told me I was the dumbest ass he had ever met." In this case, the self-disclosure is designed to help the patient discharge his aggression towards the analyst by (a) communicating that the analyst is an incompetent and an eminently suitable target of attack, and (b) that other people have attacked the analyst, and he has survived the onslaught.

Self-disclosures in the object mode

To catalyze the emergence of an object transference when the patient's conscious experience of the analyst as not similar enough to be compelling prevents the full development of the object repetition. Here, the analyst may disclose aspects of his feelings or character that are similar to a parent. For example, the analyst sees his father as selfish and the analyst as generous, and is thus unable to criticize him in the way that he needs to in order to loosen the repetition. At the right moment, the analyst might say, "Me, generous? Not many people say that! I turned away a patient just the other day because she couldn't pay my fee. What did she think I am – some kind of social service agency?" (This would be used only when the analyst has evidence, usually from the countertransference and the case history that suggests the patient is indeed experiencing incipient object transference.)

Similarly, the analyst may disclose aspects of his feelings or character to help the patient overcome his defenses/resistances to verbalizing his object feelings towards the analyst. For example, the patient feels that the analyst is a wimp, just like his father, but is holding back from verbalizing the full measure of his contempt, ostensibly because he doesn't know what the analyst is actually like. In fact, the analyst is a bit of a wimp. Here, the analyst might say, "You see me as being courageous, but in fact, I've always been a wimp. A lot of people don't like that about me." This can help the patient express feelings towards the analyst in the present as a stand in for the father.

Anaclitic self-disclosures

Most other uses of self-disclosure can be conceptualized as forms of anaclitic communication, in the sense that the analyst discloses for the purposes of meeting a maturational dependency need that has an analogue in normal development. Within this broad rubric, a number of distinct anaclitic functions can be defined.

To lower the intensity of the transference

Self-disclosure can also be used to reinforce the reasonable ego when the patient is so overwhelmed by an intense transference – usually object transference or projective identification – that he cannot work productively in the moment. For example, the patient forgot a session and is convinced that the analyst is enraged. He's completely consumed with fear; he can't talk about anything else, and his communications are filled with fantasies of being humiliated, punished, or rejected by the analyst. The analyst tries to explore the following questions: Why is the analyst so cruel, so unforgiving? Why can't he be more compassionate and loving? Why does the analyst blame the patient? Why isn't it the analyst's fault for not making the analysis more memorable? But the exploration goes nowhere: the patient is mired in a tight repetition. Any attempt to join makes the patient more anxious, and interpretations and historical questions bounce off without impact or acknowledgment. The patient's afflicted ego is in full control. In this case, the analyst might disclose that he is not angry, that he is sorry if he gave him any reason to think so, and that it pains him to see the patient in such pain. If successful, the intervention would help the patient's reasonable ego reassert control over his feelings, strengthen his reality testing, and hopefully, would reassure the afflicted ego as well.

Would this loosen the repetition on a long-term basis? This would depend on the nature of the repetition in that particular individual. In some cases, the object transference can be loosened simply by having a different experience with a differentiated object at a critical moment in the transference. In this case, it is possible that the patient always experienced criticism and rage from the parent when he made mistakes, and the difference between this and the analyst's feelings, which he does not simply demonstrate by his manner but reinforces with his explicit self-disclosure, makes the emotional exchange different enough to be curative. This would be a primary anaclitic moment in the treatment.

In other cases, however, a different enough response from the analyst wouldn't be enough; the patient might need to further express anger at the analyst qua the original parent to loosen the repetition more permanently but doesn't yet feel safe enough with the analyst to be able to do so. In these cases, the self-disclosure does not serve a primarily anaclitic function – meeting the need for an accepting, forgiving parent – and rather serves a partial anaclitic function: the patient would need to know that the analyst was not really like the parent in order to be able to say the things to him that he needed to say to the parent.

To communicate the impact that the patient is having on the analyst

For example, "When you complain like that, I tend to get either sleepy or irritable. Were you aware of that?" Oppositely "I'm absolutely enthralled when you talk about your work. What makes you think you are a boring person?" This can help the patient have understanding and insight into their effect on others, in cases when this is desirable.

To diffuse the object transference enough to help the patient understand that he is distorting the interpersonal situation and thus help to see how his transference prevents him from experiencing the world accurately

For example, "You seem to think that I'm all powerful, and that I could tell you the right thing to do in any situation. But I can't. I'm just a fallible human being, and all we can do is to figure things out together." This can further enhance the effectiveness of genetic interpretations by highlighting the difference between the past and the present.

Fostering object constancy

Self-disclosure serves a different anaclitic function when the patient needs information about the analyst in order to consistently experience him as a dependable, separate object – a person who has a separate existence from his own – a person who may leave but will also return. These disclosures help the patient to establish object constancy. Revealing the analyst's plans and whereabouts to the patient who is anxious about the analyst's absence – whether for vacations or other breaks in the treatment – is a prime example of this use of anaclitic self-disclosure. For patients who are terrified that the analyst will disappear forever, knowing where the analyst will be, what he will be doing, and when he will return, can help to establish the reality of the analyst in the patient's mind as a real person who exists even when not physically present. Similarly, telling the patient about the vacation – what he did, whether it was fun, how he feels about being back – similarly reinforces the patient's sense that the analyst is a real, separate person,[11] not a figment of the patient's mind or phantom who comes and goes. The goal is to create a foundation of safety and security in the patient's attachment to the analyst. All of this closely parallels what the attuned parent does with a child when he leaves him: telling him where he is going, when he will be back, and reassuring him that he will be thinking about him while he is gone.

Knowing the analyst as a separate person

Similar to but broader than the establishment of object constancy, self-disclosure also serves the critical anaclitic function of helping the patient know the analyst as a person separate from and apart from himself. (Some might describe this as knowing the analyst's subjectivity or as a separate locus of agency.) However, we must distinguish between self-disclosures of this sort addressed to the reasonable ego and those addressed to the afflicted ego. And we must further distinguish between syntonic disclosures that the patient experiences as pleasing, comforting, or at least neutral, and dystonic disclosures that the patient experiences as frightening, repulsive, or contemptible. As we shall see, these different types of disclosures have different impacts on the patient, depending on which ego they are addressed to and on the patient's level of development in the transference.

Syntonic disclosures

Let's first consider syntonic disclosures to the reasonable ego, which can have a mildly anaclitic function, addressed as they are to the adult aspects of the patient's dependency on the analyst. They tend to nourish the patient's conscious attachment to the analyst, increase the more conscious layers of trust in the analyst, and enhance his pleasure in the relationship with patients who desire this information from the analyst. (Not all do!) All these functions strengthen the analytic relationship, but they do not usually loosen repetitions or meet maturational needs.

Syntonic disclosures addressed to the afflicted ego, on the other hand, can have a profound impact on meeting the essential anaclitic function of helping the patient to know the analyst as a separate person and develop a stronger sense of himself as a separate person in relationship to the analyst. This is analogous to the child's experience of coming to know the parent as a separate person. Getting information about the analyst can overlap with the nurturing function of feeding the patient, in which the bits of information the analyst discloses feed the patient in an oral way while simultaneously leading him gently into the world of differentiated relationships. The pleasure and sense of connection the patient can take in getting to know the analyst can be much like the playful faces the parent and infant exchange after a joyful feed, and the increasing number of things that the child learns about his parent as he matures. The relationship with the parent is where the child first learns about another person, how to get to know another person, and how to see and experience himself as a separate person. Learning things about the parent that the child likes enables the patient to experience difference and separateness in an atmosphere that stimulates minimal tension, anxiety, or anger – thus easing him into the recognition of difference. The analyst can replicate this experience with disclosures that differentiate him from the patient but are (to the best of his knowledge) unlikely to disturb him.[12]

Dystonic disclosures

In contrast to syntonic disclosures, which tend to be satisfying, emotional communications for the patient, dystonic disclosures can be extremely painful for the patient and challenging for the analyst. Whether the disclosure seems large or small in the greater scheme of things – counterintuitively, the analyst's taste in movies might be more traumatic than his politics or his sexual orientation – it can seriously challenge the patient's ability to rely on, trust, or even maintain a relationship with the analyst.

The disclosure may not only disrupt the more purely narcissistic elements of the patient's transference[13] but also disrupt the patient's idealized fantasies about the analyst as a differentiated other.

The degree of the difficulty in assimilating these kinds of disclosures depends largely on whether the disclosure is experienced by a patient primarily in the context of the reasonable ego or the afflicted ego. Looking first at the reasonable ego, most patients (except those functioning deeply and chronically in the borderline or narcissistic spectrums) have developed a reasonable ego that has some capacity to accept – or at least tolerate – characteristics that they dislike or are disturbed by in others with whom they are close, provided there is a strong foundation for a positive relationship. However, dystonic disclosures to the reasonable ego don't usually have a significant therapeutic impact. They often create a degree of stress and discomfort in the patient and do not usually have an anaclitic function.

Furthermore, dystonic disclosures that the patient can tolerate within the context of the reasonable ego can be much more distressing when experienced by the afflicted ego, which may not be immediately apparent to either the patient or the analyst. It is not uncommon for a patient to become disturbed by something the analyst told him long after the event and that seemed to have no effect at the time.

Dystonic disclosures addressed to the afflicted ego have the greatest potential to both create significant pain and significant growth in the patient. If the timing is right, the pain and the growth are different aspects of learning that a person that he is deeply involved with – and wants to remain deeply involved with – can be different from himself in ways that he genuinely dislikes. Achieving this goal requires at least a partial acceptance – and ideally, perhaps, a full embrace – of the other's otherness, separateness, and differentness, while retaining the stability and integrity of his own sense of self. This experience may be the immediate catalyst of what is currently viewed as the highest level of relatedness and potential interpersonal intimacy – fully developed intersubjectivity[14] – in which the other is viewed and experienced as a subject, not an object – a point that was first[15] elaborated on by the developmental Ego Psychologists (Jacobson 1964; Mahler *et al.* 1975) and more recently by a number of Relationlists (Benjamin 1998; Mitchell 2000).[16] The potential benefits of this level of intersubjectivity for the patient are great. For this reason, dystonic emotional disclosures to the afflicted ego can serve a crucial anaclitic function.

However, the risks of these types of emotional communications must be recognized as well. Many patients require long periods of narcissistic relatedness, or less demanding kinds of anaclitic relatedness, before they can tolerate the full awareness of the other. These patients can be traumatized by premature dystonic disclosures. Furthermore, many patients derive tremendous benefit from the analysis and develop a high degree of intersubjectivity with people in their outside life but never relate to the analyst in a fully intersubjective way.

For all of these reasons, it is important to be cautious with these types of emotional communications and with the goal of fostering intersubjectivity in the patient directly in the analysis. Too much enthusiasm for intersubjectivity, like too much enthusiasm for any partial analytic goal – empathic understanding, resolving the Oedipal complex, or facilitating the verbalization of aggression – can blind the analyst to the many different needs that can be met in the analytic relationship.

15
CONCLUSION

We have discussed two major manifestations of emotional communication in psychoanalysis: the objective countertransference and the use of emotional communication in psychoanalytic technique.

Emotional communication and countertransference analysis

Emotional communication – the channel of communication in which information about a person's emotional state is conveyed by the induction of feelings in others – is shared with non-human mammals and with infants before the acquisition of language and persists throughout the lifespan. It is intertwined with cognitive communication, which conveys other types of information as facts.

Emotional communication is embedded in every moment of everyday relatedness and plays a particularly important role in creating and perpetuating repetitions of early patterns of relatedness.

When these repetitions are activated in the psychoanalytic relationship they are known as transference. Transference is manifested in the patient's perceptions, behavior, and experience of the analyst. When in a state of transference, the patient tends to induce feelings in the analyst that are consistent with the transference, and consistent with aspects of the patient's emotional life history. These feelings are the objective countertransference and are viewed as the interpersonal dimension of the transference. Objective countertransference allows the experience of aspects of the patient's life that he is often unable to remember and unable to put directly in words.

Understanding the objective countertransference requires an understanding of the specific feeling and the relational mode that characterize the induced feeling. The specific feeling describes what the analyst actually feels, while the relational mode defines how the patient experiences and relates to the analyst. The relational mode forms the context in which the patient's specific feeling should be understood as well as the relationship of the objective countertransference to the patient's feeling. There are five primary relational modes. One – the present-anchored mode – is largely uninfluenced by repetitions and, as such, is of only occasional focus in psychoanalysis; the four others are strongly shaped by repetitions and are the primary focus of psychoanalysis. The four repetitive relational modes are:

The narcissistic mode, in which the patient experiences the analyst as being similar to, the same as, merged with, or a twin of himself, and in which the analyst feels the same feeling as the patient, or a close analogue of the patient's feeling.

The object mode, in which the patient experiences the analyst as different and separate from himself, and as being a participant in an interpersonal exchange that is a repetition of a pathogenic experience for the patient. In the object mode, the analyst experiences herself as being separate from the patient and as having different feelings from the patient.

The projective identification mode, in which the patient experiences the analyst as having feelings or qualities that are the polar opposite of the patient's own feelings, because these feelings have been evacuated from the patient's experience and projected onto the patient's experience of the analyst. In the projective identification mode, the analyst's feelings are the polar opposite of the patient's. The projective identification mode is different than the other modes in that it is always the product of an intrapsychic defense.

The anaclitic mode, in which the patient experiences the need for feelings from the analyst that he requires in order to grow and mature, and the analyst experiences the desire and the ability to convey those feelings to the patient.

Although we have discussed a number of important types of countertransference, these are intended to serve a foundation of a typology of countertransference that will expand as understanding of both the relational modes and the range of specific feelings increases. Although, for expository purposes, I have drawn sharp-edged distinctions between the modes, the boundaries between the various relational modes often seem to overlap, yielding more complex intrapsychic and interpersonal configurations than I have described. While I believe that these are the basic relational modes, it is possible that there are other modes that I haven't considered.

The idea that girds this perspective on countertransference is that the analyst is in the best position to fully understand the patient's emotional life in all of its intensity and intricacy if she allows herself the freedom to experience any and every possible feeling in the course of her relationship to the patient. Just as Freud argued that, in order to overcome neurosis, the patient had to come to know and accept all of his thoughts, feelings, and impulses, no matter how painful, embarrassing, or socially unacceptable these might be, this perspective argues that the analyst must be able to experience all of her thoughts, feelings, and impulses about the patient in order to understand him well enough to cure him.

CONCLUSION

Emotional communication and psychoanalytic technique

While the patient's emotional communications to the analyst that underlie objective countertransference are involuntary, repetitive, and (usually) unconscious, the emotional communication in psychoanalytic technique involves conveying feelings in ways that are conscious and deliberately planned. The overall goal of using emotional communication in psychoanalytic technique is to loosen the hold of a repetition that is active in the psychoanalytic relationship – an active transference. Emotional communication serves to facilitate the activation of transference, to resolve maladaptive patterns of defense, to meet maturational needs, or to catalyze the impact of an interpretation.

There are two broad types of psychoanalytic interventions: containment, in which the analyst consciously experiences an objective countertransference feeling, and expressive interventions, in which the analyst actually expresses something – usually in spoken language – to the patient. Containment can take place in silence, or can be combined with an expressive intervention. All psychoanalytic interventions, including silent containment, involve emotional communication; all expressive psychoanalytic interventions combine emotional communication with some type of cognitive communication, and may be combined with containment as well.

Psychoanalytic interventions can affect two different parts of the patient's mind, separately or in combination: the afflicted ego – the part of the mind that lives in and participates in the repetition; and the reasonable ego – the part of the mind that is present reality oriented and stands outside the repetition. Both cognitive and emotional communication can address both parts of the mind. Different types of interventions are conceptualized as different combinations of emotional and cognitive communications, which address the afflicted and the reasonable egos in specific ways.

All interventions are based on interpretations in the epistemological sense, in that they are based on the analyst's intellectual understanding of some aspect of the patient's transference. However, an interpretation is also a particular type of intervention, and not all interventions are interpretations. Interventions that are interpretations combine a cognitive communication that conveys selected aspects of the analyst's understanding of the patient's repetition to the reasonable ego with an emotional communication addressed to either the reasonable or the afflicted ego. Other types of interventions contain no interpretative content, and some only address the afflicted ego.

The objective countertransference is the point of reference for finding the emotional communication that the patient requires in order to loosen a repetition – the curative feeling. Sometimes the curative feeling is the same as the objective countertransference, or varies only in intensity. Other times the relational mode might be the same, but the specific feeling must be changed, or vice versa. And at times the curative feeling is unrelated to the countertransference, and the analyst must find it through a purely intellectual analysis of the patient's needs, and stimulate it within herself through a process of auto-induction.

Specific types of interventions can be further classified according to their relational mode:

Narcissistic emotional communications convey that the analyst is similar to, the twin of, or a part of the patient and can facilitate the activation of transference, meet maturational needs, and/or modify maladaptive defensive patterns, and low intensity narcissistic emotional communications can catalyze the effect of interpretations. Narcissistic emotional communications are the most complex and varied range of emotional communications, and can be attuned to a wide range of specific feelings. They can be syntonic or dystonic.

Object emotional communications have a much more limited range. They convey that the analyst has a different feeling than the patient, and convey feelings that are similar to those the patient experienced in pathogenic interpersonal relationships. They can facilitate the activation of transference and can modify maladaptive defensive patterns, but do not meet maturational needs and are not used to catalyze interpretations. Object emotional communications are always dystonic, and must be used with great caution to avoid retraumatizing the patient.

No emotional communications are deliberately made in the projective identification relational mode. Other types of emotional communications are used to loosen the repetitions that are expressed in the projective identification mode.

Anaclitic emotional communications are analogous to the nurturing, loving, and protecting feelings – as well as some of the aggressive and competitive feelings – that a parent communicates to a child in the course of healthy emotional development. Anaclitic emotional communications can facilitate the activation of transference, the meeting of maturational needs, the modification of maladaptive patterns of defense, and can catalyze the effects of interpretations. Although most anaclitic emotional communications are experienced by both the analyst and the patient as syntonic and pleasurable, anaclitic emotional communications can also involve feelings that are maturational but not immediately positive.

The analyst is in the strongest position to loosen the grip of the repetitions that shackle the patient's potential when she allows herself to experience and to communicate any feeling that the patient might need in order to grow and mature.

Freud wrote (1940: 73), describing the role of interpretation in psychoanalysis: "Our knowledge is to make up for his ignorance and to give his ego back its mastery over lost provinces of his mental life." This idea is the basic principle of the classical tradition in psychoanalytic technique. Yet Freud recognized that the knowledge had to be combined with the necessary – but very restricted – catalyst of relatedness and feeling in order to be effective. The minority tradition provides another way to restore mastery of the lost provinces – through moments of relatedness conveyed through the full spectrum of emotional communication, sometimes, but not always, accompanied by knowledge.

Neither approach is superior to the other. Each has a distinct scope of action, a distinct effect on the mind. And every analyst has unique abilities and limitations, and every patient has unique needs. The goal is to find the right combination that works in each analytic relationship. The purpose of focusing on the importance and details of emotional communication in psychoanalytic technique is not to replace cognitive communication in psychoanalysis with emotional communication, but to amplify the therapeutic potential of the psychoanalytic relationship by making both forms of communication available to the analyst.

NOTES

PREFACE

1 The concept of transference is defined more precisely in Chapter 4. For the purposes of the earlier chapters, transference can be understood simply as how the patient's experience of the analyst is shaped by previous life experience.
2 Spotnitz's most important works are 1976, 1983, and 1985. However, all of his works have had a significant impact on the present work, whether or not they have been specifically referenced.
3 These parallels were noted by Winnicott in a letter to Spotnitz in 1953, commenting on an article by Spotnitz *et al.* (1953): "My attention has been drawn to your very interesting article . . . How difficult it is for us to keep touch with the literature: the consequence being that we find ourselves doing similar work from independent sources. I enclose a reprint giving an indication of some of my own work, and I think you will see that if I had known of your article earlier, I would have quoted from it" (cited in Spotnitz, 1976).
4 I have departed from his terminology partly because his terms were so similar that I've never been able to keep them straight, and partly because I trained using a different vocabulary.

1 INTRODUCTION

1 Or, more precisely (in this reference), soothe the patient's ego.
2 Unlike Sterba, Strachey does not focus on the patient's ego per se, but his concept of the patient's "sense of reality" would fall within the scope of what would later be described as an ego function.
3 Winnicott's paper was first delivered in 1947 but published in 1949.

2 THE EVOLUTIONARY AND DEVELOPMENTAL ORIGINS OF OBJECTIVE COUNTERTRANSFERENCE

1 A more comprehensive definition will be proposed in the next chapter.

3 THE CONCEPT OF OBJECTIVE COUNTERTRANSFERENCE AND ITS ROLE IN A TWO-PERSON PSYCHOLOGY

1 This could also be called (as many do) the analyst's transference to the patient.
2 Strictly speaking, it is not the countertransference itself that is objective but rather

NOTES

   the perspective that develops out of understanding the feelings in the broader context of the patient's repetitions.
3. This doesn't, of course, absolve the analyst of the responsibility to recognize the countertransference as quickly as possible, but it does require the analyst to understand it, and on the basis of this understanding, to consciously modify his interactions with the patient to resolve the repetition. From my perspective, that's the core of the analyst's job.
4. There are a number of different versions of two-person psychologies; the position described here is a somewhat generalized rendition of the Relational school, derived primarily from Aron (1996) and Mitchell (2000).
5. Nevertheless, this is not to say that the classical position was not an understandable concept in the development of psychoanalysis. Regardless of the present status of psychoanalysis as a whole as a natural science (a complex and controversial topic beyond the range of this discussion) psychoanalysis arose at a time when the natural sciences were the model for all non-religious approaches to knowledge. The idea that the patient should be understood dispassionately, uninfluenced by the analyst's feelings, was a reasonable analogy to the practice of the natural sciences – especially when we consider that psychoanalysis was (and remains!) the only discipline (that makes use of non-quantitative data) that developed a methodology for reducing the influence of the practitioner's subjectivity on her observations: the training analysis. Furthermore, while I believe that omitting the analyst's feelings from the analysis severely limits the analyst's ability to understand the patient, I do believe that this is a reasonable technical approach, even today. Some analysts are simply not comfortable working with the inherent ambiguities of countertransference analysis. Furthermore, excluding countertransference feelings of any sort from the analytic data does provide the patient with a measure of protection from the danger of wild analysis. There are many forms of psychoanalytic practice, and we are not currently in a position to say that any one form is unequivocally more effective than any other. The only position that is not reasonable is the idea that the analyst can communicate with the patient from a position of emotional neutrality. Emotional communication is an intrinsic and inevitable component of every human interaction, and it is not possible for the analyst to communicate without engaging in it. Some sort of acknowledgement of this must be present in all theories of psychoanalytic technique, even if the type of emotional communication that is allowed is extremely limited.
6. Relational theorists are clear, on the other hand, that neither the goals, tasks, nor the structure of the analytic relationship is (or should be) symmetrical (Mitchell 2000). Thus, my comments are directed only to the influence of the patient on the analyst's feelings.
7. To be more specific: I do not think it is a feature of a two-person psychology that can be usefully applied to clinical psychoanalysis. It is, however, perfectly suited to a two-person psychology that is focused exclusively on the here-and-now dynamics of interpersonal relationships. Such an ahistorical understanding of the relationship is interesting and of value for present-oriented forms of interpersonal psychotherapy but has little value for psychoanalysis, which is oriented, at least in part, towards identifying and changing historically rooted patterns of relating.
8. This sensitivity is only one factor in the analyst's overall talent for analytic work. I have worked with some supervisees who were virtually deaf to the induced feelings but were nevertheless able to do outstanding work almost exclusively with the more purely verbal content of the sessions.

NOTES

4 EMOTIONAL COMMUNICATION AND ITS RELATIONSHIP TO THE BASIC CONCEPTS OF PSYCHOANALYSIS

1 The concept of *relational mode* can be traced to Freud's (1914b: 88–89) idea that object-choice – the choice of person as a love-object – can be either narcissistic or anaclitic. When the choice is narcissistic, the other person resembles the self. When the choice is anaclitic, the other satisfies a dependency need and is (implicitly) experienced as different from the self. These are two different ways of experiencing the other person. The concept of the relational mode underlies Klein's (1946) account of projective identification; Balint's (1968) description of the mother/infant relationship as a "harmonious interpenetrating mix up"; Searles' (1965) discussions of symbiosis; Racker's (1957) concordant and complimentary identifications; ego psychological theories that describe maturation as an evolution from narcissism to object relatedness (Jacobson 1964; Mahler *et al.* 1975); Kohut's (1977) concept of the self-object; and many other theorists' accounts of different types of human relatedness. It is essentially synonymous with the term "mode of relatedness" and essentially synonymous with the term "type of object relationship." In all cases, the relational mode defines the general way the other person is experienced in relationship, within which a wide range of specific feelings are possible.

2 From the allegorical figure of poverty in Greek mythology.

3 Some people would argue that there is also an autistic relational mode. I am inclined to disagree. While there are aspects of genuine relatedness that can be described as autistic, I view some of them as aspects of primitive narcissistic experience and others as aspects of primitive object experience. True autism, however, in which the world appears to be experienced as inanimate or non-human is better conceptualized as a symptom of a malfunctioning nervous system, rather than as a relational mode.

4 The first reference to the narcissistic mode was Freud's (1914b) discussion of narcissistic object-choice, in which a person chooses another person as a love object because the other person is experienced as being similar to the self. But Freud's understanding of the mode was limited, and in other writings, he described narcissism as a mode of non-relatedness. Aichhorn (1936) first described narcissistic transference, in which the patient experiences the analyst as being a reflection of the self. Deutsch (1926) first described the concordant identification that would later be described as narcissistic countertransference, in which the analyst experiences himself as being similar to the patient. Jacobson (1964), Searles (1965), and Mahler *et al.* (1975) described symbiotic states in development, which fall within the narcissistic mode. Spotnitz (1985) further elaborated the concepts of narcissistic transference and countertransference, contrasting negative narcissistic states with positive ones. Kohut's (1977) account of the self-object experience of twinship also lies within the realm of the narcissistic mode.

5 Klein (1946) introduced the concept of projective identification as a defense, but later Kleinians, such as Bion (1959), Ogden (1982), and Rosenfeld (1988) elaborated on it as a relational mode.

6 I am using the concept of projective identification in a more restricted sense than it is used in Kleinian and Object Relations theory. In Object Relations theory, the concept has been used to describe a continuum of phenomena (Hinshelwood 1992) ranging from states in which the projected feeling is shared by the projector and the receiver, flowing fluidly between them, to states in which the feeling is expelled or evacuated into the receiver in a rigid interpersonal configuration.

NOTES

The shared, fluid states are viewed primarily as serving communication functions, while the evacuated states are viewed as serving primarily defensive functions. I am restricting the term to the evacuative/defensive states (most similar to the second and third types described by Rosenfeld [1988: 118], and classify the shared/communicative states as forms of narcissistic countertransference because there are significant differences – experiential, relational, and technical – between a relationship in which the feelings are narcissistically shared and one in which the feelings are evacuated or expelled. These are fundamentally different ways of relating. Ogden [1982], the most influential American theorist on the topic (and the clearest writer), emphasizes both the communicative and the defensive aspects of the process.

7 The first mention of the anaclitic mode is Freud's (1914b) description of anaclitic object choice, in which a person chooses another person as a love object because the other person meets a dependency need. Furthermore, Freud's (1917) idea that the non-erotic positive transference enables the patient to make use of the analyst's interpretations is the germ of this – the anaclitic concept in the analytic process. Ferenczi's (1931) technique of relating to the patient at the age that he is in the transference, and thus to meet the patient's emotional needs directly in the session, is implicitly based on the concept of the anaclitic mode. The concept also encompasses Balint's (1968) techniques for working with the basic fault, Winnicott's (1956) holding environment, aspects of Sechehaye's (1951) concept of symbolic realization, Kohut's (1971) concepts of mirroring and idealization, and Spotnitz's (1989) concept of the anaclitic transference.

8 Most repetitions involve a combination of feeling and behavior. However, it is worth noting that some repetitions primarily involve subjective feelings, which are not expressed outwardly in behavior; others involve primarily behavior unaccompanied by any subjective feeling. The usual psychoanalytic explanation of the former is either inhibition or self-control; the explanation of the latter (*acting-out*) is that the feelings are experienced unconsciously.

9 Examples of severe pathology would be unconsciousness, dementia, possibly certain forms of severe autism, and mental retardation.

10 Object relations theorists will probably disagree with this statement. However, because I am using the concept of projective identification in a more restricted sense than it is used by Object Relations theorists, the difference may be more a matter of terminology and jargon than theoretical difference. See page 307, Chapter 4, note 6.

11 It is probable that more than one of the patient's repetitions will be activated in the analysis, and various combinations are possible. On the other hand, it is also probable that not all of the patient's repetitions will be activated in the analysis. As we shall see in Chapter 10, the analyst's emotional communication can be directed only towards the repetitions that are active in the relationship, although cognitive communications may be directed towards those that are not.

12 This is to say: transference and countertransference arise from the ordinary moments of everyday human relatedness that are grounded in repetitions and, at the purely experiential level, are indistinguishable from them. What is different in analysis is that (a) the terminology is designed to enable the analyst to keep track of each party's role in the repetition; (b) the analyst has a responsibility to observe and feel the repetition while participating in it no more than is actually necessary; and (c) the setting is designed to highlight, study, and transform these ordinary moments.

NOTES

5 DIFFERENTIATING OBJECTIVE AND SUBJECTIVE COUNTERTRANSFERENCE

1 The reprise of Winnicott's phrase that I criticized earlier for being misleading is quite deliberate. There are two values in the analyst being "well analyzed": the relevant value here is that the analyst should have access to as wide a range of human feelings as possible. The second value will be discussed later in the chapter in the section on subjective countertransference.
2 This way of proceeding, in which the countertransference is treated as an association in the patient's process and is related to the material in both his current life and past memories, makes use of the same psychoanalytic logic described by Kris (1975) in his paper on the good hour.
3 At times the procedure will be reversed. The analyst will look at what is happening in the content and search his feelings for any similarities.
4 This descriptive distinction has nothing to do with the effect of the behavior on the treatment process; badly managed objective countertransference/enactment can be destructive to the case, while acting out may be neutral or beneficial to the case, albeit inadvertently.
5 Obviously, partisans of the various orientations will disagree with this section.
6 These moments are also potentially beneficial to the treatment process as well, but that will be discussed further on.
7 Greenberg (1986) independently formulated the same idea.
8 Some patients are so attuned to the analyst's feelings that they seem to be aware of, and to be affected by, all of the analyst's feelings. These patients can be damaged by subjective countertransference feelings, but they can also be damaged by objective countertransference feelings. This is a difficult analytic situation, as there is nothing to be done about it. Sometimes the only solution is for these patients to see an analyst with whom they are as compatible as possible.
9 An "incorrect" intervention is defined here as any intervention that does not have the intended therapeutic effect.

6 NARCISSISTIC COUNTERTRANSFERENCE

1 Margolis (1978) and Spotnitz (1985) include both the analyst's identification with the patient, the "concordant identifications" (Racker 1957), and the analyst's identification with the patient's objects, the "complementary identifications" (Racker 1957) within the concept of narcissistic countertransference. In contrast, the concept of narcissistic countertransference offered here includes *only* the analyst's identification with the patient's "concordant identification" (Racker 1957).
2 The fact that the feeling is about the patient is what makes this a patient-directed narcissistic countertransference. In the self-directed form of this countertransference, the analyst experiences *himself* in the same way that the patient experiences himself.
3 In this case and similar ones, "subjective" is used in its ordinary, non-technical meaning to refer to the analyst's personal, phenomenological awareness of his own feelings. When the term is used in the expression "subjective countertransference," it is used in the meaning specific to Modern Psychoanalytic theory, i.e., a form of countertransference that is derived primarily from the analyst's emotional life (Spotnitz 1985), as opposed to being induced by the patient (objective countertransference) (Winnicott 1949).
4 Searles (1965) has extensively described these kinds of experiences with psychotic and other severely disturbed patients.
5 Especially the overtly grandiose type described by Kernberg (1985).

NOTES

7 OBJECT COUNTERTRANSFERENCE

1 Margolis (1979) includes the forms of countertransference induced by the most primitive forms of object transference within the concept of narcissistic countertransference.
2 Important exceptions to this will be discussed below in the section "Countertransference in which one member of the dyad is narcissistic," in the examples in which the analyst is narcissistic and the patient is not.
3 There is no theoretical reason why this should be the case. In principle, the analyst might experience an extremely early object feeling towards the patient in an inverted object countertransference (addressed below – see "Inverted object countertransference").
4 The term enactment would be synonymous with repetition here, except that enactment implies a degree of action – whether acting in or acting out – that is not necessarily present in a repetition.
5 If the interaction between the analyst and the patient fits the first two categories (i.e., they have different feelings from each other, and they experience each other as separate), but the feelings they experience do not repeat an old dynamic, then they are not relating within the object mode. If the interaction is a positive one, with the potential to cure the patient, then it is probably anaclitic. On the other hand, pathological interactions that are not repetitions are just bad "here-and-now" relationships. They result from a bad match between patient and analyst or from subjective countertransference problems in the analyst. In either event, they are of no value to the analysis, either therapeutically or epistemologically.
6 Situations like this also beg the question of whether the wife's feeling of disappointment was induced by the patient (as mine was) or whether it was her own feeling. In this case, it also seemed to be an induction that had its origin in an older relationship.
7 As it turned out, the patient was actually not functioning as incompetently as I had thought or as she had presented herself.
8 This is the type of dynamic that Kohut (1971; Kohut & Wolf 1978) has extensively discussed as being pathogenic for disorders of the self.
9 It is important to remember that if the analyst is not in a narcissistic state, she can be disappointed with the patient without feeling like a failure herself.
10 Aggression is only one possible manifestation of the dynamic in which the patient adopts the parental role in relation to the analyst. Nevertheless, the more general dynamic of turning a passive emotional position into an active one has been present in all cases that I have heard.
11 Of course, the fact that the feelings are induced does not mean they are not realistic, but that is beyond the scope of this discussion.

8 COUNTERTRANSFERENCE IN PROJECTIVE IDENTIFICATION STATES

1 For purposes of maximum clarity, the term *projective identification* should be used to refer to the patient's experience and the patient's contribution to the transference/countertransference relationship, and some term, such as Grinberg's (1979) *projective counteridentification*, should be used to describe the analyst's side of things. But this becomes intolerably cumbersome and for that reason we will use the term broadly to include both the transference and the countertransference, as is usually done.
2 Furthermore, the narcissistic, object, and anaclitic modes are all compatible with a wide range of defenses; the projective identification mode is uniquely compatible with the defense of projective identification.

NOTES

3 It's worth noting (but largely irrelevant to this chapter) that projective identification can exist purely as an intrapsychic defense, without being manifest through emotional induction. The analyst may observe that the patient is in a defensive state of projective identification, without necessarily being involved in a transference/countertransference that is shaped by projective identification.
4 To be more precise, in Object Relations theory, the concept of projective identification has been used to describe a continuum of phenomena, described by Hinshelwood (1992), ranging from states in which the projected feeling is shared by the projector and the receiver, flowing fluidly between them, to states in which the feeling is expelled or evacuated into the receiver in a rigid interpersonal configuration. The shared, fluid states are viewed primarily as serving communication functions, while the evacuated states are viewed as serving primarily defensive functions. I am restricting the term to the evacuative/defensive states (most similar to the second and third types described by Rosenfeld [1988]), and I classify the shared/communicative states as forms of narcissistic countertransference. This is not (I hope) a purely pedantic distinction; there are significant differences – experiential, relational, and technical – between a relationship in which the feelings are narcissistically shared and one in which the feelings are evacuated or expelled i.e., these are fundamentally different ways of relating. Ogden (1982), the most influential American theorist on the topic (and by far and away the clearest writer), emphasizes both the communicative and the defensive aspects of the process. I would classify some of his examples as narcissistic countertransference and others as projective identification.

9 ANACLITIC COUNTERTRANSFERENCE

1 The needs may never have been experienced because the patient had developed defenses against experiencing them, or the needs may have been related to later levels of maturation that the patient had not attained in relationship with the parents.
2 This description of the anaclitic countertransference grew out of Spotnitz's concept (Spotnitz 1983), which was cited in Meadow (1999), and further elaborated by Bratt (1991), Ernsberger (1990), Laquercia (1992), and Liegner (1991, 1995) but differs from it in significant ways. Spotnitz emphasizes that the feelings experienced in the anaclitic countertransference are new feelings in the patient's interpersonal life, which nobody has experienced towards the patient before. While I would agree that this is sometimes the case, I believe that the key issue is not whether the feelings are new but that they are induced by the patient's unmet emotional needs at times when the patient is receptive to having these needs met. Second, Spotnitz emphasizes that these feelings arise after a long period of analysis. In Meadow (1999), he states that he might experience the anaclitic countertransference after three or four years. I, on the other hand, think that these feelings can arise at any point in the treatment. (For the most complete elaboration of Spotnitz's concept and a thorough review of the literature, see Bershatsky 2002).
3 The biology of this process is quite fascinating. Hrdy (1999) describes how prolactin levels rise in both males and females when exposed to a hungry infant.
4 Indeed, the analyst spontaneously offered the patient a sandwich and a drink that she had in the office, and they exchanged small talk as he hungrily polished it off. This, of course, is not just experiencing the desire to feed the patient; depending on one's theoretical bent, it is either using the feeling intuitively as a basis of an intervention, or it is acting-out. In either event, it was also a positive turning point in the case, as it was the beginning of his ability to verbalize his feelings of vulnerability and neediness.

NOTES

5 Bernstein (1992) has argued convincingly that loving the patient is at the root of all effective psychoanalytic practice. He describes this love as being "beyond countertransference," i.e., that it is related to the analyst's basic emotional position in his work. This distinguishes it from love in the anaclitic countertransference, in which the loving feelings are induced by the patient's specific need.
6 This experience is related to, but not identical to, Winnicott's (1958) discussion of the capacity to be alone in the presence of the other.
7 It has even been suggested that evolutionarily, female orgasm developed out of the pleasure inherent in nursing and not in genital sexuality (Hrdy 1999).

10 EMOTIONAL COMMUNICATION IN PSYCHOANALYTIC TECHNIQUE

1 This is, of course, the title of a valuable book by Kohut (1984). However, the question has been asked since the beginning of psychoanalysis.
2 Remember: we are using this example to illustrate different uses of emotional communication in technique, not the possible interpretations of a given clinical situation.
3 To be more precise, I would call this an affective interpretation and view the self-psychological empathic interpretation as a variant of it because not all affective interpretations are empathic in that way. But we will come to that in the next chapter.
4 The concept of loosening might sound like a rather paltry cure compared to words such as overcome, resolved, or outgrown. I have selected it, however, to emphasize that the repetitions are only rarely fully resolved. No matter how much analytic work is done, they retain a degree of potency, and the tendency to fall back on them remains.
5 This distinguishes a psychoanalytic intervention from other types of psychotherapeutic interventions. Non-psychoanalytic interventions may be designed to loosen repetitions (although they may be described in other language), and they may be similar to, or even identical in content to, a psychoanalytic intervention, but they are not focused on or understood specifically in terms of transference.
6 Keep in mind that emotional communications are not always expressed explicitly in language in actual interventions.
7 Furthermore, other techniques, such as the use of the couch (or not) or increased frequency of sessions, may also serve to activate repetitions. The point is not that emotional communications are the only way to activate repetitions but that it is one function that they can serve.
8 This is roughly equivalent to Sterba's experiencing ego. However, I am using the term afflicted ego to emphasize the role of the repetition in this part of the mind. Furthermore, the reasonable ego also experiences; it does not just observe.
9 Cognitive psychotherapy and classically oriented psychoanalysis that focuses exclusively on insight works best with patients who have a very strong reasonable ego; a little bit of insight goes a long way with these patients.
10 That said, it seems probable that these concepts do reflect different aspects of brain functioning. It could be said that the reasonable ego reflects cortical functioning, while the afflicted ego reflects limbic functioning. This is a grossly oversimplified way of looking at things but may still be useful in view of the fact that brain functioning to some extent is both modular and interconnected.
11 I have borrowed the term containment from Bion (1970) because his term is very close in spirit to what I wish to convey, there are some significant differences between his concept and my use of the term. Most importantly, Bion seems to

NOTES

use this concept solely in relationship to beta-elements – feelings that are extremely primitive and are not experienced or structured as thought. Here, however, the concept is applied to feelings that are at all levels of development. The term is also being used in a manner that is roughly synonymous with Winnicott's (1960) concept of holding, and Spotnitz's (1976) concept of "tolerating" the countertransference.
12 For example, a warm, accepting environment and a neutral supportive environment, as well as an environment that allows the patient to express his rage.
13 I first encountered this adage when I began my training at the Center for Modern Psychoanalytic Studies in 1980, in a class taught by William Kirman, and later by others at the institute. I do not recall that Kirman claimed to have coined it, and I never found it in print in the Modern Analytic literature. Greenberg, co-founder of the Relational School offered a similarly concise – and beautiful – formulation: "If the analyst cannot be experienced as a new object, analysis never gets under way; if he cannot be experienced as an old one, it never ends" (1986: 98).
14 Keep in mind that we are only discussing the emotional component of an intervention; these considerations need not apply to the cognitive component.
15 This is similar to Strachey's (1934) idea that mutative interpretations must address the transference. Strachey referred, of course, to the cognitive content of the interpretation, whereas I am referring to the emotional communication that accompanies the cognitive communication.
16 It might, of course, have an even better impact. Happy accidents are not all that uncommon in analysis, although probably less common than unhappy accidents.
17 Nor is it always – or even usually – expressed in the cognitive communication.
18 For example, it doesn't matter whether this is because the analyst actually can't tolerate the patient's anger, or the patient incorrectly believes (or feels) this to be the case. The effect can be the same.
19 Perhaps it's better to say, "approximately the right feeling," because the quality of the specific feeling usually changes, if only slightly, when experienced in a different mode of relatedness.

11 NARCISSISTIC EMOTIONAL COMMUNICATIONS

1 The reason that Freud and many classical analysts who followed him were hopeless about treating narcissism may be because they recognized that their techniques weren't effective in these cases and that the problem went beyond the accuracy of the interpretation.
2 Of course, the analyst might want to deliberately modulate the transference and firm up the ego boundaries, in which case a carefully formulated interpretation might work well. But then again, this is not a narcissistic emotional communication.
3 As we shall see in the next chapter, joining can also be used to make object emotional communications.
4 To be more precise: when joining was first conceptualized (Spotnitz 1976), the syntonic and the dystonic versions were not differentiated. However, the idea that a defense is reinforced until the need for it is outgrown is more relevant to syntonic joining. As we shall see, dystonic joining serves the more immediate goal of reversing self-hatred.
5 Time is compressed in this exchange. In reality, such a shift in the patient's level of comfort would probably take weeks or months, but even that is far faster than the result that might be obtained from interpreting the material.

NOTES

6 There are times when the patient's shift in feeling is due to negative suggestibility or oppositionalism; I would not describe this situation as a successful use of joining because no change has taken place in the degree of the patient's emotional freedom. This is more accurately described as manipulating the patient. This is not to say that this doesn't have its place; sometimes nothing else can get a patient to cease some destructive or self-destructive behavior. But this is case management, not maturational emotional communication.

7 As we shall see in the following chapter, there is a form of joining used in the object mode that looks very similar to dystonic narcissistic joining and seems to have the same effect, i.e., mobilize the discharge of rage at the analyst. Similar as they are, however, they are based on different modes of relatedness and play somewhat different roles in the analytic relationship.

8 If you believe in psychosomatic illness; I'm skeptical, but that's another story altogether.

9 Although it is possible for it to be more prominent in some relationships rather than others.

10 It is not, however, the whole of the afflicted ego; the other part is the part that is attacked and suffering. The reasonable ego, when it exists at all, stands back and observes the whole process, suffering too, but helpless to do anything about it.

11 The exception to this are some Modern Analysts and some Interpersonalists, who have been specifically trained (sometimes too well trained) in this area.

12 This idea does have a place in object joining (see the next chapter) but has no place in narcissistic joining.

13 There is, of course, a danger here that if the intervention is too premature, the analyst will scare the patient away or disrupt the narcissistic transference altogether by being too different from the patient.

14 I would argue that the intervention should not be classified as containment if the analyst deliberately infuses the expressive intervention with the feeling, but if the expressed feeling is extremely attenuated and indirect, then the distinction is, perhaps, academic.

15 While I admire the term *metabolize*, I think it is more usefully understood in relationship to extremely early feeling states of confusion, aggression, and anxiety – those that Bion calls beta elements – that diminish in intensity as a result of the containment process. I also find it to be appropriate to describe what takes place with projective identifications. In other instances, however, it is both too abstract and somewhat misleading, or the issue is more simply finding the courage and the willingness to accept a feeling – such as murderous rage or a dystonic sexual desire – than it is a matter of metabolizing the feeling. Such feelings are not essentially changed, toned down, or in any other way digested through containment.

12 TECHNIQUES OF OBJECT EMOTIONAL COMMUNICATIONS

1 As we shall see in the following chapter, anaclitic communications are also within the differentiated mode of relatedness. However, they do not repeat feelings from a pathological relationship and function and in general function very differently from the object communications.

2 Of course, there will be spontaneous object communications in the form of enactments, but as we will discuss later, I prefer to avoid these to the extent that it's possible to do so.

3 Some American Freudians, of course, famously attempt to make these object interpretations with complete emotional neutrality, devoid of any empathy or

NOTES

support, and claimed that this worked in the small minority of patients who were truly "neurotic" – no character pathology, no ego pathology. Given that it is almost impossible to make a verbal communication without an emotional communication, I suspect that these interpretations work when some sort of supportive emotional communication leaks through despite the analyst's best efforts to prevent it.

4 This way of working goes so against my own training and prejudices that I can't say that I have tried it often or consistently. But my sense is that in other people's hands it works much better than it does for me, or from what has been frequently reported by my supervisees.

5 They are the foundation for a good reason: this emotional blend works with most patients most of the time, at least in the very early stages of treatment. The problem, of course, is that most patients are not all patients.

6 In this case, however, the analyst will proceed very slowly, with very little affect in the communication because (a) he does not want to overly disturb defenses that may be very delicate, and (b) his hypothesis may be wrong, and he does not want to muddy the transferential waters with too much irrelevant emotional communication.

7 There is sometimes a tendency among Modern Analysts to use this line of intervention whenever the patient complains he is not making progress. However, it will be useful only when the patient makes this complaint (or doesn't make the complaint, but implies it) coupled with inhibited anger. On the other hand, the patient might make the complaint but be in need of an entirely different emotional communication, such as anaclitic encouragement, narcissistic empathy, or narcissistic mirroring.

8 Spotnitz is reported to have said that some patients have to leave any number of analysts until they have discharged enough rage that they can settle in with an analyst and talk.

9 And there is absolutely nothing wrong with that. Indeed, it is crucial that every analyst monitors the amount of stress that he experiences with each patient, and shapes his practice accordingly. If not, both he and his patients will suffer.

10 Object-oriented questions (Spotnitz 1969) are emotionally neutral questions that are about anything other than the patient's thoughts, feelings, or sensations. Their purpose is to lower the level of stimulation when the patient appears to be over-stimulated by the intensity of her feelings. This might be manifested by obsessive thinking, rumination, delusions, hallucinations, thought disorders, narcissistic self-absorption, or aggressive or sexual feelings that are interfering with the patient's ability to communicate his thoughts and feelings. They work by unobtrusively directing the patient's attention away from the contents of his mind and towards the outside world. Ideally, an object-oriented question will engage a patient's active interest. However, any question that the patient will respond to can function in this way. For example, if a patient becomes over stimulated in recounting an argument with his boss, he might be asked: "What time did that happen?" "Was anyone else there?" At first glance, these questions appear to be the opposite of more psychoanalytic questions, which are designed to help the patient to become aware of his feelings. Object-oriented questions, however, facilitate this process by helping to maintain his level of stimulation at a workable level.

13 TECHNIQUES OF EMOTIONAL COMMUNICATION WITH PROJECTIVE IDENTIFICATION

1 I should reiterate that I would classify much of what other writers refer to as projective identification as narcissistic transference/countertransference – a much easier state to work with.

NOTES

2 Although I wrote earlier that I find the term *metabolize* to be most appropriate for very early feelings, as opposed to all feelings that can be contained, I do find that it is also particularly appropriate for the intensity of projective identifications.
3 It should be noted that this can occur with any ill-timed or ill-conceived intervention, but again the risks are higher in the projective identification mode.

14 ANACLITIC EMOTIONAL COMMUNICATIONS

1 This is another difference between anaclitic communications and narcissistic communications (although it is not an essential one): narcissistic emotional communications in analysis more closely resemble those in development than do anaclitic communications. This is because anaclitic emotional communications in development are so closely intertwined with actual nurturing behavior, whereas narcissistic emotional communications in development tend to be more purely emotional interactions.
2 It should be noted that just because the anaclitic emotional communication in development is often tied with actual nurturing actions, the nurturing actions can be performed without the anaclitic feeling, which accounts for many patients' complaint that their parents did the right things but did not have the right feeling for them.
3 At the same time, caretaking behavior that is not accompanied by anaclitic emotional communication often feels cold and unsatisfying, as evidenced by so many patients' complaints that their parents did the right things but without the right feelings.
4 If the analyst were interpreting according to Fenichel's (1969) classical principle of interpreting defense before content, he would be interpreting the defensive nature of the patient's use of intellectuality rather than the content of the patient's words.
5 Although I do think that facial interactions are crucial for some patients, I'm skeptical that the more precise gaze interactions that may characterize early mother/infant interaction, as described Schore (1994), for example, which are anaclitic emotional communications, have analogues that can be deliberately expressed in psychoanalysis. I'm not convinced that these types of eye contact can be voluntarily controlled by most analysts. And even if they can be, it is even less clear if these types of eye contact can be taught. In contrast, most analysts can control the emotional communication in their voices, and a range of emotional communication can be easily modeled by teachers and supervisors.
6 I suggest to any reader who would find this surprising to consider how difficult it is for even the best parents – at least those who have jobs and/or households to manage – to consistently carve out an hour of time to give a child the sort of completely child-focused attention, undistracted by their own personal needs and feelings, that meets this developmental need.
7 To be more precise, the development of positive affect can occur in two ways. One occurs when the patient and the analyst enjoy talking about almost anything; this experience of shared enjoyment can expand the patient's ability to experience positive feeling. Or the analyst can more deliberately model positive affect, gradually titrating his own expression of pleasure and excitement so that the patient can follow his lead. This, strictly speaking, is a narcissistic emotional communication, as described in Chapter 11.
8 It's tempting to think these children grow up to be these types of patients, but I'm not sure that is the case.

NOTES

9 The term *schizotypal* was introduced after the bulk of Spotniz's work was published, and Spotnitz did not use it. However, I think that this term describes many (but not all) of the patients described in Spotnitz's work better than schizophrenic.
10 Actually, the problem that I have encountered most frequently is that many patients look like they might regress in this dramatic way when exposed to anaclitic emotional communication – or anything else about the treatment that appears to be overstimulating – but only a very few do, so there are a lot of false positives. This presents the clinical dilemma of whether to be overly cautious with most patients of this sort, and thereby slow down the progress of those who won't regress, or take greater chances knowing that over time, some patients will regress. This is the sort of dilemma that each analyst must work out on his own, in consultation with peers and supervisors.
11 Obviously, disclosing this information to a patient in a different transference state could create all kinds of problems.
12 Of course, it is always possible – and will happen – that the analyst discloses something about himself that he anticipates the patient will find syntonic only to discover that the patient experiences it as dystonic. But this is true of any intervention.
13 Of course, we are assuming that the patient is primarily in a state of anaclitic transference – or that the analyst's communication will induce an anaclitic transference – when any of these interventions are made deliberately. However, other transferential feelings may be activated by the communication, even if these were not primary when the communication is made.
14 Which, in this framework, is one type of experience that is possible within the present-anchored relational mode.
15 In the language of separation individuation, but with, I think, essentially the same meaning as contemporary theories of intersubjectivity.
16 For better or worse, I find it impossible not to see the influence of Kant's moral philosophy, and his insistence that one must treat humanity never merely as a means, but always at the same time as an end, in this formulation of psychoanalytic maturity.

BIBLIOGRAPHY

Aichhorn, A. (1936) "The Narcissistic Transference of the 'Juvenile Impostor'," in O. Fleischmann, P. Kramer, and H. Ross (Eds.) (1965) *Delinquency and Child Guidance: Selected Papers of August Aichhorn*, New York: International Universities Press.

Alexander, F. (1925) "Contribution to the Symposium Conducted at the Eight International Psycho-Analytic Congress, Salzburg," *International Journal of Psychoanalysis* 6: 13–24.

Arlow, J. (1963) "The Supervisory Situation," *Journal of the American Psychoanalytic Association* 11: 576–594.

Aron, L. (1996) *A Meeting of Minds: Mutuality in Psychoanalysis*, Hillsdale, NJ: The Analytic Press.

Atwood, G. and Stolorow, R. (1984) *Structures of Subjectivity: Explorations in Psychoanalytic Phenomenology*, Hillsdale, NJ: The Analytic Press.

Auden, W. (1979) "In Memory of Sigmund Freud," in E. Mendelson (Ed.) *Selected Poems*, New York: Random House.

Balint, M. (1952) *Primary Love and Psycho-Analytic Technique*, London: Hogarth.

—— (1968) *The Basic Fault*, London: Tavistock Publications.

Bartsch, A. and Hübner, S. (2005) *Towards a Theory of Emotional Communication*, vol. 7, issue 4, article 2. Available online at: http://docs.lib.purdue.edu/clcweb/vol7/iss4/2/ (accessed September 19, 2011).

Basch, M.F. (1983) "Empathic Understanding: A Review of the Concept and Some Theoretical Implications," *Journal of the American Psychoanalytic Association* 31: 101–126.

Beebe, B., Knoblauch, S., Rustin, J., and Sorter, D. (2005) *Forms of Intersubjectivity in Infant Research and Adult Treatment*, New York: Other Press.

Benjamin, J. (1986) "A Desire of One's Own: Psychoanalytic Feminism and Intersubjective Space," paper presented at a conference in 1985 at the Center for Twentieth Century Studies of the University of Wisconsin-Milwaukee, in T. de Laurentis (1986) *Feminist Studies, Critical Studies*, Bloomington, IN: Indiana University Press.

—— (1998) *The Shadow of the Other: Intersubjectivity and Gender in Psychoanalysis*, New York: Routledge.

Beres, D. and Arlow, J.A. (1974) "Fantasy and Identification in Empathy," *Psychoanalytic Quarterly* 43: 155–181.

BIBLIOGRAPHY

Bernstein, A. (1992) "Beyond Countertransference: The Love that Cures," *Modern Psychoanalysis* 17: 15–31.

Bernstein, J. (1981) "An Approach to the Management of Treatment Impasses," *Modern Psychoanalysis* 6: 201–220.

—— (1993) "Using the Countertransference Resistance," *Modern Psychoanalysis* 18: 71–80.

Bershatsky, D. (2002) "The Positive Anaclitic Countertransference in Modern Group Analysis," *Annals of Modern Psychoanalysis* 1: 31–91.

Binswanger, L. (1957) *Sigmund Freud: Reminiscences of a Friendship*, New York: Grune & Stranton.

Bion, W. (1959) "Attacks on Linking," *International Journal of Psychoanalysis* 40: 308–315; reprinted in *Second Thoughts: Selected Papers on Psycho-Analysis* (1967), New York: Jason Aronson.

—— (1961) *Experiences in Groups, and Other Papers*, New York: Basic Books.

—— (1962) *Learning From Experience*, London: Karnac Books.

—— (1963) *Elements of Psycho-Analysis*, London: Heinemann.

—— (1970) *Attention and Interpretation*, London: Tavistock.

Bollas, C. (1983) "Expressive uses of the Countertransference – Notes to the Patient from Oneself," *Contemporary Psychoanalysis* 19: 1–33.

—— (1987) *The Shadow of the Object: Psychoanalysis of the Unthought Known*, New York: Jason Aronson.

Boston Change Process Study Group (2008) "Forms of Relational Meaning: Issues in the Relations Between the Implicit and Reflective-Verbal Domains," *Psychoanalytic Dialogues* 18: 125–148.

Bratt, P. (1991) "Whose feelings first? Group treatment as an anaclitic intervention," *Modern Psychoanalysis* 16(2): 207–218.

Brothers, L. (1989) "A Biological Perspective on Empathy," *American Journal of Psychiatry* 146: 10–19.

Buck, R. and Ginsburg, B.E. (1997) "Communicative Genes and the Evolution of Empathy: Selfish and Social Emotions as Voices of Selfish and Social Genes," *Annals of the New York Academy of Sciences* 807: 481–484.

Cancelmo, J. (2009) "The Role of the Transitional Realm as an Organizer of Analytic Process: Transitional Organizing Experience," *Psychoanalytic Psychology* 26: 2–25.

Cardinal, M. (1983) *The Words to Say It*, Cambridge, MA: Vanvactor & Goodheart.

Chused, J.F. (1991) "The Evocative Power of Enactments," *Journal of the American Psychoanalytic Association* 39: 615–639.

Cosmides, L. and Tooby, J. (1992) "Cognitive Adaptations for Social Exchange," in J. Barkow, L. Cosmides, and J. Tooby (Eds.) *The Adapted Mind* 163–228, New York: Oxford University Press.

Damasio, A. (1994) *Descartes' Error*, New York: Avon.

Darwin, C. (1872) *The Expression of Emotions in Man and Animals*, London: John Murray.

Davis, J.D. (1994) "Love in the Afternoon: A Relational Reconsideration of Desire and Dread in the Countertransference," *Psychoanalytic Dialogues* 4: 153–170.

Deutsch, H. (1926) "Occult Processes Occurring During Psychoanalysis," in G. Devereaux (Ed.) (1953) *Psychoanalysis and the Occult*, New York: International Universities Press.

Eissler, K. (1953) "The Effect of the Structure of the Ego on Psychoanalytic Technique," *Journal of the American Psychoanalytic Association* 1: 104–143.

BIBLIOGRAPHY

Ekstein, R. and Wallerstein, R. (1958) *The Teaching and Learning of Psychotherapy*, New York: Basic Books.

Ellman, S.J. and Monk, C. (1997) "The Significance of the First Few Months of Life for Self-Regulation: A Reply to Schore," in M. Moskowitz, C. Monk, C. Kaye, and S. Ellman (Eds.) (1997) *The Neurobiological and Developmental Basis for Psychotherapeutic Intervention*, Northville, NJ: Jason Aronson.

Ellman, S. and Moskowitz, M. (Eds.) (1998) *Enactment: Towards a New Approach to the Therapeutic Relationship* (Library of Clinical Psychoanalysis), Northvale, NJ: Jason Aronson.

Epstein, L. (1982) "Adapting to the Patient's Therapeutic Need in the Psychoanalytic Situation," *Contemporary Psychoanalysis* 18: 190–217.

—— (1987) "The Bad-Analyst-Feeling," *Modern Psychoanalysis* 12: 35–45.

—— (1999) "The Analyst's 'Bad Analyst' Feelings: A Counterpart to the Process of Resolving Implosive Defenses," *Contemporary Psychoanalysis* 35: 311–325.

Epstein, L. and Feiner, A. (1979) *Countertransference: The Therapist's Contribution to the Therapeutic Situation*, New York: Jason Aronson.

Ernsberger, C. (1979) "The Concept of Countertransference as Therapeutic Instrument: Its Early History," *Modern Psychoanalysis* 4: 141–164.

—— (1990) "Modern Countertransference Theory: Some Elaborations and Clinical Illustrations," *Modern Psychoanalysis* 4: 141–164.

—— (1991) "Modern Psychoanalytic Training: The First Four Decades," *Modern Psychoanalysis* 16: 15–36.

Fenichel, O. (1969) *Problems of Psychoanalytic Technique*, New York: The Psychoanalytic Quarterly.

Ferenczi, S. (1931) "Child-Analysis in the Analysis of Adults," *International Journal of Psychoanalysis* 12: 468–482; reprinted in *Final Contributions to the Problems and Methods of Psycho-Analysis* (1980), New York: Brunner Mazel.

Fernald, A. (1992) "Human Maternal Vocalizations to Infants as Biologically Relevant Signals: An Evolutionary Perspective," in J. Barkow, L. Cosmides, and J. Tooby (Eds.) *The Adapted Mind*, New York: Oxford University Press.

Fliess, R. (1942) "The Metapsychology of the Analyst," *Psychoanalytic Quarterly* 11: 211–227.

Frank, G. (1987) "Weinstein Revisited: Should Analysts Love Their Patients?" *Modern Psychoanalysis* 12: 81–95.

Freud, A. (1966) *The Ego and the Mechanisms of Defense*, London: The Hogarth Press for the Institute of Psychoanalysis.

—— (1969) "Difficulties in the Path of Psychoanalysis: A Confrontation of Past With Present Viewpoints," in *The Writings of Anna Freud*, vol. 7, New York: International Universities Press.

Freud, S. (1905) "Three Essays in the Theory of Sexuality," in *The Standard Edition of the Complete Psychological Works of Sigmund Freud*, vol. 7, London: Hogarth Press.

—— (1910) "The Future Prospects of Psychoanalytic Therapy," in *The Standard Edition of the Complete Psychological Works of Sigmund Freud*, vol. 11, London: Hogarth Press.

—— (1912) "Recommendations to Physicians Practising Psychoanalysis," in *The Standard Edition of the Complete Psychological Works of Sigmund Freud*, vol. 12: 111–120, London: Hogarth Press.

—— (1913) "On Beginning the Treatment," in *The Standard Edition of the Complete Psychological Works of Sigmund Freud*, vol. 12, London: Hogarth Press.

—— (1914a) "On the History of the Psychoanalytic Movement," in *The Standard Edition of the Complete Psychological Works of Sigmund Freud*, vol. 14, London: Hogarth Press.

—— (1914b) "On Narcissism: An Introduction," in *The Standard Edition of the Complete Psychological Works of Sigmund Freud*, vol. 14, London: Hogarth Press.

—— (1914c) "Remembering, Repeating and Working-Through," in *The Standard Edition of the Complete Psychological Works of Sigmund Freud*, vol. 12, London: Hogarth Press.

—— (1915) "Observations on Transference Love," in *The Standard Edition of the Complete Psychological Works of Sigmund Freud*, vol. 12, London: Hogarth Press.

—— (1916) "Introductory Lectures on Psychoanalysis," in *The Standard Edition of the Complete Psychological Works of Sigmund Freud*, vol. 16, London: Hogarth Press.

—— (1917) "Mourning and Melancholia," in *The Standard Edition of the Complete Psychological Works of Sigmund Freud*, vol. 14, London: Hogarth Press.

—— (1919) "Lines of Advance in Psychoanalytic Theory," in *The Standard Edition of the Complete Psychological Works of Sigmund Freud*, vol. 12, London: Hogarth Press.

—— (1923) "The Ego and the Id," in *The Standard Edition of the Complete Psychological Works of Sigmund Freud*, vol. 19, London: Hogarth Press.

—— (1925) "Some Additional Notes on Dream Interpretation as a Whole," in *The Standard Edition of the Complete Psychological Works of Sigmund Freud*, vol. 19, London: Hogarth Press.

—— (1933) "New Introductory Lectures on Psychoanalysis," in *The Standard Edition of the Complete Psychological Works of Sigmund Freud*, vol. 22, London: Hogarth Press.

—— (1940) "An Outline of Psychoanalysis," in *The Standard Edition of the Complete Psychological Works of Sigmund Freud*, vol. 23, London: Hogarth Press.

—— (1954) *The Origins of Psychoanalysis. Letters to Wilhelm Fliess. Drafts and Notes: 1887–1902*, New York: Basic Books.

Gabbard, G. and Wilkinsin, S. (2000) *Management of Countertransference with Borderline Patient*, Northvale, NJ: Jason Aronson.

Gay, P. (1988) *Freud, A Life for Our Time*, New York. London: W.W. Norton & Company.

Geltner, P. (2000) "The Evolutionary and Developmental Origins of Patient Induced Countertransference," *Psychiatry* 63(3): 253–263.

Giovacchini, P. (1979) *Treatment of Primitive Mental States*, Northvale, NJ: Jason Aronson.

Gittelson, M. (1952) "The Emotional Response of the Analyst in the Psychoanalytic Situation," *International Journal of Psycho-Analysis* 33: 1–10.

Glover, E. (1955) *The Technique of Psychoanalysis*, New York: International Universities Press.

Greenberg, J. (1986) "Theoretical Models and the Analyst's Neutrality," *Contemporary Psychoanalysis* 22: 87–106.

Greenson, R. (1960) "Empathy and Its Vicissitudes," *International Journal of Psychoanalysis* 41: 418–424.

—— (1967) *The Technique and Practice of Psychoanalysis*, New York: International Universities Press.

Griffin, D.R. (1984) *Animal Thinking*, Cambridge, MA: Harvard University Press.

Grinberg, L. (1979) "Countertransference and Projective Counteridentification," *Contemporary Psychoanalysis* 15: 226–247.

Grotstein, J. (1981) *Splitting and Projective Identification*, New York: Jason Aronson.
Hann-Kende, F. (1933) "On the Role of Transference and Countertransference," reprinted in G. Devereaux (Ed.) (1953) *Psychoanalysis and the Occult*, New York: International Universities Press.
Hauser, M. (1996) *The Evolution of Communication*, Cambridge, MA: MIT Press.
Hayden, S. (1983) "The Toxic Response in Modern Psychoanalysis," *Modern Psychoanalysis* 8: 3–16.
Heimann, P.I. (1950) "On Counter-Transference," *International Journal of Psychoanalysis* 31: 81–84.
Hinshelwood, R.D. (1992) *Clinical Klein*, London: Free Association Books.
Hrdy, S.B. (1999) *Mother Nature: A History of Mothers, Infants, and Natural Selection*, New York: Pantheon Books.
Humphrey, H.F. (1976) "The Social Function of Intellect," in P.P.G. Bateson and R. Hinde (Eds.) *Growing Points in Ethnology*, New York: Cambridge University Press.
Jacobson, E. (1964) *The Self and the Object World*, New York: International Universities Press.
Kernberg, O. (1965) "Countertransference," *Journal of the American Psychoanalytic Association* 13: 38–56.
—— (1985) *Borderline Conditions and Pathological Narcissism*, New York: Jason Aronson.
Kirman, J. (1983) "Modern Psychoanalysis and Intimacy: Treatment of the Narcissistic Personality," *Modern Psychoanalysis* 8: 17–34.
—— (1998) "One-Person or Two-Person Psychology," *Modern Psychoanalysis* 23: 3–22.
Kirman, W. (1980) "Countertransference in Facilitating Intimacy and Communication," *Modern Psychoanalysis* 5: 131–145.
Klein, M. (1946) "Notes on Some Schizoid Mechanisms," in *Envy and Gratitude and Other Works* (1975). New York: Delacorte Press/S. Lawrence.
Kohut, H. (1971) *The Analysis of Self*, New York: International Universities Press.
—— (1977) *The Restoration of Self*, New York: International Universities Press.
—— (1984) *How Does Analysis Cure?* Chicago, IL: University of Chicago Press.
Kohut, H. and Wolf, E. (1978) "The Disorders of the Self and Their Treatment: An Outline," *International Journal of Psychoanalysis* 19: 413–435; reprinted in A. Morrison (Ed.) (1986) *Essential Papers on Narcissism*, New York: New York University Press.
Krebs, J.R. and Dawkins, R. (1984) "Animal Signals: Mind-Reading and Manipulation," in J.R. Krebs and N.V. Davies (Eds.) *Behavioral Ecology*, Sunderland, MA: Sinauer Associates.
Kris, E. (1975) *Selected Papers of Ernst Kris*, New Haven, CT: Yale University Press.
Krystal, H. (1988) *Integration and Self-Healing: Affect, Trauma, and Alexithymia*, Hillsdale, NJ: The Analytic Press.
Kumin, I. (1996) *Pre-Object Relatedness: Early Attachment and the Psychoanalytic Situation*, New York: Guilford Press.
Laplanche, J. and Pontalis, J.B. (1973) *The Language of Psychoanalysis*, London: Hogarth Press.
Laquercia, T. (1992) "The Anaclitic Environment: The Emerging Challenge for the Analyst," *Modern Psychoanalysis* 17: 35–42.

—— (1998) "Symbolic Imagery: An Aspect of Unverbalized Communication," *Modern Psychoanalysis* 20: 23–33.

LeDoux, J. (1998) *The Emotional Brain: The Mysterious Underpinnings of Emotional Life*, New York: Touchstone.

Lester, B.M. and Boukydis, C.F.Z. (1992) "No Language but a Cry," in H. Papousek, U. Jurgens, and M. Papousek (Eds.) *Nonverbal Vocal Communication: Comparative and Developmental Approaches*, Cambridge, UK: Cambridge University Press.

Liegner, E. (1980) "The Hate That Cures: The Psychological Reversibility of Schizophrenia," *Modern Psychoanalysis* 5: 5–95.

—— (1991) "The Anaclitic Countertransference," *Modern Psychoanalysis* 16: 5–13.

—— (1995) "The Anaclitic Countertransference in Resistance Resolution," *Modern Psychoanalysis* 20: 153–164.

Little, M. (1951) "Counter-Transference and the Patient's Response to It," *International Journal of Psycho-Analysis* 32: 32–40.

Loewald, H.W. (1960) "On the Therapeutic Action of Psycho-Analysis," *International Journal of Psychoanalysis* 41:16–33.

McConnell, P.B. (1990) "Acoustic Structure and Receiver Response in Domestic Dogs, Canis Familaris," *Animal Behavior* 39: 897–904.

MacLean, P.D. (1990) *The Triune Brain in Evolution*, New York: Plenum.

Mahler, M., Pine, F., and Bergman, A. (1975) *The Psychological Birth of the Human Infant: Symbiosis and Individuation*, New York: Basic Books.

Makinnon, N. (2003) *Symbolic Interaction and Knowledge Presentation: From Cognitive to Affective Models*. Available online at www.knowledgepresentation.org/Building TheFuture/MacKinnon/MacKinnonb.html (accessed October 23, 2011).

Margolis, B. (1978) "Narcissistic Countertransference: Emotional Availability and Case Management," *Modern Psychoanalysis* 3: 161–177.

—— (1979) "Narcissistic Transference: The Product of Overlapping Self and Object Fields," *Modern Psychoanalysis* 4: 131–140.

—— (1981/1994) "Narcissistic Countertransference: Further Considerations," *Modern Psychoanalysis* 6: 171–182. Also in *Modern Psychoanalysis* 19: 149–159.

Maroda, K. (1991) *The Power of Countertransference: Innovations in Psychoanalytic Technique*, Chichester, UK and New York: Wiley.

—— (1999) *Seduction, Surrender, and Transformation: Emotional Engagement in the Analytic Process*, Hillsdale, NJ: The Analytic Press.

—— (2009) *Psychodynamic Techniques: Working with Emotion in the Therapeutic Relationship*, New York: The Guilford Press.

Marshall, R. (1982) *Resistant Interactions: Child, Family, and Psychotherapist*, New York: Human Sciences Press.

—— (1991) "Comparisons, Contrasts, and Convergences," *Modern Psychoanalysis* 18: 45–57.

Marshall, R. and Marshall, S. (1988) *The Transference–Countertransference Matrix: The Emotional-Cognitive Dialogue in Psychotherapy, Psychoanalysis, and Supervision*, New York: Columbia University Press.

Meadow, P.W. (1987) "The Myth of the Impersonal Analyst," *Modern Psychoanalysis* 12: 131–150.

—— (1988) "Emotional Education: The Theory and Process of Training Psychoanalysts – Historical and Current Developments of a Modern Psychoanalytic Program," *Modern Psychoanalysis* 13: 211–388.

—— (1989) "How We Aim to Be With Patients," *Modern Psychoanalysis* 14: 145–162.
—— (1991) "Resonating With the Psychotic Patient," *Modern Psychoanalysis* 16: 87–103.
—— (1999) "The Clinical Practice of Modern Psychoanalysis: An Interview with Hyman Spotnitz," *Modern Psychoanalysis* 24 (1): 3–19.
Messer, D.J. (1994) *The Development of Communication*, Chichester, UK: John Wiley & Sons.
Mitchell, S. (1988) *Relational Concepts in Psychoanalysis: An Integration*, Cambridge, MA: Harvard University Press.
—— (2000) *Relationality: From Attachment to Intersubjectivity*, Hillsdale, NJ: The Analytic Press.
Mithen, S. (2006) *The Singing Neanderthals*, Cambridge, MA: Harvard University Press.
Morrel, A. (1992) "Countertransference and the Analyst's Response to It: Feelings About Feelings," *Modern Psychoanalysis* 17: 85–95.
—— (1994) "Notes on Anaclitic Countertransference," *Modern Psychoanalysis* 19: 75–87.
Ogden, T. (1979) "On Projective Identification," *The International Journal of Psychoanalysis* 60: 356–373.
—— (1982) *Projective Identification and Psychotherapeutic Technique*, New York: Jason Aronson.
—— (1997a) "Reverie and Metaphor: Some Thoughts on How I Work as a Psychoanalyst," *International Journal of Psychoanalysis* 78: 719–732.
—— (1997b) *Reverie and Interpretation: Sensing Something Human*, Northvale, NJ: Jason Aronson.
Ornstein, A. (1974) "The Dread to Repeat and the New Beginning: A Contribution to the Psychoanalysis of Narcissistic Personality Disorders," *Annual of Psychoanalysis* 2: 231–248.
Panksepp, J. (1998) *Affective Neuroscience: The Foundations of Human and Animal Emotions*, New York: Oxford University Press.
Pinker, S. (1997) *How the Mind Works*, New York: Norton.
—— (2003) "Language as an Adaptation to the Cognitive Niche," in M. Christiansen and S. Kirby (Eds.) *Language Evolution: States of the Art*, New York: Oxford University Press.
Racker, H. (1957) "The Meanings and Uses of Countertransference," *Psychoanalytic Quarterly* 26: 303–357; reprinted in *Transference and Countertransference* (2001), New York: International Universities Press.
Rado, S. (1951) "Psychodynamics of Depression from the Etiological Point of View," reprinted in Rado, *Psychoanalysis of Behavior* (1957), New York: Grune & Stratton.
Reich A. (1951) "On Countertransference," *International Journal of Psychoanalysis* 32: 25–31.
Rice, A. (1976) *Interview with the Vampire*, New York: Ballantine Books.
Riek, T. (1941) *Masochism in Modern Man*, New York and Toronto: Farrar & Rinehart.
Rosenfeld, H. (1987) *Impasse and Interpretation*, London: Routledge.
—— (1988) "Contribution to the Psychopathology of Psychotic States: The Importance of Projective Identification in the Ego Structure and the Object Relations of the Psychotic Patient," in E. Bott-Spillius (Ed.) *Melanie Klein Today*, vol. 1. London: Routledge.

Sandler, J. (1976) "Countertransference and Role-Responsiveness," *International Review of Psychoanalysis* 3: 43–47.
Schore, A. (1994) *Affect Regulation and the Origin of the Self: The Neurobiology of Human Development*, Hillsdale, NJ: Lawrence Erlbaum Associates.
Searles, H. (1965) *Collected Papers on Schizophrenia and Related Subjects*, New York: International Universities Press.
—— (1979) *Countertransference and Related Subjects*, New York: International Universities Press.
Sechehaye, M. (1951) *Symbolic Realization: A New Method of Psychotherapy Applied to a Case of Schizophrenia*, New York: International Universities Press.
Sheftel, S. (1998) "On the Patient's Need to Feel Loved," *Modern Psychoanalysis* 20: 35–51.
Sherman, M. (1983) "Emotional Communication in Modern Psychoanalysis: Some Freudian Origins and Comparisons," *Modern Psychoanalysis* 8: 173–189.
Slochower, J. (1996) *Holding and Psychoanalysis: A Relational Approach*, Hillsdale, NJ: The Analytic Press.
Spitz, R. (1945) "Diacritic and Coenesthetic Organizations," *Psychoanalytic Review* 32: 146–152.
—— (1956) "Countertransference," *Journal of the American Psychoanalytic Association* 4: 256–265.
—— (1963) "Ontogenisis: The Proleptic Function of Emotion," in P.H. Knapp (Ed.) *The Expression of the Emotions in Man*, New York: International Universities Press.
—— (1965) *The First Year of Life*, New York: International Universities Press.
Spotnitz, H. (1966) "The Maturational Interpretation," *Psychoanalytic Review* 53c: 166–169; reprinted in *The Psychotherapy of Preoedipal Conditions* (1976), New York: Jason Aronson.
—— (1967) "Techniques for the Resolution of the Narcissistic Defense," in B.B. Wolman (Ed.) *Psychoanalytic Techniques: A Handbook For the Practicing Psychoanalyst*; reprinted in *The Psychotherapy of Preoedipal Conditions* (1976), New York: Jason Aronson.
—— (1969) *The Modern Psychoanalysis of the Schizophrenic Patient: Theory of the Technique*, New York: Grune & Stratton.
—— (1976) *The Psychotherapy of Preoedipal Conditions*, New York: Jason Aronson.
—— (1977) "Emotional Communication and Countertransference in the Narcissistic and Borderline Disorders: A Symposium," T. Lidz, J. Masterson, H. Spotnitz, V. Volkan, moderator: P. Meadow, *Modern Psychoanalysis* 2: 149–179.
—— (1983) "Countertransference With the Psychotic Patient: Value of the Positive Anaclitic Countertransference," *Modern Psychoanalysis* 8: 169–172.
—— (1985) *The Modern Psychoanalysis of the Schizophrenic Patient: Theory of the Technique*, 2nd edn., New York: Human Sciences Press.
—— (1989) "Therapeutic Countertransference: Interventions With the Schizophrenic Patient," *Modern Psychoanalysis* 14: 3–20.
Spotnitz, H. and Meadow, P.W. (1976) *Treatment of the Narcissistic Neurosis*, New York: Manhattan Center for Advanced Psychoanalytic Studies.
Spotnitz, H. and Nagelberg, L. (1958) "Strengthening the Ego through the Release of Frustration-Aggression," *American Journal of Orthogpsychiatry* 28: 794–801, reprinted in *Psychotherapy of Preoedipal Conditions* (1976). New York: Jason Aronson.

Spotnitz, H., Nagelberg, L., and Feldman, Y. (1953) "The Attempt at Healthy Insulation in the Withdrawn Child," *American Journal of Orthopsychiatry* 23: 238–251; reprinted in *Psychotherapy of Preoedipal Conditions* (1976), New York: Jason Aronson.

Sterba, R. (1934) "The Fate of the Ego in Analytic Therapy," *International Journal of Psychoanalysis* 15: 117–126.

Stern, D. (1985) *The Interpersonal World of the Infant*, New York: Basic Books.

Stolorow, R., Brandchaft, B., and Atwood, G. (1987) *Psychoanalytic Treatment: An Intersubjective Approach*, Hillsdale, NJ: The Analytic Press.

Strachey, J. (1934) "The Nature of the Therapeutic Action of Psychoanalysis," *International Journal of Psychoanalysis* 15: 127–159; reprinted in R. Langs (1990) *Classics in Psychoanalytic Technique*, Northvale, NJ: Jason Aronson.

Tooby, J. and Devore, I. (1987) "The Reconstruction of Hominid Behavioral Evolution Through Strategic Modeling," in W. Kinzey (Ed.) *Primate Models of Hominid Behavior*, New York: SUNY Press.

Tower, L. (1956) "Countertransference," *Journal of the American Psychoanalytic Association* 4: 224–255.

Trevarthen, C. (1993) "The Function of Emotions in Early Infant Communication and Development," in J. Nadel and L. Camaioni, *New Perspectives in Early Infant Communicative Development*, London: Routledge.

Trivers, R. (1971) "The Evolution of Reciprocal Altruism," *Quarterly Review of Biology* 46: 35–47.

—— (1985) *Social Evolution*, Reading, MA: Benjamin/Cummings.

Weinstein, R.S. (1986) "Should Analysts Love Their Patients?" *Modern Psychoanalysis* 11: 103–110.

Winnicott, D.W. (1949) "Hate in the Countertransference," *International Journal of Psychoanalysis* 30: 69–74; reprinted in *Through Paediatrics to Psychoanalysis* (1975), London: The Hogarth Press.

—— (1956) "Primary Maternal Preoccupation," in *Through Paediatrics to Psychoanalysis* (1975), London: The Hogarth Press.

—— (1958) "The Capacity to Be Alone," *International Journal of Psychoanalysis* 39: 416–420; reprinted in the *Maturational Processes and the Facilitating Environment: Studies in the Theory of Emotional Development* (1965), New York: International Universities Press.

—— (1960) "The Theory of the Parent-Infant Relationship," *International Journal of Psychoanalysis* 41: 585–595.

—— (1965) "The Maturational Processes and the Facilitating Environment: Studies in the Theory of Emotional Development," *The International Psycho-Analytical Library* 64: 1–276. London: The Hogarth Press and the Institute of Psycho-Analysis.

—— (1978) *The Piggle: An Account of the Psycho-Analytic Treatment of a Little Girl*, London: The Hogarth Press and the Institute of Psycho-Analysis.

Zetzel, E. (1956) "Current Concepts of Transference," *International Journal of Psychoanalysis* 37: 369–376.

—— (1966) "The Analytic Situation," in R. Litman (Ed.) *Psychoanalysis in the Americas*, New York: International Universities Press.

INDEX

Please note that page numbers relating to notes will have the letter 'n' following the page number.

activating repetitions 169–70
affect, non-interpretative object emotional communications with 245–8
affective tone 60, 61, 63
afflicted ego 160, 161, 173, 174–6, 178, 209, 302; anaclitic emotional communications 273, 282, 285, 295; joining and mirroring 213, 223, 249
after education 272
aggression: aggressive anaclitic feelings *see* aggressive anaclitic feelings; dystonic joining 224, 225; introverted 205; object joining 251; passive 144; *see also* anger
aggressive anaclitic feelings: angry or critical 153–4; competition, jealousy and envy 154–5; sadism, contempt and exploitativeness 155–6
agitation 141, 142
Aichhorn, A. 307n
Alexander, F. 7
American psychoanalysis 9
anaclitic countertransference 137–58, 311–12n; aggressive anaclitic feelings 152–6; anaclitic inductions, types 140–7; congruence and incongruence 139–40; general features 138–9; loving patient 148–52; sexual feelings 156–8
anaclitic cry 2–3
anaclitic emotional communications 167, 272–99, 303, 316–17n; afflicted ego *see* afflicted ego; anaclitic relatedness in development and in analysis 275–7; with classical interpretations 279–82; and couch 284–7; in development versus the psychoanalytic relationship 277–8; and empathy 276–7; interpretations as 278–82; object constancy, fostering 296–7; pathological dependency risk 289–91; reasonable ego *see* reasonable ego; regression as consequence of 293; risks 289; and self-disclosures *see* self-disclosures; structure and function 274–5; talking about the day 287–9
anaclitic inductions, types: feeding 142–3; nurturing and caretaking 140–1; protecting patient from environment 143–6; protecting patient from himself/herself, in session 145–6; protecting patient from impulses inside session 146–7; soothing 141–2
anaclitic misattunement 190
anaclitic mode 41–2, 137–8, 301
anaclitic needs 171
anaclitic repetition 48
analyst: as batterer 115–16; childless 75; communication of impact of patient on 296; demonstrating patient's impact on 171; as depleted

327

parent 111–12; experiencing patient as separate 102–3; failure, feelings of 61, 62, 64; feelings of 102; impatience of 30–1; as incompetent parent 117; as indulging or controlling parent 115; knowing as separate person 297; life story 25; as neglectful parent 118; as rejecting parent 108–11; as sexual abuser 112–14; subjectivity of 26–7, 28, 32; as victim of child 116–17; as withholding parent 114–15; *see also* countertransference; object countertransference; objective countertransference

analytic process 27, 231; role of objective countertransference in 34–5

analytic relationship 7; analyst's impact on patient 29; communication of patient's impact on analyst 296; demonstration of patient's impact on analyst 171; emotional communication in 10–11; experience of other as separate 102–3; projective identification 130–1; as a repetition of a pathogenic dynamic 103–5; role of objective countertransference in 24–7; similarities between analyst and patient 94–5

analytic style 25

analyzing ego 7

anger 2, 61, 112, 268, 313n; anaclitic countertransference 147, 151, 153, 154; anaclitic emotional communications 292, 296, 298; angry or critical feelings 152–6; emotional communication and psychoanalysis 50, 51, 167, 171, 172, 175, 178, 180, 184–8, 190, 192–3, 195, 196, 198; narcissistic emotional communications 206, 207, 211, 226; narcissistic rage 189; object emotional communications 247, 249, 251, 252, 255, 256; *see also* aggression; aggressive anaclitic feelings

animal communication 11–13

anxiety 103; anaclitic emotional communications 274, 276, 280, 282, 292, 293, 294; narcissistic countertransference 81, 83, 89, 90; narcissistic emotional communications 206, 229, 231, 236, 237, 238; objective and subjective countertransference, distinguishing 57, 58, 74; projective identification states, countertransference in 135, 136; psychoanalytic technique 162, 178, 180, 194; *see also* fear

Aron, L. 306n

attention deficit disorder 144

attunement 4, 13, 121, 180; badly attuned emotional communications, effect 291–2; *see also* misattunement

auto-induction 200–2

"bad analyst feeling" 117
Balint, M. 7, 273, 307n, 308n
batterer, analyst as 115–16
behaviour, control of 76–7
Bernstein, J. 312n
beta-elements 314n
beta-screen 4
Binswanger, L. 6
Bion, W. 9, 16, 307n, 312–13n, 314n
birds 10, 11
blurred ego boundaries *see* ego boundaries, blurred
body language 2
Bollas, C. 244, 253
Bratt, P. 311n
breastfeeding 157, 277

characterological traits, of analyst 71
chimpanzees 13
classical tradition, psychoanalysis 4, 27
co-construction concept 29, 53
coenestheic functioning 4
cognitive behavioural therapy 119
cognitive communication 1; afflicted and reasonable ego 178, 179; and emotional communication 2–3, 15, 18, 159–60; functions 168; and language 14–15, 159
communication: cognitive *see* cognitive communication; emotional *see*

328

INDEX

emotional communication; infant 16–19; multi-channel 18; object countertransference 243–8; as two-way process 12
competition 154–5
concordant identification 309n
congruence: anaclitic countertransference 139–40; between content and countertransference (example) 61–5; definitions 59–61; and incongruence 105–6, 139–40; narcissistic countertransference 96, 97; object countertransference 105–6; between words and feelings 19
containment 180–2, 235–8, 258–60, 312n; combined with other forms of emotional communication 259–60; interventions 176, 177; silent 181, 237, 259–60, 262
contempt 155–6
couch 284–7, 312n
countertransference 1; anaclitic *see* anaclitic countertransference; analysis 300–4; as analyst's own feeling 54–5; comparing to content of sessions 59; comparison of theories 27–9; congruence 59–65; differential effects of positive and negative transference on 96–8; differentiating objective and subjective 53–78, 309n; enactments 68–9, 310n; identifying 56–9; introverted narcissistic transference, induced by 80–92; narcissistic *see* narcissistic countertransference; narcissistic emotional communications 236–7; objective *see* objective countertransference; in projective identification states 129–36, 310–11n; repetitions as basis of 51–2; role of emotional communication in analysis 8–9; specific feelings/relatedness modes 56; subjective *see* subjective countertransference; subjective intolerance 75; symmetrical narcissistic countertransference, induced by 98–100; in which one dyad member is narcissistic 120–3

crying, in therapy session 123, 141, 181
curative emotional communications: characteristics 182–8; finding 202–3; general features 192–4; objective countertransference as 195–6; relationship of objective countertransference to 191–200; specific features 194–200

Damasio, A. 11
Darwin, C. 10, 12, 14
dependency, pathological (risk of) 289–91
depression 91, 111, 152, 205
Deutsch, H. 8, 307n
developmental stages 42
Devore, I. 14
differentiated relational modes 39, 41–3
disclosures: dystonic 298–9; self-disclosures *see* self-disclosures; syntonic 297–8
"disgusting baby" induction 109, 111
displacement 46, 47
distortions: extroverted narcissistic countertransference 95; repetitions 46–7; subjective 72–4
dystonic disclosures 298–9
dystonic emotional communications 211
dystonic joining 224–8, 231, 249; versus object joining 255–6
dystonic mirroring 230–2, 249

ego 5, 6, 7, 18, 86, 159; afflicted *see* afflicted ego; reasonable *see* reasonable ego
ego boundaries, blurred: joining and mirroring 213, 214; modeling 232; narcissistic countertransference 80–1, 210–11; and object countertransference 103, 107
Ego Psychologists 299
ego weakness 208
Eissler, K. 273
Ellman, S.J. 16–17
emotional communication 1, 10; activating repetitions 169–70; anaclitic *see* anaclitic emotional

communications; anaclitic needs 171; badly attuned, effect 291–2; and cognitive communication 2–3, 15, 18, 159–60; concept 4; and countertransference analysis 300–4; curative *see* curative emotional communications; defenses/resistances against experiencing/verbalizing feelings 171; functions 168–71; in infant-mother relationship 16–19; and interpretation 7, 172–6; and interventions 172–6; maturational needs, meeting 170–1; narcissistic *see* narcissistic emotional communication; narcissistic needs 170–1; in non-human mammals 11–13; non-interpretative 266–71; and objective countertransference 20–1; patient's impact on analyst, demonstrating 171; and psychoanalysis *see* psychoanalysis and emotional communication; relational modes and repetitions (example) 49–51; role in countertransference analysis 8–9; supporting/catalyzing impact of an interpretation 171–2

emotional engagement 4

emotional expressions 12

emotional induction 3, 12, 47, 54

emotional relatedness, defining qualities 36–8

emotional states: in animals 12, 13; here-and-now 43–4, 61; in infants 17; objective countertransference 52; relational modes 36, 37, 38, 39, 43; specific feelings 36, 37, 38

emotions 14, 160; in non-human mammals 11–13; *see also* anger; anxiety; fear

empathy 4; and anaclitic emotional communications 276–7; patient-focused narcissistic countertransference 81, 82, 83; self-directed narcissistic countertransference 87; and sympathy 82, 176

enactments, countertransference 68–9, 310n

enjoying patient 149–50

envy 154–5

epistemology, classical psychoanalysis 27, 159

Epstein, L. 117

Ernsberger, C. 311n

evolutionary psychology 11

exhaustion 91

exploitativeness 155–6

expressive interventions 176, 177–9, 265–6; interpretation 265–6

extroverted narcissistic countertransference 80, 92–8; basic forms 94–6; countertransference induced by 93–4

extroverted narcissistic transference 92–3

eye contact 17, 316n

failure, feelings of 61, 62, 64, 87

fantasies 6, 44, 68, 90, 104, 117

fear 56, 136, 237, 295; narcissistic countertransference 81, 89, 92; object countertransference 103, 105, 121, 122, 123, 124, 125; object emotional communications 264, 292; objective and subjective countertransference, distinguishing 57, 61, 74; psychoanalytic technique 166, 174, 179, 203; *see also* anxiety

feelings: aggressive anaclitic 152–6; of analyst 54–5; angry or critical 152–6; congruence 58–9; defenses/resistances against experiencing/verbalizing 171; and language 1–2; narcissistic countertransference 79; object countertransference 102; objective countertransference concept 27–8; specific *see* specific feelings; subjective countertransference 70–8; unconscious 83; *see also* anger; anxiety; countertransference; fear; objective countertransference; transference

Fenichel, O. 316n

Ferenczi, S. 7, 160, 273, 308n

food 142–3, 275–6

freedom to function 78

INDEX

Freud, A. 124
Freud, S. 4, 27, 44, 97, 113, 121, 156, 205, 301; American Freudians 286, 314–15n; anaclitic emotional communications 272, 273, 278, 289; interpretation in psychoanalysis 303–4; role of emotional communication in psychoanalytic technique 6, 7, 8, 160, 161, 169

gaze interactions 17, 316n
Giovacchini, P. 9
Giovaccinni, P. 23
Gittleson, M. 9
Glover, E. 6
grammar 2
Greenberg, J. 309n, 313n
Greenson, R. 7, 157, 160, 280
Griffin, D.R. 12
Grinberg, L. 310n

Hamilton's Mythology 58
Hann-Kende, F. 8
happy accidents 313n
Heimann, P.I. 9, 20, 23
helplessness 86–7, 111
here-and-now emotional states 43–4, 61
heuristic principles 31
Hinshelwood, R.D. 311n
holding environment 273, 308n, 313n
homicidal impulses 16
hostile feelings 152–3
Hrdy, S.B. 141, 156, 311n

id 5, 18, 278
idealization 93, 308n
identification with the aggressor 124
impact of patient on analyst: communication of 296; demonstrating 171
incongruence 65–6; anaclitic countertransference 139–40; and congruence 105–6, 139–40; containment 236; explanations for 66; inductions 66–8, 105, 140; object countertransference 105–6
induction(s): anaclitic, types 140–7; auto-induction 200–2; "disgusting baby" 109, 111; emotional 3, 12, 47, 54; incongruent 66–8, 105, 140; narcissistic 129; in non-human mammals 13–14; object countertransference 21; objective, misinterpretations 72–4; primitive 57; reasonable ego 173–4; and repetitions 19–20; sexual 157
infanticidal impulses 156
infantile nonverbal affect system 4
infant-mother relationship 2–3, 13, 141, 276, 307n; emotional communication and language in 16–19
interpretation(s): affective 205, 206, 209; anaclitic affective 282–4; as anaclitic emotional communication 278–82; classical 205, 206, 207, 279–82; containment 180–2; and emotional communication 7; emotional communication and psychoanalytic technique 5–6; expressive 177–9; expressive interventions 265–6; as first psychoanalytic technique 168; functions 278; narcissistic countertransference, use in formulating 210–11; narcissistic emotional communication 205–9; narcissistic misattunement 189–90; object, risks of 242–3; object emotional communication techniques 240–3; and repetitions 164–8; risks 209–10; supporting/catalyzing impact of 171–2; targets 172–6; types 176–82
intersubjectivity: objective countertransference concept 28–9; present-anchored mode 42; repetitions 48
interventions: cognitive and emotional communication as components of 165–8; and emotional communication 172–6; silent 262–4
intolerance of countertransference, subjective 75
intrapsychic conflict, repetitions 46
introverted aggression 205

331

INDEX

introverted narcissistic transference, countertransference induced by 80–92

inverted object countertransference 124–7; in sexually abused patients 126–7; typical case examples 124–6

Jacobson, E. 72, 307n
jealousy 154–5
joining 213–28, 313n; dystonic 224–8, 231, 249; object 249–58; syntonic 214–24; *see also* mirroring

Kant, I. 317n
Kernberg, O. 9, 23, 88, 136, 309n
Kirman, W. 313n
Klein, M. 16, 130, 224, 307n
Kohut, H. 7, 157, 206, 221, 223, 307n, 308n, 310n, 312n
Kris, E. 309n

Laius (Oedipus' father) 154
language: and cognitive communication 14–15, 159; and feelings 1–2; in infant-mother relationship 16–19; and pre-linguistic experience 20; spoken 1, 2, 10, 15, 18; symbolic elements 2, 15
Laquercia, T. 311n
LeDoux, J. 11
Liegner, E. 311n
limit setting 145
loving patient: enjoying patient 149–50; pride and admiration 150–2; wanting patient 148–9

MacLean, P.D. 141
Mahler, M. 96, 307n
manic defense 84
Margolis, B. 309n, 310n
masochism 146, 158
maternal behavior, in non-human mammals 13–14
maturational needs: meeting 170–1; unmet 46
Meadow, P.W. 311n
melancholia 97, 205
merger *see* twinship/merger

metabolizing 237, 314n
minority tradition, psychoanalysis 5
mirroring 121, 213, 228–32, 308n; dystonic 230–2, 249; syntonic 228–30; *see also* joining
misattunement 189–91; *see also* attunement
Mitchell, S. 306n
Mithen, S. 15
modeling 232–5
Modern Analysts 23, 75, 122, 138, 211, 228, 292, 313n, 314n, 315n
Monk, C. 16–17
mothering, optimal 17

narcissistic countertransference 79–100, 131, 309n; countertransference induced by introverted narcissistic transference 80–92; extroverted 80, 92–8; interpretations, use in formulating 210–11; and object countertransference 85, 108; patient-focused 81–6; self-directed 86–92; self-involvement 80–1, 84, 86, 87; symmetrical 80, 98–100; types 79–80
narcissistic defense 121, 231, 291–2
narcissistic emotional communications 167, 204–38, 303, 313–14n; containment 235–8; interpretation/interpretation risks 205–10; joining 213–28; mirroring 213, 228–32; modeling 232–5; psychological reflection 211–32; use of narcissistic countertransference in formulating interpretations 210–11
narcissistic induction 129
narcissistic joining *see* joining
narcissistic misattunement 189–90
narcissistic mode 39–40, 44, 62, 101, 294, 301
narcissistic needs 170–1, 276
narcissistic personality 136
narcissistic repetitions 47, 48
neediness 112, 142
neglect of patient 69
neglectful parent 118
neurosis 6, 20, 27, 301

332

newborn, cry of 2–3
non-human mammals 18; emotional communication and emotions in 11–13; induction and maternal behavior in 13–14
non-interpretative emotional communications 266–71; verbal refusal (contradicting patient's projection) 266–70
non-verbal communication 2, 4
nurturing and caretaking inductions 140–1

object countertransference 8, 101–28, 131, 302–3, 310n; analyst as batterer 115–16; analyst as depleted parent 111–12; analyst as incompetent parent 117; analyst as indulgent or controlling parent 115; analyst as neglectful parent 118; analyst as rejecting parent 108–11; analyst as sexual abuser 112–14; analyst as victim of child 116–17; analyst as withholding parent 114–15; common simple scenarios 107–8; communication 243–8; conditional positive 118–20; congruence and incongruence 105–6; feelings experienced by patient and analyst 102; idiosyncratic examples 123–4, 127–8; inverted 124–7; and narcissistic countertransference 85, 108; non-interpretative object emotional communications 245–8; object relational mode, characteristics 102; patient and analyst experiencing each other as separate 102–3; patient-analyst relationship as a pathogenic dynamic repetition 103–5; piano analogy 22; simple 106–8, 123–4; theory 25–6
object emotional communications 167, 303, 314–15n; interpretation of techniques 240–3; non-interpretative 245–8; techniques 239–60
object joining 249–58; versus dystonic narcissistic joining 255–6; explicit 250–4, 257, 258; implicit 250, 254–5, 257, 258; risks of 256–8; types 250–5
object misattunement 190
object mode 41, 73, 104, 301; characteristics 102; congruence 58, 62; self-disclosures in 294–5
Object Relations theory 73, 89, 130, 307n, 308n
object repetition 48
object transference 101
object-choice 307n, 308n
objective countertransference: in analytic relationship 24–7; concept see objective countertransference concept; as curative emotional communication 195–6; distinguished from subjective countertransference 53–78, 309n; and emotional communication 20–1; as emotional state 52; as epistemological tool 34–5; evolutionary and developmental origins 10–21; intolerance, leading to errors in technique 74–5; multiple objective countertransferences 33–4; place in analytic process 34–5; practical application versus application of standard two-person model 29–33; relationship to curative emotional communication 191–200; role in a two-person psychology 22–35, 305–6n; role of analyst's subjectivity in 26–7, 28; stimulation of insight, self-understanding or awareness of interpersonal impact 243–8; when toxic 193–4; see also subjective countertransference
objective countertransference concept: definition/scope 23; formulation 23; intersubjective nature 28–9; and opposing countertransference theories 27–9
objective inductions 76; misinterpretations 72–4
object-oriented questions 315n
Ogden, T. 57, 58, 130, 307n, 308n
omission, mistakes of 75
Ornstein, A. 170
overstimulation 141

Panksepp, J. 11
paranoia 99
parent, analyst as: depleted 111–12; incompetent 117; indulgent or controlling 115; neglectful 118; rejecting 108–11; withholding 114–15; *see also* analyst; object countertransference
parenthood 149–50
passive aggression 144
pathological dependency risk 289–91
patient-analyst relationship *see* analytic relationship
patient-focused narcissistic countertransference 81–6
Pinker, S. 11, 14–15
post-traumatic stress disorder (PTSD) 151–2
prejudices 71–2
present-anchored mode 41, 42–3, 301
preverbal development 16, 66
pride and admiration 150–2
primitive inductions 57
problem-solving 142
projective counteridentification 310n
projective identification 4, 93, 307n; concept 130, 310n, 311n; emotional communication techniques with 261–71, 315–16n; examples 131–6; idealization 93, 308n; polar opposites 129, 133; projective identification states, countertransference in 129–36, 310–11n; risks of expressive emotional communications with 271
projective identification misattunement 190–1
projective identification mode 40, 301
protecting of patient: from environment 143–6; from himself/herself, in session 145–6; from impulses inside session 146–7
psychoanalysis: American 9; classical 4, 27; cognitive communication in 165; and emotional communication *see* psychoanalysis and emotional communication; epistemology 27, 159; and everyday life 52
psychoanalysis and emotional communication 3–5, 36–52, 307–8n; emotional moments and relational modes 36–43; role of emotional communication in psychoanalytic technique 5–8, 159–203
psychoanalytic technique 1; errors in, caused by intolerance of subjective/objective countertransference 74–5; role of emotional communication in 5–8, 159–203, 302–4, 312–13n
psychological reflection 211–32
psychotic states 174

Racker, H. 9, 307n
reality ego 285
reasonable ego 160, 161, 173–5, 176, 177, 178, 223, 249, 302; anaclitic emotional communications 278, 279, 280; modeling 232–3
reflection: psychological 211–32; Rogerian 212–13
refusal: silent 263–4, 266; verbal 266–70
regression 293
relational modes 300, 307n; anaclitic 41–2, 137–8, 301; basic 38–43; countertransference 56; differentiated 39, 41–3; and emotional moments 36–43; emotional states 36, 37, 38, 39, 43; narcissistic 39–40, 44, 62, 101, 294, 301; object *see* object mode; present-anchored 41, 42–3, 301; projective identification 40, 301; psychoanalytic technique 166; and relationships 43–5; and repetitions *see* relational modes, and repetitions; undifferentiated 39–40
relational modes, and repetitions 45–6; and emotional communication (example) 49–51
Relational school 306n
relationships, and relational modes 43–5
religion and spirituality 119, 120
repetitions: activating 169–70; as basis of transference and countertransference 51–2; causes 46; characteristics 47–8; concept 44, 45;

INDEX

enacted in present day relationships 46–7; and induction 19–20; and interventions 164–8; intrapsychic conflict 46; narcissistic 47, 48; objective countertransference 32; patient-analyst relationship 103–5; and relational modes 45–6; trauma 46; unmet maturational needs 46
reptiles 10, 11
reverie 4
Rogerian reflection 211, 212–13
Rogers, C. 212
role-responsiveness 4
Rosenfeld, H. 9, 307n, 311n

sadism 155–6
sadness 90–1
sadomasochism 92, 131, 199
schizophrenic patients 92, 97, 138–9, 317n
Schore, A. 17
Searles, H. 7, 20, 23, 307n, 309n
Sechehaye, M. 7, 273
Self Psychology 163
self-directed narcissistic countertransference 86–92
self-disclosures 4; anaclitic 295–6; and anaclitic emotional communication 293–4; in narcissistic mode 294; in object mode 294–5
self-experience 207
self-object 307n
separation individuation 317n
sex addiction 145–6
sexual abuse: analyst as sexual abuser 112–14; inverted object countertransference 126–7
sexual anaclitic feelings 156–8
sexual arousal 67–8
sexual inductions 157
shared/communicative states 311n
silent interventions 181, 237, 262–4
silent refusal 263–4
simple object countertransference 106–7; common scenarios 107–8; idiosyncratic, example 123–4; *see also* object countertransference
soothing inductions 141–2

specific feelings 36, 37, 38, 47, 56, 300; psychoanalytic technique 166, 187
specific intensity 168
spending patterns 85–6
splitting 130
spoken language 1, 2, 10, 15, 18
Spotnitz, H. 7–9, 20, 23, 78, 97, 121, 194, 273, 289, 292, 305n, 307n, 309n, 311n, 313n, 317n
Sterba, R. 6–7, 305n, 312n
Stern, D. 20, 101
Strachey, J. 6–7, 273, 305n, 313n
stuttering 67
subjective countertransference 20, 24; defined 24, 52, 70; distinguished from objective countertransference 53–78, 309n; distortions, subjective 72–4; effects on treatment process 76–8; feelings 70–8; intolerance, leading to errors in technique 74–5; *see also* objective countertransference
subjectivity of analyst 28, 32; role in objective countertransference 26–7
substance abuse 115
suicidal impulses 16
superego 5, 6, 107
survival needs 12
symbols 2, 15
symmetrical narcissistic countertransference 80; countertransference induced by 98–100
sympathy, and empathy 82–3, 176
syntonic disclosures 297–8
syntonic joining 214–24
syntonic mirroring 228–30

thought transference 4
Tooby, J. 14
Tower, L. 9
toxoid response 194
transference 5, 7, 162–3; active 183–4; classical theories 41; explicit erotic 147; extroverted narcissistic 92–3; introverted narcissistic, countertransference induced by 80–92; multiple transferences 238; object 101; and objective

countertransference 20, 25; positive and negative, differential effects on countertransference 96–8; repetitions as basis of 51–2

trauma 103; repetitions 46

trial identification 4

twinship/merger 39, 96, 294, 307n; narcissistic emotional communications 214, 229, 232, 235

two-person psychology 305–6n; co-construction concept 29; practical application of model versus application of objective countertransference 29–33; role of objective countertransference in 22–35; subjectivity of analyst 28

unconscious, the 45

undifferentiated relational modes 39–40

unshared emotionality, burden 223

vocalization 14, 15, 17

wanting patient 148–9

Winnicott, D.W. 7, 8, 20, 23, 153, 273, 305n, 308n, 309n, 312n, 313n

withdrawal 111

Wolf, E. 157, 223, 310n

worthlessness 263